Exploring Identity in Literature and Life Stories

Exploring Identity in Literature and Life Stories:

The Elusive Self

Edited by

Guri E. Barstad, Karen S. P. Knutsen
and Elin Nesje Vestli

Cambridge
Scholars
Publishing

Exploring Identity in Literature and Life Stories: The Elusive Self

Edited by Guri E. Barstad, Karen S. P. Knutsen and Elin Nesje Vestli

This book first published 2019

Cambridge Scholars Publishing

Lady Stephenson Library, Newcastle upon Tyne, NE6 2PA, UK

British Library Cataloguing in Publication Data
A catalogue record for this book is available from the British Library

Copyright © 2019 by Guri E. Barstad, Karen S. P. Knutsen,
Elin Nesje Vestli and contributors

All rights for this book reserved. No part of this book may be reproduced, stored in a retrieval system, or transmitted, in any form or by any means, electronic, mechanical, photocopying, recording or otherwise, without the prior permission of the copyright owner.

ISBN (10): 1-5275-3571-1
ISBN (13): 978-1-5275-3571-8

TABLE OF CONTENTS

Acknowledgements viii

Introduction 1
The Search for Self: Continuity and Mutability
Guri Ellen Barstad, Karen Patrick Knutsen and Elin Nesje Vestli

Identity and Cultural Hybridity

Chapter One 16
"Brittle identities": Identity Discourses in the Work
of Austrian Author Julya Rabinowich
Elin Nesje Vestli

Chapter Two 31
Identity, Trauma and Language Confusion in Olga Grjasnowa's
Der Russe ist einer der Birken liebt and *Gott ist nicht schüchtern*
Grazziella Predoiu

Chapter Three 48
Fractured Boundaries, Cultural Hybridity and In-between
Spaces in Norwegian Young Adult Immigrant Literature:
Maria Navarro Skaranger's *Alle utlendinger har lukka gardiner*
Wayne Kelly

Identity and Religion

Chapter Four 64
The Search for Authenticity: Religious Identity in the Norwegian Novel
Guds tjener by Tor Edvin Dahl
Guri Ellen Barstad

Chapter Five 81
"My centre not my edge": Uncanny Identity, Death,
Doubles and Medievalism in Kevin Hart's *Your Shadow*
Melanie Duckworth

Chapter Six 103
The Israelite and Saint Identity According to Polynesian Latter-day Saints
Mette Ramstad

Identity, Nationality and Language

Chapter Seven 120
The Weight of Collective Memory: Surviving in the
Inhospitable Realm of Haiti
André Avias

Chapter Eight 137
Identity, Migration and Language in Two Stories by
the German-Speaking Writer Richard Wagner from Romania
Roxana Nubert and *Ana-Maria Dascălu-Romițan*

Chapter Nine 153
Group Identity in Teenage Talk from Madrid
Annette M. Myre Jørgensen

Identity, Profession and Gender

Chapter Ten 178
"It's doable": Women's Journeys to Academia in South Africa
and Their Sense of Self
Eva Lambertsson Björk, Jutta Eschenbach, Mathabo Khau
and *Lynette Webb*

Chapter Eleven 195
Fiction as the "first laboratory of moral judgment":
Pre-service Teachers and the Development of a Professional Identity
Karen Patrick Knutsen

Chapter Twelve 215
Negotiating and Introducing Identities: The "Écriture Collective"
of Ariane Mnouchkine, Hélène Cixous and the Théâtre du Soleil
Gabriele C. Pfeiffer

Chapter Thirteen 228
Alienated and Evanescent Identities in the Contemporary World
of Austrian Author Kathrin Röggla
Alessandra Schininà

Chapter Fourteen 241
How "the Other" Becomes "Agent" through the Rupture of War:
A New Look at Jacqueline Winspear's Maisie Dobbs Novels
Jane M. Ekstam

Chapter Fifteen 255
In Search of "the message hidden in the beauty of the words":
Virginia Woolf's Novel *Mrs Dalloway*
Britt Andersen

Identity and Illness

Chapter Sixteen 276
Writing with One's Eyes: Identity and Communicative Strategies in
Masahiro Fujita's *99% Thank you* and Leo Montero's *Muñeca de trapo*
Wladimir Chávez Vaca

Identity and Childhood

Chapter Seventeen 294
"Each homeless person has a different story to tell": Homeless Identity
in David Walliams' Metafictive Children's Book *Mr Stink* (2009)
Gro-Anita Myklevold

Chapter Eighteen 309
"The right Alice": A Cybertext Perspective on Narrated Identity
in Film Adaptations of Lewis Carroll's Novels
Britt W. Svenhard

Contributors 324

Acknowledgements

The editors would like to thank Østfold University College, Halden, Norway and the Faculty of Business, Languages and Social Sciences for funding received to arrange a conference in Vienna, Austria in December 2017, and for a series of follow-up sessions held at the college in Halden, under the auspices of the Literature and Narrativity Research Group.

We truly appreciate the work that the referees have put into reading the draft manuscript, giving us insightful and constructive feedback on the texts included here. We are also particularly grateful for the patience and generous support of our commissioning editors Rebecca Gladders, Adam Rummens and their team at Cambridge Scholars Publishing.

Guri Ellen Barstad, Karen Patrick Knutsen and Elin Nesje Vestli
Østfold University College
Halden Norway

INTRODUCTION

THE SEARCH FOR SELF: CONTINUITY AND MUTABILITY

GURI ELLEN BARSTAD, KAREN PATRICK KNUTSEN AND ELIN NESJE VESTLI

Dimensions of Identity in Narratives

Exploring Identity in Literature and Life Stories: The Elusive Self grew out of a project focusing on how issues of identity are presented in different types of narratives, based at Østfold University College, Halden, Norway. It was initiated towards the end of 2015 by the Literature and Narrativity Research Group in the Foreign Language Department. The group held a conference in Vienna, Austria in December 2017, and continued with a series of symposia in the following year, where more members of the research group and scholars from other institutions were invited to participate. In addition to the Østfold University College researchers, contributors were recruited from the Norwegian University of Science and Technology in Trondheim, the West University and the Polytechnic University of Timisoara, Romania, the Nelson Mandela University of South Africa, the University of Vienna, Austria and the University of Ragusa, Italy. This volume comprises 18 chapters, selected and adapted from the three-year long project.

According to the psychologist and narratologist Michael Bamberg, identity "designates the attempt to differentiate and integrate a sense of self along different social and personal dimensions such as gender, age, race, occupation, gangs, socio-economic status, ethnicity, class, nation states, or regional territory" (2013). This definition reveals the complexity of the term. Many narratives have focused on issues of identity, from the classical Bildungsroman describing the development and education of the protagonist from childhood to adulthood, to postmodern studies of the fragmented self in literature and life stories.

The initial context of the Bildungsroman was Germany in the late 18th century, and these novels recorded the development of a (usually male) protagonist, maturing through a process of acculturation. Ultimately, the protagonist was integrated harmoniously into the surrounding society (Karafilis 1998, 63). As Maria Karafilis argues, today, "the goals of such a text are naïve and, in fact, impossible to achieve in postmodern societies that deny the existence of a unified self" (ibid.). Instead, contemporary narratives seem to affirm "an era of alienation from the society whose values in former times might have confirmed selfhood" (Breandlin 1984, 75, cited in Karafilis ibid.). The Bildungsroman and other narrative genres have had to develop to accommodate new forms of being and socio-economic conditions in our globalized, yet fragmented world.

Our work in this project focuses mainly on contemporary literature or life stories, actualizing this postmodern conundrum. The overarching research question in this volume is: How is the sense of self negotiated in narratives that problematize identity formation and transformation? Our point of departure is first, and foremost narratives in which a subject is confronted with major life changes and has to adjust to new situations or contexts. The fictional characters and the informants in the different narratives discussed in the contributions experience existential challenges, in which they must consider how to balance between being positioned or positioning themselves in terms of identity. This requires negotiation between old and new positions and already established perceptions, both their own and those of others.

The majority of the studies here address identity as it is thematized in literary narratives, but others also include analyses of other types of narrative: e.g., life-writings, pathographies, interviews, reading logs, language corpora, film, and theatre. The texts discussed are thus based on both the stories of fictional characters and on the life stories of actual individuals. They all include elements of identity negotiation, realized in different fashions. The contributors approach identity formation in terms of a number of the various dimensions listed in Bamberg's definition of identity above (2013). Rather than arranging the chapters in terms of genre here, they are organized in groups in terms of the major dimensions of identity they share thematically: Identity and Cultural Hybridity; Identity and Religion; Identity, Nationality and Language; Identity, Profession and Gender; Identity and Illness; and Identity and Childhood. However, these themes cross each other in unexpected ways, and the chapters are therefore organized in terms of their *dominant* thematic issues rather than isolated, single issues.

The question of personal identity has engaged philosophers for centuries, and a common dilemma in the approaches found in the Western tradition is how one can preserve sameness in a sense of self, faced with the constant change inherent in the biological human condition (Ritivoi 2005, 231). More recently, Paul Ricœur has discussed this continuity/change dilemma: "Let me recall the terms of the confrontation: on one side, identity as *sameness* (Latin *idem*, German *Gleichheit*, French *mêmeté*); on the other, identity as *selfhood* (Latin *ipse*, German *Selbstheit*, French *ipséité*)" (Ricœur 1994, 116). Here Ricœur describes individual identity as having two sides. *Mêmeté* describes the permanence of the self, whereas *ipséité* denotes the constantly evolving nature of selfhood.

The way we think about selfhood and identity is also constantly evolving. The humanist model, for example, defined the "self" as "a conscious being who had the power of logic and rationality to discover the truth about the workings of the world, and who was able to act and think for himself or herself, independently of external influences, and also able to think reflexively about the status of his or her own being" (Klages 2011, 89). In contrast, in poststructuralist thought, the idea of identity or selfhood is no longer considered to be something that is natural or innate; instead it is something that is socially constructed (ibid., 88). However, different disciplines seem to concur that identity is constructed through the stories we tell ourselves, and each other about who we think we are; narrative configurations create meaning out of the chaos of reality. As Ricœur maintains, we come to grips with our own identities by creating our own life stories, inspired by literature and drawing on literary elements:

> self-understanding is an interpretation; interpretation of the self, in turn, finds in the narrative, among other signs and symbols, a privileged form of mediation; the latter borrows from history as well as from fiction, making a life story a fictional history, or if one prefers, a historical fiction, interweaving the historiographic style of biographies with the novelistic style of imaginary biographies. (1994, 114, footnote 1)

Making sense of our lives and our sense of selfhood means structuring the events in our lives. Any stability in identity, however, is an illusion; and as

Ricœur has pointed out, one's life story is inevitably incomplete as long as one is still alive. In this connection, Ritovoi asks whether it is possible to make sense of the plot without knowledge of the way the narrative ends (2008, 232)? In contrast to life stories, literary narratives tend to convey a sense of an ending, which again sheds light on our understanding and interpretation of the whole story (Kermode 2000).

Literature "is the space in which questions about the nature of personal identity are most provocatively articulated" (Bennett and Royle 2009, 130). Narration is a privileged genre for identity construction especially because it requires us to situate characters in space and time. A narrative consists of both a "story" and a "plot". Whereas a story merely presents a chain of events, the plot presents stories that are not only chronologically related, but also related in terms of cause and effect (Forster 1962, 92). Narrating also "enables speakers/writers to disassociate the speaking/ writing self from the act of speaking, to take a reflective position vis-a-vis self as character" (Bamberg 2013). This disassociation or defamiliarization raises awareness, opening new spaces for re-negotiation of the identity. This applies to fictional characters and autobiographical stories, but also equally well to the identity negotiations of readers or viewers.

As previously stated, identity processes are dynamic. They are the result of negotiations and social interactions: "'Identity negotiation processes' refer to those activities through which people establish, maintain, and change their identities" (Swann and Bosson 2008, 465). However, there will always be encounters with others or new situations in which the status and role of a person are challenged, leading to incongruence. The image of the self must then be re-negotiated. Identity is not established once, and for all, but is under constant revision because we are members of a society and a culture. Cultural identity "is a matter of becoming as much as being [and] belongs to the future as much as to the past" (Hall 1990, 435). Incongruence in identity processes can lead to unease, but can also open up an in-between space where a new identity can be negotiated. This in-between space gives room for creativity; this existential uncertainty triggers experimentation, playing on the edge where one can challenge, expand, cross, or even move boundaries. It is in these creative spaces that the negotiation of identity takes place.

The contributors here examine the transformation processes that take place in the narrow space between past and future, in other words in the in-between spaces, where the individual is struggling to position or establish her- or himself between the two proverbial stools. Thus, the identity discourses discussed in this volume reflect the tension between being forced into or assigned a role, consisting of the expectations and conceptions of others, or of life itself, and the need to establish one's own role or space. Several contributions deal with the concept of "the other" (see e.g. Beauvoir 1997 in connection with gender or Said 1978 in connection with culture) the stranger. Among other recurring issues are hybrid identities (Bhabha 2004) as well as what could be called a homeless identity (McCarthy 2013).

It has also been pointed out that broadly speaking, "questions of personal or individual identity are indissociably bound up with language" (Bennett and Royle 2009, 131). A number of the contributors (KELLY; JØRGENSEN; PREDOIU; NUBERT and DASCĂLU-ROMITAN), focus on language as a constitutive factor in identity formation and transformation (Bucholtz and Hall 2004). It is, for example, interesting to examine the effects of hybrid identities, in the space between two or more languages or sociolects. The anthology analyzes narratives from several language areas, first and foremost English, French, German, Norwegian and Spanish. It also covers narratives from several countries and regions: Australia, Austria, Azerbaijan, France, Germany, Great Britain, Haiti, India, Israel, Japan, Polynesia, Norway, Romania, Spain and South Africa.

Identity and Cultural Hybridity

The first three chapters (VESTLI, PREDOIU and KELLY) examine novels which thematize identity crises brought about by the situations of immigrants and refugees as well as integration issues affecting the identity of second generation immigrants. We see what can happen when people have to leave their homes, their languages and their cultures behind. Furthermore, the situation of the children of these immigrants is problematic, positioned as they are between two distinct cultures, often with opposing values. Some of the characters are unable to tackle the challenges and perish; others take advantage of the in-between spaces and develop hybrid identities.

In "'Brittle identities': Identity Discourses in the Work of Austrian Author Julya Rabinowich", ELIN NESJE VESTLI focuses on hybrid identities in three contemporary novels written by Julya Rabinowich. VESTLI shows how the female protagonists in *Spaltkopf* (2008), *Die Erdfresserin* (2012) and *Dazwischen: Ich* (2016), all from migration backgrounds and contextualized in transgenerational and transnational family histories, feel uprooted and struggle to find their place in a new country with a new social framework. Rabinowich uses complex narrative structures to thematize the notion of in-between, not as a static space, but as a dynamic process in which one can negotiate and struggle in choosing one's own way.

GRAZZIELLA PREDOIU examines two novels written by Olga Grjasnowa, a German author, born in Azerbaijan in a Russian-Jewish family. In "Identity, Trauma and Language Confusion", PREDOIU discusses identity discourses in *Der Russe ist einer der Birken liebt* (2012) and *Gott ist nicht schüchtern* (2017). She shows how the author depicts young people who, due to international political conflicts, are forced to break up from their country of origin and try to settle elsewhere. The problems of migration are exacerbated by complex family stories, shaped through persecution and traumas passed down from one generation to the next. Grjasnowa portrays a cosmopolitan, but rootless generation, whose members PREDOIU interprets as nomads or commuters, all stuck in a non-place.

In his chapter "Fractured Boundaries, Cultural Hybridity and In-between Spaces in Norwegian Young Adult Immigrant Literature: Maria Navarro Skaranger's *Alle utlendinger har lukka gardiner*", WAYNE KELLY discusses how the concept of cultural hybridity may be applied to Navarro Skaranger's novel from 2015. In this literary debut, Navarro Skaranger, a young, second-generation immigrant author, describes the life of young adults, most of them with immigrant backgrounds, in one of Oslo's suburbs. In relating her story, the author uses so-called "Kebab-Norwegian", a sociolect that many young Norwegians, not only those with immigrant backgrounds, can relate to. KELLY discusses how literature may contribute to managing integration and assimilation, and how novels like Navarro Skaranger's can contribute to our understanding of our changing societies.

Identity and Religion

Religion is often crucial in the formation of an individual's identity. It can give a person a sense of belonging, but can also restrict their perceived freedom, leading to a crisis in faith (BARSTAD). Religious beliefs often reflect on death and the afterlife. DUCKWORTH examines poems that demonstrate how the idea of death is utterly central to identity. Socialanthropologists and religion scholars also see the importance of religion in terms of a collective identity (RAMSTAD).

In "The Search for Authenticity: Religious Identity in Norwegian Author Tor Edvin Dahl's *Guds tjener*", GURI ELLEN BARSTAD focuses on the representation of religious identity in this Norwegian Bildungsroman from 1973. The protagonist, Anders, embarks on a spiritual journey outside his familiar Pentecostal milieu. He spends some time in an in-between space before taking the decisive plunge into a secular world full of promises, returning home with new knowledge and insight. The novel draws on and problematizes existentialist concepts such as freedom, choice, anxiety and responsibility. Understanding that he has "to be" before he can "become", the character reflects on the relationship between authenticity and religious identity.

In "'My centre not my edge': Uncanny Identity, Death, Doubles and Medievalism in Kevin Hart's *Your Shadow*", MELANIE DUCKWORTH discusses a series of poems addressed to and spoken by "your shadow". The shadow is the body's constant companion–it is discovered at birth, and accompanies the body throughout life until the body and its shadow are united forever in the grave. While death can be seen as the ultimate erasure of self, the shadow poems show that it is in fact central to one's identity. In her chapter, DUCKWORTH uses the notions of "the uncanny" and "the double" to explore the fraught connection between identity and death. This also enables a consideration of the collection's use of two different strains of medieval imagery, both of which are preoccupied with death and identity: Catholic medieval mysticism, and the memento mori tradition, which feeds into the Gothic. The power of the collection comes from its combination of playful literal description, metaphor, black humour, uncanny foreboding, and a mystical desire for transcendence. The shadow remains a slippery, unsettling, companionable, and ultimately faithful reflection of the self.

METTE RAMSTAD discusses the development of a "Saint" identity in East Polynesia, catalyzed by the work of missionaries from the Church of the Latter Day Saints (LDS or Mormon) during their first sojourns in the region in the mid-1800s. In her chapter, she explores narratives found in historical and ethnographic accounts that focus on the construction of a Polynesian LDS identity and its Israelite connection. Furthermore, she draws on contemporary East Polynesian Latter-day Saints narratives (1950–1995), and interviews which explore personal experiences and popular religious understandings of Christianity. East Polynesian converts were able to combine traditional beliefs in the influence of the spirits of deceased family and ancestors with their new LDS religious beliefs. The "Saint" identity, as a chosen and privileged people with a genealogical connection to the tribes of Israel, remains appealing to many LDS Polynesians today.

Identity, Nationality and Language

Just as religion can define the collective identity of a community, shared historical memories contribute to a collective national identity (AVIAS). An individual's identity within a national context can, however, be challenged if one belongs to a minority, in terms of for example ethnicity, language or age (AVIAS; NUBERT and DASCĂLU-ROMIȚAN; JØRGENSEN).

In "The Weight of Collective Memory: Surviving in the Inhospitable Realm of Haiti", ANDRÉ AVIAS examines the relationship between identity and culture/history in three Haitian novels, all to different degrees documentary: *Tout bouge autour de moi* by Dany Laferrière, *Ballade d'un amour inachevé* by Louis-Philippe Dalembert and *Bain de lune* by Yanick Lahens. None of the three authors has French as their native language, but they have chosen to write in French. Culture and history combine to create a community's collective memory. Haiti has had its share of earthquakes, violence, oppression and political unrest, and AVIAS shows how the inhabitants' ability to survive as well as their narrative about it have become an important part of their collective identity. He focuses not only on the battle for physical survival but also on traditional Haitian spirituality as a means of mental survival.

In their chapter "Identity, Migration and Language in Two Stories by the German-Speaking Writer Richard Wagner from Romania", ROXANA NUBERT and ANA-MARIA DASCĂLU-ROMITAN discuss the two texts *Ausreiseantrag* (1988) and *Begrüßungsgeld* (1989), written by Richard Wagner. The author, who migrated to West Germany in 1988, comes from the German-speaking minority in Romania. Both texts are partially autobiographical, and the existential crises that the protagonist, the author Stirner, lives through both in Romania, where he is politically persecuted and in West Germany, where he is considered an alien, mirror Wagner's own experiences. The chapter explores the individual's struggle to define his own identity and the connection between identity and language, including regional variations.

ANNETTE M. MYRE JØRGENSEN examines how language codes contribute to the constitution of a group identity among teenagers. She argues for the significance of different codes in the analysis of so-called *vague language* (VL) in teenage conversations in Madrid, where the informants narrate events to their peers. She uses examples from the COLAm-corpus (www.colam.org), and a pragmatic linguistic approach. These teenagers' interactions are interspersed with codes that are in-group identity markers, making their speech nearly incomprehensible for the people around them. Examples of vague language are presented in JØRGENSEN'S study in order to show that these expressions work not only as a communicative strategy, but that they also create bonds between members of the group and express their in-group social identity: "a same age group" affiliation with their peers. She therefore concludes that contrary to popular belief, vague language is not motivated simply by sheer laziness or by an unwillingness to think.

Identity, Profession and Gender

JØRGENSEN'S study draws on the language of teenage informants. The contributions of BJÖRK, ESCHENBACH, KHAU and WEB as well as of KNUTSEN also use informants. The former chapter deals with what can be called "life stories" (cf. Bruner 1990), whereas the latter analyzes reading logs where students comment on their reading of a novel. Both chapters focus on professional identities, since work is an essential part of individual identity. Work is also thematized in PFEIFFER, SCHININÀ and EKSTAM. BJÖRK et al. and EKSTAM write about gender as part of our identity in addition to discussing the importance of professions and working life. BRITT ANDERSEN goes beyond gender roles to discuss how discourses of sexualities are negotiated in narratives.

EVA LAMBERTSSON BJÖRK, JUTTA ESCHENBACH, MATHABO KHAU and LYNETTE WEB are interested in first generation academic women in South Africa and the journey they took to academia. This obviously involves changing identities. In individual, semi-structured interviews with three women, Buhle, Jane, and Mpho, who come from different ethnic backgrounds, they posed questions related to their life stories. First, they focused on the interviewees' hopes for the future as young girls. Secondly, they were asked about challenges and highlights during the journey, and finally, about how they viewed their journey from their present vantage point as academics. They find that these women managed to break free from the fixed gendered script of African woman and its repetitive patterns. In their life stories about the journey towards academia, they position themselves, and are positioned as different from others. In this vying for positions, they are able to construct a new sense of self.

In "Fiction as the 'first laboratory of moral judgment'", KAREN PATRICK KNUTSEN examines the relationship between reading fictional narratives and students' development of their professional identities as future teachers. Paul Ricoeur (1994) argues that literature functions as a laboratory where we experiment with judgments of approval and condemnation; when reading narratives, we come to grips with our own identities and values by creating our own life stories, inspired by literature and drawing on literary elements. KNUTSEN examines 86 teacher trainee reading logs where students respond to Anglo-Indian writer Bali Rai's teenage novel *(Un)arranged Marriage* (2001). Students commented on dysfunctional families, arranged marriages, the importance of education, racism and the tolerance of difference, contrasting their own experiences with those of the protagonist. The moral judgments they make in their logs suggest that they have become more aware of their own identities and development as future teachers.

In "Negotiating and Introducing Identities: The 'Écriture Collective' of Ariane Mnouchkine, Hélène Cixous and the Théâtre du Soleil", GABRIELLE C. PFEIFFER focuses on professional identity in the theatre. Against the background of the history of the Théâtre du Soleil, PFEIFFER examines how the directrice Ariane Mnouchkine and her ensemble established and developed a collective ensemble identity, based on the idea of collaborative work in all aspects of their productions. In spite of this collaborative ideal, the special competence of individual ensemble members is fundamental in ensuring the quality of their work. To exemplify their concept of professional identity PFEIFFER discusses the artistic meeting between the ensemble and the French feminist writer Hélène Cixous, who has been collaborating with the theatre since the 1980s.

In the next chapter, ALESSANDRA SCHININÀ examines a number of works by the Austrian writer Kathrin Röggla: *wir schlafen nicht* (2004), *die alarmbereiten* (2010), *besser wäre: keine* (2013) and *Nachtsendung* (2016). SCHININÀ argues that Röggla shows how alienation can lead to the loss of self in a globalized work environment. Her characters–who are office and NGO workers, computer scientists, interpreters, politicians, managers and the like–live in a permanent and conscious state of self-representation, which is characterized by the omnipresence of the media and a sense of precariousness. Their identities increasingly dissolve and, in the end, they move like ghosts or zombies in disturbing urban landscapes and non-places. These characters are determined and trapped by a system that impedes free, individual development. Literature and literary discourse thus become Röggla's tool for denouncing dominant economic discourses and for reflecting on social identities, on the loss of liberty, and on the essential democracy needed for the autonomous, conscious development of identity.

JANE M. EKSTAM has chosen to focus on Canadian writer Jacqueline Winspear's female detective Maisie Dobbs in a series that follows the protagonist from girlhood to adulthood, set against the background of the two world wars. The books delineate the gradual development of Maisie's identity from being "the other" to becoming an active "agent" in her own life. Maisie is "the other" in three main respects: social class, gender, and profession (there were few female private investigators in the inter-war years). Her development illustrates the huge changes taking place in female identity formations during this turbulent period. Starting in a working-class family, and later working as a domestic servant, Maisie changes her status (and identity) forever. She becomes a successful, educated, and self-assured professional. Throughout this mythical narrative, however, Maisie retains a strong core identity based on her natural empathy with victims of injustice, and, to some extent, with the perpetrators of foul deeds.

EKSTAM'S chapter, as we have seen, describes the way gender expectations complicated a fictional woman's professional choices during the first decades of the 20th century. BJÖRK ET AL.'S interviews with female academics from South Africa deal with how societal expectations tend to restrict behavior and enforce conformity to current gender norms, making it difficult for South African women to choose academic careers, even in the 21st century. BRITT ANDERSEN, like EKSTAM, has chosen to focus on a historical narrative. She discusses how sexual orientation is negotiated in a narrative from 1925, namely Virginia Woolf's innovative modernist novel *Mrs Dalloway*. Gender and sexual orientation are two distinct aspects of our identity: gender identity is personal, based on our internal experience of naming our gender. Sexual orientation, in contrast, is interpersonal and involves who we are physically, emotionally and/or romantically attracted to (e.g. Butler 1990; Foucault 1990). When Woolf was writing, same-sex love was a tabooed issue; in Sir Alfred Douglas' words it was "the love that dare not speak its name". In her close reading of the novel, ANDERSEN shows how Woolf nevertheless thematizes sexual orientation through her highly associative, stream-of-consciousness technique, and through the use of doubling, or parallel characters. She focuses particularly on the character Miss Kilman, who has often been over-looked by readers and critics alike, and argues that she has an important function in the narrative as she helps to delineate the sexual identity of the protagonist Clarissa Dalloway.

Identity and Illness

WLADIMIR CHÁVEZ VACA is also concerned with "life stories". He addresses two so-called pathographies–or narratives of illness–which raise questions of identity, since a person is undoubtedly changed after being diagnosed with a serious or fatal disease. He draws on two books; the first is Japanese writer Masahiro "Hiro" Fujita's *99% Thank you* (2013), and the second is Spanish writer Leo Montero's *Muñeca de Trapo* (2013). Both writers tell the stories of their own illness; they have both been diagnosed with the incurable disease Amyotrophic Lateral Sclerosis (ALS) that progressively weakens the muscles, causing paralysis and, in its final stage, death by respiratory failure. The disease is capable of stealing the patient's voice; it darkens and overwhelms their powers of speech. CHÁVEZ VACA finds that formulating their testimonies as pathographies can help patients in their quest to regain control of the situation and come to terms with their new identities as terminally ill or radically changed.

Identity and Childhood

The two last chapters focus on identity formation in childhood. GRO-ANITA MYKLEVOLD discusses the construction of a homeless identity in the contemporary children's book *Mr Stink* (2009) by British writer David Walliams. She notes that childhood plays an important role in identity development and children's literature often grapples with issues related to identity. MYKLEVOLD examines how Walliams' child protagonist Chloe interprets the "individual biography" (Giddens 1991) of a homeless character, Mr Stink, and how the narrative contradicts or confirms stereotypical images of such a large, heterogeneous group as the homeless community. She also discusses the metafictive devices that Walliams uses, showing how they relate to the construction of Chloe's identity as a promising writer. MYKLEVOLD pursues the following research questions: How can a child protagonist's perceptions of a homeless person's identity say something about the (in)tolerance of contemporary society? And, how can metafictional children's literature assist readers in becoming more tolerant towards ambiguity and marginalized groups?

In "'The right Alice': A Cybertext Perspective on Narrated Identity in the Film Adaptations of Lewis Carroll's Novels", BRITT W. SVENHARD argues that the medium of film can function as a tool that can convey the multi-level structure of cybertexts, thus creating a new, cultural narrative model for the construction of identity. She examines Tim Burton's *Alice in Wonderland* (2010), and James Bobin's *Alice Through the Looking Glass* (2016), both based on the classical children's tales of Lewis Carroll. SVENHARD explores the dream motif in Burton's film and the memory motif in Bobin's, linking both to theories on narrativization and identity construction. The classical fantasy stories about *Alice* in both films are used to emphasize how cybertext structures can shape viable models for life narratives and identity construction.

As the chapters in this anthology demonstrate, the self is indeed elusive. Literature and life stories, however, allow us to explore identity processes, shedding light on the roles different social and personal dimensions can play in the negotiation and integration of the sense of self. Our contribution has been revealing the wide variety of stories that thematize this search for the elusive self across nationalities, languages and genres. The stories we tell ourselves and others about who we are can help to preserve a sense of sameness, or *mêmeté*, and simultaneously help us understand the continual evolution of identity, or *ipséité*, in Ricœur's (1994) terms.

References

Bamberg, Michael. 2013. "Identity and Narration." In *The living handbook of narratology*, edited by Peter Hühn et al. Hamburg: Hamburg University Press. Available through: http://sub.uni-hamburg.de/lhn/index.phh?title=Narratology&oldid=2050 [Accessed 25.01.2018].
Bennett, Andrew and Nicholas Royle. (2009) [1995]. *An Introduction to literature, criticism and theory*. London, etc.: Pearson/Longman.
Bhabha, Homi K. 2004. *The Location of Culture*. London: Routledge.
Breandlin, Bonnie H. 1984. "*Bildung* in Ethnic Women Writers." In *Denver Quarterly* 17/4: 75–87.

Bucholtz, Mary and Hall, Kira. 2004. "Language and Identity." In *A Companion to Linguistic Anthropology*, edited by Alessandro Duranti, 369–394. Malden, Oxford, Carlton: Blackwell.

Butler, Judith. 1990. *Gender Trouble. Feminism and the Subversion of Identity*. New York, London: Routledge.

de Beauvoir, S. 1997. *The Second Sex*. London: Vintage Classics.

Forster, E. M. 1962 [1927]. *Aspects of the Novel*. London and New York: Penguin.

Foucault, Michel. 1990 [1976]. *The History of Sexuality: Volumes 1-2*, Harmondsworth: Penguin.

Hall, Stuart. 1990. "Cultural Identity and Diaspora." In *The Post-Colonial Studies Reader*, edited by Bill Ashcroft, Gareth Griffiths and Helen Tiffin, 435–438. London: Routledge.

Karafilis, Sandra. 1998. "Crossing the Borders of Genre: Revisions of the 'Bildungsroman' in Sandra Cisneros's *The House on Mango Street* and Jamaica Kincaid's *Annie John*." In *The Journal of Midwest Modern Language Association*, 31/2 (Winter): 63–78.

Kermode, Frank. 2000 [1966]. *The Sense of an Ending. Studies in the Theory of Fiction with a New Epilogue*. Oxford: Oxford University Press.

Klages, Mary. 2011 [2006]. *Literary Theory: a Guide for the Perplexed*. London and New York: Continuum.

McCarthy, Lindsey. 2013. "Homelessness and identity: a critical review of the literature and theory" from *People, Place and Policy Online*, Vol. 7, No. 1: 46–58. Sheffield: Sheffield Hallam University. Available through: http://extra.shu.ac.uk/ppp-online/wp-content/uploads/2013/09/homelessness_identity_review_literature_theory.pdf [Accessed 23.05.2018].

Ricoeur, Paul. 1994 [1992]. *Oneself as Another*. Trans. Kathleen Blamey. Chicago and London: Chicago University Press.

Ritivoi, Andreea D. 2005. "Identity and Narrative." In *Routledge Encyclopedia of Narrative Theory*, edited by David Herman, Manfred Jahn and Marie-Laure Ryan, 231–235. London and New York: Routledge.

Said, Edward W. 1978. *Orientalism*. New York: Pantheon Books.

Swann, William B., and Jennifer K. Bosson. 2008. "Identity negotiation: A theory of self and social interaction." In *Handbook of personality psychology: Theory and research*, 3rd ed., edited by Oliver P. John, Richard W. Robins, and Lawrence A. Pervin, 448–471. New York: Guilford Press.

IDENTITY AND CULTURAL HYBRIDITY

CHAPTER ONE

"BRITTLE IDENTITIES": IDENTITY DISCOURSES IN THE WORK OF AUSTRIAN AUTHOR JULYA RABINOVICH

ELIN NESJE VESTLI

Introduction

"Mich interessieren brüchige Identitäten" (Paterno 2014).[1] With this statement, Julya Rabinowich sums up her previous work. Her protagonists, most of them from migration backgrounds, appear "brittle" in many ways. They are on the move, crossing borders that are both real and metaphorical. Uprooted and transplanted,[2] as the author also characterizes herself, they struggle to find a way to grow new roots without totally letting go of the old ones, to re-position themselves in a new setting. In the following, I will look into the literary identity discourses in Rabinowich's novels *Spaltkopf* (2008 [*Splithead*]), *Dazwischen: Ich* (2016 [In-between: I, my trans.]), which show several parallels, and finally *Die Erdfresserin* (2012 [The Woman Who Ate Dirt, my trans.]), Rabinowich's darkest and most radical novel to date.

Biography and Literary Work

Julya Rabinowich was born into a Jewish-Russian family in St. Petersburg in 1970; the family migrated to Austria in 1977. Rabinowich is a trained artist from the University of Applied Arts in Vienna; her graduation portfolio consisted of a cycle of paintings entitled *Spaltkopf* (2006),[3] or *Splithead* in its English translation, the same title she chose for her debut novel, inspired by her own migration experiences. Moreover, her work as a simultaneous translator (Russian-German) during psychotherapy sessions for refugees in Vienna influences her writings; the refugees' stories, which she translated while working as a state-approved interpreter between 2006 and 2012, leave literary traces, especially in *Die*

Erdfresserin (in which the author pictures herself as a translator with her characteristic dark page haircut, (cf. Rabinowich 2012, 155)) and in *Dazwischen: Ich.*

Rabinowich made her debut as a writer in 2003 with an early version of *Spaltkopf* (cf. Schwenns-Harrant 2014, 65), for which she was honoured with the annual award from "edition exil", an Austrian literary support program for authors with migration backgrounds. Today she stands her ground within Austrian contemporary literature. Whereas the three novels discussed in this chapter deal with the negotiation of identity in the context of transnational biographies, she turns in a quite different direction with *Herznovelle* (2011) and *Krötenliebe* (2016). The tautly composed *Herznovelle*, the title of which gives associations to Arthur Schnitzler's *Traumnovelle*, thematizes the identity crisis of a well off, but bored wife. *Krötenliebe* deals with the Austrian icons Alma Mahler and Oskar Kokoschka as well as with the Austrian-Jewish biologist Paul Kammerer, first acclaimed as the new Darwin, then framed as a fraud, who embodies the Jewish "Leerstelle" in the Austrian official memory. With these novels, full of intertextual references to the Wiener Moderne, Rabinowich writes herself into the Austrian literary tradition.[4]

In-between?

Already in her debut novel Rabinowich uses the notion of in-between, falling between the two proverbial stools, a metaphor she radicalizes by comparing her situation to lying on a bed of nails (cf. Rabinowich 2011a, 12). Her novel for young adults uses this metaphor as its title: *Dazwischen: Ich*, In-between: I. The notion of in-between,[5] apparently indispensable in discussions of contemporary migration literature, is however both inaccurate and controversial, as pointed out by literary scholars, such as Leslie Adelson, Jim Jordan and Sandra Vlasta. As early as 2001, Adelson disagreed with the metaphor used in the sense of creating a "bridge 'between two worlds'" (Adelson 2001, 246). She argued that this paradigm of bridging two worlds "is designed to keep discrete worlds apart as much as it pretends to bring them together" (ibid.) and thus denies the dynamic nature of cultural transformation. With reference to Adelson, Jordan characterizes "the two worlds paradigm, complete with stools and bridges" (Jordan 2006, 497) as a "cliché" (ibid., 489). He refutes "a model of two fixed entities, with the migrant subject either suspended in motion or trapped between them" (Jordan 2006, 490). Sandra Vlasta also disputes the idea of "zwei intakte, in sich abgeschlossene Welten, die durch klare Grenzen voneinander geteilt sind" in her work on German-Turkish literature (Vlasta 2009, 103).[6] In her research on identity discourses in contemporary German-Turkish novels she points out the dynamic character, the permeability or mixture rather than the depiction of an existence between disparate spheres of life (cf. ibid, 104).

Based on this briefly outlined argument I will discuss Rabinowich's use of the metaphor of in-between in the context of the identity discourses in her literary work. The concept of hybrid identity, which goes back to the cultural theorist Stuart Hall, is relevant for my reading. The notion of a hybrid identity (cf. Griem 1998) aims to describe the composite identity of migrants, who have a bond to their country of origin, to which they are not able to (or do not wish to) return, and who thus adapt to the new country, to its culture and language, but not through full assimilation. As my point of departure I use Silke Fürstenau and Heike Niedrig, who apply the concept at an individual level and define hybrid identity as "einen spezifischen diskursiven Modus der Selbstverortung im (dominanten) national-kulturellen Repräsentationssystem" (Fürstenau, and Niedrig 2007, 247).[7] Their study is not based on a deficit assumption, but on the proposition that:

> 'neue, dauerhafte Formen und Inhalte von Selbstvergewisserungen und von sozialen Positionierungen', die insofern 'hybrid' seien, [...] die 'Elemente der Herkunfts- *und* der Aunkunftsregion' aufnähmen und 'zu etwas Eigenem und Neuen [sic!] transformierten". (ibid., 248)[8]

Spaltkopf

Spaltkopf is told from the perspective of the girl Mischka, who–together with her parents and grandmother–is allowed to leave the Soviet Union for Austria as a Jewish contingent refugee. The plot revolves around Mischka's experiences in Vienna in the late 1970s and 1980s and is expanded with childhood memories from the Soviet Union. The novel ends with her first visit in post-Soviet Russia when she is expecting her first child. After a prologue, the development of the protagonist unfolds in the following two, detailed parts. In this introduction, laid out as four lessons, a complex travel motif is established: "Ich mache also eine Reise. Ich bin eigentlich nie angekommen, weder bei meiner ersten noch nach der zweiten" (Rabinowich 2011a, 9),[9] expanded by a reference to the game hopscotch: "mein Spiel ist das Tempelhüpfen von Land zu Land" (ibid.).[10] In hopscotch, a game played mostly while standing on one leg, one advances through good balance and brave jumps, and one succeeds only by taking detours, in the sense of concentric movements and repeated attempts at self-positioning. By establishing this metaphor in the prologue, Rabinowich implies a difficult process of identity development, at the same time as she puts the protagonist in an agentive position: not trapped, but balancing on one leg, contemplating the next jump.

The external circumstances of Mischka's socialization are complex: the story begins with her exclusion and repression in the Soviet Union, continues with her experiences of the unknown West and her integration process in Vienna; on top of this she has to learn a new language. In addition, her family history is intricate. Through the traumatic and partly repressed fate of Mischka's grandmother, who was a victim of anti-Semitic pogroms in Tsarist Russia, a transgenerational family history of persecution emerges. As a result, the family's provenance is a taboo, not only in public, but also within the family itself. Mischka learns of her Jewish origin only through coincidence: "Juden, das sind wir" (ibid., 62).[11] The transgenerational family trauma, a result of denial as a condition of survival, is manifested in the image of the split head, an image handed down in the family, which expresses the trauma in a circuitous way, evoking fears based upon the experience of alterity for generations. Mischka learns about the image of the split head, but not what it represents. The split head is a metaphor of seemingly incompatible existences (cf. Niedermeier 2009); it is manifested in the novel as a second narrative voice and symbolizes the many layers of repressed memories through generations as well as the seemingly unbridgeable schism between external regulation and self-esteem, which prohibits an autonomous and realistic self-positioning. The power of the split head may only be restrained by looking it in the eye. Mischka finally succeeds in doing so, when she, after years of hesitation, again visits Russia where she finds herself again speaking (and dreaming in) Russian and by looking at herself in the mirror.

Even though Vienna–with its Mozartkugeln and Barbie dolls–fascinates her, Mischka soon becomes familiar with the experience of alterity, of being "the other". Obsessed with the desire for belonging, she compensates for her alleged strangeness by trying to distinguish herself positively from other migrant children in her class, for example by speaking German better than they do and through participation in the Catholic lessons. Over-adjustment follows, mimicry understood as the "desire to emerge as 'authentic' through mimicry" (Bhabha 1994, 88):

"Adoptiert werden will ich. Endlich Teil dieses Landes sein. Die richtigen Dinge tragen, tun und sagen. Das künstlich erblondete Haar über eine knochige Schulter werfen" (Rabinowich 2011a, 86);[12] she desires a visible transformation, which is impossible for the dark-haired, chubby girl, a reaction that the author–considering her own development–characterizes as "Integrationswut" (Schwenns-Harrant 2014, 60). [13] Later, during puberty, Mischka behaves auto-aggressively, developing eating disorders, dropping out and joining socially marginalized groups, for example as a punker and a squatter in Berlin in the late 80s, living on the edge of society.

An important subject in the contemporary transnational family novel is increased family tension as a result of the challenges due to migration. Not only does the protagonist herself suffer from the traumatic experience of migration and the difficulties of integration, but her family ties barely endure the struggles of everyday life in the new country. In the foreign environment, her relatives are the only people she truly knows, but at the same time family life forms the stage where battles are fought and frustration is voiced (cf. Schweiger 2012). Thus migration-related conflicts often turn out to be part of the power struggle between parents and children, for example when the child masters the new language and the social codes better than the parents. Additionally, puberty in the novel is depicted as a second emigration (cf. Rabinowich 2011a, 82) since Mischka's pubertal rebellion is directed not only against the authority of her parents, but also against the Russian values they voice. The daughter's emancipation makes excessive demands on the father, who sees his authority as paterfamilias in danger. "Mein Vater, eigentlich liberal und offen, fällt ins tiefste Patriarchat zurück. [...] Alle Freiheiten, die mir bisher gewährt wurden, werden von meiner Periode hinweggeschwemmt" (ibid., 80–81).[14] The conflicts end when her father leaves for Russia, where he unexpectedly dies–leaving his daughter feeling guilty and lost.

The novel traces the protagonist's complex journey, both in the literal world and in the transcendent sense. In this way, the travel motif highlights the challenges of migration and adolescence. Mischka's journey consists of several self-positionings, partly one-legged (playing hopscotch), partly on shifting ground (cf. ibid, 183), choosing the bed of nails (cf. ibid., 12, 181) over the two proverbial stools–if you do not want to get hurt, you must not lean on the solid surfaces. At the same time, however a linguistic self-positioning takes place. Through the declaration "ich schreibe" (ibid., 11),[15] she makes a linguistic conquest, implementing the metaphor of translation as a border crossing. Her earlier rejection of the Russian language, which she felt was forced upon her by her parents, crumbles. When she enters a new phase of life through the birth of her own daughter, she allows the repressed language to surface in her dreams: "Ich träume auf Russisch neuerdings" (ibid., 144).[16] The conquest of the German language is no longer opposed to her dreams in Russian, they both belong to her. With one leg in each language, she finally recovers her balance.

Dazwischen: Ich

Rabinowich's first novel for young readers uses her play *Tagfinsternis* (2014) as its point of departure. The play explores the conflicts in a family living in a refugee accommodation, showing how the resultant mental stress affects the relations between them and challenges their self-esteem. The conflict culminates when the father decides to return to their country of origin, now a battle zone, to support his brother, thus jeopardizing their asylum application and the future of the whole family. The young daughter, in the play a minor character, turns out to be the protagonist and first-person narrator in *Dazwischen: Ich*; the novel is composed as her diary.

The teenager Madina lives together with her parents, a younger brother and an aunt in a refugee accommodation in a German-speaking country. At the beginning of the novel, they have been living there for approximately two years, and during this time Madina has developed into a young woman. Her discovery of her own body and her startling first, timid experience of love are familiar features of the adolescent novel. Her development is overshadowed by the bleak atmosphere of the refugee lodgings, the lack of private space and their uncertain future. Their application for asylum has not yet been processed, and their future is on hold.

In contrast to her parents, who spend the whole day in the cramped lodgings, Madina attends school and thus experiences a respite. She quickly learns German, and with the help of her best friend, Laura, she gradually finds her place in the new country, although she is always aware of a certain distance to her classmates–based on her different upbringing and experiences. Her parents, on the other hand, isolate themselves, especially her father, who increasingly reflects on his cultural and religious origin: "Wir werden jetzt traditionell, damit ja niemand vergisst, wer wir sind" (Rabinowich 2016, 112).[17] In this way, he hopes to preserve his authority as paterfamilias, which he feels is endangered by the customs of the new country. For reasons that are logical only for him, he refuses to learn German and thus paradoxically turns out to be dependent on his daughter, who must act as interpreter between her parents and the authorities, a humiliation which he in turn tries to compensate for by enforcing even stricter educational measures. This accelerates Madina's pubertal conflicts with her parents: she loves her father and understands his concern for her, but she wants to set the course for her future herself, as is customary in the new country: "Damals fand ich das in Ordnung [dass die Frauen die Hausarbeit machen, während die Männer sich ausruhen]. Heute nicht mehr" (ibid., 39).[18] She does not care about simple, short-term compromises, like being allowed to wear pants or to stay overnight at Laura's house, she wants to make future-oriented and long-term decisions: "Ich will hier leben" (ibid., 247).[19]

Compared to *Spaltkopf*, the complex social and cultural framework in *Dazwischen: Ich* has been simplified, as is to be expected considering the target group of readers. To make the plot as exemplary as possible, we are not told which country Madina originally comes from or what language is her native tongue; her religious affiliation is only indicated by references to wearing a headscarf (which she is not forced to do). The traumatizing events that forced her family to flee concentrate on specific, memorable images in the form of flashbacks, such as the death of her best friend, which demonstrates how the traumatic impact focuses on interpersonal relationships rather than political analyses or statements. The repeated flashbacks are triggered by harmless events, such as fireworks, and thus exemplify the permanent emotional stress under which refugees live in a context that is comprehensible for young readers. The uncertainty of the future, not being able to make plans, the repeated questioning by the authorities as well as clumsy and malicious comments at school contribute to the emotional insecurity in Madina's daily life. However, the author avoids a black-and-white portrait by including significant contrast figures that positively contribute to Madina's development, such as the clerk who confirms her in her new self-confidence: "'Du machst das toll […]. Solche wie dich können wir hier gut brauchen.' Und wirklich, es klingt blöd, aber ich denke: Das weiß ich" (ibid., 252).[20]

Even though Madina is strong-willed, gifted, and has few, but supportive friends, she is faced with a complex threshold that she must cross: to a new home, to a new language, to a new stage in her life. And this symbolic threshold seems to involve both the proverbial two stools and bridges of no return: on one side are her old home and cultural affiliation, on the other a shore with a yet unknown future, but at least a future she will be able to determine for herself. As in *Spaltkopf*, this transition is emphasized by a variation of leitmotifs such as thresholds, borders, gangways and landings–metaphors corresponding with the fateful journey she made as a refugee, slowly but surely replacing the traumatic memories of death and fear with vigorous images of self-determination. Through the example of her friend Lynne's father, who is originally from Turkey, Madina experiences a counterpart to the backward-looking behaviour of her father and is thus encouraged to find her own way. She finds guidance in her own imaginary space. As a mental refuge, she imagines a fairy-tale forest to which she retreats when the demands become overwhelming. As the inner-family conflict grows, her dreams offer a space where she can try out different trajectories of self-development. The imaginary journey that she makes in her dreams is dangerous, but finally leads to the insight that there is no journey that can return her to her native country and the child she once was. Ahead of her is only the future. Finally, she sees herself "auf der Kommandobrücke, das Steuerrad in meinen Händen. […] Ich bin die Steuerfrau" (ibid., 243),[21] as commander in chief in her own life, and takes her destiny in her own hands. When her father decides to return to the war zone to support his remaining relatives, Madina decides to choose her own destiny. Symbolically she cuts off her long pigtails. She occupies the vacancy in the family created by the departure of her father, which also includes taking responsibility for others as well as standing her own ground: "Ich werde dableiben" (ibid., 255).[22]

Die Erdfresserin

Die Erdfresserin traces the destiny of an illegal prostitute in Vienna. The first-person narrator, Diana, comes from the former Soviet republic Dagestan and supports her family–her mother, sister and her handicapped son back home–with her income in Austria. When she is caught in a police raid and faces deportation, a policeman protects her; in return, she takes up with him, the relationship however remains characterized by increasing dependency. When he dies after severe illness and she is left with nothing, Diana suffers a mental breakdown and is hospitalized. The novel ends with her flight from the hospital; she wants to return to Dagestan on foot to help her son.

A short prologue, in which the first-person narrator is fighting her way through the wilderness, disappearing into nothing, foreshadows the end of the novel. In the following part, "Davor",[23] the conversation therapy prescribed in hospital frames her memories from her childhood and the time spent in Vienna before her breakdown. In the second part, "Danach",[24] which starts with her escape from the hospital, fragmented memories and chaotic impressions of her being on the run, straying through foreign woods and crossing borders form a structure in which the boundaries between reality, memories, dream and nightmare are blurred. In the end, she disappears: "Ich gehe weiter. Ich gehe tiefer. Tiefer. Tiefer. Ich gehe. Ich gehe. Gehe. Gehe" (Rabinowich 2012, 236),[25] probably into her death (cf. Schwens-Harrant 2014, 73). Her self-dissolution is traced narratively: the text becomes increasingly fragmented, the use of the pronoun I ultimately ceases, and the text is no more; it seeps into the earth (cf. Ekelund 2015, 205).

As an illegal prostitute, Diana lives on the verge of society. However, in contrast to her friend Nastja, who also works on the streets and so desperately wants to fit in that she bleaches her hair so radically that it falls out, Diana embraces her own marginalization with an aggressive attitude. She demonstratively flags her self-assertion as she repeats that she is not one to give up. Economic emergencies determine her actions; she cannot afford sentimentality, she frequently and accusingly tells her therapist. It would be too simple, however, to reduce the novel to criticism of strict asylum procedure, which does not acknowledge economic need. Embedded childhood memories show that Diana's marginalization does not come from migration alone, but is rooted in a sense of alterity, which Rabinowich characterizes as "eine aus innerer Zerrissenheit selbst gewählte Fremdheit" (Geets 2011).[26] It seems obvious that Diana, since the disappearance of her father when she was a child, has occupied the empty space after her father's departure, and taken over the responsibilities of the head of the family. Thus she is the one who makes a daily living, the one who is needed, but not necessarily the one the family loves: "Ihr lebt mehr als gut von meiner Hölle" (Rabinowich 2012, 14),[27] she accusingly says to her sister. Consequently, her travels abroad to earn money resemble hunting,[28] which fits the name Diana, the goddess of the hunt, perhaps not her given name, but the name of her choice: "Sie können mich meinetwegen Diana nennen. [...] Diana und nichts" (ibid., 156).[29] Through her acceptance of her otherness, she–on one hand–acquires a great strength, "Es gibt welche, die liegen bleiben. Ich gehöre zu denen, die aufstehen und weitergehen" (ibid., 5);[30] the external constraints–for instance the death of Leo, which deprives her of a safe place to stay, "Das [Wohnungs]Schloss ausgetauscht und meine Schlüssel nutzlos geworden" (ibid., 148)[31] –however teach her that her self-determination has its limits.

Rabinowich provides her protagonist with an unusual biography with several insidious "Leerstellen". As a result a female character emerges, whose development is characterized by a traumatic experience of loss and an emotional coldness due to secrets in her dysfunctional family. Her theatre studies, specializing in directing, probably inspired by her forbidden reading during childhood, have given her an extensive classical literary education, but it remains an education with few prospects of remuneration. As a theatre director to be, she is used to standing her ground, to asserting herself, not only defining her own position, but also those of others. As the given circumstances however decrease the scope for individual development, her behaviour slips into aggression and auto-aggression; the fact that she prostitutes herself, may also be seen as an act of auto-aggression. Eventually she sees her own face in the mirror–a leitmotif in Rabinowich's work–in the form of a snake's head, or a Gorgon, a female creature in Greek mythology, whose gaze could turn others into stone, a threatening look that frightens everyone who sees her. Confronted with her own gaze in the mirror Diana feels threatened and ducks from the danger that emanates from herself (cf. ibid., 96). She is dangerous, not only for others, but most of all she is a threat to herself.

In *Die Erdfresserin* the border between dream and reality is even more blurred than in *Spaltkopf*; the novel "erschöpft sich keinesweg in seiner realistischen Dimension" (Hofmann and Patrut 2015, 143).[32] Special attention should be drawn to the many mythological references. Even the title indicates the mythical dimension of the novel. The earth, a leitmotif, stands for the earth-bound, for Diana's wish to belong, to feel at home, and is a counter-movement to her uprooting and her increasing psychological illness. At first the earth seems to heal, later her efforts turn into self-destruction, for example, when she–in the literal sense of the word–eats dirt; she literally loses the ground under her feet. Her distinctive desire for earth, not only touching it, but also eating it, is a craving well known in native populations in for example Africa (known as geophagy) and is combined with her idea of the golem, a mythological creature connected to Judaism. A golem is a homunculus, created from mud or clay, brought to life and controlled by a human being. The golem which Diana creates as she strays through the dark woods does not however remain under her control. He follows his own will, repeatedly disappears, then comes back to finally lead the way, but only ending up back in the mud, from which she originally created him. There he lets her see herself once again as a Gorgon with snakes in her hair, reflected in a puddle of water ("Der Atmen rührt kleine Wellen auf, das Haar gerät in unruhige Bewegungen, verwischt, setzt sich erneut zusammen. Dampf breitet sich darüber, ich verschwinde im Nebel" (Rabinowich 2012, 5).[33] "Ich folge meinem Schatten" (ibid.).[34] Thus, she regresses, dissolving gradually.

In-between

The three protagonists discussed here are contextualized in transgenerational and transnational family histories; they are challenged not only by migration, but also by familial silence and taboos. In this respect, Rabinowich's work connects with one of the comprehensive trends in German contemporary literature. Mischka's, Madina's and Diana's attempts to stand their own ground are therefore not only made difficult by their migration backgrounds or by the clichés and prejudices they are faced with, but also by complex family constellations.

Rabinowich shows hard-won positions, which are associated with high emotional costs. The processes that Mischka and Madina go through are characterized by both adaptation and rebellion, which ultimately results in the juxtaposed position of the ambiguous "Angekommen, aber nicht daheim" (Rabinowich 2011a, 12),[35] as expressed in *Spaltkopf*. Even though the identity discourse in *Dazwischen: Ich* appears in a language adapted for its young target group, Madina's dilemma is absolutely existential and echoes *Spaltkopf*: "Um anzukommen, muss man zuerst richtig weggehen" (Rabinowich 2016, 112).[36] Both protagonists depict their own struggles for self-positioning with metaphors like "Nagelbrett" (Rabinowich 2011a, 12)[37] or "zwischen allem" (Rabinowich 2016, 118).[38] This in-between state is, however, not a static space, but a space in which one can negotiate both on an individual and family level as well as on a social level. Nor do leitmotifs such as thresholds, gangways or landings suggest a permanent in-between state, as is clearly expressed by Madina's many speculations about where she wants to spend her future; they emphasize instead the dynamic process underlying the more sophisticated metaphoric narrative in *Spaltkopf*, aimed at a different target group. In Rabinowich's debut novel this dynamics is expressed not least through the elaborated linguistic biography of the protagonist in which both Russian and German might coexist, a linguistic conquest which echoes Rabinowich's own position: "In der Sprache allerdings fühle ich mich sowohl angekommen als auch daheim" (Schilly 2008).[39] In contrast to Mischka and Madina, who both have a future-oriented perspective, despite the open endings of the novels, *Die Erdfresserin* traces a psychogram of radical ego dissolution.

Rabinowich's protagonists are in many ways living on the edge, balancing while trying to find their own way, feeling uprooted and insecure, but all the same their brittleness seems to give them strength and open their eyes for the possibilities around them. Even if you are in one sense or another in-between, you are not necessarily trapped. Sometimes a simple, one-legged jump can move you forward–as is the case with Mischka and Madina–who succeed in transforming their initial disunity into something independent and new. Considering the perspective from the margins might be well worthwhile, Rabinowich once stated (cf. Rabinowich 2010, 7). The marginal position is not only "als Begrenzung zu verstehen. Er ist auch ein Ort, an dem Begegnungen und Vermischungen stattfinden und etwas 'Neues' entstehen kann" (Schwaiger 2016, 101).[40]

Notes

[1] "I am interested in brittle identities" (my trans.).
[2] Rabinowich uses the image "entwurzelt und umgetopft", uprooted and transplanted, on her homepage, cf. http://www.julya-rabinowich.com/leben.html [Accessed 26.02.2019].
[3] Cf. http://julya-rabinowich.com [Accessed 26.02.2019].
[4] Current state of research on Rabinowich's authorship cf. Vestli 2016.
[5] Cf. Bhabha 1990, 211.
[6] "two intact, self-contained worlds, separated by clear boundaries" (my trans.).
[7] "a specific discursive mode of self-location in the (dominant) national-cultural representation system" (my trans.).
[8] "'new, lasting forms and contents of self-assurances and social positions' which are 'hybrid' in so far as the 'elements of the region of origin and of the region of origin' and 'transformed into something independent and new'" (my trans.). The quote within the quote comes from Ludger Priess (2000): "Transmigranten" als ein Typ von Arbeitswanderern in pluri-lokalen sozialen Räumen. In Migration, gesellschaftliche Differenzierung und Bildung, edited by Ingrid Gogolin, and Bernhard Nauck, 415–447, 418. Opladen: Leske + Budrich.
[9] The English quotations from *Spaltkopf* are from the translation by Tess Lewis 2011, *Splithead*. "So, I'm travelling. I never did arrive, not on my first trip, not after my second" (3).
[10] "My game is hopscotch from one land to another" (3).
[11] "The Jews, that's us" (59).
[12] "I want to be adopted. To finally be part of this country. To wear, say and do the right things. To toss bleached-blonde hair over a bony shoulder" (85).

[13] "'integration fury" (my trans.).
[14] "My father, actually open and liberal, regresses to staunchest patriarchy. [...] All the freedom I'd previously been granted was washed away with my period" (79–80).
[15] "I write" (6).
[16] "I have started dreaming in Russian" (165).
[17] "We are now becoming traditional so no one will forget who we are" (my trans.).
[18] "At that time, I found it all right [that the women do the housework while the men rest]. Not today" (my trans.).
[19] "I want to live here" (my trans.).
[20] "'You're doing great [...]. We need persons like you here.' And really, it sounds stupid, but I think: I know that" (my trans.).
[21] "on the command bridge, the steering wheel in mine hands. [...] I am the woman in charge" (my trans.).
[22] "I will stay" (my trans.).
[23] "Before" (my trans.).
[24] "Afterwards" (my trans.).
[25] "I move on. I move deeper into the woods. Deeper. Deeper. I walk. I walk. Walk. Walk" (my trans.).
[26] "a self-chosen marginalization which dates back to her inner self-consciousness" (my trans.).
[27] "You live more than well on my hell" (my trans.).
[28] She sends her prey – mostly money, but also medication, back to Dagestan, cf. Rabinowich 2012, 90.
[29] "You may call me Diana [...] Diana and nothing" (my trans.).
[30] "There are some who are left behind. I belong to those who get up and go on" (my trans.).
[31] "The [apartment] lock was exchanged and my keys were useless" (my trans.).
[32] "does by no means exclusively take place in the realistic dimension" (my trans.).
[33] "Her breathing stirs up small waves, the hair falls into restless movements, blurs, and sits down again. Vapour spreads over, I disappear in the mist" (my trans.).
[34] "I follow my shadow" (my trans.).
[35] "I'm not home. I have arrived" (7).
[36] "To get there, you have to walk away first" (my trans.).
[37] "bed of nails" (12).
[38] "between everything" (my trans.).
[39] "In the language, however, I feel both that I have arrived and that I am at home" (my trans.).
[40] "to be understood as a limitation. It is also a place where encounters and mingling take place and something 'new' can emerge" (my trans.).

References

http://www.julya-rabinowich.com/leben.html [Accessed 26. 02.2019].
Adelson, Leslie A. 2001. "Against Between–Ein Manifest gegen das Dazwischen." In *Unpacking Europe*, edited by Salah Hassan, and Iftikhar Dadi, 244–255. Rotterdam: NAi Publishers.
Bhabha, Homi. 1990. "The Third Space." In *Identity. Community, Culture and Difference*, edited by Jonathan Rutherford, 207–221. London: Lawrence & Wishart.
—. 1994. *The Location of Culture*. London, New York: Routledge.
Ekelund, Lena. 2015. "Nomadinnen in Österreich." In *Österreichische Gegenwartsliteratur. Text+Kritik, Zeitschrift für Literatur*, Begründet von Heinz Ludwig Arnold, IX/15, 198–207.
Fürstenau, Sara, and Heike Niedrig. 2007. "Hybride Identitäten? Selbstverortung jugendlicher TransmigrantInnen." In *Diskurs Kindheit- und Jugendforschung*, Vol. 3, 2007: 247–262.
Geets, Siobhan. 2011. "Werkzeug Sprache: Mehrsprachige Autoren sind selten." In *Die Presse*, 13.9.2011, http://diepresse.com/home/panorama/integration/693007/Werkzeug-Sprache_Mehrsprachige-Autoren-sind-selten [Accessed 26.02.2019].
Griem, Julika. 1998. "Hybridität." In *Metzler Lexikon Literatur- und Kulturtheorie. Ansätze–Personen–Grundbegriffe*, edited by Ansgar Nünning, 220–221. Stuttgart, Weimar: Metzler.
Hofmann, Michael and Iulia-Karin Patrut. 2015. *Einführung in die interkulturelle Literatur*. Darmstadt: Wissenschaftliche Buchgesellschaft (=Günter E. Grimm, and Klaus-Michael Bogdal (ed.): Einführungen Germanistik).
Jordan, Jim. 2006. "More than a metaphor. The passing of the two worlds paradigm in German-language diasporic Literature." In *German Life and Letters* 59-4 October 2006, 0016-8777 (print): 1468-0483 (online), 488–499.
Niedermeier, Cornelia. 2009. "Der Aufbruch in die (eigene) Fremde." In *Der Standard*, 25.3.2009.
Paterno, Petra. 2014. "Die menschliche Note fehlt." Interview. In *WienerZeitung* 14.1.2014.
Rabinowich, Julya. 2010. "Das Unbehagen in der Migrantenliteratur." In *preistexte* 10, edited by Christa Stippinger, 7–9. Wien: Edition Exil.
—. 2016. *Dazwischen: Ich*. München: Hanser.
—. 2011a. *Spaltkopf*. Wien: Deuticke.
—. 2011b. *Splithead*. Translated by Tess Lewis. London: Portobello.
—. 2012. *Die Erdfresserin*. Wien: Deuticke.

Schilly, Julia. 2008. "Dann hätten wir bald viele Würstelstand-Literaten." In *Der Standard*, Wien, 19.11.2008.
Schwaiger, Silke. 2016. *Über die Schwelle. Literatur und Migration um das Kulturzentrum exil.* Wien: Praesens.
Schweiger, Hannes. 2012. "Sprechen 'Spaltköpfe' mit 'Engelszungen'? Identitätsverhandlungen in transnationalen Familiengeschichten." In *Immer wieder Familie. Familien- und Generationenromane in der neueren Literatur*, edited by Hajnalka Nagy, and Werner Wintersteiner 157–172. Innsbruck, Wien, Bozen: StudienVerlag. (=Schriftenreihe Literatur. Institut für Österreichkunde 26).
Schwens-Harrant, Brigitte. 2014. "Es muss verändert werden." In *Ankommen. Gespräche mit Dimitré Dinev, Anna Kim, Radek Knapp, Julya Rabinowich, Michael Stavaric*, edited by Brigitte Schwens-Harrant, 53–85. Wien, Graz, Klagenfurt: Styria.
Vestli, Elin Nesje. 2016. "Julya Rabinowich." In *Kritisches Lexikon zur deutschsprachigen Gegenwartsliteratur*. München: Verlag Text+Kritik.
Vlasta, Sandra. 2009. "Das Ende des 'Dazwischen'–Ausbildung von Identitäten in Texten von Imran Ayata, Yadé Kara und Feridun Zaimoglu." In *Von der nationalen zur internationalen Literatur. Transkulturelle deutschsprachige Literatur und Kultur im Zeitalter globaler Migration*, edited by Helmut Schmitz, 101–116. Amsterdam, New York: Rodopi (=Amsterdamer Beiträge zur neueren Germanistik, 69).

Chapter Two

Identity, Trauma and Language Confusion in Olga Grajsnowa's *Der Russe ist einer der Birken liebt* and *Gott ist nicht Schüchtern*

Grazziella Predoui

Born in Azerbaijan in a Russian-Jewish family which later emigrated to Germany, Olga Grjasnowa has to date published three novels: *Der Russe ist einer der Birken liebt* (2012 [A Russian is a person who loves birches, my trans.]), *Die juristische Unschärfe einer Ehe* (2014 [The judicial ambiguity of a marriage, my trans.]) and *Gott ist nicht schüchtern* (2017 [God is not shy, my trans.]). Her protagonists, Masha, Amal and Hammoudi are nomads, cross-border commuters and migrants–men and women who leave their countries of origin due to war, expulsion, and religious persecution, to search for substitute homes and peace. They are drifters and failures, people who are negotiating new identities, transcending national, cultural and ego-boundaries in times of heightened refugee and migratory movements. The author examines their exceptional, traumatic circumstances, showing how family traumas are passed on from one generation to the next, and how these families collapse as a result of the shocks of war, migration, persecution and the end of political systems. She describes the experience of immigration to Germany through the eyes of a cosmopolitan, but also rootless generation of young people.

In this chapter, I focus on two of Grjasnowa's novels, *Der Russe ist einer der Birken liebt* and *Gott ist nicht schüchtern*, tracing the identity negotiations of the protagonists, their traumatic experiences in leaving their native countries, with the alienation, loss of language and loss of roots this entails. All of the protagonists migrate between different countries and find that they belong neither here nor there.

The novel *Der Russe ist einer der Birken liebt*, awarded the Klaus-Michael-Kühne prize, handles motifs such as national and linguistic boundaries, border experiences and crossings, the feeling of estrangement and the negotiation of identities which takes place in the crossing of cultural thresholds. The book is divided into four parts, with different settings: the first two parts take place in Frankfurt am Main with flashbacks to Baku–through which the traumatic past of the protagonist, Masha, is introduced. The third part takes place in Tel Aviv and the fourth in Palestine, all places in which Masha tries to cope with her trauma. The parts are sub-divided into short chapters, in which the narrator relates episodes of her life story. The story begins on the day her partner Elias is involved in a sports accident which leads to his death, and ends with the turning point in her life crisis. Numerous flashbacks interrupt the chronological course of the action and offer insight into Masha's childhood, her isolation in Germany, her education and her circle of friends.

The three countries where the action takes place serve different purposes: Azerbaijan is the site of her fragmented childhood memories with their accompanying trauma. Germany is associated with both alienation and socialization; we hear about her encounters with a number of young people with cosmopolitan, mobile, hybrid identities. Israel is where she searches for her Jewish roots and tries to escape from the grief stemming from the loss of Elias. These three countries and the three venues of Frankfurt, Baku and Tel Aviv create a network of cross-border structures, populated by people of different origins, cultures, religions and languages, where traces of successive conflicts are visible everywhere. The mechanisms of hatred and exclusion familiar to Masha from Azerbaijan are repeated in Germany and in Israel, where the dichotomy between Jews and non-Jews influences daily life and politics. The theme of identity is omnipresent, along with the motifs of exclusion, persecution and expulsion.

Concepts of Identity

A review in the *Neue Züricher Zeitung* characterizes the text as a "hochtouriges Identitätskarussel"[1] (Plath 2012). The title of the novel itself also alludes to the theme of identity, as it is derived from a conversation about national stereotypes found in Chekhov's drama *Drei Schwestern* (1900 [*Three Sisters*]), where the birch tree functions as a metaphor for the Russian soul (Andre 2012). In response to Masha's question about what

Russians are like, a character answers: "Wie Leute die Birken lieben" (Grjasnowa 2013, 5).[2] His stereotypical description of Palestinians is "Wie Leute die gewohnt sind, lange zu warten" (ibid., 265).[3] Catani argues that the novel's central theme is the "postkoloniale Kritik an identitätsstiftenden Zuschreibungen, die das Subjekt religiös, geschlechtlich und ethnisch möglichst eindeutig zu klassifizieren suchen und kulturelle [Diversität im Ansatz ausblenden]"[4] (Catani 2015, 95).

Masha dominates the plot, the view of German society unfolds from her perspective, as well as the view of life in Israel and of her childhood. As the daughter of Azerbaijani immigrants, who are Jewish, but do not speak Hebrew, she is "ein menschliches Mosaik, zusammengesetzt aus unterschiedlichsten ethnischen Teilchen",[5] as Ludmilla Weber (2017) argues–she moved to Germany during the struggles around Nagorno-Karabakh. 14,000 inhabitants of Armenian origin fled, the conflict spread to "Gewalt, Vertreibungen, Vergewaltigungen und Pogrome auf beiden Seiten" (Grjasnowa 2013, 46).[6] The hatred of other ethnic groups was fueled artificially by nationalist parties; it mutated from Armenian resentment towards Russians, to hatred of Jews and everybody else.

Breaks and new beginnings run like threads throughout her story, through her family history and the lives of her few friends, testifying to the fragility of political and social systems. Her life is characterized by the friction inherent in her migrant identity. When she is asked about her strange roots, she reacts bitterly–"spürte ich, wie mir die Gallenflüssigkeit hochkam. Schlimmer wurde es […] beim Adjektiv postmigrantisch" (ibid., 12)[7]–we learn that she has been demoted two classes at school because of her lack of language skills.

The already traumatized student learns that "Sprachen Macht bedeuteten. Wer kein Deutsch sprach, hatte keine Stimme, und wer bruchstückhaft sprach, wurde überhört" (ibid., 37).[8] Due to her divergent cultural background and deficient German, this sensitive girl experiences exclusion. She becomes almost mute, and feels homeless and alienated. "1996 war ich in Deutschland. 1997 dachte ich zum ersten Mal über Selbstmord nach" (ibid., 40).[9] The trauma of her shattered childhood and losing her home is expressed in two simple sentences, laconically suggesting her probable fate. However, Masha does not take refuge in the traditional role of the migrant as victim; she wants to travel, she has a gift for languages and studies to become an interpreter. Learning foreign languages helps her bridge the inner gap and fill the emptiness inside her. Her language skills are quite astonishing:

> In der Schule hatte ich Englisch, Französisch und ein wenig Italienisch gelernt [...] Danach hatte ich mich für ein Dolmetscherstudium eingeschrieben und in meiner Freizeit Italienisch, Spanisch und ein bisschen Polnisch gelernt, aber für die slawische Sprachgruppe konnte ich mich nie sonderlich begeistern. (ibid., 31)[10]

In becoming a professional interpreter, Masha consolidates her transition from one culture to another as a pattern of action (Klatt 2013, 221), and acts transculturally as a migrant between different spaces. Madlen Kazmierczak (2016, 255) emphasizes the fact that the concepts of native country, ethnicity, nationality, culture or religion are of secondary importance in Masha's identity formation. Cultural and national borders have lost their validity for her and she does not accept religious traditions. When the Palestinian Ishmael asks her about her faith, Masha replies that she does not believe in God, culture or nation: "Weißt du, in meiner Kindheit gab es einen gepackten Koffer zu Hause, für den Fall der Fälle" (Grjasnowa 2013, 276).[11] She is not interested in being assimilated as a German citizen, but prefers her multiple, heterogeneous cultural identity. She has never practiced the Jewish faith and does not want to be recognized as a Jew. She lives in a third place, in the in-between, where her cultural identity is produced in the intersections between the spheres of class, gender, race, nation, and location. In *The Location of Culture* (2011), Homi Bhaba defines the area of culture as that of transnationalism. A person's identity is not rooted in an internal system, but in the encounters with divergent tendencies that affect her. Referring to the spatial dimension, Bhaba states that postcolonial subjects do not live in a defined space that shapes their identity, but in a "third space" that is neither the first of the initial culture nor the second of the former colonial power. This third, hybrid space encompasses both spaces and is simultaneously extraterritorial (Bhaba 2011).

Andreas Thamm (2017) recognizes in Masha a "Kristallisationspunkt der Kulturen", eine "hochintelligente Kosmopolitin, ein Bindeglied zwischen Ost und West."[12] Under the dazzling surface of a woman gifted in languages, for whom languages represent signposts and who completed her studies more quickly than her peers, and who, like Julya Rabinowich's protagonist from the migration novel *Spaltkopf* (2008, *Splithead*), is also trained as an interpreter, hides a doubly traumatized young woman. The different threads of the narrative are all tied to trauma, threads which Chris

Wilpert (2015, 66) describes as tracing transgenerational and transhistoric trauma. The unexpected loss of her friend Elias leads Masha to take up a job offer, travelling from Germany to Israel. This in turn triggers another personal trauma, the recovery of memories connected to the pogroms in January 1990 in Baku, which intersects with the trauma experienced by her family. Thus, the trauma experienced in her native country leaks into her life in her adopted country.

The post-Soviet civil war and the bloody conflicts between Armenians and Azerbaijani have shaped Masha's childhood, and she re-experiences the wartime trauma of massacres carried out in the name of ethnic cleansing. As a girl, she witnessed how a young Armenian woman was blown out of a window and smashed bloodily on the pavement. This image haunts Masha throughout the novel, the victim's light-blue dress reminding her of the disaster. But it is the death of Elias that recalls the memory, propelling Masha into a deep life and identity crisis, intertwining the old bloody image with the new traumatic experience. The loss affects Masha physically as well as mentally and rekindles her post-traumatic stress disorder, which she has suffered from ever since she saw the woman collapsing beside her on the street, bleeding to death. The first flashback occurs during a conversation with Elias, who asks about the pogroms which led to her emigration. The first time Masha speaks of the horrific mass murders, she has not yet contextualized the events; she describes the events from a third person perspective, even though the child she is speaking about was herself. The traumatic childhood event is deeply rooted in her subconscious; her reality becomes increasingly brittle and permeable to the repressed childhood memories after her lover's traumatic death. Her painstakingly constructed reality breaks down again, causing her to transcend her own limits: she plagues herself with reproaches and self-doubts, breaks down inside, has to cope with the pain of loss and reacts with illness, mental torment, oblivion and psychotic suppression. "Mein Immunsystem gab kurz nach dem Begräbnis auf […]. Mein Körper wollte nicht mehr weitermachen. […]. Ich lebte im Vakuum" (Grjasnowa 2013, 115).[13] Her panic attacks, breathlessness and fainting, vomiting and weight loss are the physical manifestations of her psychic decay, a "flackernde Folge von Angst, Hilflosigkeit, Verzweiflung, Einsamkeit" (Buchholz 2012).[14] The job offer in Tel Aviv as an interpreter for a German company offers a timely, geographical escape from personal trauma. The journey to Israel can be read on the one hand as an escape from inner images, grief and anger over the death of Elias and on the other hand as the search for her identity and her Jewish roots.

Israel is a place where different religions and ethnic groups meet, where violence is ubiquitous, due to the hostility between Israelis and Palestinians. Masha is confronted with Israeli violence and the harassment of the authorities in a grotesque manner on her arrival at the airport, when her laptop is considered suspicious and thus destroyed. This brutality continues in Israel; her distant kinsmen suffer from identity problems similar to her own–they isolate themselves and do not adapt to the new culture. The men of the family look into the camera with a defeated expression, in an environment marked by their old USSR belongings.

In Tel Aviv, Masha breaks down even more than she did in Frankfurt, because her loss haunts her and she cannot work through it. She covers her deeply injured soul beneath pseudo-feminist behavior, a lesbian relationship and parties: "Ich wollte [...] mich häppchenweise verlieren und nie wieder aufsammeln" (Grjasnowa 2013, 225).[15] Neither the spatial distance from Germany nor the nightlife or the beach of Tel Aviv can alleviate her suffering. Wherever Masha goes, she is perceived as a stranger. It seems as if she is always between worlds, conscious that she belongs nowhere. Her alienation is portrayed through Masha's everyday life, the landscapes or memories of other countries are tangible wherever she is. Azerbaijan can never be her secure childhood home, Germany never becomes home, and her solitude accompanies her in Israel. There is no spatially defined home that can safeguard her sense of self. Masha moves in many linguistic and cultural worlds and does not want to belong to any specific place: "Eigentlich hielt ich nichts von vertrauten Orten, der Begriff Heimat implizierte für mich stets den Pogrom" (ibid., 203).[16] Thus, her native country is rendered dysfunctional by the traumatic experiences of death, loss and loneliness and these existential experiences make home seem sinister. The existential native country is represented in the novel only as a lack, as a deficiency, but a fleeting feeling of security comes over her in Tel Aviv, because a taxi ride brings back memories of the Baku of her childhood:

> Als ich im Taxi durch Tel Aviv fuhr und im Radio laute orientalische Musik kam [...] fühlte ich mich zu Hause. Es war ein längst vergessenes Zuhause, ein Mosaik aus der Landschaft, der Temperatur, der Musik, den Geräuschen und dem Meer [...] bis ich merkte, dass ich zu Hause mit den Orten assoziierte, die mich an Baku erinnerten". (ibid., 253)[17]

Catani emphasizes the fact that "das religiöse, politische und kulturelle Niemandsland, in das Mascha sich [...] zurückzieht, um allen Identitätszuschreibungen entfliehen zu können, erweist sich als keines, das tatsächlich Halt bietet" (Catani 2015, 106).[18] This is confirmed in the conclusion of the novel, which ends in a non-place in the middle of a field near a Palestinian airport. Totally lonely and disoriented, Masha is disturbed by post-traumatic memories. She visualizes Elias's accident and hears the sound of an impacting body. She calls her ex-boyfriend Sami, declaring that she is bleeding, her physical decay corresponding to her disorientation. It remains unclear what happens to Masha, but this ending suggests that she will remain trapped in a threshold state between reality and fantasy.

Nomadic Identities In-between

Not only Masha's relationships with Elias and Tal, but also her other friendships, are presented in the novel as "interkulturelle, gegen- und gleichgeschlechtliche Begegnungen" (Kazmierczak 2016, 254).[19] Her friends have negotiated nomadic identities like hers, "Grenzgänger-Figuren, die eine transnational dominierte Biographie ebenso ausstellen wie ein transkulturell geleitetes Wertesystem" (Catani 2015, 98).[20] Masha socializes with marginalized groups only, people like her with migrant backgrounds. She has ambivalent erotic experiences with men as well as with women, reflecting her "religiöse und kulturelle Unentschlossenheit" (ibid.).[21] Her sexual ambivalence corresponds with her lack of belonging because "Transkulturalität und interkulturelle Begegnungen in dem Roman in […] persönlichen Biographien, in Bars und in Betten stattfindet" (Klatt 2013, 220).[22] In many social relations, she rejects genuine intimacy and retreats to her "Zynismus und Lakonie changierenden Weltsicht zurück" (Catani 97).[23]

Her friendships are intercultural meeting spaces, encompassing people with hybrid identities, who are also homeless, with injured identities. These characters, situated in the in-between, are found only in these chance encounters; they too have nowhere to live and put down roots; they move through cities like Paris, Frankfurt, Beirut, and Tel Aviv. Her close friend Elias, whose loss triggers her identity crisis, is German, but beneath the apparent harmony of his dignified home lie latent conflicts, the façade crumbling. He has also had a rupture in his identity because of an alcoholic father and is portrayed as an inner-German migrant from east to west. Masha's best friend Cem has a migration background; his parents are from Turkey, he was born in Frankfurt, studied at the University of Istanbul, he is a specialist in cultural theory, does not care about religious or ethnic affiliations and is also a homosexual. "Er war der erste aus seiner

Familie, der studierte und besseres Türkisch als seine Eltern sprach" (Grjasnowa 2013, 56).[24] But he is excluded in Germany, marked as a stranger and marginalized. In order to be liberated from the linguistic periphery, he has decided "ihre viel bewunderten Sprachen besser zu sprechen als sie und es ihnen zu zeigen, samt ihrer kulturellen Hegemonie" (ibid., 221).[25]

Masha's Azerbaijani-Russian-German-Jewish-self finds a counterpart in Sami, with his paradigmatic, modern migrant history. He was born in Beirut, grew up in Switzerland and France, and is now writing his doctoral thesis on German Idealism in the USA. He is waiting for his passport in Frankfurt. He commutes between the Arab, German and American cultures, without knowing where he belongs. "Ich bin weder hier, noch dort. Wenn ich wenigstens wüsste, wie lange ich bleiben muss. Ich würde […] irgendetwas tun. Nicht im Transit vor mich hin vegetieren" (ibid., 86).[26] Thus, the prevalent construction of identity, based on transculturality and transit permeates the novel. Masha, Cem, and Sami belong to an educational elite, and they use their exceptional language skills, their independence and mobility professionally (Kazmierczak 2016, 252). In Tel Aviv, Masha meets the sibling couple Ori and Tal, who grew up in London. She falls in love with Tal, who like Masha, is a heterogeneous and contradictory personality. She is serving her military service in an elite unit, leaves it prematurely and is picked up as a drug addict by an Israeli relief organization in India. Afterwards, she fights for her ideals in Israel as an "Aktivistin, Kommunistin und Feministin" (Grjasnowa 2013, 197),[27] driven by what she had done. When it comes to questions about their own pasts, Masha and Tal's mutual relationship fails because no real closeness can arise on either side.

Masha maintains relations with nomads like her, who do not have clear-cut identities, who often travel, staying in "heterotopic places" (Augé 1994, 92), in transition, in coffee bars, hotels, bars and public places, where people are more likely to be on the road or on the run. These breaks in identity are manifested at the text level in all the temporarily available rooms, at hotels, on terraces and in restaurants, where Masha can build only fleeting relationships. These buildings and sites can be classified as non-places, according to Marc Augé who describes them as "Raum, der keine Identität besitzt und sich weder als relational, noch als historisch bezeichnen lässt" (ibid., 94),[28] –spaces which create loneliness. These non-places fulfill the posttraumatic function of protection and healing (cf. Klatt 2013, 216), creating an illusion of home that helps her to deal with death and childhood trauma, as Andrea Klatt argues (cf. ibid., 225). In this way,

Masha resembles Irene, in Herta Müller's *Reisende auf einem Bein* (1989, *Traveling on one leg*) who responds to the cold reception she receives as an emigrant by wandering aimlessly in non-places. She feels connected to the people who live out of step with the majority in society, because her experiences have trained her to see those who are marginalized. She herself flees from her past, her ex-girlfriend Sibel is pursued by her family and is on the run, and Masha's Palestinian acquaintance Ismael flees from his Islamic past.

When Masha goes jogging on Christmas Eve on the banks of the Main River she notes: "Auf der Straße waren nur Moslems, Juden und ein paar einsame Christen" (Grjasnowa 2013, 108).[29] In this series of identities, reduced to religious labels, we see the potential of all the lines of power in the novel. We learn about the conflict in the Nagorno-Karabakh region between Muslim Azerbaijanis and Christian Armenians, the conflict between Israelis and Palestinians, and different German perspectives on these conflicts–solidarity with Israel as well as anti-Zionism. In the end, the conflicts in Germany center on key words such as "migration background" or "integration", which the narrator calls the "dominant culture" ("Leitkultur") as a model for assimilation. Masha's childhood trauma in Baku sensitizes her to the difference between the majority society and the ideological authority of firmly attributed identities (Wilpert 2015, 71).

The implications of these splintered identities are tied to the irreversible political catastrophes that frame the novel: on the one hand, those between the Israelis and the Palestinians and on the other hand, that of her native country Azerbaijan, both in the context of ethnicity. The violence against the other is embedded in the extermination machinery of National Socialism with its racial policy. Masha remembers her grandmother, a survivor of the Holocaust, who pointed out how the cruelty of the atrocities in Baku continues to be repeated: "Alles wiederholt sich, murmelte sie. Alles wiederholt sich. Alles wiederholt sich" (Grjasnowa 2013, 283). Thus, several political issues collide: the Middle East conflict, the post-Soviet warlike conflicts between Armenians and Azerbaijani, and the xenophobia and nationalism of migrants in Germany and Israel. The novel also questions the importance of one's native country and origin in a postmodern world, where dealing with one's own migration history seems to be obligatory, especially in light of refugee movements in recent years.

Deprived of One's Native Country, Identity and Language

Grjasnova's latest novel, *Gott ist nicht schüchtern*, takes place partly in Damascus in the middle of the Arab Spring and the Syrian Civil War of 2011 under the dictator Bashar al Assad, before moving on to Beirut and Turkey. The last part turns to the refugee crisis in Germany. The author stays true to the themes of migration and the clash of cultures and discusses the current problem of escaping from wars in the Islamic countries in the Middle East to Europe.

Grjasnova's third book is about torture and the war, escape, expulsion, asylum and the alienation refugees feel in Germany. While the first part of the novel centers on Syria and tells about the attacks on the system, the second is devoted to the protagonists' lives after the Syrian crisis and thematises their escape to Beirut, to Turkey and finally to Europe, in a dinghy which crosses the Mediterranean Sea. The third part is set in Berlin; here the protagonists are confronted with the feeling of being in-between, their lack of citizenship and loneliness.

The book is about modern nomads, the fate of the refugees, but also about boundaries and their significance for the individual. It describes the desire for a place "wo es die Grenzen nicht mehr gibt oder zumindest, wo sie einfacher zu überwinden sind" (Plath 2017).[30] This sentence relates to the motto of the third part of the novel, quoting Bertolt Brecht's *Refugee Conversations*: "Der Pass ist der edelste Teil von einem Menschen. Er kommt auch nicht auf so einfache Weise zustand wie ein Mensch" (Grjasnowa 2017, 277).[31] The characters belong to the middle and Syrian upper classes, are involved in the hustle and bustle of the times and leave their native country for political reasons. They fall into nothingness, failing due to a whim of fate.

The two characters Amal and Hammoudi present two different approaches to reality until the violence tears both their lives apart, driving them out of their comfortable bourgeois lives into an existence marked by terror and poverty. Their completely different paths intersect only sporadically, at the beginning in Damascus and at the end of the novel in Berlin, but they share in the same tragedy. The young Amal has a degree in English literature and is studying dramatic art. She comes from a wealthy family and enjoys a privileged status in Syrian society thanks to her father's wealth. She has her own home, money, designer clothes and is free from material worries. But her carefree life is just a sham: "Amal hatte es satt, ihr Bruder hatte es satt, ihre Freunde hatten es satt. […] Sie hatten die

Korruption, die Willkür der Geheimdienste, die eigene Machtlosigkeit und die permanenten Demütigungen satt." (ibid., 18).[32] The omniscient eye of power and the way it controls the people suggests that "Bashar-al-Assad ist größer als Gott, zumindest suggeriert das seine Omnipräsenz […] und sei es in Form von Porträts, die in jedem Winkel des Landes hängen" (ibid., 19).[33] In Amal, her fundamentally seditious potential is anchored in "an Obrigkeiten zu zweifeln und den autokratischen Politikstil Assads zu bekämpfen" (Böhm 2017).[34] However, because of her sympathy with subversive forces, she quickly attracts the interest of the secret services. She takes part in demonstrations against the regime, is seized and humiliated, beaten, deprived of the protection of her bourgeois identity, and is saved only through her father's intervention.

This female character is contrasted with the young Syrian physician Hammoudi, who was trained as a plastic surgeon in France but returned to Damascus because of his expired passport. The fact that his passport has not been renewed and his confrontations with the chicanery of the corrupt medical mafia plunge him into a deep life crisis: "Die Rückkehr nach Syrien ist die größte Niederlage seines Lebens, also kann er sie sich nicht eingestehen" (Grjasnowa 2017, 44)[35] […], "[e]r distanziert sich immer mehr von allen, denn er möchte nichts über Syrien hören, er möchte einfach nur zurück" (ibid., 46).[36] The Syrian intelligence service interprets his occidental background as suspicious, while he begins to assume his Syrian identity, participating in demonstrations, because he is angry at the arbitrariness of the regime. Hammoudi pursues an adventurous and life-threatening "career" as a doctor for the resistance movement against Assad, which operates provisional clinics in private rooms in Deir-az-Sour near the Iraqi border. His fate resembles that of Amal, for whenever these protagonists, Amal, her brothers Ali, Youseff and Hammoudi leave their dwellings and emerge on the streets they feel spied upon, persecuted and threatened. The spiraling violence tears the lives of the characters apart, turning their safe bourgeois existence into a life permeated with fear.

Deprived of Home and Family

The brutalization of everyday life forces the characters to become nomads and flee. Amal flees first to Beirut, then to Turkey and ends up in Germany. Hammoudi crosses the sea in a dinghy and witnesses the deaths of many people. Their fates are intertwined towards the end of the novel. Deprived of both family and citizenship, they make their way to Germany with difficulty, and the author deals extensively with their escape routes, and crossings in crowded, inflatable boats. They are emotionally damaged because the regime has inscribed itself too deeply within them.

The book points to the refugees' impending loss of identity; they are not recognized as citizens in Europe, and nobody in Germany seems to be interested in their origins, stories or their current struggle to survive. The various identities of the refugees are manifested through Grjasnowa's complex literary structure. The descriptions of several possible flight routes from the Middle East to Germany and the role that chance plays in terms of escaping successfully are accentuated. She focuses on the plurality of possible forms of existence, which can arise when normal lives are disrupted and people are forced to become refugees. Amal and Hammoudi, two traumatized people, meet at a hotel due to their common language and origin. Amal tells about her sea-crossing and how she saved a child from drowning. She is now raising it as her own. Hammoudi sums up his traumatic experiences as follows: "Ich habe zugesehen, wie neunhundertsiebzehn Menschen starben" (ibid., 301).[37] In this part of the novel, the language turns stereotypical and stenographic and reflects the loneliness she experiences in Germany: "Das Leben hier ist einsam" (ibid., 305).[38] Amal has lost her privileged, carefree lifestyle, she is not proficient in German, and has also lost a significant part of her identity, as she no longer has any family or friends. Thus, she clings to the child she has saved all the more desperately. When she watches women passers-by on the street, she feels that she is no longer a part of everyday life. She looks at their clothes and hairstyles, aware of who is in a hurry, who has the time to stand in front of shop windows–just as she did in Damascus a few months ago. Suddenly she realizes that she is no longer part of this everyday interaction and that these women perceive her as a stranger. Passers-by see her as only one of countless refugees, exhausted, her face marked by hardship, with no home and wearing cast-off clothing.

> Amal hasst es, sich als Flüchtling durch die Stadt zu bewegen. Sie hasst ihre ganze Existenz. Sie hasst es, sich nicht auf Deutsch verständlich machen zu können und dass in den Behörden niemand [...] in der Lage ist, auch nur das primitivste Englisch zu sprechen. Sie hasst es, als Muslimin und Schmarotzerin angesehen zu werden, und sie hasst sich selbst. Die Welt hat eine neue Rasse erfunden, die der Flüchtlinge, Refugees, Muslime oder Newcomer. (ibid., 281)[39]

Amal, who led a privileged life until the outbreak of the revolution, has not just fallen out of society because she has not yet learned the new language. The escape has deprived her of her native country and closeness to family and friends. Furthermore, a significant part of her personal identity has been taken from her, her lifestyle, the obvious status she had in her former life. Her life story and career are no longer visible to the passers-by (Porombka 2017).

The novel takes place in non-places, especially in the portrayal of the refugee crisis: the reception center for refugees, the transitional lodgings of migrants with travel bags, at the airport and in aircraft–places where long-term contacts are not possible. All of the stories are tragic. Although Amal's small family has grown accustomed to Germany and learned the language, it has not settled in. Hammoudi is killed in a bomb attack in the East German province to which he was assigned. But long before this physical death, he was dead inside. Here we see the omnipresence of violence; the western world is no safer than the Islamic world. The capitalism of Western societies is criticized and Westerners' orientation towards individualism and economic success denounced.

Amal and Hammoudi are likely to experience almost everything that can happen to people in Syria, who, though hesitantly, oppose the regime. The fates of the novel's characters are tragic; they have failed, and a new beginning in Germany seems impossible. Language barriers, lack of acceptance, identity problems, and the absence of social relationships are a hindrance. While Grjasnowa's first book still allows salvation, the novel *Gott ist nicht schüchtern* is more pessimistic. These young, well-educated, cosmopolitan characters find themselves uprooted. The terror they experience casts them out of society; those who survive flee to a new place, but find no home. The surgeon Hammoudi cannot cope with his meaningless existence in a refugee asylum in German, and predictably, terror strikes again, ending his life.

Notes

[1] "A high speed identity carousel" (my trans.).
[2] "Like people who love birches." (my trans.).
[3] They look like "people who are used to waiting for a long time" (my trans.)
[4] "postcolonial criticism of identity-shaping attributes which attempt to delineate the subject as clearly as possible, in terms of religion, history, and ethnicity, while hiding cultural diversity in doing so" (my trans.).
[5] "a human mosaic made up of the most diverse ethnic particles" (my trans.).
[6] "violence, expulsions, rape and pogroms on both sides" (my trans.).
[7] "I felt the bile come up. [...] the adjective post-migrant made it even worse" (my trans.).
[8] "Languages meant power. He who spoke no German had no voice, and whoever stuttered was overheard" (my trans.).

[9] "I was in Germany in 1996. In 1997, for the first time, I thought about suicide" (my trans.).
[10] "At school, I had learned English, French and a little Italian. [...] Afterwards, I had enrolled in an interpreter's program and learned Italian, Spanish and a bit of Polish in my spare time, but I was never particularly enthusiastic about the Slavic language group" (my trans.).
[11] "You know, during my childhood, there was always a packed suitcase at home, just in case" (my trans.).
[12] "crystallization point of cultures", a "highly intelligent cosmopolitan, a link between East and West" (my trans.).
[13] "My immune system gave up shortly after the funeral on [...]. My body did not want to go any further. [...]. I lived in a vacuum" (my trans.).
[14] "flickering sequence of anxiety, helplessness, despair, solitude" (my trans.).
[15] "I wanted [...] to lose myself bit by bit and not ever get picked up again" (my trans.).
[16] "Actually, I did not care about familiar places at all; the term home always implied the pogrom for me" (my trans.).
[17] "When I drove in the taxi through Tel Aviv and on the radio loud Oriental music came [...] I felt at home. It was a long forgotten home, a mosaic of landscape, temperature, music, sounds and the sea [...] until I realized I was at home with places that reminded me of Baku" (my trans.).
[18] "the religious, political, and cultural no man's land, into which Masha withdraws herself [...] in order to be able to escape all identity ascriptions, does not prove to offer any support" (my trans.).
[19] "intercultural, equal and opposite sexual encounters" (my trans.).
[20] "cross-border figures exhibiting a transnationally dominated biography as well as transcultural value system" (my trans.).
[21] "religious as well as cultural indecision" (my trans.).
[22] "transcultural and intercultural encounters in the novel take place in [...] personal biographies, in bars and in beds" (my trans.).
[23] "world-view, which fluctuates between cynicism and laconicism" (my trans.).
[24] "He was the first of his family who studied and spoke better Turkish than his parents" (my trans.)
[25] "'show them by speaking their much admired languages better than they do themselves, in spite of their cultural hegemony'" (my trans.).
[26] "I am neither here nor there. If at least I knew how long I have to stay. I would [...] do something. Instead of vegetating in transit" (my trans.).
[27] "activist, communist and feminist" (my trans.).
[28] "A space that has no identity and can neither be described as relational nor as historical" (my trans.).
[29] "On the street were only Muslims, Jews and a few solitary Christians" (my trans.).
[30] "where borders no longer exist or at least where they are easier to overcome" (my trans.).
[31] "The passport is the noblest part of a human. It also does not materialize as easily as a human being" (my trans.).

³² "Amal was tired, her brother was tired, her friends were tired. [...] They were fed up with the corruption, the arbitrariness of the secret services, their own powerlessness and the permanent humiliation" (my trans.).
³³ "Bashar-Al-Assad is larger than God, at least his omnipresence suggests [...] in the form of portraits that hang in every corner of the country" (my trans.).
³⁴ "doubting the authorities and combating the autocratic policy style of Assad" (my trans.).
³⁵ "The return to Syria is the greatest defeat of his life, and he cannot get over it" (my trans.).
³⁶ "He is distancing himself more and more from everything; he does not want to hear about Syria, he just wants to get back" (my trans.).
³⁷ "I have watched how nine hundred and seventy people died" (my trans.).
³⁸ "Life here is lonely" (my trans.).
³⁹ "Amal hates moving as a refugee through the city. She hates her whole existence. She hates not being able to make herself understood in German, and that in encounters with the authorities no one [...] is able to speak even the most primitive English. She hates being seen as a Muslim, a parasite, and she hates herself. The world has invented a new race, that of refugees, Muslims, or newcomers" (my trans.).

References

Andre, Thomas. 2012. "Olga Grjasnowas Debüt: Der Russe ist einer, der Birken liebt." In *Hamburger Abendblatt*, 9.02. 2012. https://www.abendblatt.de/kultur-live/article107735420/Olga-Grjasnowas-Debuet-Der-Russe-liebt-Birken.html [Accessed 13.07. 2017].

Augé, Marc. 1994. *Orte und Nicht-Orte: Vorüberlegungen zu einer Ethnologie der Einsamkeit*. Frankfurt/Main: Suhrkamp.

Bhabha, Homi. 2011. *Die Verortung der Kultur*, Tübingen: Stauffenburg Narr.

Böhm, Marcus. 2017. "Olga Grjasnowa: Gott ist nicht schüchtern." In *KulturErnten*. http://www.kulturernten.com/olga-grjasnowa-gott-ist-nicht-schuechtern/ [Accessed 17.09. 2017].

Buchholz, Hartmut. 2012. "Ohne Heimat. 'Der Russe ist einer der Birken liebt'". In *Badische Zeitung*. http://www.badische-zeitung.de/literatur-rezensionen/ohne-heimat-der-russe-ist-einer-der-birken-liebt-64980194.html [Accessed 15.09. 2017].

Catani, Stephanie. 2015. "Im Niemandsland. Figuren und Formen der Entgrenzung in Olga Grjasnowas Roman Der Russe ist einer, der Birken liebt (2012)." In *Über Grenzen: Texte und Lektüren der deutschsprachigen Gegenwartsliteratur*, edited by Stephanie Catani, and Max Friedhelm, 95–111. Göttingen: Wallstein.

Grjasnowa, Olga. 2013. *Der Russe ist einer der Birken liebt*. München: DTV.

—. 2017. *Gott ist nicht schüchtern*. Berlin: Aufbau.

Kazmierczak, Madlen. 2016. *Fremde Frauen. Zur Figur der Migrantin aus (post)sozialistischen Ländern in der deutschsprachigen Gegenwartsliteratur*. Berlin: Erich Schmidt.

Klatt, Andrea. 2013. "Heterotope Heilsamkeit der Nicht-Orte bei Olga Grjasnowa und Christian Kracht." In *Provisorische und Transiträume. Raumerfahrung Nicht-Ort*, edited by Miriam Kanne, 215–230. Berlin: Lit Verlag.

Plath, Jörg. 2012. "Olga Grjasnowas erfrischendes Romandebüt Der Russe ist einer der Birken liebt. Hochtouriges Identitätskarussel." In *Neue Zürcher Zeitung*. 13. 03. 2012. https://www.nzz.ch/hochtouriges_identitaetskarussell-1.15713595 [Accessed 4.08. 2017].

—. 2017. "Vom Irrsinn und von Grenzen."

http://www.deutschlandfunkkultur.de/olga-grjasnowa-gott-ist-nicht-schuechtern-vom-irrsinn-und.974.de.html?dram:article_id=381762 [Accessed 4.03. 2018].

Porombka, Wiebke. 2017. "Roman über Syrien-Flüchtlinge. Wellenschlag vom Tod entfernt." In http://www.faz.net/aktuell/feuilleton/buecher/rezensionen/belletristik/der-roman-gott-ist-nicht-schuechtern-von-olga-grjasnowa-15009241-p2.html [Accessed on 12.10.2017].

Thamm, Andreas. 2017. "Kristallisation der Kulturen. Ein beachtliches Debüt: Olga Grjasnowa hat mit 'Der Russe ist einer, der Birken liebt' einen Roman geschrieben, der auf der Höhe der Zeit nicht weniger als alles verhandelt." In: http://literaturkritik.de/public/druckfassung_rez.php?rez_id=16527 [Accessed 4.08. 2017].

Weber, Ludmilla. 2017. "Zu Hause in der Fremde." In http://culturmag.de/rubriken/buecher/olga-grjasnowa-der-russe-ist-einer-der-birken-liebt/48277 [Accessed 20.08. 2017].

Wilpert, Chris. 2015. "Traumatische Symbiose. ‚Juden, Moslems und ein paar einsame Christen' in Olga Grjasnowas Der Russe ist einer, der Birken liebt." In *Heimat–Identität–Mobilität in der zeitgenössischen jüdischen Literatur*, edited by Christina Olszynski, Jan Schröder, and Chris Wilpert, 59–77. Wiesbaden: Harassowitz.

CHAPTER THREE

FRACTURED BOUNDARIES, CULTURAL HYBRIDITY AND IN-BETWEEN SPACES IN NORWEGIAN YOUNG ADULT IMMIGRANT LITERATURE: MARIA NAVARRO SKARANGER'S *ALLE UTLENDINGER HAR LUKKA GARDINER*

WAYNE KELLY

Fractured Boundaries and the Negotiation of Identity

Growing up as a young, second-generation immigrant involves living with the worldview of the first generation immigrant parent or parents and their communities, while managing competing voices in the country of one's birth and upbringing. Various encounters between multiple worldviews, traditions and cultural discourses in a multi-ethnic environment affect a rapidly increasing proportion of young people in modern Norway. In the process of developing an understanding of life, self and one's identity, they face various challenges and must find a balance between mixed or hybrid cultural backgrounds. Cultural differences can inhibit communication and understanding, but at the same time, they can open up an in-between space where a new, hybrid identity can be negotiated. Similarly, the residents or citizens of the broader community, as part of the various encounters, also go through processes, developing understanding and integrating changes in their individual and communal sense of identity.

A central aim of this chapter is to consider how the broad concept of cultural hybridity may be applied to an example of Norwegian young adult immigrant literature: Maria Navarro Skaranger's, *Alle utlendinger har lukka gardiner* (2015 [All Foreigners have Closed Curtains, my trans.]). This debut novel, written by a young, second-generation immigrant author is narrated from the perspective of Mariana, an even younger, second-generation immigrant. Its relatively unique point of view illuminates a number of issues in the world of immigrant youth in Norway. Additionally it is written in a distinctive sociolect, or multi-ethnolect–so-called "Kebab-Norwegian"–that many young Norwegians are familiar with or can relate to. After a brief description of the setting in *Alle utlendinger har lukka gardiner* (henceforth referred to as *Alle utlendinger*), and some brief consideration of narrative and identity in light of the text, we will consider the key terms fractured boundaries, cultural hybridity and in-between spaces, applying them in a discussion of the novel and its general social context.

Skaranger's short novel, narrated in the first person, presents diary-like vignettes from the life of a young teenage girl who lives in a multi-ethnic setting. It centers on a suburb, Romsås, part of Grorud in the northeastern part of the Norwegian capital, Oslo. The suburb has a high proportion of first and second-generation immigrant inhabitants (new settlers), and "ethnic" Norwegians are in minority. The same statistics apply, of course, in the local school population, where the protagonist, Mariana, is in eighth grade. At home, most of the student population speaks a language other than Norwegian. In the narrative, only a few of the many characters are ethnic Norwegian. The majority of the characters live in apartment blocks, with many interactions taking place in the apartment block grounds. The narrator's father is a Catholic from Chile and her mother is Norwegian. The majority of her peers and neighbors are from different ethnic backgrounds, and the neighborhood presents a microcosm of a growing segment of Norwegian society.

Marie-Laure Ryan points out that narrative can be seen, generally, as a strategy by which we plot, convey a description of, or represent a series of events (Herman et al. 2011, 22). Furthermore, the plotting or ordering of actions depicts to some extent how an individual acts or makes choices in given circumstances, and in this sense, narrative helps to shape identity where identity is a representation of individual as well as collective acts or actions. An individual identity, it might be added, changes or alters with the advent of new encounters. In Skaranger's novel, a series of events depicting encounters between different cultures and generations highlights both individual and collective identity formations.

Individuals have a multiplicity of identities in their various roles, meaning among other things, that identities cannot be upheld without Others. Mikhail Bakhtin, whose widely influential range of ideas related to literary analysis–including understanding of the concept of the self–maintained that the self can only exist in the presence of an "Other". Michael Holquist notes that for Bakhtin "the self is dialogic; a relation"; it depends on an interaction with an "Other" and such interaction is part of what drives a narrative and is integral to identity formation (Bakhtin, cited in Holquist 2002, 19). Bakhtin's ideas on dialogism and the relational self can be related to issues raised in *Alle utlendinger*. Holquist notes that for Bahktin, "Literary texts, like other kinds of utterance, depend not only on the activity of the author, but also on the place they hold in the social and historical forces at work when the text is produced and when it is consumed" (Holquist 2002, 68–69). Skaranger's novel takes the pulse of contemporary identity formation amongst young people living in a particular spatial and historical context: a multiethnic neighborhood of Oslo in the first decade of this century.

Alle utlendinger illustrates many aspects of dialogism in relation to how narrative and identity are connected and impact individual and collective identities. The setting is a contemporary urban environment where multicultural and ethnic communities alter the narratives and identities of other communities or the broader community generally, giving *Alle utlendinger* its social and historical context. The recent inclusion of some extracts from the novel in some Norwegian school textbooks (Opsahl and Røyneland 2016, 51) indicates at least one way in which it is "consumed". Its use of language ("Kebab-Norwegian") as a marker of group identity demonstrates its discursive capacity in facilitating the establishment of a collective or individual sense of identity.

Identities are constantly "reconstituted", remaining subject to ongoing "self-narrations". Cultural identity, according to Stuart Hall, "is a matter of becoming as much as being [and] belongs to the future as much as to the past" (Hall 1990, 435). Identities he writes, "have histories, [they] come from somewhere, but like everything which is historical, they undergo constant transformation" (ibid.). Skaranger's text, is written in diary-like vignettes where the protagonist self-narrates her identity. She and the characters around her all undergo constant change as the narrative unfolds. Darden, a bully, defends a victim; Ibra, an enemy, shows affection; Matias, often frightened, shows some bravery. With each of these events, the characters' identities are changed. The school class as a whole, though full of cliques and cultural differences, stands united in difficult moments such as the drowning of one of their classmates. The cultural differences within the group and the neighborhood are neutralized by the emergence of common vulnerabilities and needs. The diary-like quality of the novel and its use of a unique dialect increase its authenticity. Through the recollections of the protagonist, accounts of scenarios as they unfold, or various dialogues, the text shapes the individual identity of the characters, as well as the collective and cultural identity of the community in which the text is set.

Cultural Hybridity

As noted, a central consideration in this chapter is how the broad concept of cultural hybridity may be applied to *Alle utlendinger*. With this in mind, one may ask what cultural hybridity is, and why it is useful as a heuristic in our understanding of issues in modern multicultural society and within the frame of young adult immigrant literature? In "Cultural Hybridity and International Communication" Marwan Kraidy refers to a range of thinkers from Bhabha to Derrida to Bakhtin, and the recognition of the historical and ongoing pervasiveness of cross-cultural encounters. He refers to the maddening elasticity of the concept of "hybridity" and ventures concern regarding what he says "can be described as an academic stampede" toward usage of the concept (Kraidy 2005, 2). He begins with a quote from Tomlinson: "[...] cultural hybridization is one of those simple-seeming notions which turns out, on examination, to have lots of tricky connotations and theoretical implications." However, he goes on to argue that, "the analytical potential of 'hybridity' has not been fully exploited" and suggests that despite the challenging complexities:

> Hybridity is one of the emblematic notions of our era. It captures the spirit of the times with obligatory celebration of cultural differences and fusion, and it resonates with the globalization mantra of unfettered economic exchanges and the supposedly inevitable transformation of all cultures. (ibid., 1)

Emerging literary genres such as young adult immigrant literature and texts like *Alle utlendinger* help show the concrete potential and impact of cultural difference.

Pnina Werbner and Tariq Modood in *Debating Cultural hybridity: Multicultural Identities and the Politics of Anti-racism* describe how "Hybridity is celebrated as powerfully interruptive" (2015, 1). Despite the challenging nature of the various complexities mentioned above, Werbner and Modood see hybridity as a facilitator of change. They argue that:

> [...] while there may be many routine cultural mixings and collages [...] the *ethical* and *political* power of cultural hybridity [has the capacity] to effect real, emancipatory change, particularly in defence of minority cultural and human rights. Cultural mixings are thus conceived of [...] as conjoined with social responsibility and care for the other, respect for difference and a challenge to established inequalities and hierarchies. (ibid., Preface xv)

Alle utlendinger represents an example of how literature, including young adult immigrant literature, can raise awareness of the potentially positive transformative impact cultural hybridity can have in different communities. Through the actions of a young second generation immigrant, her peers and friends, the reader gains insight into some preoccupations and developing social perspectives of young people at the threshold of areas where cultural difference, hybridity and increasingly cosmopolitan worlds are clearly evident. The narrative sheds light on the emergent situation among migrant youth, and the communities in which they live, where stereotyping and the negative elements of "othering" hopefully will have less of an impact in the future.

In his foreword to Werbner and Modood's (2015) text, Homi Bhabha considers the immense empowering capacity of cultural hybridity. He writes:

> Hybridity is a form of incipient critique; it does not come as a force from 'outside' to impose an alternative *a priori* ground-plan on the pattern of the present. Hybridity works with, *and within*, the cultural design of the present to reshape our understanding of the interstices–social and psychic– that link signs of cultural similitude with emergent signifiers of alterity. The 'difference' that constitutes the subject of hybridity can be temporal, political, racial, sexual, social or economic. These forms of 'difference', reconfigured as spontaneous discrimination or systemic inequality, are neither historically synchronic nor ethically and politically equivalent. What the minoritarian presence reveals are the limits of pluralist 'progress'. (Werbner & Madood 2015, ix)

Alle utlendinger thematizes many of the changing social contexts and collective identities in a growing number of multicultural, multi-ethnic regions. Young people, who represent the future, also represent a culturally hybrid demographic element of the community, and a microcosm of the growing situation both in Norway and globally. By presenting a narrative of the experience of young immigrants in Norway,

Alle utlendinger empowers those living in culturally hybrid contexts, building reader interest and awareness and, possibly, greater acceptance and tolerance. Each vignette raises different issues. Christian girls date Muslims, young people fight back against homophobia and cultural differences in the classroom become the norm rather than the exception. Of course, conflicts continue, and generally, in increasingly mixed environments, each conflict impacts notions of identity. Inevitably, change occurs and the paradigm, over which elements constitute cultural differences, shifts, as do power structures. Hence, an increasingly central power evident in the immigrant-dominated communities is "hybridity".

In-Between Spaces–A Third Space

Cultural hybridization in a community is enacted, as Bhabha and others argue, in a "Third space". This Third space may be seen as a space outside of the first space of a hegemonic power and the second space of the minority or subaltern power. The boundary areas separating first and second space encounters are referred to as the in-between spaces. These in-between spaces represent the threshold where conflict (contrasting or non-correlative worldviews or voices) and transformation (alteration or evolution of identity) may occur as a result of the fracturing of boundaries. In *The Ethics of Travel* (1996) Syed Islam raises the importance of boundaries and in-between spaces as the location where cross-cultural conflict and potential for transformation occurs. He notes, "The question of the boundary looms large in cross-cultural discourse, and the implications are enormous" (Islam 1996, 4). Islam refers to "fractured boundaries", which may be seen as the threshold where conflict between notions of identity occur and where the opportunity for transformation may emerge.

In *Alle utlendinger* misunderstandings between homophobic young Muslim boys and an engaging history teacher, well-liked by the narrator and other students, results in the teacher, Frode, leaving; rather than all parties mutually benefitting. On the other hand, the potentially fractured boundaries of sensitive language use, including the use of religious terms such as "inshallah" ("God willing") or "Allah" occurs throughout the text without serious consequence. In other contexts, globally, misuse of terms such as "Allah" has brought violent reaction from fragments of the Islamic community while within the day-to-day discourse of young people in *Alle utlendinger* the same term is used flippantly in matters of relative triviality without incident, for the most part. In contrast, the broad use of religious terms in everyday discourse contributes to a sense of youth cultural identity. The various uses of so-called "Kebab Norwegian" have a bonding effect–separating youth from the older "Other".

Bhabha sees the boundaries signified by cultural difference, "where meanings and values are (mis)read or signs are misappropriated", as the space where change or transformation may occur (Bhabha 1988a, 156). He refers to times of "cultural uncertainty", and times of what he calls "significatory or representational undecidability" as times of possible "liberation". In this way, cultural uncertainty, despite sounding worrisome, is an important aspect underlying social change. Bhabha also refers to Franz Fanon who notes in *The Wretched of the Earth* that "it is to the zone of occult instability where the people dwell that we must come" (ibid., 155). For Bhabha, it seems, a time of "cultural uncertainty" is the crucial time of identity formation and transformation and in this sense narrative has a transformative role. Like a phoenix from the flames, in a sense, from fractured boundaries or the deconstruction and rupturing of old boundaries, emerges a Third space of what may be referred to as cultural hybridity.

Approaching the in-between spaces of cultural difference or conflict is the first step in approaching a threshold or area of cultural uncertainty. Specific actions that occur in *Alle utlendinger* such as: stepping into a foreign environment; accepting an invitation to the home of an unknown other; travelling to an unknown place unprepared; accepting an offer of help or offering to help; addressing an unknown other; or simply stepping outside of one's comfort zone into an activity entailing some degree of risk or uncertainty, are simple examples of approaching in-between spaces or new borders and territories. *Blackwell reference online* describes the idea of the threshold as:

> A term much used in anthropology and literary and cultural theory to designate a space or state which is situated in between other, usually more clearly defined, spaces, periods or identities. The threshold, the foundational metaphor, occupies a liminal space between the inside and outside of a house; dawn and dusk hold liminal positions between night and day; transgender and intersex people assume liminal identities in relation to the established categories of gender. The latter example is suggestive of how liminality might be disruptive of dominant discursive frameworks: it defies boundaries and erases the differences upon which regulatory frameworks depend. In postcolonial theory, for instance, the concept has been employed to consider how the contact zone exists as a cultural space in between that of the colonizer and the colonized; in these

liminal spaces of transcultural exchange, the colonized subject may find resources and strategies for self-transformation that upset the fixed polarities of colonial discourse. (*Blackwell* 2013)

The liminal or interstitial is evident in *Alle utlendinger* where various multi-ethnic first and second-generation immigrants traverse spaces in-between social norms and protocols of groups that identify with differing values. Such contexts may be referred to as an encounter with an unknown other. The "Other" may be a person, group, collective identity, situation, or even role or a responsibility previously not familiar to the "self", entering an in-between space or grey zone. For example in *Alle utlendinger* in the chapter titled "Asylmottak" (Immigrant transit processing centre–my trans), one of the few ethnic Norwegian classmates, Nora, is tidying up after work on a group project. Unwittingly she screws up and throws out the used rough paper drafts, one of which has "Allah" written on it. At this point, one of the Muslim boys in her group, Ibra, becomes agitated. He calls on the other boys from his group to confront Nora during recess. Mariana, the protagonist, describes the situation:

> [...] når skulle vi rydde Nora selvfølgelig kasta arket, og Ibra bare: du kan ikke kaste det når det står Allah, du må brenne det, og Nora bare: hæ, det er et kladdeark, og Ibra bare: det står Allah på det, og Nora bare: så hvis jeg tegne et strekmann så er det Muhammed da? for å si tilbake ikke sant, og det var da tredje verdenskrig begynte, for etterpå vi gikk i friminutt, og da alle muslimsgutta, wollah, hele asylmottak stillet seg i ring rundt og nesten skulle banke hun, og bare: rasist!!!!!! Det så helt ut som krigssone, nesten de kunne begynt å steine Nora. Og så helt fra himmelen Dardan kom inn i ringen og bare: gutta, dette har vært stort misforståelse, og alle bare: hæ, fordi Dardan alltid er drittsekk ellers, og han bare: Nora ikke sa noen ting, brødre, hun ikke mente noe vondt, og siden Darden har sin egen lille b-gjengen, ringen bli oppløst i løseste lufta og folk stakk. [...] stakkars Nora. Men en ting er sikkert: vi vet hvem Darden er keen på. (Skaranger 2015, 29)[1]

This incident describes an encounter in the confusing in-between spaces of religious understanding and tradition. The boy Ibra no doubt is confused, and overreacts. At the same time, Nora shows a certain naivety. Ironically, it is the gang leader, Darden, who stops the commotion, pulls Ibra into line and says it was merely a misunderstanding. Darden is typically one of the main instigators, provoking and bullying other students, but on this occasion, he steps in as a hero. The protagonist suggests this is likely because he has a crush on Nora, which slightly changes the whole scenario in terms of Darden's motivation. However, the scene illustrates a type of in-between space characteristic in the daily lives of a segment of Norway's immigrant and "culturally hybrid" youth. These young people will shape the future. Although some of the issues taken up in *Alle utlendinger* at times seem less important or trivial–the concerns of teenagers–they also focus on their capacity to negotiate, empathize, tolerate or accept; such in-between spaces offer them opportunities to rehearse these abilities. The result of this particular incident (one of many described in the text) is a slightly altered identity among everyone involved, illustrating how in-between space, conflict and fractured boundaries lead to a new Third space and the continual development of a hybrid identity.

The protagonist in *Alle utlendinger* inhabits multiple spaces in the text. Geographically, she inhabits her home, the classroom, and the school grounds. Outside of Romsås, other spaces include the city centre pedestrian street (Karl Johans gate), a Somali father's syntactically odd "Grønt og Frukt butikk" ("Vegetable and Fruit shop"),[2] or even Social Media. Other spaces include the presence of family, friends or peers or the space of authorities including police, teachers and wardens. Friends, family or peers are also found in similar spaces geographically, physically, metaphorically or real and imaginary. More broadly, community or collective identity in *Alle utlendinger* is evident politically, economically and socially in school: on Norwegian Constitution Day (May 17) and during various festival activities, funerals and elections. Spaces also arise in terms of religious issues, peer pressure or language (Kebab-Norwegian). The spaces between become clues identifying the protagonist, and other characters. Various individual and collective identities are defined within these contexts, which nurture further in-between spaces. How they are occupied helps determine how various identities evolve.

As mentioned, the text is presented through diary-like vignettes; giving momentum to a relentless, fast-paced, daily narrative of identity-shifting encounters. Another feature of the narrative that stands out is the way it uses language. One of the main ways the narrative generates an understanding of the broader community, youth identity and the protagonist is through its previously mentioned use of the special teenage sociolect or multi-ethnolect referred to as "Kebab-Norwegian". In an article entitled "Reality rhymes: Recognition of rap in multicultural Norway", Opsahl and Røyneland refer to Kebab-Norwegian as a "multiethnolectal speech style" (2016, 45) adopted by many Norwegian young people, particularly those with an immigrant background. A "multiethnolectal speech style" is described by the authors as:

particular speech styles that are characterized by the inclusion of linguistic features from many different varieties, used by people with several ethnic backgrounds, to express their minority status and/or as a reaction to that status to upgrade it. (Opsahl and Røyneland 2016, 45)

The term "Kebab-Norwegian", or more specifically the word "kebab", holds cultural associations and connotations shared by most Norwegians. It is a typical type of fast food served at cafes and restaurants typically run by recent immigrants, especially from the Middle East. "Kebab-Norwegian", developed in "multi-ethnic and multi-lingual environments in Oslo", has been adopted widely, not just by immigrants, but also by other Norwegian young people in many contexts.

Opsahl and Røyneland describe it as initially viewed negatively, but recently accepted more broadly for various reasons. One reason is that Norway as a general rule has a history of tolerance for dialects and sociolects, given that the country has an enormous variety from region to region. Additionally, and perhaps most significantly, it is because the dialect has been successfully adopted by certain influential elements of youth culture including hip-hop artists and rappers, often from immigrant backgrounds. Further, the dialect has become so pervasive that it has been included in school textbooks, in the form of rap lyrics as a means of studying language cultures. In the same way, and for similar reasons, extracts from *Alle utlendinger* have also been included in some school textbooks and materials, as previously mentioned (ibid., 51).

The first-person protagonist and her peers use a range of slang terms, incorrect word order, and "Arabic loanwords" throughout the text. For example, throughout the text the protagonist and her friends seamlessly use terms like "Wollah" ("Honest to God" / "I swear"), "Inshallah" ("God-willing"), or "ekte potet" (genuine potato / ethnic Norwegian person). Opsahl and Røyneland mention that *Alle utlendinger* is "framed as the first novel written in 'Kebab-Norwegian'" (Opsahl and Røyneland 2016, 51).

In *Alle utlendinger* each chapter entails some kind of encounter with a new issue or situation which alters or contributes in a new way to an understanding of the identity of the protagonist, as well as the transient, grey and ever-evolving parameters of cultural identity generally. The incidents described reflect issues related to religion, school, elections, ethnic background, bullying and new accounts of the identity of both the protagonist and the community. It is not possible to pin any of the characters or groups down to a fixed identity. Clashes, conflicts and issues on the borders of miscommunication or conflicting viewpoints in different contexts, mean boundaries are fractured constantly and the sense of identity is in constant flux or transition, or as Stuart Hall writes, "production":

> [...] instead of thinking of identity as an already accomplished fact, which new cultural practices then represent, we should think, instead, of identity [constituted within, not outside, representation. (Hall, in Mongia, 1997, 110)

Bhabha also writes about the limitations and dangers of a certain "fixity" in our understanding of "identity" and the close relation of such "fixity" to stereotyping. He describes "stereotyping", which is based, to a large extent, on fixedness or rigidity of ideas and viewpoints of the "Other" as a strategy for imposition of hegemonic discourse and the subsequent power and influence it acquires. He writes, "An important feature of colonial discourse is its dependence on the concept of 'fixity' in the ideological construction of otherness" (Bhabha, in Mongia 1997, 37). In *Alle utlendinger* we see a number of traces of such "fixity" throughout the text and the process of revealing such notions through the narrative helps to unveil the dangers of stereotypes. This is evident in the "Shtogge potet" [Ugly potato / Norwegian, my trans.] protesting in the main street of Oslo (Karl Johans gate) that "alle utlendinger må ut" (Skaranger 2015, 15) [all foreigners must get out of Norway, my trans.]. We also see it among the parents–Mariana's father is not happy that his daughter may choose to marry a Muslim. Such "fixity", often driven by stereotyping or fear of the unknown other, inhibits the opportunities for transformation that can result from cultural differences, fractured boundaries and in-between spaces among individuals or communities.

Concluding Remarks

Alongside population growth, climate change, environmental issues, war, economic shifts in power, financial crises, poverty and the global division between rich and poor, migration is a massive and growing global concern. These issues are intrinsically related. At no period in history have there been more people on the move, nor have there been so many efficient but also inefficient, dangerous means and routes by which people can move. In 2015, UN figures report that there were 244 million migrants globally. This represents 3.3% of the world's population, and represents a 41% increase in numbers from 2000 (UN 2016).

In Norway, according to statistics provided by Opsahl and Røyneland; "15.6 percent of the Norwegian population of 5.1 million inhabitants [have] immigrant backgrounds" (Opsahl and Røyneland 2016, 47). Further, since most opportunities exist in Oslo, "approximately 33 percent of the Oslo population are foreign born or Norwegian born with foreign born parents." This new society is "increasingly culturally and ethnically mixed, due to the labour and refugee-driven immigration of recent years" (ibid.). One of the many concerns of the mass movement of population is the settlement process. That is, the process that occurs after arrival, when immigrants settle. The social, political, and economic structures within the receiving country are impacted in multiple, interlinked ways. Due to the numbers and the vast differences represented by immigrant groups and receiving communities, more effective strategies for managing difference are increasingly important. Storytelling, narratives and literature represent one such important strategy.

Literature is a force by which ideas are spread and understanding can be generated across invisible distances and barriers; metaphorical, cultural and otherwise. Cultural differences at times underlie invisible barriers and impede communication and understanding. However, they also present thresholds and in-between spaces that open opportunities for transcending issues of breakdown in cross-cultural discourses and communication. In this way, literature may be seen as a means of managing integration and assimilation. Further, with this in mind, it is also fully conceivable that young adult immigrant novels such as *Alle utlendinger* have an important contributing role in the understanding of ever-evolving societies.

Etching out a framework for understanding oneself and one's place in the world is a challenging task of constant redefinition. One of the challenges of our increasingly crowded planet is the encounter with cultural difference. Part of the implication of living with less physical space may be the need to find greater tolerance and understanding within these in-between spaces. While there are many ways through which communities may come to terms with the changes that large-scale migration brings in first and second-generation immigrant settlement, literature and narratives play key roles in nurturing understanding, and fostering adaptation and adjustment. As is evident in the young adult immigrant literary text *Alle utlendinger*, literature can facilitate individual and collective understanding of the self and the world and thereby help address challenges at the thresholds or boundaries where different selves meet different "Others". These borders or boundaries might be found at cultural cross-sections related to different backgrounds and circumstances in terms of ethnicity, tradition, religion, gender, or upbringing. They may arise from situations of varying socioeconomic, political or geographical circumstances–or combinations of all or some of these. Cross-cultural discourse, including lack of understanding or empathy, may well lead to a fracturing of boundaries, but ultimately this also proves to be the path by which transformation of individual or communal worldviews, may take place. That is to say, the same in-between places and liminal areas that engender spaces of uncertainty and conflict are also the spaces where opportunity for change, transformation or transcendence lie and "newness" occurs.

Notes

[1] "[...] when we went to tidy up, Nora of course threw out the papers and Ibra says: you can't throw that out when it says 'Allah', you have to burn it, but Nora says: hahh, it's just notes, and Ibra says: it has Allah written on it, and Nora says: so if I draw a stick figure is that Mohammed? And with that, World War III breaks out, then, when we went out for recess, all the Muslim boys, 'Wollah', the whole asylum stood in a ring around her and were ready to beat her up, shouting: racist!!!!!! It was like a warzone, next thing they would have stoned Nora. Then out of the heavens Darden came into the ring and says: boys, it was just a misunderstanding, and they all: hahh, because Darden's normally a shithead, but then he says: Nora didn't mean anything, brothers, she didn't mean any harm, and because Darden has his own 'b-gang', the ring broke up and people left [...] poor Nora. But, one thing is certain: we know who Darden is keen on" (my trans.).
[2] The common collocation in Norwegian would be "Fruit and Vegetable shop".

References

Abrams, M. H. 1999. *A Glossary of Literary Terms,* 7th Edition. Boston: Heinle & Heinle.
Ashcroft, Bill, Gareth Griffiths and Helen Tiffin. 2006. *The Post-Colonial Studies Reader.* New York: Routledge.
Bhabha, Homi K. 1988. "Cultural Diversity and Cultural Differences." In *The Post-Colonial Studies Reader,* edited by Bill Ashcroft, Gareth Griffiths & Helen Tiffin, 155–157. London: Routledge.
—. 2004. *The Location of Culture.* London: Routledge.
—. 2015. "Foreword." In *Debating Cultural Hybridity: Multicultural Identities and the Politics of Anti-racism,* edited by Pnina Werbner and Tariq Madood. IX-XIII. London: Zed books.
Blackwell Reference online. 2013. "A Dictionary of Literary Theory" http://www.blackwellreference.com/public/tocnode?id=g9781444333275_chunk_g978144433327513_ss1-49 [Accessed 27.2.2019].
Brah, Avtah. 1996. "Thinking Through the Concept of Diaspora." In *The Post-Colonial Studies Reader,* edited by Bill Ashcroft, Gareth Griffiths, and Helen Tiffin, 443–446. London: Routledge.
Brettel, Caroline B. and James F. Hollifield. 2011. *Migration Theory: Talking across Disciplines.* New York: Routledge.
Hall, Stuart. 1990. "Cultural Identity and Diaspora." In *The Post-Colonial Studies Reader,* edited by Bill Ashcroft, Gareth Griffiths, and Helen Tiffin, 435–438. London: Routledge.
Herman, David, Manfred Jahn and Marie-Laure Ryan, eds. 2008. *Routledge Encyclopedia of Narrative Theory.* London: Routledge.
Herman, David, ed. 2011. *The Cambridge Companion to Narrative.* New York: Cambridge University Press.
Holquist, Michael. 2002. *Dialogism.* London: Routledge.
Islam, Syed Manserel. 1996. *The Ethics of Travel.* New York: Manchester University Press.
Kraidy, Marwan. 2005. "Cultural Hybridity and International Communication." In *Debating Cultural Hybridity: Multicultural Identities and the Politics of Anti-racism,* edited by Pnina Werbner & Tariq Madood, 1–14. London: Zed books.
Mack, Michael. 2012. *How Literature Changes the Way We Think.* London: Continuum International Publishing Group.
Mongia, Padmini. 1996. *Contemporary Postcolonial Theory: A Reader.* London: Arnold, A member of the Hodder Headline Group.

Opsahl, Torill and Unn Røyneland, Unn. 2016. "Reality Rhymes–Recognition of Rap in Multicultural Norway." *Linguistics and Education* 36, 45–54.
Skaranger, Maria Navarro. 2016. *Alle utlendinger har lukka gardiner.* Oslo: Forlaget Oktober.
U.N. 2016. "Sustainable Development Goals" July 12. http://www.un.org/sustainabledevelopment/blog/2016/01/244-million-international-migrants-living-abroad-worldwide-new-un-statistics-reveal/ [Accessed 27.2.2019].
Werbner, Pnina and Tariq Madood, eds. 2015. *Debating Cultural Hybridity: Multicultural Identities and the Politics of Anti-racism.* London: Zed books.

IDENTITY AND RELIGION

CHAPTER FOUR

THE SEARCH FOR AUTHENTICITY: RELIGIOUS IDENTITY IN NORWEGIAN AUTHOR TOR EDVIN DAHL'S *GUDS TJENER*

GURI ELLEN BARSTAD

This chapter aims to explore the representation of religious identity in Norwegian author Tor Edvin Dahl's novel *Guds tjener* (1973) [God's servant]. The main character, Anders Renstad, a young man in his thirties, tries to determine who he is by reminiscing about his past. His identity is inseparable from his religious background in the Pentecostal congregation of Hebron in Oslo. Through the narrator's memories, the reader follows Anders from childhood to adulthood, and through different existential and religious stages. While the child is perfectly "churched", the adolescent distances himself gradually from Hebron. Having lingered for a while in a confusing existential space in between, he finally crosses the border and plunges into a secular life of liberty and endless choices. However, the close of the novel suggests an experience of "coming home" which has been interpreted in various ways.

Guds tjener created quite a sensation in 1973, when it was first published. The reviewers were unanimous in their appraisal. The novel's message about the Pentecostal movement as a social revolt was well received, and the class perspective was easily transferable to other contexts as well. Some considered it one of the most important Norwegian novels of the 1970s. In 1974, it was even nominated for the Nordic Council's Literature Prize.

Guds tjener has several layers. Scholars have recognized and focused on the conflict between socialism and Christianity (Ustvedt 1975), and between the individual, the congregation and the secular society (Gulliksen 1975). The novel has been defined as "social-realistic" (Rottem 1997), and as a story about human beings in crisis (Nes 1980). Helge Dahl points at similarities between religion in *Guds tjener* and Marxism in a novel by Dag Solstad.[1] More recently, Helje Kringlebotn Sødal has concentrated on the novel's representation of spiritual revivals (Sødal 2014).

As mentioned, my focus will be on the religious aspects of the novel. In what follows, we will look into different stages of the character's development. Existentialist concepts like freedom, choice, anxiety, responsibility and authenticity are central in describing the protagonist's quest. I will argue that regardless of the novel's social focus, *Guds tjener* is also–and perhaps more importantly–a reflection on the relationship between authenticity and religious identity and on what it means to be "God's Servant".

One of the reasons why *Guds tjener* aroused such great interest was its unusual religious setting. For the first time the public got an inside view of a religious milieu mainly known through rumors and mockery. The author grew up in the Pentecostal congregation of Salem in Oslo, and when he was writing *Guds tjener* he was still an active member. The novel is not autobiographical, though, even if the description of Hebron draws on life and experiences in Dahl's home church.

Sødal (2014) situates *Guds tjener* in a wider tradition of Norwegian "revival literature", including some of the greatest Norwegian authors like Arne Garborg and Alexander Kielland. We could add Henrik Ibsen as well with his intransigent pastor in *Brand* (1866). While Garborg and Kielland describe strict Lutheran lay people and power loving pastors in the 19th century, the 20th century author Ronald Fangen refers to the Oxford movement of the 1930s, which he knew from the inside. Sødal rightly points out that revival descriptions often emphasize the negative aspects of revivalist Christianity. *Guds tjener* has another approach; it has a different focus.

Furthermore, the novel may be seen as the first of several Scandinavian works bearing on Pentecostals. Per Olov Enquist's *Lewis resa* (2001) is a fictionalized biography about the Swedish Pentecostal leader, Lewi Pethrus. In Norway, other works by Tor Edvin Dahl as well as novels by Levi Henriksen include references to Pentecostalism. In 2013, Heidi Sævareid published her critical young adult novel, *Spranget* (The leap), based on her own experiences. In a larger international perspective, *Guds tjener* has been compared with James Baldwin's semi-biographical novel *Go Tell it on the Mountain* (1953) which builds on Baldwin's own experience in a Pentecostal assembly. When asked about the similarity, Dahl answered that he had not yet read the American novel at the time he wrote *Guds tjener*.

The Religious Setting

Guds tjener gives a realistic description of life in a Pentecostal congregation during the period 1945-1972 (Rudolph 1975, 491). The Pentecostal movement is a worldwide charismatic movement with a large number of branches and independent churches. It started officially as a revival in Azusa Street, Los Angeles in 1906. There were rumors about supernatural manifestations of the Holy Spirit. Records of sensational healings and strange phenomena like glossolalia (speaking in tongues) attracted the crowds. The revival came to Oslo via the Methodist Pastor Thomas Ball Barratt, and from Norway, it penetrated the entire European continent. Pentecostal theology is described as a "theology of encounter" (with God). It is "praxis-oriented and experiential" (Warrington 2008, 16). "We know that God is here!" proclaims the revivalist preacher in *Guds tjener* (123),[2] and the narrator affirms: "The promises we gave were not empty, we offered no philosophy, no theology, we offered the resurrected Christ" (149).[3] The personal born-again experience is vital. The new believer receives a new identity, confirmed by baptism by immersion. The particular mark of the movement is baptism in the Holy Spirit, a special empowering experience normally accompanied by speaking in tongues.

A Short Presentation of *Guds tjener*

The protagonist Anders was born in 1943. He grows up on the eastern side of Oslo, at the time a typical working class area. Anders' father benefits from a social promotion when he becomes a truck driver. When he was still a baby, Anders had a twin brother, Terje. His mother, Christine, suffered from severe depression and one day she accidentally killed Terje, while trying desperately to silence his endless crying with a pillow. After this tragic event, she spent two years in a mental hospital, a place to which she was to return regularly throughout her life. Anders describes his mother as distant and unpredictable, switching abruptly from coldness to exuberance and back again. She both scares and attracts him. Terje remains a stable and important part of Anders' identity; he considers his dead brother a better and more capable person than himself, and he needs him in order to be a complete person. He feels guilty about Terje's death without reason. He identifies with Cain, the Old Testament figure who murdered his brother Abel. He attributes a mole near his eyebrow with symbolic meaning as a mark of Cain.[4] The novel alternates between descriptions of home and church; even though they are intertwined, they represent two different worlds. At the age of fourteen, during a school excursion, Anders comes to a turning point in his life. In his desire to be accepted, he joins some of his classmates who plan to break into a cabin. Anders tries smoking for the first time, and he waits outside the cabin, while his friends break in and steal a deck of cards. At first, Anders is thrilled to feel the boys' acceptance, but in the aftermath, he is devastated and tells his pastor, Tore Henningsen, about it. Confronted with Anders' vulnerability and unlimited confidence the pastor feels helpless and instead of dealing with the boy's feelings, he focuses on the mere facts and on God's forgiveness. Anders feels betrayed, and for many years, he resents the pastor for being unable to prevent him from sliding even further away into confusion. This is the beginning of a process, which leads to his gradual alienation from Hebron. Many years later, a nightmarish sexual experience adds to his confusion. Another crucial episode takes place in a cemetery, where he suddenly "understands" that there is no transcendence, and that everything is equally true or false.

As an adult, Anders marries Lillian, Tore Henningsen's daughter, and life takes a new and dramatic direction. Their marriage turns out to be a disaster. For some time, Anders has entertained an obsessional dream about freedom and permissiveness outside Hebron, a dream that he now embraces more and more. Alcohol, card playing and movies become symbols of this freedom. Lillian resists at first, but feels more and more neglected, and ends up adapting to her husband's new lifestyle. Their marriage develops from bad to worse and finally Lillian takes her own life. Anders is successful in his work as a teacher but in his private life, he is miserable. The freedom he had wanted so desperately is not exactly what he had imagined, and he starts asking himself critical questions. What exactly does freedom mean? Who is he? He understands that unlike his mother whose anguish was always genuine, he himself has been an inauthentic player in life, and he exhorts himself to "wake up" (318).[5]

At the end of the novel, Anders and his father pay Christine a visit at the mental hospital. In what seems like a spontaneous act, Anders suggests they pray for his mother's healing. The three of them kneel down and Anders, who is no longer used to praying, asks that not only Christine, but "all of us may come home".

A Claim for Honesty

The novel begins with Anders' firm determination to remember and understand the past: "Well? Shall we get started?" (7)[6] These opening words function as his point of departure. While reminiscing, he can observe his mother's pale figure in the twilight. Is her presence real or is she only visible for his inner gaze? In any case, in addition to her real role as Anders' mother, she seems to assume metaphorical meaning. In his remembrance process, she serves as a signpost and a focal point. She is both his inner conversation partner and a mirror where he sees his own reflection. The narrative is not chronological but a collection of important moments and feelings that the narrator tries to arrange into a meaningful configuration.[7] Because he spent his childhood searching for his mother even when she was physically close to him, her genuineness and indirect guidance are what he needs now to reach his goal; coming to grips with who he is. The authenticity he recognizes in her at the end of his narrative is also the culmination of his own introspection. His mother's metaphorical meaning is underscored by the vocabulary used to describe her. As a child, Anders noticed her whiteness and knife-like sharpness, which made her cold and distant. On another level, these characteristics connote a blank piece of paper, sharp as a knife. The sharpness also qualifies the intense light that sometimes seems to surround her. The whiteness exhorts the narrator to tell his story based on a new consciousness, its sharpness and brutal light demand unyielding honesty. It is not only about telling a story, it is a journey, where the destination is a new consciousness of his own identity.

In Anders' existential and religious journey narrative, there seems to be a pattern of recurrent concepts and experiences whose meanings change depending on where he is in the process. The end of the novel seems to be the synthetic result of a dialectical dynamics between the experiences and positions of Anders' childhood / early adolescence and his adult life.

Childhood

Anders' childhood memories are concentrated on his home and the congregation. The description highlights differences between a religious and a secular lifestyle in the 1950s and 1960s, especially in a low-church context. Between the lines, the novel also addresses the difficulties in communication when it comes to religious experiences. Finally, it gives a description of Anders' sensory approach to faith.

Life in Hebron

Secular novels and popular culture frequently confuse Christianity with moralism. The religious character may be a hypocrite, a controlling killjoy, a pervert or an ecstatic with a limited sense of reality. This is not the case in *Guds tjener*. Certainly, Pentecostals of the 1950s and 60s did not believe in drinking alcohol, playing cards, dancing and watching movies, and Anders admits that he was a difficult friend to have because of all the restrictions. In exchange, the congregation offers joy, warmth, fellowship and solidarity. As a child, Anders' identification with Hebron is total, and he remembers belonging to the congregation with his entire being. This feeling was even stronger at times of revival: "I was *in* it. I *was* the revival" (146).[8]

Anders is an artistic child who experiences his environment first, and foremost, through his senses. More than words, colors,[9] music and voices speak to him on a deeper level. Thus, the contrast between home and church becomes evident through his perceptions. While his mother is associated with white, coldness and grey, Hebron is described with warm colors like brown and yellow. The adjective "warm" is recurrent in his memories. When the church family gather, the walls' hardness seems to change into a warm, steaming forest floor (40). In a similar way, Sunday school is a warm place (76) and Jesus a white, warm figure with brown hair and a red garment. The landscape surrounding him is warm, yellow and light green and the heaven above is pink. While listening to the Pastor's soothing voice Anders imagines a soft, friendly and smiling landscape (24). He remembers the music and the songs that used to create a "cloud of tunes and happiness!" (85).[10]

These perceptions characterize Anders' form for spirituality, but his memories also include typical theological identity markers like his "born again"-experience followed by baptism by immersion and baptism in the Holy Spirit. A number of details tell the informed reader that Hebron is not a Lutheran State church. As a baby, Anders has been dedicated, not baptized. The atmosphere is loud and expressive. People participate actively with spontaneous feedback to the preacher during the sermon. Joyful hallelujahs, prayers in tongues, and testimonies often fill the sanctuary. There are tears and laughter. The believers lift their hands during prayer (which was then unusual in other denominations). Encounters with God may be narrated with humor. The desire to "see the fire burning" (132),[11] reveals a milieu relating to the tongues of fire on the day of Pentecost. When Anders, aged nine, decides it is time to "cross the border", and be "born again", he knows and feels he is a sinner. He accepts the invitation and approaches "the altar" to be prayed for and "led to Christ". It is a public act celebrated by the whole congregation. He takes on a new identity and a new position in Hebron. While his born-again experience and baptism where the old Adam is symbolically buried are described in a rather neutral and objective manner, his baptism in the Holy Spirit on the other hand is emotional and powerful and fills him with boldness. His natural shyness is totally gone when he surprises himself by crying "Hallelujah!" with a loud voice. Testifying is part of his new identity, and he does so at school. His classmates' mockery is an expected reaction, but that is how it is.

Life outside Hebron

Being different is an important part of Anders' identity. A chapter devoted to his childhood simply starts with the words "Two worlds" (73).[12] The expression refers to the contrast between the unstable home atmosphere and the child's playful relationship with his friends at Sunday school. Additionally, it emphasizes the cultural difference between seculars and believers. It is Sunday morning. Anders is alone in the empty tram, heading off to Sunday school. The short trip feels like a journey between two different worlds where he is moving in a "vacuum", in a vague space in between. The tram is travelling down one of the capital's main streets. The reader's attention is drawn to a meeting tram, which is packed with people, on their way to a joyful day somewhere "out in Nature". These two journeys in opposite directions have a symbolic meaning. Anders moves "in the reverse direction" compared to the surrounding secular world and to what most Norwegians do on a Sunday morning.

As he grows older, the gaze of the outside world affects him more directly. Through reports in the newspapers, the inside life of the church becomes visible to all, but in a distorted way. At a time of revival, inquisitive or sensation-seeking journalists visit Hebron and the result is

> articles in the newspapers accompanied by photos. The headlines in red or black: THE MIRACLE MAN IN VOGT'S STREET or GOD'S POWER OR FRAUD? We could see our own faces strangely distorted by the hard black and white photos. Everything seemed different. The photographer had not tried to catch what we really experienced, but only the sensational, the unusual, the frightening. We saw close-ups of crying people, of some who had fallen to the floor and lay like corpses down by the chairs. We had seen this–it had really happened–but it seemed so different, so baffling,

like this, as photos. Some of the boys in my class asked me about it, but I refused to tell them anything. They wanted to know if I had fainted and a bunch of other stupid things. (153)[13]

The photos show people "slain in the Spirit".[14] Touched by the power of God, they have fallen to the floor. However, the photos show only the surface, not the spiritual experience, which underlies it. The situation makes visible the tension or incompatibility between narratives from widely opposed positions. The gaze from an outside perspective accentuates the strangeness of the scene, and widens the distance between the two worlds. Anders experiences a double de-familiarization: the others' curious gaze and his own puzzlement when he both does and does not recognize what he sees. For a moment, he perceives the situation from a distance.

The incident can serve as a meta-commentary on the insufficiency of one-dimensional representation in capturing depth and multiplicity. It tells us that facts are only facts, not necessarily the truth. Why does Anders refuse to answer his schoolmates' questions? Is he simply annoyed by their ignorance or does his unwillingness point to the difficulty in describing spiritual experience? The whole situation is an example of incommunicability.

The episode also reveals a different religious landscape than the familiar Lutheran one. It refers to a charismatic spirituality which may be physical in its form and which allows emotional and supernatural manifestations. It points to the minority status and identity of Anders, his family and their denomination, and the majority's unquestioned "right" to intrude into their space without trying to understand. Moreover, the incident shows how integrated Anders is in his own reality when he calls his friends' questions "stupid". He appears secure in his identity and in knowing something the others know nothing about. He is not perplexed by the experience itself but by the strangeness of the photos.

On another level, the incident refers to a challenge on a general basis: how can religious experience be described and communicated? This has always been the mystic's dilemma. Words prove insufficient. "The religious experience is pretty hard to describe",[15] says the narrator in Per Olov Enquist's *Lewis resa*. "They could only resort to their own words" (Enquist 2003, 458),[16] "Which words could you possibly use in order to describe immensity?" (ibid., 459).[17] Elsewhere in *Guds tjener* the narrator differentiates between the distance between words and experience and between words and reality. But this time the gap is unimportant because the believers in Hebron share the same experience: "The words did not mean that much, or they referred to something else, to something more real than the words" (149).[18] "We knew that it meant something else than what it seemed to mean" (149).[19] Both physical manifestations and words may refer to another, invisible reality which language in its purely instrumental form seems unable to transmit.

Thus, Anders' childhood memories revolve around his different worlds, home and Hebron, where he has his identity. But he is also conscious of a third space which he thinks of as "the other side", that is secular reality. Indirectly his memories address the relationship between minority and majority, the conflict between appearance and truth, religious experience and the difficulties in transmitting an intangible reality. In the next stage of his life, a certain number of these elements will assume a new meaning.

The Space In-between

The years from 14 to 20 represent a transitional period in Anders' life. He enters a puzzling space in-between, where some of the typical traits of his childhood are transformed into what may seem like their counterpart. The predominance of the senses gives way to reflection; his relationship to Terje is felt to be a hindrance to his own development; a feeling of fullness is replaced by an existential void. This dissolution indicates a tension between past and future, and may be a normal stage in a person's development towards adulthood. Sødal characterizes *Guds tjener* as a Bildungsroman, a novel where the character leaves home to learn about the world and about life, and returns later, well-endowed with greater insight and wisdom. For Anders, the journey is also a period of religious "homelessness" and confusion. The world outside Hebron comes closer, and his new self-reflection makes it difficult to dissociate life's different spaces.

The school outing is the starting point of Anders' homeless identity. His complicity during the break-in changes his conception of who he is and he is destabilized. When the pastor fails to put his world together again, he feels betrayed and starts perceiving his environment differently: "The landscape lost its colors" (183).[20] Hebron's warm magic (81) is broken, and gradually the congregation becomes less important to him than before. This may suggest a farewell to a childlike faith. However, the novel emphasizes the feeling of betrayal, not the loss of faith. On a metaphorical level, the colorless and homogeneous landscape may indicate that from now on he will be responsible for his own "colors", or for his own life. They will no longer be bequeathed spontaneously via the others' soothing voices.

Fullness and Void

A couple of years after "the betrayal", Anders has an almost metaphysical experience of vertiginous emptiness. This is the counterpart of the religious experience of his childhood's colorful and warm fullness. It may seem like a religious experience without a god, a revelation that fills him with a feeling of freedom and endless possibilities. He realizes that he can move in either direction, or take either road.

Simultaneously, the sensual immediacy of his earlier approach to the world is gradually replaced by a distanced and critical view of Hebron and the restrictive lifestyle he grew up with. He has discovered another "fullness", without constraints. He makes new experiences. However, the darker side of his new freedom is symbolized by an erotic experience with a girl he meets randomly. The meeting has a special significance. Anders first mistakes her for a girl in Hebron he used to be attracted to. Now, in his newfound freedom, he indulges in a sexual encounter with the unknown girl. The experience turns out to be violent and nightmarish, and Anders will later blame this incident for his failed marriage.

Anders Renounces Terje

His former closeness to his dead twin brother now feels like a burden, and he realizes that he will have to "kill" him in order to become a whole person. The separation is concretized by the removal of his mole, which had started to grow. Nevertheless, this separation creates another void, and he feels the need for another "cocoon into which he can place his self" (200).[21] He is liberated from the mark of Cain that tied him to Terje, but he still has to build his own identity. During the procedure of eliminating the mole, Anders refers explicitly to the importance of the moment: he loses his identity. He refers to a famous scene in Ibsen's play, *Peer Gynt*, where Peer is peeling an onion, a metaphor of his identity… or the lack of it. In the end, Peer realizes that the onion has no core. This reference gains deeper meaning in the next stage of Anders' life.

Reflection and Search for the Gaze of the Other

Being able to experience a situation from another's point of view is a part of a self-reflexive process. It is an antithetical attitude to the child's sensuous approach. Once Anders was surprised when confronted with the others' reaction to the newspapers' reports about Hebron. Now he actively seeks outside opinions. His entire identification with his milieu is replaced by an interest in the critical outsiders' point of view, and he reads books and articles criticizing the Pentecostal movement. The neutral vocabulary of these works helps him to create a distance to his former life and to dissociate himself. Another case of dissociation takes place when he invites his non-Pentecostal friend, Hans, to a service. When Hans, after an emotional outburst from a lady next to him, suddenly gets up and leaves the room, Anders is first surprised, then he gets an understanding glimpse of the situation from the outsider's point of view: "Anders realized that what to him was ordinary, yes, really familiar, could seem brutal and scary to others. For the first time he saw the meetings from the outside, or tried to" (198).[22] Even though he had gradually distanced himself from Hebron, it seemed that he had not yet become "the Other", his perception had not really changed. Now, something radical becomes evident; his own gaze is changing.

As mentioned above, this stage is one of both homelessness and excitement. Anders is looking for a new foundation. When he marries Lillian, he believes that he has found what he was searching for: "I believed that I had come home" (254).[23]

A New Consciousness

Homecoming? The feeling is short-lived. The narrator's question, "Who is Anders?"[24] (198) becomes more crucial. After Lillian's death, his private life seems purposeless, and he realizes that he has become a slave of his own dream of freedom. In addition, his memories seem to betray him.

Memory Deconstructed

"The memory lies on purpose" (258),[25] says the narrator. He accuses himself of being a liar. The lies concern his childhood, his relationship with Lillian and with her father, Pastor Tore Henningsen. Anders' attempt to gather episodes from his life into a coherent narrative seems to fail, mainly because some of those narratives contradict each other.

Nevertheless, "Memory is at the heart of the way most people think about personal identity".[26] Anders seems unable to determine exactly who he is, but he is trying to get to the core of the problem by penetrating the layers of illusion.

In several memories, he is a victim. He remembers his childhood as cold and lonely. "I am condemned, I am an outcast. My whole life people have looked down on me, some because I was a Pentecostal, and the Pentecostals because I refused to accept that they owned the whole truth" (260).[27] According to this narrative, his rebellion had been hindered by a fear of loneliness and accusations that he was being deceived by the devil. He asks a rhetorical question: "Who can ever escape from his childhood environment"? (259).[28] However, later another picture comes to his mind. He is thirteen years old, and gives his testimony in a Christian meeting. The narrator sees himself as secure, calm, and smiling, answering a person who asks him about his faith with confidence. The word "secure" (306)[29] is underscored, and the narrator asks himself if he had really forgotten this event. It comes to mind after a dark memory of his last conversation with Lillian and her vain attempt to connect with him. The contrast between the two memories shows the two extremes in Anders' life. The rhetorical question above had a negative twist. Applied to the second childhood memory, not escaping may appear as something desirable. The adult might be able to reconnect with his childhood; it may even be a necessity: the narrator refers to an article he has read about sea turtles who have gone astray and distanced themselves from their natural environment. Disoriented, they are unable to function normally.

The memory of Tore Henningsen's so-called betrayal is another "truth" that the narrator deconstructs: he realizes that the real traitor in this story was his own illusion about freedom. He asks himself whether he himself is the real traitor and even contends that he had tried to punish Tore Henningsen by destroying his daughter.

Freedom Deconstructed

Anders' self-examination makes him think of himself as an inauthentic player. Like the disoriented turtles, he has gone astray. "The answer is not to find in what we can be but in what we are" (274).[30] The concepts of being and becoming echo Sartrian existentialism's "existence precedes essence". The individual must consciously create his identity and determine a meaning for his life.

"Paralyzed and helpless, I felt that it was the dream of freedom that persecuted me and not the opposite" (255).[31] He ponders the concept of freedom and concludes that the notion of a reasonable and tolerant freedom is just "a polite vacuum" (300),[32] a dream about nothing, and the opposite of fellowship and solidarity. Real freedom is not an empty void without any constraints. In existentialist thinking, referred to indirectly in the novel, freedom is associated with the freedom of choice. For Kierkegaard, the awareness of freedom is a source of anxiety, for Sartre an experience of "nausea". An authentic person faces life's choices and the void of freedom without delusions and without hiding or pretending. Moreover, faced with his choices, he has a well-founded feeling of anxiety. "The self is essentially intangible and must be understood in terms of possibilities, dread and decisions. When I behold my possibilities, I experience that dread which is 'the dizziness of freedom', and my choice is made in fear and trembling" (Kaufmann 1975, 17).[33] The authentic person takes responsibility for his own choices. The narrator translates this thinking into Christian terminology when he takes a growing responsibility for his own actions and life: he himself is the one who "has sinned" (265).[34]

Anders criticizes the tendency to embrace any dream of freedom uncritically. To be is not to remain always the same, but to be real and genuine, to refuse to be a player.

The Leap of Faith or the Return of a Sea Turtle

The background for Anders' final homecoming is a word "duel" between himself and Tore Henningsen. For a long time, Anders is the stronger. He talks about the decline of the Pentecostal movement, which has betrayed the working class and become a middle class movement. He is an articulate student referring to sociology and history within a socialist frame of reference. The pastor is unable to argue with him on a theoretical level, and feels helpless. However, he has his own weapon. Changing the subject, he simply asks: "–But what about the power of God?" (309).[35]

The argument makes Anders stop and think. It stretches behind the construction of words and theory where he has been moving for a long time, what the narrator calls his "own theoretical figure skating show" (303).[36] The reference to God's power in this context is both a reference to the experiential knowledge Anders had as a child where his perceptions were an important part of his spirituality, and an appeal not to neglect a kind of knowledge, which is as real as the knowledge he can express in words and opinions. To reach authenticity he has to move beyond words: "Now Anders is struggling in order *to be* [...]. Here, now. Without hiding behind postures or opinions" (318).[37] The prayer at the end of the novel is an attempt "to say something true, something real" (318).[38] In other words, to become a true "God's servant".

The novel never suggests that Anders had intended to leave his faith. On the contrary, the narrator reflects on his unconscious selfishness and on the fact that his search for a superficial kind of freedom had led him astray without him understanding that it turned him away from God. In the end, he affirms: "No one can play around with God. The day that you are, you become. The day you are, He comes down, and *stays*" (318).[39] He concludes that "The only free human being is God's servant, the human being who knows that there is no truth, not even a world outside God" (301).[40] The void has again acquired new meaning, it is a place of divine fullness and reminds us of Kierkegaard's famous image of plunging into 70 000 fathoms of water.

Anders then seems to reconnect with his childhood when he reconnects with God in a new conversion and embraces his identity from an adult's conscious perspective. His kneeling is a reconnection with and a parallel to his childhood experience in Hebron. It is not necessarily a return to Hebron, but a turning away from the player's position, which, according to the narrator, is the position of "the individualist who has lost faith in his dream of happiness" (318).[41] According to Kierkegaard, in "the conversion experience", "the decisive move is not purely intellectual but a matter of will and feeling [...] as well. Such is the nature of the so-called 'blind leap' of faith that catapults one into the religious sphere of existence" (Flynn 2006, 10).

Notes

[1] *Gymnaslærer Pedersens beretning om den store politiske vekkelse som har hjemsøkt vårt land* (1982). (Professor Pedersen's story about the great political revival that has flooded our country).

[2] - *Vi vet at Gud er her!* Since Norwegian is read only by a small group of people, I have chosen to use the English translation in the main text. The novel has not been translated into English, so all translations of quotations from the text will be mine.

[3] Våre løfter var ikke tomme, vi tilbød ingen filosofi, ingen teologi, vi tilbød Jesus Kristus oppstanden.

[4] There are different interpretations of the significance of the mark (or the curse) but according to the Bible, the mark was meant to protect Cain.
[5] *Våkn opp.*
[6] Nåvel? Skal vi begynne?
[7] According to Paul Ricœur (1985, 1990), we need narrativisation to figure out who we are. Putting together disparate events into a meaningful plot may enable us to understand our past, present and future.
[8] Jeg var *i* det. Jeg *var* vekkelsen.
[9] Gulliksen 1975, 479–482.
[10] en sky av toner og lykke!
[11] se ilden brenne.
[12] To verdener.
[13] billedreportasjer og store overskrifter i rødt eller svart: MIRAKELMANNEN I VOGTS GATE og GUDS KRAFT ELLER SVINDEL? Vi kunne se våre egne ansikter merkelig fordreid i de harde svart-hvitt bildene, alt virket annerledes, fotografene hadde ikke prøvd å fange inn det vi virkelig opplevde men bare sensasjonen, det uvanlige, det skremmende. Vi så nærbilder av gråtende mennesker, av noen som hadde falt om og lå som døde nede ved stolsetene. Vi hadde sett dette–det hadde hendt–men det virket så annerledes, så uforståelig, *slik*, som bilder. Noen av guttene i klassen spurte meg ut, men jeg ville ikke fortelle noe; de ville vite om jeg besvimte og mange andre dumme ting.
[14] Term used in Pentecostal and Charismatic circles when a person falls to the floor, overcome by the power of the Holy Spirit.
[15] Den religiøse opplevelsen er jo ganske vanskelig å beskrive.
[16] De hadde bare ordene sine å ty til.
[17] hvilke ord kunne man bruke for å beskrive det umåtelige?
[18] Ordene betydde ikke så mye, eller de sto for noe annet; for noe virkeligere enn ordene.
[19] Vi visste at også dette betydde noe helt annet enn det det lød som.
[20] Landskapet mistet fargene.
[21] Et annet hylster å sette sitt jeg i.
[22] Anders forsto at dette som for ham var vanlig, ja, virkelig *fortrolig*; på en annen kunne virke brutalt og skremmende. For første gang så han møtene utenfra, eller prøvde å se dem.
[23] Jeg trodde jeg hadde funnet hjem.
[24] Hvem er Anders?
[25] Hukommelsen lyver med overlegg!
[26] Klein and Nichols. http://dingo.sbs.arizona.edu/~snichols/Papers/MemoryandSense of Personal Identity.pdf (Accessed 15.02.2018).
[27] Jeg er en fordømt, en utstøtt, hele mitt liv har folk sett ned på meg, noen fordi jeg var pinsevenn og pinsevennene fordi jeg ikke ville godta at de satt inne med hele sannheten […].
[28] Hvem kan noensinne få rett overfor sitt barndomsmiljø?
[29] trygg
[30] Svaret ligger [ikke] i hva vi kan bli men hva vi er.

³¹ [i det øyeblikket] følte jeg også lammende og hjelpeløst at det var drømmen om friheten som forfulgte meg og ikke jeg den [...].
³² Et høflig vakuum
³³ The author refers to Søren Kierkegaard.
³⁴ som syndet
³⁵ - Men hva med Guds kraft?
³⁶ Egne teoretiske kunstløpoppvisninger.
³⁷ Anders kjemper etter *å være* nå [...]. Uten å springe bak positurer eller meninger.
³⁸ Si noe sant, noe virkelig.
³⁹ Ingen kan spille med Gud. Den dagen du er, blir du. Den dagen du er, stiger Han ned, og *blir*.
⁴⁰ Det eneste frie mennesket er Guds tjener, det mennesket som vet at det finnes ingen sannhet utenfor Gud, at det ikke engang finnes noen verden utenfor Gud.
⁴¹ Individualisten som har mistet troen på lykkedrømmen.

References

Dahl, Helge. 1986. "Politisk og religiøs tro." *Ergo*, Vol. No. 3: 131–139.
Dahl, Tor Edvin. 1975. *Guds tjener*. Oslo: Gyldendal.
Enquist, Per Olov. 2001. *Lewis resa*. Stockholm: Norstedts.
—. 2003. *Lewis reise*. Oslo: Gyldendal. (Translated into Norwegian by Bodil Engen).
Flynn, Thomas R. 2006. *Existentialism. A Very Short Introduction*. Oxford: Oxford University Press.
Gulliksen, Øyvind. 1975. "Fragmenter av et kristenliv? En analyse av Tor Edvin Dahls roman *Guds Tjener*." *Kirke og Kultur*, Vol. No. 8: 474–488.
Kaufmann, Walter. 1975. *Existentialism from Dostoevsky to Sartre*. New York, London, Scarborough: The New American Library.
Klein, Stanley and Nichols, Schaun. "Memory and the Sense of Personal Identity." http://dingo.sbs.arizona.edu/~snichols/Papers/MemoryandSenseofPersonalIdentity.pdf. [Accessed 18.03.2019].
Nes, Solrunn. 1980. "Mennesker i krise. Analyse av Tor Edvin Dahls *Guds tjener*." *Kirke og Kultur*, Vol. No. 4: 230–243.
Ricœur, Paul. 1985. *Temps et récit* III. Paris: Seuil.
—. 1990. *Soi-même comme un autre*. Paris: Seuil.
Rudolph, Anne Beate. 1975. "Miljøet i Guds tjener." *Kirke og Kultur*, Vol. No. 8: 489–491.
Sødal, Helje Kringlebotn. 2014. "Når vekkelse blir skjønnlitteratur." In *Fra svar til undring. Kristendom i norske samtidstekster*, edited by Øyvind T. Gulliksen and Årstein Justnes, 83–101. Oslo: Verbum Akademisk.
Ustvedt, Yngvar. 1975. *Dagbladet*. Reproduced on the book cover of *Guds tjener*. Oslo: Gyldendal.
Warrington, Keith. 2008. *Pentecostal Theology. A Theology of Encounter*. New York: T & T Clark.

Chapter Five

"My Centre Not My Edge": Uncanny Identity, Death, Doubles and Medievalism in Kevin Hart's *Your Shadow*

Melanie Duckworth

In a poem called "My Death", first published in *The Lines of the Hand* (1981), the Australian poet Kevin Hart describes "a shadow // I follow / Or follows me / And leads me to my centre, not my edge" (2002, 19). Here he presents the idea of death as utterly central to identity. This image of death as a shadow is developed further in Hart's unsettling yet lovely poetry collection *Your Shadow* (1984), which uses images of light and the uncanny "double" of the shadow to explore ideas of selfhood, death and belonging. A series of poems entitled "Your Shadow" and "Your Shadow's Songs", which form a dialogue between a person and their shadow, comprise the core of the collection. At times, the shadow is addressed or described, and at others, the shadow itself speaks. The shadow is at once an effect of the light, a reminder of death, and a constant companion. The poems about "your shadow" are meditations on self-identity: one's shadow is an image of oneself, an ethereal reminder of the physicality of one's presence in the world.

As Andreea Deciu Ritovoi notes, Ricoeur has pointed out "the inevitable incompleteness of one's life story for as long as one is alive. Yet without knowledge of how the narrative ends," she asks, "how to make sense of the plot?" (2008, 232). In one respect, however, the end of the story is always known, and it is always the same. If the narrative of identity only makes sense once we know its conclusion, Kevin Hart's poetry reminds us that we *do* know the conclusion, but try hard not to think about it. "Your shadow", on the other hand, does not forget. "It is the thing / Beside you when you wake, a cold sheet / As delicate as your skin" (Hart 2002, 52). It is always already there, cold, like a shroud:

> At daylight
> It is already obsessed,
> Wearing black as if expecting your funeral
> And trying to be a grave. (2002, 70)

With sly humour, precise description, and deepening foreboding, Hart creates an image of the shadow as a kind of "double". "Your shadow" is an image of the self, but apart from the self, haunting the daylight world of solid things. It is at once utterly familiar, and disconcertingly strange. It is, in Freud's terms, *uncanny*. As Freud explains, the uncanny "is undoubtedly related to what is frightening—to what arouses dread and horror", but he qualifies: "the uncanny is that class of the frightening that leads back to what is known of old and long familiar" (2001, 930). Nicholas Royle, at the beginning of his extensive study of the uncanny, emphasises that "the uncanny is not simply an experience of strangeness or alienation. More specifically, it is a peculiar commingling of the familiar and unfamiliar" (2003, 1). As such, the uncanny is also intimately connected to the idea of the self:

> It is impossible to think about the uncanny without this involving a sense of what is autobiographical, self-centred, based in one's own experience. But it is also impossible to conceive of the uncanny without a sense of ghostliness, a sense of strangeness given to dissolving all assurances about the identity of a self. (Royle 2003, 16)

Hart's shadow fits all the qualities described above: it is familiar and strange, intimate and terrifying.

> How quiet he is, your friend,
> And how attentive to your each need–
> As the ocean caresses the shore
> As the bee trembles beside a blossom… (Hart 2002, 64).

Like a stubborn ghost, it cannot be escaped. At noon the sun, "furious, / Burns it within an inch of life", "[b]ut watch: it returns, freshened by failure and rest" (ibid., 70). The uncanny nature of Hart's shadow is related not only to its premonitions of death, but also to the fact that is an image of the self made strange. "One day you will become / That other man, the silent one, the one in black" (2002, 64).

The "uncanny" nature of the shadow comes through even in the way Hart talks about the poems. Interviewing Hart in 1995, John Kinsella asked him to explain the "dichotomy" of the shadow poems: "There is a duality here; [the shadow] is part of you. It is necessary, but it retains an independence, it is separate from your earthly manifestation, your physical entity. Can you explain that dichotomy?" (Kinsella 1997, 261). Hart declined:

> I've never fully understood those shadow poems. When I wrote them–a fair whack of them back in the early eighties –I found that in some cases it was the shadow speaking to me, not me to the shadow. When that was happening, the shadow always referred to itself in the third person. And I've never fully been able to work that out . . . Even now I don't understand those poems fully. I remember they came to me with the force of necessity, but I have no idea where they came from or what the need was. (Kinsella 1997, 261–262)

This comment positions the poems themselves as strange and somehow uncanny: Hart has never "fully understood" them, he has "no idea where they came from" or why he needed to write them. They almost appear to come from the shadow itself.

Freud shows that uncanny, *unheimlich*, actually sometimes means the same thing as its opposite, *heimlich*, or "homely". *Heimlich* means both "free from fear" and, in a different sense, "something hidden and dangerous" (2001, p. 934): "Thus *heimlich* is a word the meaning of which develops in the direction of ambivalence, until it finally coincides with its opposite, *unheimlich*. *Unheimlich* is in some way or other a sub-species of *heimlich*" (ibid.). Appropriately, the shadow poems riff uneasily upon the concept of home:

> You are, as always,
> Standing on the brink of something new,
> And your shadow
>
> Waits behind, paring its nails,
> And it will follow you
> Across the earth, until it brings you home. (ibid., 52)

The uncanny often involves a blurring of boundaries between life and death, as Freud quotes Ernst Jentsch: "doubts whether an apparently animate being is really alive; or, conversely, whether a lifeless object might not in fact be animate" (ibid., 935). It can be experienced in relation to madness and epilepsy, dolls and manikins, silence and darkness, repetition, doubles, and hints of the supernatural.

The idea of the double, or the *doppelgänger*, is the central way in which Hart embodies the uncanny in this collection. A shadow is always a double, and the double always involves a splitting and questioning of self. In addition to the shadow itself, "doubling" can be found throughout the collection, in relation to mirrors and photographs, and in poems in which the poet attempts to come to terms with the deaths of his father and his sister. The uncanny also provides an interesting perspective on the religious, mystical and Christian aspects of Hart's verse. Christianity is usually seen as incompatible with the uncanny, but in these poems, the Christian and the uncanny are merged. Christ is even figured as a kind of "double". Although the poetry gestures towards Christian theology and eschatology as ultimately capable of providing a resolution to the problems of death and fractured identity, the collection as a whole retains the obscured, sometimes frightening perspective of the here and now: shadows, mirrors, loss and yearning. We see, in St Paul's words, "through a glass, darkly".

Gary Catalano points out the importance of light as well as shadow in the collection *Your Shadow* (1986, 25), and David McMooey notes the "medieval intensity" of the poems (1995-1996, 110). In "Exploring the Shadow of *Your Shadow*", Lachlan Brown reads Hart's shadow in three ways: "Firstly the representational shadow, secondly the shadow of death, and thirdly a kind of theological shadow, which speaks some interesting things onto the other two shadows" (2007, 106). In doing so he traces references in Hart's poetry to the representational shadows of Plato's cave, and discusses the association of the shadow with death in relation to Heidegger's concept of Dasein. Finally he puts these in context with the Christian imagery of darkness and light, which Hart draws on in multiple ways. In this chapter I will show how the sense of the uncanny, which pervades the collection, enables Hart to interrogate the connection between death and identity. Hart has often spoken of a preoccupation with a mystical "unknown", and it is through the *uncanny* nature of this collection that he achieves one of his most successful engagements with it. One way in which the poems engage with both the Christian and the uncanny is through their disparate range of mystical and medieval sources. The epigraph of the collection is a quotation from the 16th century St John of the Cross, and the poems also reference the fourteenth-century Meister Eckhart, and a fifteenth-century medieval lyric about "death". The shadow poems themselves echo medieval debate poems between the body and the soul. Thus, Hart combines theological, mystical sources of "negative theology" with more popular and more grotesque medieval images of death, which have fed into "uncanny" traditions of the Gothic. My approach of reading the poems in the context of the "double" enables a focus on the Gothic elements of Hart's poetry, elements which can easily be ignored or downplayed when reading the poetry from a purely Christian or mystical perspective. Ultimately the power of Hart's poetry lies in the way it straddles the physical and the philosophical, the mystical and the Gothic. Hart's poetry shows that in this world at least, identity is not fixed, the self is not whole. "Your shadow" becomes a quiet reminder not only of death but of the strangeness of living in the world.

The Double

The notion of the double is the most compelling and developed way in which the collection explores uncanny elements of identity, death and religion. The presiding image of the collection, the shadow, is by its very nature a double, creating ghostly repetitions of objects as light falls on them. As John Herdman explains:

> The human shadow and reflection have always been seen as extensions of the personality and have carried a numinous charge. They were long regarded as in some sense spiritual doubles, ultimately perhaps representing the soul, and vital to the wholeness and integrity of the individual. (1991, 2)

Sigmund Freud and Otto Rank's conception of the "double", *der Doppelganger*, has been an influential concept in the study of Gothic fiction, and is related to the unsettling idea of a "second self". Its most well-known literary examples include Robert Louis Stephenson's *The Strange Case of Dr Jekyll and Mr Hyde*, Fyodor Dostoevsky's *The Double*, and the work of E. T. A Hoffman. Rank and Freud speculate that the idea of a "double" was initially related to a desire for immortality, but it has become an uncanny "harbinger of death" (Freud, 2001, 940). The double has connections with "reflections in mirrors, with shadows, with guardian spirits, with belief in the soul and the fear of death" (ibid.). All of these images occur in Hart's shadow poems. "Your shadow" is

> The blueprint
> For the monster in your head,
> The sideshow mirror
> whose black humour is all too true. (Hart 2002, 52)

As Royle puts it:

The double is uncanny. It is weird, eerie, spooky, strangely disorienting to think about. It is uncanny because it involves a strangeness contaminated with sameness, difference as repetition. It is one thing *and* something else. The double is a matter of life and death. On the one hand, it seems to illustrate or promise immortality: you can be repeated, replicated, duplicated. The life of an individual is no longer precariously confined to a single body. On the other hand, it is the very disordering of identity. The individual is no longer individual. There is a dividing of the one, division within the self. Seeing your double you are obliged to suppose that your own identity is dissolving or has already come to an end. The double thus comes to figure as, in Freud's phrase, "the uncanny harbinger of death" (2014, 123).

The notion of the "double" is invoked viscerally in Hart's choice of imagery. In one poem Hart qualifies that he doesn't mean "the one in mirrors" or "the one shut up in photographs" (2002, 64), but:

> The one without a face,
> Who sways with your each movement, the snake-charmer;
> Who keeps his ear to the ground,
> Who puts on stilts when evening comes.
>
> This is the one
> The sun has given you for company;
> A fallen guardian angel,
> A butterfly stuck to its chrysalis… (ibid.)

Describing the shadow as "the one without a face" transforms a benign description into a grotesque, nightmarish image. Of course shadows do not have faces, but a being without a face is a cause for some alarm. The image of a "butterfly stuck to its chrysalis" is also unsettling, first because of the idea of the entrapped, encumbered butterfly, and secondly for the realization that the inert, encumbering chrysalis is the image for the body or the self. The poems alternate between precise and playful descriptions of real shadows, personifying them, and transforming them to metaphor.

For Freud, the role the double plays in regards to identity formation is linked to its roots in what he sees as a childish or "primitive" wish for immortality:

> Such ideas, however, have sprung from the soil of unbounded self-love, from the primary narcissism which dominates the mind of the child and of primitive man. But when this stage has been surmounted, the 'double' reverses its aspect. From having been an assurance of immortality, it becomes the uncanny harbinger of death. (2001, 940)

This, he claims, is the root of its uncanny nature. The double is initially meant to preserve the ego, but ends up frighteningly dismantling it. The above quotation resonates in *Your Shadow* in a number of different ways. The story of Narcissus, who falls in love with his own reflection, is a foundational trope of the "double". Freud speaks of a "primary narcissism", but Rank discusses the story in more detail, as an example of "the ruinous and the erotic" aspects of the double (1971, 67). He summarises: "Narcissus, who was equally unresponsive to youths and maidens, caught sight of himself in the water and became so enamoured of the handsome boy so splendidly reflected that the longing for this image caused his death" (ibid.). The poems that make up the poem-sequence "Your Shadow's Songs" are prefaced by a quotation from the Narcissus story in Ovid's *Metamorphoses*: "*sit tibi copia nostri*", which means "I yield to you" (Hart 2002, 76). In Ovid's version, the nymph Echo falls in love with Narcissus, who, already in love with his own reflection, spurns her advances and cries: "I will die before I yield to you". She echoes only: "I yield to you" (Ovid 1987, 63). In the context of these poems, the quotation has multiple resonances. The proud defiance of "I will die before I yield to you" is the attitude of the body, which struggles to escape the shadow's embrace. Ironically, the body will indeed yield in death. The echo, "I yield to you", is the shadow's voice, as the shadow continually yields to the body that casts it. This epigraph thus epitomizes the fraught and intimate relationship the poem goes on to explore.

The figure of the child, the narcissist, and, arguably, a form of "primitivism" all feature in the poems. The image of the child recurs several times:

> Come closer, it is a trap-door
> Into the secret earth, and one day soon
>
> You will go there
> To meet the child you were, covered in dirt. (Hart 2002, 46)

This image of a child covered in dirt is on one level a nostalgic picture of a carefree child playing outside, perhaps even recalling the ways in which children play with their shadows. The thought of one day soon going under the earth and being covered in dirt is also, however, deeply creepy. Here death is presented as a way of accessing your true identity, which is linked with your childhood self. Unlike Freud's double, however, Hart's shadow is not created from a desire for immortality; it is born along with the child. The poems repeatedly link the shadow to both birth and death. It is "a gift, a birth right, your baby shawl / Now growing into a shroud" (ibid.). In the words of the shadow itself:

> My brother, when you fed on blood
> Our mother smiled to feel each kick,
>
> You slid into a world of light
> And found me in the doctor's arms... (ibid., 78)

The above quote attests to a shared identity–"you fed on blood", but "*our* mother smiled". Our shadow and our mortality are essential parts of our identity–they are there from birth, from the beginning.

An intense awareness of childhood, birth, and intrauterine existence is also at stake elsewhere in the collection. The shadow is not the only double present in the poems. Other potential "double" pairings are siblings, and fathers and sons. In a prose poem about his father's death, "The House", Hart writes of driving back to his childhood home, where he finds the surreal scene of the tree he had climbed as a child, "leafless now, and from each branch there hung faces of the family, men with moustaches and pipes, women with faces fine as spiderwebs" (ibid., 74). Members of his family are reduced to miniature doubles, strange likenesses hung from a tree. The uncanny scene continues as he approaches the house from the perspective of the newly dead:

> I came upon the house from behind, and saw it as the dead must see their lives, as something odd and ungainly to have won such love. Tired now, I found my former room, crammed with old furniture and dustmotes gliding though the moonlight. Lying down I began to slip away from the world, becoming the size of myself in a photograph, myself reflected in an eye. Like father, I could see my life from the other side–unfinished, all hidden errors exposed–like a needle pushed through embroidered cloth. (ibid.)

Here the speaker finds himself shrinking to "the size of myself in a photograph, myself reflected in an eye". Engulfed by the proximity of his father's death, Hart's own identity shrinks to that of a double, a reflection, a photograph, as he views his own life from the other side.

Perhaps the most heartbreaking double of all is that of Hart's stillborn sister, Marion. In "For Marion, My Sister", Hart writes of trying to retrieve impossible memories of the sister who died in utero before he was born: "I say your name / Though it reminds me of nothing, like water" (ibid., 56). Despite the impossibility of imagining her, he begins to see himself as her double:

> I tell myself
> I have seen you in the mirror
> Before I see myself, a boy-girl face
> That weds us before I think.
> This will not do,
> My face is different
> And I must have it whole. . . (ibid.)

His reflection in the mirror uncannily merges with the ghost of his sister. He tries to shake himself free of the guilt of being born alive when his sister was not, and claims his face as his own:

> I have not stolen it, sister,
> And cannot give it back.
> I do not know
> Why you were chosen
> And I was not, I cannot understand
> What brings you, thirty years too late,
> Back from the other world: only
> Tonight I feel you
> As our mother once felt you,
> Trapped in a cage deep within me,
> Beating steadily
> With articulate, insistent fists. (ibid., 56-57)

From seeing his sister as an uncanny double in his own reflection, Hart moves to feeling her deep within himself, "trapped in a cage", as his mother once felt her. The experience described here is both tragic and uncanny. According to Freud:

> To some people the idea of being buried alive by mistake is the most uncanny thing of all. And yet psycho-analysis has taught us that this terrifying phantasy is only a transformation of another phantasy which had originally nothing terrifying about it at all, but was qualified by a certain lasciviousness–the phantasy, I mean, of intra-uterine existence. (2001, 946)

The fact that Hart includes imagery of both graves and wombs does not necessarily mean that he endorses Freud's correlation of the two, but the poems' continual oscillation between the darkness before birth and the darkness after death link the two as strange and unknowable aspects of our own identity. For the stillborn baby, like Hart's sister, the womb that gives life becomes the site of suffocation and death. She dies before she gets to meet her shadow.

The double, as Hart conceives it here, has to do with death, mortality, and identity. Like the face of his sister, which haunts his own reflection in mirrors, the shadow sings of death and a fracturing of self. At the same time, however, the shadow affirms existence and life–it is cast by a solid, living body. The shadow is undoubtedly uncanny, but it is also something more. Throughout the collection, the image of the shadow is held in tension with images of the sun, the good and pleasurable things of this world, and the hope of redemption, in particular the mysterious Catholic doctrine of the resurrection of the body.

The Christian Uncanny

Hart's poetry has frequently been read in the context of his religious and philosophical background. He is not only a poet, but a philosopher and prominent literary critic, and the author of monographs on Jacques Derrida and Maurice Blanchot. In *The Trespass of the Sign* (1989), he seeks to reconcile Derrida's deconstruction with a tradition of negative theology stretching back through the Middle Ages to Augustine and Pseudo-Dionysius. In *Christian Mysticism and Australian Poetry*, Toby Davidson reads Hart as a participant and an innovator in a tradition of Christian mysticism in Australian poetry. Hart converted from "nominal Anglicanism" to Catholicism in 1980, just four years before *Your Shadow* was published (Davidson, 2013, 188). The collection is prefaced by a quotation from the sixteenth-century Spanish mystic, St John of the Cross:

> If an object is opaque and dark, it makes a dark shadow; if it is transparent and delicate, its shadow is transparent and delicate. Thus the shadow of a dark object amounts to another darkness in the measure of the darkness of the object, and the shadow of something bright amounts to something else that is bright according to the brightness of the object. (Hart 2002, 44)

Taken out of context, as they are in Hart's epigraph, St John's words appear a curiously scientific description of light, transparency and opacity. The words invoke shifting planes of darkness and light, emphasized by the repetition of the words "transparent and delicate" and the opposition of dark and bright objects. This monochromatic spectrum brings to mind differing shades, textures and strengths of light: glass, lace, gauze, and the silken, slippery shadows themselves, "as delicate as your skin" (ibid., 52). These images are a fitting introduction to Hart's collection, which uses shadows as images of death: "Your body's very own black flower" (ibid.); but contrasts this with a continuing love for the bright things of the world, such as "sunlight / Basking on the wooden floor / With an animal pleasure" (ibid., 63). In *The Living Flame of Love*, St John writes about the shadow of God on the soul, a bright "enkindled" shadow, as God is bright: "For when a person is covered by a shadow, it is a sign that someone else is nearby to protect and favour" (2017, 168). The bright shadow is a sign of God's glory, God's protection, and also of the limitations of vision. John of the Cross's use of light and shadow touches on the negative theologian's territory of the fragility of image and representation: God's brightness is experienced as shadow. These spiritual aspects of light and shadow resonate in the poems of *Your Shadow*. Alongside this possible spiritual interpretation, however, the poems retain an intense awareness of the physical world, as well as a darker, Gothic, almost surreal preoccupation with the shadow as an intimate and frightening reminder of death.

The relationship between the uncanny and religion is somewhat fraught. Nicholas Royle points out that "[i]t is, in fact, one of the unstated assumptions of Freud's essay that the uncanny is to be theorized in non-religious terms. The experience of the uncanny, as he seeks to theorize it, is not available or appropriate to, say, a Jewish or Christian 'believer'" (2003, 20). For Freud, religion enables us to be "at home in the uncanny". Religion acts as a kind of buffer against uncanny feelings. Hart's shadow poems, however, operate within a Christian, Catholic framework, but remain undoubtedly "uncanny". Christ himself is presented as kind of double in several of the poems. The opening poem of the collection, "The Ten Thousand Things", speaks of "The true man's face, once hidden by your own" (Hart, 2002, p. 45). In "A Silver Crucifix on my Desk", Christ's face is presented as a mirror:

> . . . Each year
> I grow
> Toward your age,
> A face moving towards a mirror,
> I measure myself against you, a child
> Beside his father. . . (ibid., 88)

In addition to the imagery of "doubles" inherent in mirrors and fathers, the poem refers to shadows and clocks:

> By evening
> I no longer look your way, but watch
> Your shadow
> Steal towards my hand, I hear you talk
> In the clock's dialect

And my pen
Becomes an ancient nail. . . (ibid., 87)

This shadow is not exactly "bright" or "enkindled": it speaks of suffering, death, and time running out. In "The Companion", Christ is presented as a shadowy presence that haunts the speaker every night:

There is a man who will not let me sleep,
Each night he comes and trembles by my side.
He cannot be touched yet wind disturbs his hair,
He cannot touch yet shadows cover me. (ibid., 84)

This poem is a pantoum, a four-stanza poem structured like a villanelle in that entire lines from each stanza are repeated in the following stanzas. In this way the poem itself performs a doubling and mirroring, as well as achieving a curious incantatory effect. By presenting Christ as a double in this way: a shadow, a reflection, a face once obscured by your own, the poems hint at a conversion narrative, and a reassessment of identity. The idea of Christ as double ties in with Christian theology of Christ standing in for humanity in his death on the cross. As an image, however, Christ as *double* retains a note of unsettling strangeness, elusiveness, and an awareness of self as fractured and incomplete.

The collection as a whole circles around not only the inevitability of death but a strange, repressed desire for it, framed in the poems as the "will to change". Hart presents the world itself as aching towards transformation and fulfillment. In human terms, however, this transformation will come through death. The poem "The Will to Change" speaks of the world, and objects and bodies within it, "leaning into the future", desiring to be transformed (ibid., 62). The end of the poem riffs on an uncited passage from Meister Eckhart. Here the self yearns to discover its true self beyond death:

Come, be quickened,

Like a river approaching the rapids,
You must see
You are moving towards yourself, the one

Who will give up this world
As the afternoon blossoms from the cool morning,
As the flame reaches from the wood. (ibid.)

Here death is imagined not as shadow but as light. The images of the flowing river and the flame's self-sacrifice are taken from the fourteenth-century mystic, Meister Eckhart:

> Solomon says that all waters, that is, all creatures flow and return to their source. [...] So I say then that similarity, begotten of the One, draws the soul into God, as He is one in His hidden unity, for that is the meaning of 'one'. We have a clear illustration of this: when the physical fire kindles the wood one spark receives the nature of fire and becomes like the pure fire, which without any medium clings to the lower heavens. Immediately it forgets and deserts father and mother, brother and sister on this earth, and it darts up to the heavenly father. [...] In addition, it is to be noted that this small spark not only forsakes and forgets father and mother, brother and sister on earth, but it leaves, forsakes and denies itself also, being drawn by love to its real father, the sky, for it must necessarily be extinguished in the cold air. (1994, 124-25)

Despite their unacknowledged medieval sources, Hart's images retain an inevitability and lightness. Instead of reproducing the density of Eckhart's allegory, Hart's verbs "blossoms" and "reaches" lose the strained and negative connotations of Eckhart's "forgets", "forsakes", "deserts" and "denies". Eckhart's theological "One" becomes Hart's colloquial "the one who". The themes and images of the medieval mystic inform the modern poem, but in such a way that the contemporary sounding surface of the poem is unruffled.

"The will to change" can thus be aligned with the uncanny concept of the "death drive", which Freud discusses in *Beyond the Pleasure Principle* (1959). In "Toscanini at the Dead Sea", Hart speaks of "a century of Europe // Almost in love with death", and observes:

> How everything we love moves to one end,
> Inevitable yet unexpected, a will to change
> That somehow raises us above the end. (2002, 85)

This touches on the central tension of the collection: the desire to see death as not only inevitable but wholesome, good and necessary, the gateway to the true self and Christian transcendence, while at the same time acknowledging a sensible human resistance to such an idea. The poem concludes with the necessity of making "desire our home" (ibid.). But a lot of the time, death remains frightening, haunting, unwanted. Thus the entire Christian premise of life beyond death is, from another perspective, deeply uncanny.

Medievalism

Mladen Dolar argues that the concept of the uncanny emerged after the Enlightenment because uncanny and numinous experiences were no longer accorded their own "socially sanctioned place" as "sacred and untouchable":

> There is a specific dimension of the uncanny that emerges with modernity … [I]n premodern societies the dimension of the uncanny was largely covered (and veiled) by the area of the sacred and untouchable. It was assigned to a religiously and socially sanctioned place … With the triumph of the Enlightenment, this privileged and excluded place (the exclusion that founded society) was no more. That is to say that the uncanny became unplaceable; it became uncanny in the strict sense. (Dolar 1991, 7, quoted in Royle 2003, 22)

As discussed above, Hart's work as a whole orientates itself towards the Middle Ages partly through an engagement with Christian mysticism. This is evident in *Your Shadow* in the epigraph from St John of the Cross and allusions to the fourteenth-century mystic Meister Eckhart in the poem "The will to change". In addition to this, however, as the poems' connection to the unsettling notion of the "double" makes clear, Hart makes use of another strain of medievalism–that of the Gothic. As Peter Otto points out, by the middle of the nineteenth century, the word "Gothic" "could designate the barbarous world from which the modern has emerged; a primitive (natural) world able to renovate a lifeless modernity; and the sense that the modern is unable to divide itself from the barbarous past" (2005, 19). Thus, in the form of the Gothic, the Middle Ages itself operates as a kind of uneasy "double" of the modern world. These two forms of medievalism, one connected to a mystical tradition, the other Gothic, darker, more grotesque, with links to the medieval tradition of *memento mori*, form two poles from which Hart balances contradictory attitudes towards death. In one aspect death is friendly, necessary, an essential part of one's identity, and in another it remains unwanted, spooky and terrifying, but unavoidable all the same.

The dialogue format of Hart's shadow poems, as well as the way the shadow appears as a representation of death, bring to mind medieval debate poems between body and soul. These were a popular genre during the Middle Ages, and usually consisted of the soul berating the body for its attachment to earthly things, which are revealed to be useless in the face of death. As the genre developed, however, in poems such as "Als I lay in a winteris nyt", the body started arguing back (Conlee 1991, xxvi).

Michael-Andre Bossy describes two different varieties of these discussions: those that describe a good soul and a reluctant body, and those in which the soul and body are both guilty (1976, 145). In each case, however, the conversation takes place with the understanding that death is near, the body is mortal, and the soul will soon be held to account. Conversations between the body and the soul attest to a double, fractured identity–the self is split into two bickering halves. Medieval body-soul debates, then, could also be seen as examples of a "split" identity, and a kind of "doubling".[1] The self and the shadow in Hart's poems cannot be equated with the body and the soul, but Hart's poems and the medieval lyrics share an intense awareness of mortality, and dramatize the struggle between resisting and accepting it. They both depict identities that are split–selves, divided into parts sufficiently separate that they can argue, resist and console one another.

Thomas L. Reed suggests that one of the most interesting features of Middle English debate poetry is its "aesthetics of irresolution": "these poems [...] often seem less interested in settling a winner than in the apprehension or appreciation (in the multiple senses of the words) of the differences that give rise to the debate" (1990, 2). In *Your Shadow* Hart does not simply imitate the medieval genre, but adapts it for his own purposes. The self and the shadow, who converse in the poems, are not precise translations of the body and the soul, or even the body and death. This is confirmed in "Your Shadow's Songs" by the way the shadow refers to the soul: "I know you all too well, this head / That holds its thoughts like mercury, // This soul composed of ice and steam…" (2002, 78). The shadow claims more intimacy with the body than the soul itself: "I sleep with you, your bony arms / Holding me closer than your soul" (ibid., 79). The shadow operates as a constant reminder of mortality, but if it symbolizes death, it is a personal and intimate death–not alien to the self, but an essential part of it. Two of Hart's later poems, each entitled "Soul Says", also allude to the medieval body soul debates, describing a body distracted by the physical world while "soul" counsels it to look beyond it. "You ear and eye and mind, you others too– / I say, / Come be gathered in a word..." (ibid., 160) The body continues to be distracted but the end of the poem reaches a compromise: "One day, soul says, // One day, I say, // One day, / The eye and mind will listen, and abide" (ibid.). The haunting quality of Hart's shadow poems is intensified by the fact that his shadow is not purely allegorical–it is a physical reality, a companion, and belongs to the world of light and solid things as much as we do.

While Hart does not make any explicit references to medieval body/soul debates in *Your Shadow*, in "Till Sotell Death Knocked at My Gate", Hart responds to a fifteenth-century religious poem about the suddenness of death, the need for repentance, and the enduring glory of paradise. The title of Hart's poem is taken from its second stanza:

> This lyfe, I see, is but a cheyre feyre;
> All thyngis passene and so most I algate.
> To-day I sat full ryall in a cheyere,
> Tyll sotell deth knokyd at my gate,
> And on-avysed he seyd to me, chek-mate!
> lo! how sotell he maketh a devors–
> and wormys to fede, he hath here leyd my cors. (Brown 1962, 236)

The original poem has its fair share of black humour, as death declares "chek-mate!" to the speaker who has been sitting royally on a chair, unaware of the vulnerability of his position. In no time at all, death has divorced soul from body, and given the corpse to worms. The poem rues the transience of life, which turns out to be nothing more than a fleeting cherry fair, itself an image of transience, desired and fleeting. Hart's version takes the popular image of death knocking on your door, and sees in it a loophole:

> Don't let him think you're home: lock all the doors,
> Cut off the telephone, and plug both ears;
> Divorce your wife–she might make a mistake;
> Let all your mail pile up outside; put out
> Some bottles of rancid milk beside the gate. (2002, 86)

If death doesn't know you're home, it seems, he won't be able to find you. The poem continues in this vein for another five stanzas, in the tone of one friend giving secret advice to another: "This plan will only work for one or two ... // Remember, if it fails you don't know me, / You don't know where I am" (ibid.). By twisting a rueful medieval acceptance of death into a modern evasion of death, which itself looks suspiciously *like* death, Hart draws attention to the modern unease about representations of death and its place in society.[2]

Like several medieval models, Hart's tripartite body, soul and shadow, and his multiple "body, mind, and others too", construct a self-identity built of multiple constituent parts. The shadow represents an aspect of the self, mortality, that the rest of the self wishes to banish or ignore. Gothic medievalist portrayals of death are one way to represent this. Body soul debates describe what happens to one's identity when one finally dies and has to face what has hitherto been avoided. In contrast to this, the tradition of Christian mysticism seeks a true form of identity in union with God, beyond a fragmented earthly experience of self. Hart's shadow poems hold in tension these ways of viewing the body, death, darkness, light, and our place in the world.

Conclusion

As we have seen, the shadow is very literally a "double", an "uncanny harbinger of death" (Freud 2001, 940). But it is more than this. Your shadow "will not hurt you, it simply shows / That you are not alone, / That what you fear is part of you…" (Hart 2002, 46) In this chapter, I have traced the myriad ways "doubling" ricochets throughout the collection: shadows, reflections, a dead unborn sister, medieval poems and the face of Christ himself. According to Royle, "Freud himself contends that the 'constant recurrence of the same thing' is a powerful element in many literary texts and is what can help to give them their uncanny character" (2003, 89). This is evident in this collection even in the titles of the poems themselves: there are no less than four poems sharing the title of "Your Shadow". The shadow is a reminder of death, and it is only beyond death that the dualism of the body and the shadow can be resolved, an event that the poems imagine in both personal and eschatological terms. In "The Last Day" a "ploughman in Europe … will watch his shadow / Run back up his spine" (Hart, 2002, 89):

> It will be morning
> For the first time, and the long night
> Will be seen for what it is,
> A black flag trembling in the sunlight. (ibid.)

For the mystics, true identity is to be found in forsaking the world and embracing God. For the shadow, true identity is to be found in acknowledging physicality and mortality, and in embracing ambivalence. The self, it seems, will remain split until death:

> Our God has cast us in this world
> Not into hell: one flesh, two minds,
>
> Identified in the one light,
> And swept together in the same wind

> Till death when all of life contracts
> About you, like your shadow at noon. (ibid., 78)

This resolution remains beyond our reach, however, so the poems counsel to "make desire your home".

The collection is compelling, however, not because of a mystical reconciliation with death, but because of the uncanny way it charts the relationship between death and the self. At times it veers into surrealism, which "[a]s Hal Forster has persuasively argued in his book *Compulsive Beauty*, . . . was above all concerned with the uncanny" (Royle 2003, 97). In "Your Shadow's Songs", the shadow peers into the body's dreams:

> I sleep with you, your bony arms
> Holding me closer than your soul,
>
> So that I creep into your dreams
> And see things as they are for you:
>
> The hospital of sharpened knives
> Where animals couple in greasy straw;
> Where surgeons place a bawling child
> Upon a slide toward the grave;
>
> A body you must try to eat
> That grows much larger with each bite,
>
> Whose face you will never see, although
> You know full well it is your own. (Hart 2002, 79)

Images familiar from the rest of the collection–babies, graves, weird doubles–are intensified here. The shadow observes what the surrealist Andre Breton called: "a vertiginous descent within ourselves, the systematic illumination of hidden places and the progressive darkening of all other places, the perpetual rambling in the depth of the forbidden zone" (Breton, quoted by Hart 1993, 47). Hart himself is slightly wary of surrealism. He writes: "Surrealism tries to grasp the unknown, and in doing so transforms it into the bizarre. Its greatest successes are those works that begin from its doctrines and then turn partly against them" (Hart 1993, 48). This observation could be a fair description of the collection as a whole, with its unconventional pairing of uncanny doubles and Christian mysticism. In "Your Shadow's Songs", a poem in six parts, the tempo increases and the fears hinted at in the other shadow poems are magnified, until once again the pace relaxes, and the shadow is revealed, finally, as a friend.

The strange love poems of "Your Shadow's Songs" run a gamut of emotions from fear and black humour to intimacy and acceptance. Most touching of all is when the shadow voices its own uncertainties:

> Whose world is this? I walk with you
> And try to think of earth as home;
> [...]
> I follow you, you follow me,
> Across the fragrant earth's slow curve
>
> This solid shadow cast by God.
> Whose world is this? Not mine, not yours. (ibid., 79)

Here the transience of the world is put into stark relief: neither the body nor its shadow are at home here. The home made strange is a trope of the uncanny. This theme of homelessness, and of belonging, ultimately, to a realm beyond death, also recurs in the writings of the mystics. St John of the Cross's *Dark Night of the Soul*, for example, describes a journey to meet God beyond the dark veil of the world, and, as we have seen, *The Living Flame of Love* describes God's love experienced as shadows (2017, 168). The poems of *Your Shadow*, however, perform a kind of double movement: reaching towards death but also reaching towards experiences of fullness in this world. The shadow is not the soul. The shadow is the body's fleeting imprint on the world. And it is towards the world that the shadow directs the gaze of the self at the end of "Your Shadow's Songs": "Don't worry ... There is so much within your reach: // The sun's home in the honeycomb, / The quiet waters, the fragrant field" (Hart 2002, 81).

Notes

[1] In reality the relationship between body and soul in the Middle Ages was more complex than this, and changed over time. Aquinas, for example, proposed a "tripartite" soul modelled on the Trinity. Caroline Walker Bynum has argued persuasively against the assumption that the Middle Ages had a purely dualist approach to the body and the soul by showing how central the body itself was to medieval thought and identity: "So important was the literal, material body that by the fourteenth century not only were spiritualized interpretations firmly rejected; soul itself was depicted as embodied. [...] But the 'other' encountered in body by preachers and theologians, storytellers, philosophers, and artists, was not finally

the 'other' of sex or gender, social position or ethnic group, belief or culture; it was death." (Bynum 1995, xviii)

[2] This perception of medieval and modern attitudes toward death echoes views expressed by Philippe Ariès in *Western Attitudes Toward Death: From the Middle Ages to the Present*, trans. by Patricia M. Ranum (Baltimore: Johns Hopkins University Press, 1974). Ariès argues that during the Middle Ages death was seen as familiar and "tame", while in modernity society has become increasingly estranged from an accepting relationship with death.

References

Ariès, Philippe. 1974. *Western Attitudes Toward Death: From the Middle Ages to the Present*. Trans. by Patricia M. Ranum. Baltimore: Johns Hopkins University Press.
Bossy, Michel-Andre. 1976. "Medieval Debates of the Body and Soul." *Comparative Literature*, 28.2: 144–63.
Brown, Carleton (Ed.). 1962. *Religious Lyrics of the XVth Century*. Oxford: Oxford University Press.
Brown, Lachlan. 2007. "Exploring the Shadow of *Your Shadow*". *JASAL Special Issue 2007: Spectres, Screens, Shadows, Mirrors*: 106–116.
Bynum, Caroline Walker. 1995. *The Resurrection of the Body in Western Christianity, 200–1336*. New York: Columbia University Press.
Catalano, Gary. 1986. "The Weight of Things: The Poetry of Kevin Hart." *Overland* 104: 23–26.
Conlee, John W. (Ed.). 1991. *Middle English Debate Poetry: A Critical Anthology*. East Lansing: Colleagues Press.
Davidson, Toby. 2013. *Christian Mysticism and Australian Poetry*. Amherst, New York: Cambria Press.
Dolar, Mladen. 1991. "'I shall be with you on your wedding night': Lacan and the Uncanny." *October* Vol. No. 58: 5–53.
Eckhart, Meister. 1994. *Selected Writings*, edited and translated by Oliver Davies. London: Penguin.
Freud, Sigmund. 2001. "The 'Uncanny'." *The Norton Anthology of Theory and Criticism,* 929–52. General editor Vincent B. Leitch. New York and London: Norton and Company.
—. 1959. *Beyond the Pleasure Principle,* edited and translated by James Stratchey. New York and London: Norton and Company.
Hart, Kevin. 2002. *Flame Tree: Selected Poems*. St Leonards: Paperbark Press.
—. 2000 [1989]. *The Trespass of the Sign: Deconstruction, Theology and Philosophy*. New York: Fordham University Press.
—. 1993. "After Poetry 17, A Quarterly Account of Recent Poetry: The Unknown", *Overland* 131: 42–48.
Herdman, John. 1991. *The Double in Nineteenth-Century Fiction: The Shadow Life*. New York: St Martin's Press.
Kinsella, John. 1997. "Interview with Kevin Hart: Melbourne, 22 October" *Salt: On-line* 10: 265–75.
Martin, Raymond and John Barresi. 2006. *The Rise and Fall of Soul and Self: An Intellectual History of Personal Identity*. New York: Columbia University Press.

McCooey, David. 1995–6. "'Secret Truths': The Poetry of Kevin Hart." *Southerly*, 55.4: 109–21.
—. 2003. "In Dialogue with Kevin Hart", *Double Dialogues* 5.
Otto, Peter. 2005. "Romantic Medievalism and Gothic Horror: Wordsworth, Tennyson, Kendall and the Dilemmas of Antipodean Gothic." In *Medievalism and the Gothic in Australian Culture*, edited by Stephanie Trigg, 19–40. Turnhout: Brepols.
Ovid. 1987. *Metamorphoses*, translated by A.D. Melville. Oxford: Oxford University Press.
Rank, Otto. 1971. *The Double: A Psychoanalytic Study*, translated and edited by Harry Tucker Jr. Chapel Hill: University of North Carolina Press.
Reed, Thomas L. Jr. 1990. *Middle English Debate Poetry and the Aesthetics of Irresolution.* Columbia and London: University of Missouri Press.
Ritivoi, Andreea Deciu. 2008. "Identity and Narrative." *Routledge Encyclopedia of Narrative Theory,* edited by David Herman, Manfred Jahn, Marie-Laure Ryan, 231–235. Abingdon: Routledge.
Royle, Nicholas. 2014. "Freud's Double." In *A Concise Companion to Psychoanalysis, Literature and Culture.* Edited by Laura Marcus and Ankhi Mukherjee, 122–136. Chichester: Wiley Blackwell.
—. 2003. *The Uncanny*. Manchester: Manchester University Press.
St John of the Cross. 2017. *The Collected Works of St John of the Cross*, third edition, translated by Kieran Kavanaugh, OCD and Otilio Rodriguez, OCD. Washington: ICS Publications.

CHAPTER SIX

THE ISRAELITE AND SAINT IDENTITY ACCORDING TO THE POLYNESIAN LATTER-DAY SAINTS

METTE RAMSTAD

The Church of Jesus Christ of Latter-day Saints (LDS or Mormon for short) is an American church with millenarian and prophetic characteristics and a vigorous proselytizing agenda with a large missionary force. The church has a strong, unified global agenda but also emphasizes its status as a local faith in Polynesia.

The LDS church established its first non-English-speaking mission in Polynesia in 1844 on Tubuai (Tahitian mission). LDS missions opened up among the Hawaiians in 1850 and among the Maoris of New Zealand in 1882. The church grew rapidly during the pioneer period, despite the fact that the new members and missionaries faced opposition and persecution from the governments and previously established mission churches. The LDS church is one of the largest church denominations today in Hawai'i, French Polynesia and New Zealand.

In the past, a crucial factor of identity in Polynesian families was knowing the names of one's ancestors through genealogy. With the coming of Christianity, and the abolition of different island rituals, some Polynesians felt they had lost this genealogical connection with their ancestors' spirits which could tie them to the Christian God they had accepted. However, the LDS missionaries offered a new identity narrative for the Polynesians in their interpretations of the *Bible* and their scripture, the *Book of Mormon*.

The LDS church believes that it is fulfilling the biblical prophecy of identifying the tribes of Israel in the contemporary world and saving the living descendants through conversion and baptism. The emphasis is on blood affinity, which can guarantee certain God-given privileges and blessings. Prominent pioneer missionaries initiated the identification of ethnic groups, and LDS prophets followed up in public speeches. They aim to unite mankind in one spiritual family, connecting all people to the first human father Adam and to the Heavenly Father. This idea is not just a Polynesian phenomenon, but applies globally. This is based on LDS interpretation of what they consider is fulfillment of end-time prophecies about the mission of Elijah turning the hearts of the children to their (fore)fathers in Malachi 4:5-6, and the gathering of the house of Israel in Jeremiah 23:3; Ezekiel 20: 33-36. LDS patriarchs give blessings to LDS members around the globe, revealing which tribe of Israel each LDS member is connected to by bloodline or adoption.

The Maoris were especially eager to find the link that could relate them to the Israelites in the *Bible* when the LDS missionaries started proselytizing among them. One could say that the missionaries showed the Polynesians how they were linked to God through ancestry. This was possible through the genealogy found in the *Book of Mormon* going back to Israel, and then in the *Bible* going back to Adam. The goal for the LDS is that each member will ultimately learn the names of all of his or her ancestors in a genealogy line all the way back to Adam. LDS theology is positive about traditional local beliefs as a source in identifying the connection with Israel. Local members at the grass-root level are encouraged to draw on their traditional heritage based on oral narratives in their presentation of ancestors and their origins.

Polynesian LDS members have accepted a "New Saint" identity and genealogical connection to one of the lost tribes of Israel. All members of the church define themselves as saints, and the term "latter-day", signifying the end of time, distinguishes between biblical saints and modern saints. East Polynesian LDS members combine traditional beliefs in the influence of deceased family and ancestor spirits with the LDS church's views on spirits of deceased family and ancestors, temple ordinances for the deceased and faith in eternal family units (Ramstad 2003).

In this chapter, I explore narratives found in historical and ethnographic accounts that focus on the construction of a Polynesian LDS identity and its Israelite connection. Furthermore, I draw on contemporary East Polynesian Latter-day Saints narratives (from the 1950s until 1995), and interviews which explore personal experiences and popular religious understandings of Christianity. Many of the latter narratives were collected during fieldwork on the North Island of New Zealand, the Hawaiian Islands and French Polynesia–the Society Islands, the Tuamotu Islands, and Tubuai in the Austral Islands between 1993 and 1995 (Ramstad 2003). Informants had been LDS convert members for shorter or longer periods, and represented various age groups. Oral history narratives often reflect the ideological, meaning-making activities of a people and aid the negotiation of identity. Whereas several Hawaiian and Maori church leaders eagerly accepted the Israelite connection, convert informants in the 1990s gave a variety of other reasons for joining the church.

Polynesians as Israelites: Historical and Ethnographic Accounts

The first LDS prophet Joseph Smith stated that "The *Book of Mormon* is a record of the forefathers of our western tribes of Indians" (Joseph Smith 1976, 17). According to LDS belief, the Lamanites were descendants of Laman and Lemuel, who journeyed with their father Lehi and their other brothers, among them Nephi, from Jerusalem to the promised land of America. Lehi was a descendant of Joseph, one of the twelve tribal leaders of Israel, through Joseph's son Manasseh. Lehi's sons married Ishmael's daughters who were descendants of Joseph's son Ephraim. Mormon in the *Book of Mormon*, one of the last Nephites who survived the great war between the Lamanites and Nephites, was purported to have written to the surviving Lamanites.

> Know ye that ye are of the house of Israel, [...] Know ye that ye must come to the knowledge of your fathers [...] And ye will also know that ye are a remnant of the seed of Jacob; therefore ye are numbered among the people of the first covenant *(Book of Mormon*, Mormon 7:1–2, 5, 10).

The *Doctrine and Covenants* repeat this promise to the future Lamanites; they will blossom like a rose before the Lord's second coming (49:24).

In the *Book of Mormon* there is another account about Hagoth, a shipbuilder, who departed twice "into the west sea by the narrow neck which led into the land northward" (*Book of Mormon*, Alma 63:5–8). Hagoth was a Nephite, and sailed with many other Nephites, including women and children. They were never heard of again according to the *Book of Mormon*. The LDS church's general authorities, historians and missionaries have added much lore to this meager account. The LDS believed that Hagoth reached one of the Polynesian Islands, most likely Hawai'i, and the story explains the connection between the Polynesians and the Nephites in the *Book of Mormon*. The LDS consider the Nephites to be distant relatives of the Lamanites–who are believed to be the ancestors of the American Indians of today. The Polynesians have been described as both Lamanites and Nephites, but mostly the former by LDS authorities and missionary leaders in the 19th and early 20th centuries. *The Book of Mormon,* which the LDS missionaries presented to the Polynesians, was considered to be an account of their ancestors on the American continent. Later, missionaries throughout Polynesia claimed that the Polynesians were a branch of the house of Israel, related to the Lamanites or American Indians. These missionary statements reached church headquarters in Utah, where they were affirmed and expanded on by prophets and apostles, who uttered them as prophecy.

The prophet leader Brigham Young was the first general authority to state publically in 1853 that the Polynesians were descendants of Abraham. George Q. Cannon wrote in Hawai'i right after missionary work started there:

> [...] they are the seed of Israel, and to them peculiar promises have been made.
>
> [...] the soul of a Sandwich Islander or a Lamanite is as precious in the sight of the Lord as the soul of a white man (Cannon 1882, 22).

Missionary William Farrer, Cannon's companion, wrote that it was common to refer to, and address the Hawaiians as descendants of Israel. He also reminded them of the "promises of the Lord to their fathers" (Farrer March 7, 1852).

Missionary Benjamin F. Johnson wrote in 1853 that the Hawaiians "appear to be of the same stock as the tribes on the mainland, yet they are unlike them, caused doubtless by their different surroundings." (1947, 171) Later, an article in the LDS journal *Juvenile Instructor* of October 1, 1868, took up the topic of Polynesian origin, and used the fair complexions of the different islanders as evidence for an American connection, claiming that they "have never mixed with other darker races but are the pure original stock." Here we have two contradictory statements; Johnson claims the Polynesians of Hawai'i did not physically resemble the Indians, while the *Juvenile Instructor* claims that the physical resemblance was good evidence of the connection. Similarities between

Israelites and Polynesians were also used as evidence for an Israelite identity for the islanders.

Benjamin Cluff, Jr., another missionary on Hawai'i, stressed the importance of ocean currents as proof of voyaging from the American continent. He also examined the Hawaiian voyaging legends:

> Among the many legends referring to the first settlement of Hawaii several bear out the American origin, one as follows: Hawaii-loa, a great chief, sailed westward and guided by the Pleiades, discovered the Hawaiian group. (1899, 2)

Cluff said that old Hawaiian legends referred to the creation, the flood, and Cain and Abel in the *Bible* (1899, 1). He seems to have been aware of Hawaiian ethnographic accounts on Hawai'i-loa. In addition, there are examples of comparisons between Polynesian and American Indians' traditions used to verify a connection.

James Brown, missionary to French Polynesia, was the first to write that the Polynesians descended from Hagoth in the *Book of Mormon*. In October 1852, Brown spent some time on Rapa, one of the most remote islands in the Austral group in French Polynesia. There were no Mormons on Rapa at that time, and the people on Rapa were rather hostile toward him. Brown recounted how he came across a large gourd, or calabash vine, and a watermelon patch. He had never seen these plants on any of the other islands he had visited. He asked the Rapans "where they got the seed of the vegetables" and was told "our forefathers brought them here" (Brown 1902, 276–277). The Rapans told Brown that their forefathers "came from the rising of the sun. It was a big land, so big they did not know its boundary. It was a land of food, and of great forests of big trees, and great fresh waters that were filled with fish." They had been lost in fog and blown ashore on Rapa. "They used to say that if they could get back to their fatherland they could find metal to make fish spears and hooks with." Commenting on recent history: "When the first white men's ship came in sight we tried to go to it, thinking we could get some fishing tackle therefrom." Brown noted, "Read the Book of Mormon, 63rd chapter, 5th to 9th verses. Was the ship that Hagoth built the same that was wrecked on the island of Rapa? The reader may form his own conclusions" (ibid). It is likely that 25 years of Christian mission influence had colored the Rapans' accounts of their ancestors by 1852, even though Rapa was not as influenced by western cultures due to its remoteness.

The Hawaiian LDS church magazine *Ka Elele Oiaio,* operating from 1908 until 1911, had two articles purportedly written by a Hawaiian LDS, which also explain the origin of Hawaiians in America and Israel. One of the articles was entitled "Are the people of Hawai'i from Israel?" It has a list of twenty-four points with references mainly to Old Testament scriptures describing laws and customs practiced in Israel, which were considered the same as those found in Hawai'i. The article concluded that the Polynesians had a very similar lifestyle to the old Israelites (Platou 1911, No. 72, 561). Although there are several examples of missionaries maintaining that the Polynesians were of the house of Israel in letters, diaries, magazine and newspaper articles, there are few written sources showing missionaries using this doctrine when they preached to the Polynesians about the LDS church in the earliest mission period in the Eastern Polynesian islands (Ramstad 2003).

Benjamin Duncan McAllister – who was a recorder at the Hawaiian LDS temple–wrote several articles in 1920–21 about the origin of the Polynesians, and their connection to the American Indians. He was first influenced by a group of visiting LDS Maori chiefs attending the temple (Jay 1920). He concluded that the Polynesians had no knowledge of the Christian religion before the coming of the Europeans. He reasoned that this was because their American ancestors came to the Pacific Islands before the Christian era (before Christ visited America around 33 AD, according to the *Book of Mormon*), therefore their religious traditions were of an Israelite character, concerning the creation, the flood, and the tower of Babel. From this one could possibly deduce that their ancestors left America before they had been visited by the great white God, therefore they would not have any idea of a white God visiting when they came to Polynesia. He used diffusionist theories to explain how cultural traits, religious customs and beliefs spread from one area to another through migration.

William Cole, former missionary amongst the Maori and church genealogist, believed that when the Polynesian LDS had completed their lines of genealogy back to *Book of Mormon* times, they might expect to have pedigrees from themselves back to Father Adam. He also believed that God's Spirit had prompted the Polynesian ancestors to preserve their genealogies (according to Cole & Jensen 1961, 39, 41).

Cole and Jensen (1961, 164, 166) wrote that the church had performed temple ordinances for the Hawaiian "ancestors" Papa and Wakea and their offspring, all of whom traditionally were viewed as gods. The LDS church has temple records showing that ordinances were performed for Papa and Wakea on January 6, 1920, shortly after the opening of the temple in Hawai'i. The ceremonies were all carried out by a Hawaiian female member, according to records at the La'ie Family History Center, Oahu, Hawai'i that I examined. Later on, temple ordinances were performed for the Maori progenitors by Maori members according to other temple records and Cole and Jensen. Some of these Maori progenitors were the same as Papa and Wakea, namely Rangi and Papa.

LDS church historian Britsch concluded that the main reason why so many Polynesians were converted so rapidly (in the 1800s) was because the LDS gospel had a "familiar ring in the Polynesians' ears" because of the idea of a genealogical connection to the ancient Nephites–the "white/fair skinned" branch of the Lehi family (1981, 38– 46). American Indians in LDS theology are viewed as descendants of the Lamanites–the "dark skinned" branch of the Lehi family and as genealogically related "distant cousins" of the Polynesians, who are viewed as descendants of the Nephites. Polynesians simply "remember" the "familiar sound" of the LDS missionary gospel. This belief indicates that the so-called Israelite blood ties enabled the Polynesians to recognize the similarities between the LDS gospel and the religion of the Israelites in the *Bible*, a religion that, according to the LDS, was the religion of their migrating ancestors.

Polynesian Latter Day Saint Views on being Israelites: (Past and Present)

Becoming an LDS entails, among other things, accepting a new narrative about the origin of one's ancestors. LDS often think of themselves as a peculiar people set apart by their special religious prohibitions, belief system and temple ordinances. A convert enters a church organization that is both hierarchical and egalitarian in the sense that it gives all worthy male members the priesthood. The convert gains an identity based on a new way of living as well as a new past. Like most religions with a millenarian hope and a prophetic base, the members of the LDS church identify themselves as the elect and chosen people of God. Here I discuss my fieldwork interviews, and those of Polynesian LDS leaders and scholars, where Polynesians tell about their relationship with the LDS church.

Most of the Polynesians I interviewed were not aware, prior to their conversion, of the LDS belief that the Nephites were the ancient ancestors of the Polynesians. There was only one informant in Hawai'i–an inactive LDS–who emphasized that he was convinced about joining the church because he found out that the church suggested that Christ visited both America and Hawai'i, and that the well-known Hawaiian god Lono was Christ. He had seen a missionary film before his baptism about Christ in the Americas that described the *Book of Mormon* incidents (Hawaiian male, June 1995 in Ramstad 2003).

Another Hawaiian LDS man from a LDS family was confident about his Hawaiian ancestors' spiritual insights based on their genealogical blood ties to the Nephites of the *Book of Mormon*. He said that the *Book of Mormon*'s original language (reformed Egyptian according to LDS belief) was the same language as the Hawaiians knew. Therefore the Hawaiians were the only people who knew how to translate the *Book of Mormon* because they knew the language. He concluded that the Hawaiians had gone through "dark ages" when their Nephite religion had been corrupted (Hawaiian male, June 1995 in Ramstad 2003).

There is a marked pride in idealized ancestors amongst many Hawaiian and Maori LDS. Ancestors were sometimes portrayed as having lived in a golden age, much better than the present. Yet another Hawaiian LDS man connected his ancestors' knowledge of astronomy to their genealogical link to Abraham. It seemed as if his conviction and interest in this topic stemmed from his awareness of the LDS church teachings about the creation of other planets and galaxies (Hawaiian male, 40s, 1994 in Ramstad 2003).

In general, the Hawaiian and Maori LDS that I interviewed were more interested in the American and Israelite connection than the French Polynesians. Most of the LDS informants in French Polynesia did not express particular interest in an American connection or migration legends from their area. The Maori LDS seem to be the Polynesian people who are most concerned with the American and Israelite connection. Voyaging legends between the island groups are more common for Maori LDS in their private family accounts and at prominent *marae*–religious and social gathering places (Jensen 1970; Meha 1962). One reason is that opening phrases at most *marae* meetings concern the migration and origin of the Maori. Since New Zealand was one of the islands settled last, the Maoris seem to have always been aware that they came from somewhere else, that their remote homeland was not *Aotearoa.* Nowadays many Maori accept and believe in the synthesized version of the migration of the great fleet of ancestors.

During my fieldwork, I also collected accounts about ancestors' conversions to the LDS church. One elderly Maori woman told me about how her grandmother, who lived until she was over 100 years old, had received a message in the 1890s from her deceased mother in a dream. The message was that she should look for two foreign men using the sign of the upraised hand who would come with a new church. American LDS missionaries used to pray in this fashion.

> It was through her-grandmother that we become members, because she got the vision of her mother, and her mother told her that two pakehas were going to come, and when they pray they raise their right hand, and this is where the Maori got that Ringatu sign anyway from the first place, from when they were in America. In the *Book of Mormon.* They were members when they first arrived. They come from Jerusalem. [...] Even though we were just Maoris to the Pakeha, but **_to them we were the true blood of Israel_** [...] because the church has, because they know we are the true blood of Israel. Not only through that dream, but through the *Book of Mormon.* Our history, they went to America and came out here to the islands. [...] They came out in families, they were all favored because they were the children of Israel (New Zealand, female, 80s, June 1994 in Ramstad 2003, my emphasis)

Blending of Traditional and LDS Elements

The LDS church has positively approved of various blendings of traditional and LDS elements of religious practices and beliefs, especially those elements that might confirm the LDS belief that the ancient Polynesians were Israelites. However, the LDS, like most other churches, have condemned and disapproved of certain traditions deemed negative and in contradiction with LDS practices and beliefs. The LDS uphold everything which is "praiseworthy, edifying and good" in every culture, according to their articles of faith (The Articles of Faith 1:13, in Pearl of Great Price 1982: 61; NT: Philippians 4:8). Some Polynesian LDS believe that the church has shown more approval of their culture than other churches in the area.

The contemporary LDS church and the Polynesian LDS seem to look more favorably on certain elements of tradition, which in the pioneer period were considered as a hindrance to a saintly life, both by church leaders and staunch members. Today many traditional elements have lost their original meaning for many Polynesians. Their allegiance is not as torn between traditional family gods and the church. Some of these traditional elements have become nostalgic relics of the past, important in the conscious preservation of the renaissance of the various Polynesian island cultures. Some younger and middle-aged LDS converts spoke positively about their traditions. In most contemporary cases, the traditional beliefs form a smaller part than the LDS elements in people's worldviews. Some people seem to cope well with two sets of beliefs and practices that *can* contradict each other. Others discard traditional belief elements. Often this happens in connection with authority allegiance and new commitment tests when receiving priesthood callings and temple recommendations.

A prominent Hawaiian LDS man who had grown up in an LDS family with long traditions in the church, and deep roots in the Hawaiian culture, told me that his family seemed to have raised him in a workable blending of Hawaiian tradition and LDS church beliefs. This was his view of his heritage.

> I could see that there were changes, that once upon a time they did have the truth, because the foundation is there, but it was much like the *Bible* today, you have many different interpretations. (Hawaiian male, 50s, June 1995 in Ramstad 2003)

Clinton Kanahele was a prominent Hawaiian LDS who tried to make a workable blending between traditional beliefs and beliefs he understood as representative of Israel in the *Bible*. He grew up in Hana, Maui. Later he became the principal of the first public elementary school in La'ie. Kanahele carried out several interviews in Hawaiian with elderly LDS in 1970. Kanahele eagerly expressed his opinion that Hawaiians were related to Israelites while conducting his interviews with other Hawaiians. He pointed to similarities between Hawaiian and Old Testament customs that seemed to strengthen his belief that the "Hawaiians are God-fearing people; we are God-observing people" (H (C. K.), 5, female, elderly, 1970). According to Kanahele, Hawaiins traditionally upheld the laws of God as found in the Old Testament because they were descendants of Israel. The genealogical link to Israel strengthened their identity of being descendants of a God-fearing people. Kanahele explained his view of the American-Israelite origin:

Some people believe they are from America, and the people of America came from the land of Israel where they had lived and from there the progenitors came and landed in America, and some of them came and landed on these islands of the Pacific and came here (to Tahiti, Samoa), to New Zealand and such places. (H (C. K.), 4, female, elderly, 1970)

Kanahele saw connections between Hawaiian customs and those of the Israelites. He mentioned that circumcision, which he considered to be in accordance with the *Bible*, was still practiced among some Hawaiian LDS around the turn of the century (H (C. K.), 6, elderly, 1970). Another tradition, that of wailing as a sign of love at funerals, or when meeting family and friends one had not seen for a long time, was common in Hawai'i, and an elderly female pointed out in an interview that this was a custom of the Israelites of former times, indicating that the Polynesians were from the nation of Israel (H (C. K.), 5, female, elderly, 1970). Additionally, Kanahele asked his informants about funeral rites. They told him that after they came home from a funeral they

Sprinkled [...] with salt water. A bowl [...] of salt water was outside the door. You stopped at the steps. Before you entered, someone would sprinkle salt water over you (H (C. K.), 6, elderly, 1970). [...] Formerly when all the people left, the house was sprinkled with salt water, and all the people who had been to the funeral were sprinkled likewise. (H (C. K.), 5, female, elderly, 1970)

According to Kanahele's interpretation of this custom, the removing of defilement by sprinkling water had an Israelite origin (H (C. K.), 5, female, elderly, 1970).

Kanahele also believed the Hawaiian practice of sacrificing produce and animals to the gods originated with their Israelite ancestors and was not simply based on superstition. These common traditions strengthened Kahahele's belief in the Israelite connection.

Pageants: Acting out the Israelite Connection

Historical pageants of the early missionary period have been staged by LDS in Hawai'i, New Zealand, and French Polynesia. These pageants were viewed as important missionary tools. Some of the pageants were staged at big public theaters, but most of them were performed outdoors. Most of them were great audience successes. Several informants have told me that the more recent ones had a great effect on some friends who were not members. The pageants aroused emotional feelings for ancestors and for Christ. White members wrote and directed plays based on historical missionary records and other church literature. The pageants' main focus was the meeting between the first LDS missionary (ies) and one or two prominent early Polynesian investigators who were in most cases chiefs. The LDS pageants demonstrate how the LDS in the islands accept, interpret, and present their ancestors in the framework of the new LDS identity as descendants of a group of people described in the *Book of Mormon,* who had once dwelled on the American continent, the Nephites. The conversion accounts, which best fit the idea of the familiar ring of the LDS gospel, are presented in the New Zealand and Hawai'i pageants. The pageants are abbreviated versions of the accounts about the first encounters and therefore tend to jumble together names, events and chronology.

The LDS on Maui have put on a pageant at Pulehu for some years. The pageant depicts Hagoth's migration from America to Hawai'i, the abolition of the *kapu* system and the arrival of the Calvinist and LDS missionaries. It seems as if much of the pageant is based on white LDS church leaders' and missionaries' statements. I watched a member's video of the pageant in Maui in 1994. The pageant strongly reinforces the Nephite American identity of the Polynesians. It culminates when a Hawaiian LDS missionary goes to Latin America on a mission. He is seen as fulfilling a promise to warn his distant "cousins" the Lamanites about the true origin of both ethnic groups. A person dressed as Christ makes a dramatic entry as if floating high up in the air, illuminated in the dark. This made a great impression on the audience, and other people nearby who saw "Christ appear." The main message was that Christ loved all humanity so much, that he even visited the Americas and the ancestors of the Hawaiian people, the Nephites.

The pageant, which I witnessed in Tahiti for the church's 150th anniversary in 1994, did not focus on historical sources in the script. Instead, it focused on the paramount chiefs' humorous ridicule of the first LDS missionaries and a hospitality reception with a dance show. The chief of Tubuai finally accepted the LDS church when the missionaries told him that the *Book of Mormon* was a record of the ancestors of the islanders (Ramstad 2003; 2006).

Genealogy, Temple Work and the Influence of Deceased Family

Recent church leaders have admonished their members many times about the responsibility they have for their deceased ancestors. The LDS church envisions that it is fulfilling the prophecy of identifying the tribes of Israel in the contemporary world and saving the living remnants by conversion and baptism. Members are also encouraged to bring salvation to the deceased souls of ancestors through genealogy work and temple ordinances of sealing and proxy baptism. Many converts experience a cultural renaissance through the genealogical work that the church requires of them. Most of my informants had not considered the similarities between the LDS, traditional genealogy, and cosmologies prior to joining the church, either because they were ignorant of traditional beliefs, or because they were not interested in them. Some had to be pushed a lot before they started collecting and preserving their genealogy, since it involved a lot of work.

Most Polynesians know about their own grandparents or even great grandparents' names through orally transmitted accounts in the family. Some of the Polynesian converts who had worked on their genealogies showed great enthusiasm and pride in finding out more about their roots. Many felt strongly that they were doing important work by tying themselves to their deceased relatives through the temple sealing ordinances, which meant that they would live as a family in unity in the hereafter. They were happy that they also had the chance to save their ancestors who had not been Christians, through proxy baptism for the souls of the deceased in the temple. Many of the Polynesian LDS whom I spoke with believed they could be influenced by their deceased family members. It is possible to view this belief in continued contact with deceased family as a continuation of traditional beliefs. Belief in contact with the spirit world is a workable blending of LDS and Polynesian elements.

It is perhaps easier for a Polynesian to integrate traditional ancestral beliefs into the official LDS belief system and ordinances because the LDS put so much emphasis on religious ordinances and genealogical work for the souls of the deceased. It is also easier to accommodate traditional beliefs of influence from the spirit world with the LDS idea of a temporary spirit world with a thin veil separating it from the physical world. People with special spiritual sensitivity can sometime glimpse the souls of the spirit world. Some of the souls of the deceased are also according to LDS scriptures called by God to be guardian angels.

Almost all my informants confirmed that they considered it possible that the living family could meet the deceased at a temple ordinance. The temple was often viewed as the only appropriate place for such contact, since its sanctity somewhat guarantees its goodness. Several LDS said they felt or saw the presence of the spirits of deceased family members in the temple. Most informants also believed that it was possible that deceased family could contact their living family through dreams. Some of them recounted personal dreams, or relatives' or friends' dreams, about ancestors giving messages in dreams. A majority of these messages focused on genealogical advice, helping the living to find lost names, or confirming that they accepted the temple ordinances carried out for them. The Polynesian LDS felt their non-LDS relatives who were in the spirit world could know the truth about the spirit world and therefore acknowledge the LDS church. Many LDS informants claimed that their church was the only one that believed in eternal families.

A Hawaiian man, a convert, dreamed that he saw a long line of close and distant ancestors. He recognized the first part of the line as ancestors he had done temple work for, but the line was still very long, so much work remained. The line was led by a Hawaiian chief dressed in traditional clothes. He dreamed that this chief stepped forward and dropped his chiefly clothes as if he had received the temple ordinances that would give him salvation (Hawaiian male, 40s, March 1994 in Ramstad 2003).

A Hawaiian woman, who had grown up in the church, gave her testimony at a meeting where she stated she was grateful for the local LDS pageant which she considered to be the account of the ancestors. She claimed temple work had been done for all the Hawaiian kings, including Kamehameha I, and their spirits had accepted these ordinances. The Hawaiian kings as departed spirits were anxious to see the Hawaiians united. She had been asked why she was not part of any Sovereignty party. She had replied: "we are of the house of Israel who were the Hawaiian ancestors." She was happy to belong to the house of Israel. She related an interesting account about the presence of spirits in the temple. When temple work was done for Kamehameha I, he supposedly appeared to the prophet of the church. The prophet later witnessed about this incident in the Salt Lake City temple in Utah. She said that many Hawaiian LDS sent in genealogical names in the 1960s, and that all the spirits had accepted the gospel. She ended by saying that Kamehameha I was pleased on the other side, in the spirit world, that his family is united by LDS temple ordinances. I was very interested in finding out more about which prophet had claimed to have this experience with Kamehameha in the temple. She thought it was George Albert Smith, or Heber J. Grant. She could also tell me her genealogy went back all the way to Jesus (Hawaiian female, 60s, June 1995 in Ramstad 2003).

Concluding Remarks

As these narratives show, early LDS missionaries brought stories to the Polynesians that catalyzed their genealogical identification with the lost tribes of Israel, particularly the American Nephites. The official policy of the LDS Church is to encourage and perpetuate the various cultural heritages, reflecting all the national and ethnic backgrounds in the worldwide church. Pride in cultural heritage is linked to the idea of genealogy, acting upon and fulfilling biblical prophecies as part of unifying the family spiritually, carrying out temple ordinances and preparing for the Millennium. For East Polynesian LDS, it was easy to combine traditional beliefs in the influence of the spirits of deceased family and ancestors as this harmonized with their original religious beliefs. Today, the "Saint" identity, as a chosen and privileged people with access to knowledge and responsible for leading God's work on earth, remains appealing.

References

Book of Mormon. Salt Lake City: The Church of Jesus Christ of Latter-day Saints.
Britsch, R. Lanier. 1981. "Maori traditions and the Mormon Church." *The New Era* June: 38–46.
Brown, James. 1960 [1902]. *Giant of the Lord: The Life of a Pioneer*. Salt Lake City: Bookcraft.
Cannon, George Q. 1879/82. *My First Mission*. Salt Lake City: Juvenile Instructor Office.
Cluff, Benjamin Jr. 1899. *Myths and Traditions of the Hawaiians*. An address at the Fourth Annual Reunion of Polynesian Missionaries, held at Lagoon, Davis Co., Utah, July 24, 1899. Published by the General Committee.
Cole, William A. & Jensen, Elwin W.1961. *Israel in the Pacific*. Salt Lake City: Genealogical Society.

Doctrine and Covenants. Salt Lake City: The Church of Jesus Christ of Latter-day Saints.

Farrer, William. 1821-1906. *Biographical Sketch, Hawaiian Mission Report and Diary 1821-1906.* Typescript. Unpublished. Laie: Brigham Young University, Pacific Collection.

Jay, Mike. 1920. "And it came to pass. Mystery of origin of Pacific races one step nearer solution by discovery of Maoris that their ancestors came from Hawaii." In *Honolulu Star Bulletin* June 5th 1920.

Jensen, Elwin W. 1970. Memo: *The Pohuhu- Matorohanga Genealogy Mss. Notes and story about John H. "Te Whatahoro" Jury who was the scribe, and about the "Pohuhu" and "Matorohanga"* Maori Mss, written in Wairarapa about 1863.

Johnson, Benjamin F. 1947 (1853). *My Life's Review.* Independence: Zion's Print & Publ.

Ka Elele Oiaio. 1911. LDS Church Magazine for the Hawaiian Mission.

Kanahele, Clinton. 1970. Oral Interviews in Hawaiian with English translation, typescript. Unpublished. Laie: Brigham Young University, Pacific collection.

Meha, Stuart. April 15, 1962. "Origin of the Maori People in New Zealand". In *Family Book of Remembrance.*

McAllister, Duncan. 1920-1921. "Important Appeal to Native Hawaiians and other Polynesians." *Improvement Era no. 8 June 1921:703–712, Honolulu Star Bulletin* June 5th and 28th, August 9th and 17th 1920.

Ramstad, Mette. 2003. *Conversion in the Pacific. Eastern Polynesian Latter-day Saints' conversion accounts and their development of a LDS identity.* Kristiansand: Høgskoleforlaget.

—. 2006. *Latter-day Saints in French Polynesia 1994- 1995. East Polynesian Latter-day Saint Conversion Accounts and Culture.* Documentary DVD-film.

Smith, Joseph Fielding. 1976. *Teachings of the Prophet Joseph Smith.* Salt Lake City: Deseret Book.

Temple records. 1880s–1930. From Hawai'i and New Zealand. La'ie Family History Center.

The Pearl of Great Price. 1982. The Articles of Faith by Joseph Smith. Salt Lake City: The Church of Jesus Christ of Latter-day Saints.

IDENTITY, NATIONALITY AND LANGUAGE

CHAPTER SEVEN

THE WEIGHT OF COLLECTIVE MEMORY: SURVIVING IN THE INHOSPITABLE REALM OF HAITI

ANDRÉ AVIAS

Introduction

The history of Haiti and its people is in many ways extraordinary and enlightening. Since the discovery of the island by Columbus in 1492 and its independence in 1804, the country has suffered through many ordeals. I shall return to these ordeals during the course of this chapter, in which I hope to direct our attention to Haiti, its history, and its culture. In order to do so, I shall analyze three books by Haitian authors. Each of these books speaks of this country, of its people enduring multiple disasters, and of a collective identity linked to the memory of a foundational history, in its own way.

I begin by approaching the question of identity from a theoretical perspective. Thereafter, I present the three authors and their three selected works. Finally, my analysis shall attempt to elicit certain aspects of Haitian identity, and how Haitian literary writing is influenced by its origins. The question of identity shall be explored here in terms of survival–physically as well as mentally and symbolically–specifically as the survival of identity in an inhospitable environment.

The three authors I have selected are Dany Laferrière, Louis-Philippe Dalembert, and Yanick Lahens. Their respective works are *Tout bouge autour de moi* [*Everything Is Moving Around Me*] (2011), *Ballade d'un amour inachevé* [Ballad of an Unconsummated Love, our trans.] (2013) and *Bain de lune* [Moon Bath, our trans.] (2014).

1. Cultural and Identity Context

1.1 I and the Other

It is not simple to approach such a vast topic; we shall certainly have to limit the issue. If we focus initially on the aspect of individual identity, an author such as Ricœur may first of all give us some bases for our reflections:

> Let me recall the terms of the confrontation: on one side, identity as *sameness* (Latin *idem*, German *Gleichheit*, French *mêmeté*); on the other, identity as *selfhood* (Latin ipse, German *Selbstheit*, French *ipséité*). (Ricœur 1992, 116)

According to Ricœur, individual identity has two sides: that of the permanence of the self, or *mêmeté*, combined with a self that acts and is thus always evolving, yet remains faithful to its commitments, or *ipséité*. From this, it follows that a relationship to another person, who functions as a mirror, is fundamental to the maintenance and confirmation of the self. Furthermore, the instinct to search for identity through people who are similar to oneself–"identicité"–entails the need to belong to a group, although we must not forget that the individuals who make up the group are all different:

> Even though personalities may be *similar*, two men endowed with the same *habitus*–even if they were twins–would never be *identical*, because at every moment of their existences, they distinguish themselves, revealing a dissonant, divergent *ipséité*. *The identical is not human.* Humanity is plurality and *ipséité*. The encounter with another person, the 'relationship with the Other', because it is at the heart of sociological thought, involves the unveiling of the identical as an illusion, constructed from the close and the similar in order to refuse to accept plurality, to push it back behind borders of strangeness. (Truc 2005)

Ricœur also suggests that we include within this reflection the idea of narrative identity: "The decisive step toward a narrative conception of personal identity is made when one moves from action to character" (1992, 170). There is therefore ample room for literature and fictional characters within a reflection on identity. However, literature has a close and complex relationship with reality, and a comparison of the two demonstrates these differences:

> What is to be said, first of all, about the relation between author, narrator, and character, whose roles and voices are quite distinct on the plane of

fiction? When I interpret myself in terms of a life story, am I all three at once, as in the autobiographical narrative? (Ricœur 1992, 159–160)

With Columbus's discovery of America, there was an encounter; there was a colonizer, a "discoverer" of a new world; there were the indigenous peoples who had lived there for millennia, with their customs, their languages, and cultures. This encounter did not turn out to be peaceful. The entire world of the natives was quickly destroyed by all-powerful, pitiless, Europeans; their civilization was wiped out and they were replaced by Africans, who, in turn, had been uprooted and snatched away from their own world.

Todorov refers to this relationship between "them and us"–and asks: are we different from them?–at the end of his work. Leaping across history, he moves from the conquest of America to the Classical and Romantic Ages to highlight the search for a European "me". He writes:

> [...] we want *equality* without its compelling us to accept identity;[1] but also *difference* without its degenerating into superiority/inferiority. We aspire to reap the benefits of the egalitarian model *and* the hierarchic model; we aspire to rediscover the meaning of the social without losing the quality of the individual. (Todorov 1999, 249)

The search for similarity (or identicité) allows for the formation of particular social groups and common cultures in opposition to others. To speak of Haiti, of its people and their history, of these authors and their works, is also to speak of ourselves; we are the descendants of colonizers. Knowing oneself requires knowing the other, an affirmation built upon centuries of experience with our self-absorption. Here I also cite Todorov:

> And just as the discovery of the other knows several degrees, from the other as object, identified with the surrounding world, to the other as subject, equal to the *I* but different from it, with an infinity of intermediary nuances, we can indeed live our lives without ever achieving a full discovery of the other (supposing that such a discovery can be made). Each of us must begin it over again in turn; the previous experiments do not relieve us of our responsibility, but they can teach us the effects of the misreading of the facts. (Todorov 1999, 247)

To summarize, Ricœur and Todorov tell us that our identity is (at least) double, simultaneously containing a permanent component–"the origin"– and a dynamic one–"who I am today?". Identity must always be written in the plural. To this personal identity, we also add our symbolic, collective identity. In our Haitian context, with all of the specific representations that it entails, our authors necessarily have many points in common. The French language, the language of the other, is one of these points.

1.2 The French Language

For our authors, or others in the Francophone world, the relationship to the French language is most often problematic, but of a very variable nature. Chadian author Nimrod writes: "[...] we are writing for countries that do not yet exist, we are writing for a national readership to come [...] In truth, France ensures us a patronage that is worth another" (2007, 228, our trans.).

However, further on he uses the idea of hybridization, an idea that indicates collaboration between several elements rather than an opposition between plural identities:

> We are hybrids; it is vain to wish at all costs to drive out the African in us. [...] This literature, called African, owes everything to French literature. In any case, it owes to it the initiation of a modern tradition. (Nimrod 2007, 232–233, our trans.)

One can understand that the relationship to the French language is not simple for writers from former French colonies. However, for different reasons, many of them use French in their publications without this being objectionable. Therefore, it would seem that French is today, in practice, an *extranational* working language, which grants access to new worlds, whether real or imaginary. The term hybridization is often used to underline the fusion between multiple identities without them necessarily being conflicting. Some writers would thus consider the language that they use to be their own–that is to say, their own personal creation. This goes for Maryse Condé, who declares, "I love to repeat that I do not write in French or in Creole, but in Maryse Condé" (2007, 205).

What can be said about our authors and their use of French, which is not their mother tongue? Our three authors come from rather privileged families; their parents are teachers or politicians, and they have had access to education. They have appropriated the French language in their work. Based on this, they have decided to write, and even to make writing their careers. Furthermore, we note that the writing profession has a high status in the Haitian imagination. Laferrière himself has said, and repeated in several works, that foreigners are often surprised by this creative vigor in

Haiti (cf. 2011).

This leads me to a few points about the quality of the language used by our authors in these three books. They all write in fluent, standard French that is refined and respects grammatical rules without becoming "white writing" (like Camus).[2] On the contrary, their writing is often poetic and always sensitive: emotion is always present. One might find this style somewhat old-fashioned, compared to contemporary writing in France.[3] Their modernity is in their textual composition, and in the themes they choose to write about. Could this compositional originality perhaps be considered to be a specific feature of Haitian culture?

2. The Authors and their Works

2.1 Dany Laferrière

Dany Laferrière is a Canadian writer originally from Haiti (born in Port-au-Prince in 1953), the son of an opponent of the regime of François Duvalier, also known as Papa Doc. He grew up in his grandmother's house in Petit-Goâve, far from the Haitian capital. As a journalist under the dictatorship of Baby-Doc, he was forced to go into exile and leave for Montreal. There, he worked at different factories until the publication of his first book in 1985. He won the 2009 Médicis prize for his novel *l'Enigme du retour* [*The Enigma of the Return*]. Laferrière was inducted into the Académie Française in 2013.

***Tout bouge autour de moi* [*Everything Is Moving Around Me*]**

This work has the form of a spontaneous and partially chronological diary, with entries almost daily, based on the author's reactions and behavior following an earthquake. The author/narrator/character recounts what he is seeing, and how he is living, doing so mostly in the present tense. We move forward with him, step by step, from the fatal moment: January 12th, 2010, at 4:53 p.m.

This documentary novel appears to position itself around the personal–and very human–reactions of the author: first, surviving, trying to feel safe in the initial moments while still fearing new tremors; then, making contact with his people, calling his family to hear their news, then leaving in search of friends; observing the situation, measuring the disaster, remarking upon the behavior of some of the unfortunate; and then secondly, observing the aid being organized, the arrival of the media, the first testimonies, the first images; finally, his analytic reaction when faced with this situation: what to do, what to say, what to think? Can a lesson be learned from this? In language that is at once concrete but also full of emotion and poetry, the author reveals all of his love for this island and this people, which no catastrophe can bring to its knees. It is a life lesson he teaches us. He calls the final passage of his book, its conclusion, "The tenderness of the world." Therein he expresses the need to retain certain strong images from his personal experience. We shall cite this final passage:

> Cette petite fille qui, la nuit du séisme, s'inquiétait à savoir s'il y avait classe demain. Ou cette marchande de mangues que j'ai vue, le 13 janvier au matin, assise par terre, le dos contre un mur, avec un lot de mangues à vendre. […] Haïti continuera d'occuper longtemps encore le coeur du monde. (Laferrière 2011, 182)[4]

This is a message to people that anything is possible; it is a strong sign of a people that wishes to survive, no matter what happens. I have presented this book first, as a backdrop for what we shall show in the other two works.

2.2 Louis-Philippe Dalembert

Louis-Philippe Dalembert was born on December 8, 1962 in Port-au-Prince (Haiti), the son of a primary school teacher and a school principal. He spent the earliest years of his childhood in Bel-Air, a working-class quarter of the capital, surrounded by women: his mother's cousins, his great-aunts, and his maternal grandmother. A world traveler (America, the Caribbean, North Africa and sub-Saharan Africa, the Middle East, Europe), this self-described vagabond lived for a dozen years in Paris, where he completed his university studies and worked as a professional journalist. For his book *Ballade d'un amour inachevé*, he won the Algue d'Or Jury Prize in 2014.

Ballade d'un amour inachevé

Here, the genre is completely different. Indeed, here we have what initially might seem to be something of a rehash of a classic love story. In this book, Dalembert builds his story around the romantic relationship between the two main characters: Mariagrazia and Azaka. The entire narrative is in fact a presentation of their love, from their first meeting to their marriage and the beginning of their life together. However, other stories append themselves to this one, such as Azaka's difficulties in an Italy that is not very welcoming for those they call the "excoms", or the immigrants; and there is also the impact of disasters upon the characters' fates. Indeed, one might consider the novel to contain three different stories: (1) the main story about Azaka's life in Italy; (2) an inserted story about Azaka's childhood in Haiti during a devastating earthquake, when he was saved by an Italian rescue worker; and (3) a tragic story about an earthquake in Italy that devastates Aquila and takes the life of his pregnant wife. The baby, however, is saved. The division into parts is rather original: whereas the central inserted part about the earthquake in Haiti constitutes a complete unit, the two other stories are presented parallelly and develop linearly as subsections until they all reach a common end.[5] The first story is the most substantial in terms of the number of pages and its contents, filled with the life of the two characters. The third story, in contrast, is succinct and simply tells about some of the aftermath of the earthquake, with the reactions of the inhabitants, the officials, and the funeral.

2.3 Yanick Lahens

Born in Haiti on December 22, 1953, Yanick Lahens left for France at a very young age. There, she completed her secondary studies, as well as her higher education in the Arts. Upon her return to Haiti, she taught at the École Normale Supérieure until 1995. Yanick Lahens lived in Port-au-Prince, where she took an active part in cultural activities and citizen actions. Today, she divides her time between writing, teaching, and her work as a speaker in Haiti and abroad. *Bain de lune* is about family tragedies, country beliefs, and the violence borne by the men and women of Haiti. In 2014, she won the Prix Femina for this book.

Bain de lune

This work is also presented as a novel, but it is more than that: it must be placed midway between a novel and a historical documentary. It is initially a historical novel because it narrates the lives, and many unforeseen developments therein, of two families in a remote part of the country, covering a period of more than 80 years. It is also a historical document because it scrupulously provides a framework describing life on the island realistically for a very long period–from the American occupation through the 2000s. Moreover, through its numerous metaphors and rich imagery, the writing is both poetic and sensitive. Like the other two books, it conveys a love for this island and its people.

One particularity of this book is that its author uses a series of Creole words and expressions, many in connection to the Voodoo religion, and she adds a glossary at the end of the book, giving it a pedagogical aspect. Surely, what is most striking in this family saga is the poverty, the struggle against hunger, but also the transmission of traditions, family solidarity, uncontrollable events such as hurricanes, political upheavals, and the violence of the powerful. And it is in this context that the two families cross paths, one family of submissive peasants, the other of landowners who steal the land of others and rape their daughters with impunity. But love changes the course of the story: Turtelin Mésidor falls in love with the young and beautiful Olmène Lafleur, who bears him a son. Thus, the two families are forever united, although this does not lead to much change during the course of the story, which ends with the death of their granddaughter Cétoute.

3. Themes and Textual Composition

3.1 The Scene of Utterance

There appears to be a powerful link between the themes presented in these works and the ways in which they are written. One could see this as a *mise en scène* of stories, what Maingueneau calls the *scene of utterance* (2010). This contains three complementary planes: the encompassing scene (the context), the genre scene (the genre), and the scenography (the textual composition).

The *encompassing scene* corresponds to the discourse to which the text belongs, that is to say, the space and human activity in which it is necessary to place the text in order to situate and to interpret it. The importance of the historical framework and the symbolic links to Haitian ancestors are determining factors. Of course, the encompassing scene is not enough. We must also look at the genre level. The choices that authors make regarding norms are like their personal signatures. Scenography is a unique composition of a concrete text, the result of the structuring of the text within the situational context of the story. Within the framework of a genre, the text will unfold its narrative to give life to a story, a plot, and characters. Moreover, these three works have all of the original compositional characteristics that we shall explore.

Laferrière's work, although it is an account from a personal diary with documentary content, nevertheless has qualities and a style that one can qualify as literary. The author is at once narrator and actor because he is present on the island during the earthquake. From a compositional perspective, the narrative follows a psychological and partly chronological order–that is to say, the narrator gives an account of his reactions and describes what he sees over the course of time. Logically, after having experienced the earthquake and initially finding safety, he searches for news of his people before expanding his vision to the whole island and its inhabitants.

In Dalembert's novel, although the plot is simple, the scenography is complex, with spatiotemporal movements back and forth between Italy and Haiti, between the past of Azaka and that of his wife, their love story, and the context of the earthquakes. Two independent and chronological stories encase each other. The use of the tenses chosen for each section makes the reading somewhat complex, moving from the conditional to the past and then to the present. The author also plays with the choice of narrator, as we move from a male narrator to a female one, both being heterodiegetic with an internal focus (cf. Genette 1972), which is to say that we see and hear through the main character. On rare occasions, the author speaks to us directly, highlighting a framework, an environment, a story into which the characters are moving. The author divides his novel into different sections, called "Breathing" and "Scream". It is mostly in the "Breathing" sections that the author sets the action in the present tense.

Lahens' novel breaks down into two stories that are parallel in their linear, scriptural presentation. Even though one temporally antecedes the other, they come together at the end of the book. In order to visually demarcate them, the author uses an italic font for one of the stories. We have a double narrative: by this, I mean a double narrative focus, as there are two different narrators. The narrative of the italicized chapters uses an "I" that speaks in the present tense, whereas the other chapters use a collective voice, a "we", which speaks to us the most often. To this, Lahens also sometimes adds an external narrator who remains at a distance, an observer. This collective presence, whether at the forefront or in the background, this narrative recited by a "we", whether explicit or not, occurs in our three books: in Lahens, it is the familial "we" of the lineage, in Laferrière, the "we" of the victims, and in Dalembert, the "we" of the immigrants confronted by the inhabitants of the town.

3.2 Physical Survival of Destiny

I am convinced that the *survival instinct* is an important, if not the most important theme,[6] in our three works. This instinct and the historical fate of the descendants of slaves form a collective memory that cannot be dismissed.

It is clear that with these authors–people of color, an essential detail of their identities (and I think for example of Dalembert's character, Azaka, the *excom* in Italy; when Mariagrazia's family wishes to inquire about him, they say that "one can't miss him")–one cannot imagine their books not including, in one way or another, a link to their native cultures and their collective memory. The history of these people is that of Africans transported and exploited as slaves in America. This is quite obvious in Lahens' book, which, when discussing Voodoo and familial genealogy, skillfully displays the link between the ancestor *Franginen*[7] and the foreseen return of the dead crossing the ocean to Guinea. This encompassing scene (cf. above) occupies a preponderant place in the memory of our authors. In two of the three books, the past and the present exist simultaneously in the spatiotemporal framework. In Dalembert, the present exists explicitly in one section of the book and implicitly in the rest.

The scenographies hinge on the plots of the three books, each different, but also so similar that they establish a link among themselves. In all three, the narrative is formed by natural and human disasters: it is about the earthquake for Laferrière and Dalembert, and about a hurricane, bad weather, and social unrest for Lahens. Is this ultimately a matter of destiny–of inevitable destiny? Dalembert is the best example of this: Azaka, who survived an earthquake in Haiti, also survives one in Aquila, only to be attacked and left for dead by racists. It is the same in Laferrière, who is present at the time of the earthquake and who admires the calm strength of the Haitians in the face of misfortune and their instinct for survival. Over the course of Lahens' narrative, one understands that her objective is to fight destiny, and to refuse all fatality. The death of Cétoute, killed by her cousin Jimmy, will finally bring her brother Abner to awareness. He contacts the police, something that was never done in the past by the poor and oppressed peasants, who always defended themselves with silence and could never trust the State authorities. This is surely a small sign of hope on which Lahens hopes to conclude this country saga. In their own ways, Dalembert and Laferrière also bring a small ray of hope for the future: the former by leaving Azaka's situation unknown and giving him a son; the latter with his almost trivial comments about life being lived again in Haiti, about children who are having fun and laughing again, about women who are returning to work. However, all three authors do so with moderation and a slight hint of doubt. They do not dare display their need for hope, because experience has shown them that, in Haiti, the elements and the people are rarely clement.

3.3 The Supernatural and Spirituality, or Mental Survival

These three works also share a close relationship to the supernatural and to spirituality. This is perhaps what strikes the reader the most over the course of time. Once the reader has finished the book and goes back over the stories, what gives him a special feeling is this always latent relationship with the hereafter. Death is always present in the three books–and it is also a central theme. There is a kind of a dialogue with death, with the *invisibles*, the dead who have not yet passed on to "the other side", with whom one can speak and ask advice. This is most significant in Lahens' book, where the position of Voodoo is important, and where the entire story, centering on the death of Cétoute, is told from the young girl's point of view. This is unsettling; for a long time, one doubts that she is dead because of the fact that she is the one recounting what she sees and what is happening around her, how the people around her behave and react. The author skillfully creates an ambiguity that makes the reader feel ill at ease and thus opens up a gateway to the supernatural. One also understands the full importance of this relationship with ancestors for Haitians: this respect and these beliefs appear as a mystical and powerful instance that can help them to survive in this inhospitable world. In this way, they maintain a spiritual connection with their African ancestors and an African past that is still part of their present. The image that the narrative presents of the dead returning to Africa by crossing the Atlantic Ocean is almost enchanting. There is also an important passage about a Voodoo ceremony, which the narrator describes in a detailed, documentary fashion. One first sees all of the preparations: the sale of a pig to procure the food and the necessary accessories, as well as the cleaning of the *démembrés* and of the *badji*, then the construction of the *Agwé*[8] boat. Once the day arrives, the drums begin to beat. Food and alcohol are placed before an altar. The first Catholic prayer is said, the names of the Lord, Mary, Jesus, and the Holy Ghost pronounced like magic words. "We pray to the saints, we pray to the *Loas*"[9] (84, our trans.). Then come the Creole songs, one after another, asking forgiveness of the gods. The bottle of *trempé* (a mixture of herbs and alcohol) is passed around. The participants begin to go into a trance. They then ask *Legba* to open up the doors to the *invisibles*. Each participant then feels possessed by a god and gives voice to him with his own mouth, miming it with dance. Orvil, the master of ceremonies and head of the family, begins to speak as Agwé's representative. Finally, the boat filled with food and gifts for Agwé is launched in the water and quickly disappears in the waves, marking the end of the ceremony.

In his role as an observer, Laferrière's perception of the hereafter is different but still very obvious. Several times, the author refers to the people around him praying or singing religious songs in chorus:

> Des centaines de personnes prient et chantent dans les rues. C'est pour eux la fin du monde que Jéhovah annonçait. Une petite fille, près de moi, veut savoir s'il y a classe demain. (Laferrière 2011, 25)[10]

And on the relationship with God and their need to feel His presence, so as not to be alone, abandoned by everybody he writes:

> Dieu c'est pour se convaincre qu'ils ne sont pas seuls sur terre, et que leur vie n'est pas uniquement ce chapelet de misères et de douleurs. (...) Ils ont compris qu'il ne faut pas trop lui demander. Si ses moyens spirituels sont infinis, ses moyens matériels sont limités. S'ils ont perdu leur maison, ils lui rendent grâce d'avoir épargné leur vie. (Lafferière 2011, 128)[11]

He also amuses himself by criticizing all of the faithful, no matter their sect, because of their attempt to salvage honor from the earthquake by maintaining that they were the first to announce it. However, he leaves the Voodoo worshippers aside, explaining that they want to avoid being accused of being responsible for the disaster. Throughout his book, he skillfully shows the close relationship that Haitians have with their gods, and the presence of these gods in their daily lives. The announcers of the end of the world are also present in different places in the city, ceaselessly shouting that the end is very near: "'Cette terre ne nous appartient pas. Nous sommes des locataires. Le propriétaire vit à l'étage', fait-il en pointant le ciel. 'Et il est déçu de notre comportement'" (Lafferière 2011, 104).[12]

We observe that Dalembert has showcased two very interesting quotations at the beginning of his book. They express his thoughts and at the same time are keys for interpreting his text. The first is a passage from the Apocalypse of John, chapter 6, verses 12-14, in which disasters and the movement of an entire island are announced, undoubtedly an allusion to

Haiti. This is a very concrete reference to the Bible, to Christianity, which foreshadows an important aspect of the narrative. While the second epigraph also tells of the traumatizing event of an earthquake, it is presented more rationally by Darwin (*The Voyage of the Beagle*, 1839) in the scientific travel diary he kept during his world trip aboard the HMS *Beagle* from 1831 to 1835. In this quotation, Darwin laments the fact that "in an instant, an earthquake upends the most stationary ideas", perhaps thinking of the great earthquake in Lisbon. Obviously, owing to their epistemological foundations, these two quotations oppose each other. By quoting Saint John and Charles Darwin on the same topic, the author points to two visions of the world and our lives that open for different ways of understanding and reacting to these events. He also indicates the choice each Haitian has: whether to rely upon God or different divinities and accept things how they are, or to consider the events in a rational manner.

From the beginning, the narrative also pursues this game of double referencing: "Longtemps après [...], certains jureraient avoir senti la veille une forte odeur de soufre dans l'atmosphère" (Dalembert 2013, 15).[13] From a chemical and geological perspective, sulfur is naturally present during volcanic eruptions; from another, symbolic, perspective, it is traditionally associated with the idea of hell. There are many signs of the future disaster. But although the reader can divine in part what is to come, he cannot grasp the consequences, and this creates a certain suspense, the expectation of a tragic event. This completely transforms the reception of the book, which otherwise could have appeared to be a simple novel about the love between an Italian and an immigrant. Rather early on in the novel (ibid., 35), after a night of the first tremors, Mariagrazia dreams that Azaka has been carried off by a tsunami. She takes the dream seriously, and it troubles Azaka to see his wife in tears.

The numerous epigraphs in this book form a kind of indirect story, foreshadowing the events to come in the main story. They give important interpretative clues to the reader. They are either clearly connected to the idea of earthquakes, whether to a Biblical passage announcing misfortune (Zachariah 14:5, announcing the coming of God), or a Hemingway quotation, a point of happy calm on the beauty of the location halfway through the book. Finally, the Catholic Church is also present during the symbolic and publicized funeral. Faced with this, Azaka feels nothing but bitterness. He rejects the mise en scène of a liturgy in which he does not believe.

4. Collective Identity and Scenography

The identity of every individual is crafted around a collective and personal history, beginning from an attempt to fuse a social life with an interior life. If we compare the three books, we notice a number of points in common. Firstly, the frame–the texture–which serves as the backbone, the support for the three books' narratives, is almost the same: in Laferrière's and Dalembert's books, it is explicitly the matter of earthquakes, and in Lahens', it is the matter of a hurricane, to which a series of disasters and misfortunes of every kind, whether natural or manmade, are added over a longer period. In this way, these works distinguish themselves in the literary landscape and indicate their cultural origin.

The three books construct and draw their legitimacy from this common historical background. But, implicitly, there is more in these three works, which contain aspects of Haitian mythology in which the position given to action is important. This action is often dangerous, violent, and indeed, heroic. That is because a fundamental quality and character of the Haitian world is heroism, dating back to the time of independence and the struggles for power. This ineluctably leads to a story that is sometimes slightly epic in form, even though the heroes are neither immortal nor divine. But, as in Lahens, they are at times in contact with the hereafter, and their collective and familial life brings them a feeling of communion with a mythical past. Thus, it follows that destiny should be an essential theme in the narrative, as in Dalembert ("One can't escape one's destiny", he writes), as well as the fatality of life for poor peasants, as in Lahens, and the concrete reality of misfortune, as in Laferrière.

A central element of the scenography is also the game of temporal variation, connecting the past to the present. Our authors seem to handle this game with ease. They play, like Dalembert, with the variation between the linear timeline of the reading, the timeline of the story (or stories), presented in a surprising to-and-fro, and the tenses of the verbs, which also vary between the present and the past, and indeed, the future and the conditional. In Lahens, two stories follow each other at different rhythms– one in the present, the other in the past–before chronologically converging at the end of the novel.

Conclusion

In comparing these three contemporary authors of the beginning of the 21st century and three of their works written recently (between 2011 and 2014), our objective has been to reveal some points in common that might allow us to find a significant, communal identity. But the authors seem to feel some discomfort in putting themselves forward too much, a self-defensive reflex like that of Lahens' peasants, who still feel great pride in their past, their history, and the battle fought over centuries, from generation to generation. This epic story, of which they are so proud, is an essential part of their collective memory.

The question of identity can be found in our authors like the resurgence of a mythical past of the survival of a people, and of their history, of surviving present and future misfortunes–a common destiny–which fits in well with the central theme of the three books. Survival for a Haitian is at once a question of physical survival but also one of metaphysical survival, of preserving one's identity and the identity of one's community. Despite all of the ordeals that this people has undergone, from slavery to the fight for independence to modern-day fights for democracy and economic survival, the Haitians hold their heads up high.

Obviously, one sees in this a human constant, common to many peoples and social groups oppressed by the world and by history. These works seem to show that this is a constant of Haitian identity. One can still see a recollection of a culture and of African and oral traditions. That is because culture is triumphant, bound to the duty of memory, to the religion of the elders–a culture that allows its people to hold on to a bit of hope in the face of implacable nature and destiny.

Notes

[1] Here, in the sense of similarity.
[2] In the extreme: a neutral style. See Barthes in *Writing Degree Zero* (1955).
[3] In France, immigrant literature is relatively limited due to the absence of an "Arab" group (Cf. Charles Bonn, 127).
[4] "This little girl, who, on the night of the earthquake, troubled herself to find out if there was school the next day. Or that mango seller that I saw on the morning of January 13, sitting on the ground, her back against a wall, with a batch of mangos to sell [...] Haiti will continue to occupy the heart of the world for a long time yet" (our trans.).
[5] We shall see that this approach is similar to the one used by Lahens.

[6] It was not possible to present all of the themes within this chapter.
[7] Cf. term by which Lahens calls the Guinean ancestors.
[8] Démembré: part of the property that contains the lineage's spiritual attributes; badji: sanctuary of the voodoo temple; Agwé: ocean divinity.
[9] Loa: god in the Voodoo divinity.
[10] "Hundreds of people pray and sing in the streets. To them, this is the end of the world that Jehovah announced. A little girl near me wants to know if there will be school tomorrow" (our trans.).
[11] "God is for convincing themselves that they're not alone on this Earth, and that their life is not only this rosary of misery and pain. They have learned not to ask for too much. If His spiritual means are infinite, His material means are limited. If they have lost their homes, they give thanks to Him for having spared their lives" (our trans.).
[12] "'This earth does not belong to us. We are tenants. The owner lives upstairs', he says, pointing to the sky. 'And he is disappointed in our behaviour'" (our trans.).
[13] "A long time later […], some swore that they had smelled a strong odor of sulfur in the air" (our trans.).

References

Barthes, Roland. 1955. *Degré zéro de l'écriture*. Paris: Éd. du Seuil.
Bonn, Charles. 2016. *Lectures nouvelles du roman algérien*. Essai d'autobiographie intellectuelle. Paris: Essai, Classiques Garnier.
Condé, Maryse. 2007. "Liaison dangereuse." In *Pour une littérature-monde*, edited by Michel Le Bris, Jean Rouaud, 205–216. Paris: Gallimard.
Dalembert, Louis-Philippe. 2013. *Ballade d'un amour inachevé*. Paris: Mercure de France.
Darwin, Charles. 1997 [1839]. *The Voyage of the Beagle*. London: Wordsworth Editions Limited.
Genette, Gérard. 1972. *Figures III*. Paris: Seuil.
Laferrière, Dany. 2007. "Je voyage en français." In *Pour une littérature-monde*, edited by Michel Le Bris, 87–101. Paris: Gallimard.
—. 2011. *Tout bouge autour de moi*. Paris: Grasset.
—. 2013. *The World is Moving Around Me: A Memoir of the Haiti Earthquake*. Translated from the French by David Homel. Vancouver, Canada: Arsenal Pulp Press.
—. 2009. *l'Enigme du retour*. Paris: Éditions Grasset & Fasquelle.
—. 2011. *The Enigma of Return*. Translated from the French by David Homel. Vancouver, Canada: Douglas & McIntyre.
Lahens, Yanick. 2014. *Bain de lune*. Paris: Sabine Wespieser éditeur.
Maingueneau, Dominique. 2010. *Manuel de linguistique pour les textes littéraires*. Paris: Armand Colin.
Nimrod. 2007. "Pour une littérature décolonisée." In *Pour une littérature-monde*, edited by Michel Le Bris & Jean Rouaud, 217–235. Paris: Gallimard.
Ricoeur, Paul. 1990. *Soi-même comme un autre*. Paris: Seuil. [English: *Oneself as another*. 1992. Chicago: University of Chicago Press].
Todorov, Tzvetan. 1982. *La conquête de l'Amérique, la question de l'autre*. Paris: Le Seuil. [English: *The conquest of America*, 1999. Translated from the French by Richard Howard: Harper & Row].
Truc, Gérôme. 2005. Une désillusion narrative? De Bourdieu à Ricœur en sociologie. Tracés. *Revue de Sciences humaines*, Vol. 8 | 2005, 2009. URL: http://traces.revues.org/2173; DOI: 10.4000/traces.2173. [Accessed 18.03.2019].

CHAPTER EIGHT

IDENTITY, MIGRATION AND LANGUAGE IN TWO STORIES BY THE GERMAN-SPEAKING WRITER RICHARD WAGNER FROM ROMANIA

ROXANA NUBERT AND ANA-MARIA DASCĂLU-ROMIȚAN

Introduction

Our sense of self is closely tied to the language(s) we speak. As Andrew Bennett and Nicholas Royle point out, "questions of personal or individual identity are indissociably bound up with language" (2009, 131). This chapter focuses on how one's sense of self is affected when one speaks a different language than that of the majority culture one lives in. The individual is in a sense marginalized, an outsider. Here we discuss two stories by the German-speaking writer Richard Wagner, who lived in Romania and belonged to the German-speaking minority, but later emigrated to the Federal Republic of Germany, just as his protagonist, the writer Stirner, does in the stories we analyze. Language affects Stirner's sense of selfhood and his identity as a writer in both locations: in Romania because he is a member of a minority of German-speaking writers, and in Germany because his German is colored by his dialect of the Banat Swabians.

Wagner belongs to the generation of writers from the Banat, in Romania, who started writing at the end of the 1960's and the beginning of the 1970's. He is a founding member and mentor of the influential Aktionsgruppe Banat,[1] which led the revival of German literature in postwar Romania. The merit of these writers, as Wagner underscores, is that they have drawn attention to the Banat as a cultural region: "das Banat [...] und die Banater Schwaben und alles, was sonst noch damit zusammenhängt, das kennen sie [die Leute in Deutschland] nicht [...]

Deshalb interessiert es mich auch, darüber nachzudenken, was bedeutet diese Region in der Moderne, kulturell auch" (Wagner, cited in Jass 1996, 2).[2]

Herta Müller, who was awarded the Nobel Prize in literature in 2009, was not a member of the Aktionsgruppe Banat, has however through her work contributed decisively to its prominence. Literature from Romania written in German may be considered to be an integral part of German literature, thanks to this group of authors; they understand its idiosyncrasies, due to the extreme conditions under which it is produced, and its possible effects. The group thus achieved an impact the German literature from Romania never had experienced before.

Wagner emigrated to the Federal Republic of Germany in 1987. His status as an emigrant meant that he was exiled from Romania, however, as a German-speaking Romanian he, like many of his compatriots, often reported that they felt alienated as a social minority within the Romanian cultural environment. The dominant feeling is that they do not belong either in Romania or in Germany; they do not belong anywhere. In his story *Begrüßungsgeld*[3] (1989) his protagonist opposes the label immigrant:

> Anfangs wehrte er sich gegen die Bezeichnung Emigrant. Emigration, wieso? Er hatte immer deutsch geschrieben und hielt, was er schrieb, für einen Teil der deutschen Literatur. Auch waren die Rumänen nie der Meinung gewesen, daß die Literatur ihrer deutschen Minderheiten zur rumänischen Literatur gehört. Sie ignorierten sie eher, sie hielten die Literatur ihrer Minderheiten für eine kulturpolitische Angelegenheit des Regimes und die Leute, die sie schrieben, für übergeförderte Möchtegernliteraten. (Wagner 1989b, 63)[4]

Richard Wagner's autobiographical stories *Ausreiseantrag*[5] (1988) and *Begrüßungsgeld* (1989) reflect the sad unfolding of Richard Wagner's own life story and refer to the specific "Niemandsland" (ibid., 78)[6] of the German writer. At the centre of both stories, which appeared immediately after his emigration to the German Federal Republic, we find the writer Stirner, who faces the difficulties of both living as a German author in the Romanian Banat and of being a German writer from Romania in his new homeland. Both stories speak of a double linguistic loss: the loss resulting under the pressure of the communist dictatorship in Romania and that caused by the shock of his sudden estrangement in the German Federal Republic. What Wagner shows in these stories is how emigration means not only parting with one's native country, but also not being recognized as German in West Germany–a painful process, which is exacerbated by the fact that the protagonist is a writer. At the same time, Wagner's protagonist is confronted with the realities of the Romanian and German Federal Republics.

Ausreiseantrag

In the story *Ausreiseantrag* Richard Wagner describes the writer Stirner. As to earn a living he works who a journalist with a German-speaking newspaper, who loses his job because he refuses to adapt to the political censorship in Romania. He then decides to submit an emigration application together with his wife, Sabine. The story is comprised of notes on the protagonist's observations and experiences, which resemble those of the author himself. As noted, Wagner, too, wrote in German in Romania before his departure for the German Federal Republic. As a representative of a minority, he had been enclosed in a linguistic ghetto, addressing a limited readership. He was also a practicing journalist: "Stirner begriff sich als Schriftsteller. Er schrieb deutsch. Gedichte, kurze Prosa. Es war die Sprache einer Minderheit. Er hatte mehrere Bücher veröffentlicht, aber er lebte nicht davon [...] Er arbeitete für eine Zeitung, für eine deutschsprachige. Als Korrespondent" (Wagner 1989a, 6).[7] In many places in the text we can identify circumstances resembling those in Wagners's life in Timişoara during the mid-1980's; one recognizes for example a number of places in the city, such as the Opera Square or the Greek-Orthodox Cathedral.

Stirner experiences a moment when his native language and the language he writes in, is transformed into a foreign language against the backdrop of Romanian daily life. When, for example, he wants to render tramway dialogues he has overheard, he has to translate and "der Dialog verlor seinen Reiz" (ibid., 78).[8] As a member of the German speaking minority and as a writer he is a "Ausländer" (ibid.).[9] The degeneration of concepts perpetrated by the mass media affects Stirner's journalism negatively. He is forced to quit his job at the newspaper's editorial office because his articles are no longer wanted. He has protested because words praising the state and the party have been slipped into his texts. This is exactly what revolts Stirner; the glorification of the state has delved so deeply into the language that words have become "doppelgesichtig" (ibid., 40),[10]–they create double vision. The main character is now "ohne Anstellung" (ibid., 98),[11] as one used to say in communist Romania, exactly like his wife, Sabine, who lost her position as an interpreter, when she refused to turn informer against her male and female co-workers. The allusion to Herta Müller's fate is obvious.

> Als Sabine noch in jenem Maschinenbaubetrieb arbeitete, kam eines Tages ein großer blonder breitschultriger Mann mit wasserblauen Augen zu ihr. [...] Vielleicht könnten Sie uns, [...] er schob ihr ein Blatt Papier zu und fing an zu diktieren: Ich verpflichte mich hiermit. Das unterschreibe ich nicht. Und überhaupt, was Sie von mir wollen, gehört nicht zu meinen Dienstpflichten. (ibid., 30)[12]

And just as Sabine, Müller worked as a German Teacher without permanent employment: "Sabine arbeitete als Deutschlehrerin. Sie unterrichtete Deutsch als Fremdsprache. Sie hatte keine feste Anstellung. Seit Jahren nur Vertretungen. Mal an dieser, mal an jener Schule" (ibid., 6).[13]

As a writer, Stirner is sensitive to language distortion; he suffers because the individuality of language is lost. What bothers him most is the situation in which nothing can be written about the dismal monotony, about the "allgemeine [...] Leere" (ibid., 27),[14] which holds sway over the country. The newspaper is required to report on "das Positive [...], die Leistungen" (ibid., 23),[15] fulfilling its role as "ein Organ der Partei" (ibid.).[16] The task of the newspaper, as explained by the editor-in-chief, is to present "die Weisungen der Partei" to the readers (ibid.):[17] "Er schrieb für die Zeitung, und er schrieb für sich selbst, für seine Bücher. Was er für seine Bücher schrieb, entfernte sich immer mehr von dem, was er für die Zeitung schrieb" (ibid., 6).[18]

The more unsuccessful the regime became, the more shameless the mendacious words in the media became and the harsher the laws became. This situation affects Stirner's writing. He cannot identify himself with what is happening around him. The protagonist discloses the repressive methods and the exclusive country houses of the regime and records the movements of a population marked by a war of nerves, where everybody is busy simply getting through their day, resisting the cold, getting hold of basic groceries and catching the tram. Under these circumstances, Stirner has the feeling that he will soon no longer be able to write anything. He is living in a state of near acute isolation, which threatens him with the total loss of reality as well as with the loss of his capacities of perception. There is an important moment in his story, where the narrator mentions the contradictions between the regime's demand for realistic literature and the need of the younger authors to take part in constructive criticism. Here one recognises the leading ideas of the Aktionsgruppe Banat, and the group's mentor, Wagner: "In einem Regime, das die Sprache okkupiert, kann man nicht Meinungen äußern. Wollte man eine realistische Literatur schreiben und sagte man das, befand man sich bereits auf dem Terrain des Regimes. Denn auch das Regime forderte eine realistische Literatur" (ibid., 40).[19]

The protagonist is a communist party member (cf. ibid., 61) just like Wagner himself. The regime itself turns him into an enemy of the people; they have transformed Romania into a huge stage. And on this stage only those who cheer for the national leaders during mass rallies belong; newspapers only pretend to inform the public of ongoing news; restaurants are forced to serve whatever they can get hold of, and when they do have food, they are only open until 9 o'clock p.m.; at cinemas people queue up, in spite of the fact that the kind of movies they want to watch have not been shown for ages. It has become very hard to differentiate real life from simple survival in a country which looks deceivingly similar to a country, (cf. ibid., 5): "Die Wörter waren längst enteignet. Clowns tummelten sich auf der offenen Bühne des Regimes und warfen mit den Wörtern um sich" (ibid., 40).[20]

It is within this context we must interpret Stirner's attitude regarding the Romanian language. He has reservations against the Romanian language; it embodies an official language in which the empty sentences, the big lies collide against each other (cf. ibid., 29). This aspect also motivates Stirner's decision to write his books in German, he recognizes that he would never write in Romanian (cf. ibid.).

The problem of language is essential, particularly because Stirner is a writer by profession. Stirner's dream of his lecture in Bucharest is central in the story. The building in which the lecture is supposed to take place turns into a cemetery little by little. It is a cemetery of empty, meaningless words, because, as Kory states, the totalitarian regime robs the words of their own meaning and thus they no longer refer to reality (cf. Kory 2012, 133).

> Alle redeten bloß. Auch Stirner fing an zu reden. Aber keiner antwortete ihm. Da merkte er, daß die Anwesenden nicht miteinander redeten, sondern jeder für sich. Man verstand auch nicht, was sie sagten, und wenn man versuchte, einen Schritt näher zu treten, stand man schon wieder in einem Ausgang. Man hörte nur diesen gleichmäßigen, gedämpften Wortlärm. Stirner redete, und er merkte, daß er selber nicht verstand, was

er sagte. [...] Das Geräusch der Wörter setzte sich ungestört fort. (Wagner 1989a, 42)[21]

In the story, the main character analyses the categories of writers in communist Romania in the 1980's. Topping this hierarchy of categories was the committed author–the type of author who is completely indoctrinated with party ideology–, and this is evident in his texts: "die Linken können nicht schreiben, das sind bloß verkrachte Schriftsteller, soziales Engagement, Quatsch, wo bleibt die Ästhetik, das ist nichts als Proletkultismus, Propaganda." (ibid, 46)[22] In the second category of writers–"diese vorsichtige Sorte" (ibid., 65)[23]–we find authors who express "subversive Gedanken" (ibid., 65)[24] in a very cunning way in their texts. These writers, whom Stirner does not like at all, were the masters of subverting between the lines what everybody knows. The dissidents, whose works were banned from publication, form a third category of writers living in Romania in those days. The protagonist himself "gehörte zu den geduldeten Autoren, nicht verboten, geduldet" (ibid., 56)[25] who were not banned, because he had published something, even though not many copies were printed: "Das hieß, man konnte ab und zu noch etwas veröffentlichen. Vielleicht auch nur, um es dem Ausland zu zeigen. Seht, wir drucken sie. Sie sind nicht verfolgt. Wir drucken auch so was. Wir sind zwar nicht froh damit, aber es kann erscheinen" (ibid.).[26]

Stirner instinctively asks himself who would want to read these books and who is convinced by the idea that these works will be bought up and pulped by the Securitate,[27] so that they could print other books, using the same paper.

Wagner describes the mechanisms of brain-washing perfectly in the penultimate chapter of his story. The disillusioned Stirner's feelings of hate and impotence are expressed in his dream vision. His words echo the empty forms of the state language and lines from the party press: accusations, denunciations and curses. The call for truth and freedom becomes a repetitive chorus signifying nothing.

The choice of the protagonist's name is no coincidence: "Stirner ist ein sprechender Name: Man assoziere den ‚Denker', der den Widrigkeiten des Daseins ‚die Stirn bietet' [...]" (Perchy: 1989, IX).[28] But to confront someone, you have to have the courage; and you also have to be able to see and identify the reality. As a German writer in communist Romania, Stirner doubts the contradiction between appearance and essence and decides to emigrate from what tries to appear as a workers' paradise, but which is without reality (cf. Neidhart 1988, 89) to the Federal Republic of Germany:

> Es war schon lange kein Sinn mehr da. [...] es kommt die nächste Not, es kommen die nächsten Wochen ohne Milch, die Tage ohne Brot, die Abende ohne Strom, es kommt der nächste Medienmüll, [...], die nächste Erniedrigung und die übernächste. Es war genug. Stirner blickte über das Stadion. Dahinter war die düster dampfende Industrie. Das schweigende Land. Er stand auf, ging zum Schrank, hob die Schreibmaschine auf den Tisch, legte den Deckel beiseite, spannte zwei Bogen Papier ein, Kohlepapier dazwischen, fing an zu tippen: An das Paßamt. Wir stellen hiermit den Antrag zur endgültigen Ausreise. Unsere Gründe sind. (Wagner 1989a, 136)[29]

Begrüßungsgeld

With *Begrüßungsgeld* Wagner continues his story *Ausreiseantrag*. In this book, the protagonist also follows in the author's biographical footsteps. The title signals the content and context of the story. The protagonist lands in a transit camp in Nuremberg, where he receives financial aid and German citizenship. He succeeds in overcoming the red tape hurdles of resettlement, settling down with his wife Sabine in West Berlin where he tries to write again.

The choice of Stirner's place of residence is no coincidence. Living on the border, near the Berlin wall, is definitely uncomfortable for somebody who has to adapt to a new system step by step: "Weil er in Berlin lebte, hatte er immer, wenn er sich in Westdeutschland befand, den Eindruck, im Ausland zu sein. Bei jeder Reise die Paßkontrollen. Jede Reise war eine Auslandsreise" (Wagner 1989b, 77).[30] The specific atmosphere of this divided city can be seen as emblematic of his existence. The difficult decision to emigrate from Romania, his anxiety and guilt feelings, which recur in his dreams, and especially his painstaking attempts to overcome various hurdles that prevent him from resuming his writing can all be identified with the divided city, Berlin, as Stirner states: "Jemand zeigt mir die Stadt, und ich zeige ihm mein Leben" (ibid., 7), "Die Orte hatten mit meinem Leben zu tun" (ibid., 80).[31]

A feeling of always being "auf der Flucht" (ibid.),[32] characterizes Stirner's new status as an immigrant. Alienation and loss of orientation shape him: a part of him seems to have popped up in the Federal Republic of Germany and the rest of him seems to have lagged behind in Romania. He is always looking for information in German newspapers, but also buys Romanian newspapers and red chili peppers, and a grove of trees reminds him of the Banat. When riding on public transportation, he inadvertently tucks away his newspapers, because he was used to hiding his German language newspapers from the other passengers in Romania. He is continuously aware of the time lag between the two countries: "Er sah auf die Uhr. Es war sieben. In Rumänien ist es acht, dachte er" (ibid., 105).[33]

The protagonist's thoughts constantly fluctuate between the new and the old homeland; he suffers because he has no identity of his own which can manifest itself through language, feelings and thoughts: "In Rumänien haben sie immer gesagt: Du Deutscher, sagte Stirner. Hier bin ich der Rumäne" (ibid., 72).[34] Shortly after his arrival in the West, his attitude as a writer in the society is not yet clarified, he feels unsure: "Ich spiele mit meinen Beobachtungen wie mit einem Feuerzeug. Ich kann noch nicht darüber schreiben" (ibid., 18).[35] Stirner, searching for his sense of geographical belonging, has to learn, step by step, how to overcome the effects of being uprooted from Romania and re-planted in Germany: "Deutsch sprach er mit einem fremden Akzent" (ibid., 51).[36]

This learning and translation procedure is illustrated in *Begrüßungsgeld* especially on the level of language. With a routing slip in one's hand one is supposed to visit offices in the transit camp, to fill in forms and answer questions. For Stirner the "Beamtendeutsch" is practically the same as "Behördenrumänisch" (ibid., 10).[37] The usual question which they ask him is whether he speaks German. They also give him a Romanian-German dictionary along with the welcome money, heightening his feeling of homelessness, which the protagonist experiences. He realises how deceptive his relationship to the German language was in Romania: "Das Deutsche war bloß aus der Entfernung eine Sicherheit gewesen. Sich am Deutschen festhaltend, lebte er in der rumänischen Fremde. Und jetzt, in Deutschland? Niemand ist des Anderen Sprache" (ibid., 44).[38]

Stirner, who not only feels, but actually is German, is irked by the fact that he is considered to be a foreigner on account of his Banat pronunciation: "Deutsch sprach er mit einem fremden Akzent. Sind Sie Schweizer, wurde er gefragt. Nein, sagte er, und schon hatte er sich verraten. [...] Er mühte sich mit seiner Aussprache ab" (ibid., 51)[39] and "[er] sah sein Gesicht im Spiegel. Es war das Gesicht eines Fremden" (ibid., 65).[40]

He cannot come to terms with the fact that the German he uses in thinking and feeling has taken on another significance for him in Germany; it takes on a different meaning than it had when he used German in Romania. For Stirner, who wrote in German while living in Romania, this is a confusing experience: why has his own language changed its function in his new homeland? Previously, the German language had been a topos of his identity, a means of distancing himself from the ruling elite, who spoke Romanian, and their institutions. In the West, German is omnipresent; as the language of the majority, it encompasses both the public domain and the domain of private life:

> Plötzlich war überall nur noch die deutsche Sprache. Es war ungewöhnlich für ihn, für den das Deutsche doch etwas Privates gewesen war. Die Sprache, in der man miteinander redete, in der man las. Man entfernte sich aus der Öffentlichkeit, indem man deutsch sprach. Sein Deutsch hatte nicht die Obszönität der Losungen, der Schlagzeilen. Die Mächtigen sprachen rumänisch. Nun war das über Nacht alles anders geworden. (ibid., 119)[41]

Due to his separation from his past Stirner's native tongue suddenly turns into a foreign language: "Sätze von früher waren lächerlich. Immer öfter" (ibid., 84).[42] "Sein Deutsch wurde anders. Er merkte es. Er sagte nichts" (ibid., 104).[43]

The comparison between Romania and West Germany brings out this language switch. During the dictatorship, each word had its clearly established reference, but in the west, the language seems to become unclear. This is emphasised by ad slogans, which remind Stirner of communist propaganda. Every linguistic utterance becomes irrelevant and exchangeable in the west:

> Jetzt war er im Niemandsland. Es gehörte ihm nichts. Er redete zwar die gleiche Sprache wie die Leute hier, aber er redete wie einer, der von außen kommt. Seine Sätze wirkten wie übersetzt. Er schrieb, aber es zielte auf nichts. Er war jetzt mit seiner Sprache allein. (ibid., 26)[44]

Emigration definitely has more severe consequences for a writer than for other immigrants. A strong feeling of loneliness accompanies Stirner, when he calls his own home for example, although he knows that there is no one in; when he has last-minute holiday resorts offers announced several times; or when he asks a stranger, a retired lady, for permission to read his poems out loud to her. The protagonist is subjected to an intense process of language appropriation. Stirner records his literary exercises in a notebook, which he subsequently crosses out. Pulver states that this notebook represents a kind of book in a book, in which the short story recounts its own genesis, and namely in a simple and self-evident way (cf. Pulver 1989, 39). Stirner memorises fashionable phrases, ad slogans, language abbreviations, words unknown to him like "blood orange", "child identity card" (cf. Wagner 1989b, 104), "application for phone holder's change of address", "mail forwarding request" (cf. ibid., 57) and empty phrases found in daily language, in hopes of adapting his Banat German to that spoken in the Federal Republic of Germany. In this way, a learning process unfolds that reminds one of the rote learning of school children and it is exactly for this reason that it is effective. Sometimes these linguistic peculiarities arouse his mistrust and he muses:

> Am Kiosk standen sie und aßen Bratwurst mit Pommes frites. Oder Pommes, wie sie sagten. Er dachte öfter darüber nach, ob er das nicht auch so sagen sollte. Aber wenn er an der Reihe war, sagte er doch jedesmal Pomfrits. Das war korrekt, und das kennzeichnete ihn als Ausländer. Manchmal beobachtete er, ob die Verkäuferin überrascht war. Nein, sie war es nicht. Bestimmt, man sah ihm doch den Ausländer an. Na und, sagte er sich. Warum sollte man ihm nicht den Ausländer ansehn. Warum sollte er ein Wort falsch aussprechen müssen, nur um als Einheimischer zu gelten, als Deutscher. (ibid., 53)[45]

The main character opposes the new words until he notices that he has unwittingly internalised them: "Es war eine ferne Sprache in ihm, gegen die er sich zu sperren suchte, die er aber insgeheim wünschte" (ibid. 62).[46]

By gradually overcoming his past, Stirner regains the language little by little. For he knows that he is dependent on the language if he is to be able to handle the new reality, in order to be able to write anything at all: "Er konnte wieder schreiben, er war wieder zu Beobachtungen fähig. Was er sah, konnte er jetzt auch wieder einordnen. Das Raster war noch sehr fragil, aber daß er wieder schreiben konnte, machte ihn ruhiger" (ibid., 136).[47]

Wagner's story is not coherent: it records the haphazard observations of the protagonist and not the events that frame the experience. According to Jürgen Jacobs the text is a mosaic of reflections, memories, impressions and quotations (cf. Jacobs 1989, 89). This is added by fragments from the language of the authorities, which give the overall impression that the protagonist is performing a monologue. An outsider agrees to what he hears and sees:

In der U-Bahn beobachtete er Leute [...] Er wollte alles über sie wissen. Er wollte es, weil er nichts über sie wußte. Er stellte sich neben die Leute, die sich miteinander unterhielten, schnappte Satzfetzen auf, er schaute, was die Leute lasen. Er suchte Schlüsse zu ziehen aus dem, was er erfuhr. Er wurde den Eindruck nicht los, daß ihm alles verborgen blieb. (Wagner 1989b, 34)[48]

Stirner "lebte in einer Gegenwart, die für ihn keine Wurzeln hatte" (ibid., 62).[49]

Concluding Remarks

In both of the texts analyzed here, Wagner's own life serves as a model, with an exemplary character. The protagonist Stirner functions as the author's alter ego. *Ausreiseantrag* shows how the protagonist despairs because of the discrepancy between reality and appearance. He realizes that he has developed into an enemy of the state bit by bit; emigration is the only solution to his problems. His life is all about being affected by his subjective feelings, and he realizes that he slowly turns into the public enemy the Romanian authorities see in him. For him, as a public enemy, the only possibility if he wants to live a life of integrity, is to leave Romania, to write the application for leaving the country.

Begrüßungsgeld foregrounds the issues of the immigrant, describing the split identity of the protagonist in an exemplary way: in Romania Stirner is German, in the Federal Republic of Germany he is Romanian; during a visit to the German Democratic Republic he is seen as a westerner. This major point is illustrated in the way the stories represent the intensive dispute with the problem of language. When he lives out the boundaries of his minority German in Romania, he lands in West Berlin in a no man's land (cf. Wagner 1989b, 78), where he finds his German in a state between speechlessness and reality description (cf. Krause, 1997, 26). Stirner abandons his usual German language and approaches an alternate German language. However, he observes that he must resign himself to his own biography. Stirner wants to escape from his past. The memories of his past help him drive away the experiences in Romania. His attitude signals that he is looking toward a new future.

Notes

[1] Aktionsgruppe Banat was a famous group of authors, who were active in Timişoara between 1972 and 1975 and who exerted a decisive influence on Herta Müller. To this group belong: Anton Bohn, Rolf Bossert, Werner Kremm, Johann Lippet, Gerhard Ortinau, Anton Sterbling, William Totok, Richard Wagner, and Ernest Wichner. The group was influenced by Brecht's Marxist ideology and showed an inclination towards linguistic experiment according to the model of the Vienna group (cf. Nubert 2006).

[2] "the Banat [...] and the Banat Suabians and everything else that still has to do with it, and they [the people in Germany] do not know this [...] That is why it interests me, too to reflect on what this region means in modern times culturally speaking, too" (our trans.).

[3] "Welcome Money" (our trans.).

[4] "In the beginning he kept clear from the label 'immigrant'. Immigration, how come? He had always written in German and considered what he wrote to be a part of the German literature. Not even the Romanians had ever been of the opinion that the literature of the German minority belonged to the Romanian literature. They rather ignored them, they looked upon the literature of their minority as a cultural & political issue of the regime and looked upon the people, who wrote it, as overstrained would-be literary persons" (our trans.).

[5] "Emigration Application" (our trans.).

[6] "No man's land" (our trans.).

[7] "Stirner considered himself as a writer. He wrote in German. Poetry, short fiction. It was the language of a minority. He had had several books published, but he did not live off them [...] He worked for a newspaper, for a German-speaking one, as a correspondent" (our trans.). This corresponds with Wagner's biography: Until his emigration he published several volumes in Romania: *Klartext. Ein Gedichtbuch*, 1973; *die invasion der uhren. Gedichte*, 1977; *Der Anfang einer Geschichte*, 1980; *Hotel California I. Gedichte*, 1980; *Hotel California II. Gedichte*, 1981; *Anna und die Uhren. Ein Lesebuch für kleine Leute mit Bildernn von Cornelia König*, 1981; *Gegenlicht. Gedichte*, 1983; *Das Auge des Feuilletons. Geschichten und Notizen*, 1984. And between 1979–1983 he worked as a correspondent in the weekly paper "Karpatenrundschau", situated in Kronstadt/Braşov; he was responsible for the Region Banat.

[8] "the dialogue has lost its charm" (our trans.).

[9] "foreigner" (our trans.).

[10] "diplopic" (our trans.).

[11] "without a job" (our trans.).

[12] "When Sabine was still working at that machine building plant, one day a large broad-shouldered man with watery-blue eyes came to her. [...] Maybe you could help us, [...] he thrust a sheet of paper in front of her and began to dictate: 'I hereby pledge to...'. This I will not sign. And in general, what you demand of me does not belong to my job duties" (our trans.). The machine building plant resembles the

Tehnometal machine building plant, where Herta Müller worked between 1976 and 1979 as an interpreter.

[13] "Sabine worked as a teacher of German. She taught German as a foreign language. She did not have a permanent position. For years only substitute teaching positions. First at this school, then at that school." (our trans.).

[14] "general void" (our trans.).

[15] "positive elements, achievements" (our trans.).

[16] "Mouthpiece of the party" (our trans.).

[17] "the party directives" (our trans.).

[18] "He wrote for the newspaper, and he wrote for himself, for his books. What he wrote for his books distanced itself from what he wrote for his newspaper" (our trans.).

[19] "In a regime which occupies language, one cannot utter opinions. If one wanted to write realistic literature and one said it, then one found himself already on the home ground of the regime. For the regime, too, asked for realistic literature" (our trans.).

[20] "The words had been long expropriated. Clowns were romping about on the regime's stage and were tossing words around them" (our trans.).

[21] "Everybody just talked. Even Stirner began to talk. But nobody answered him. Then he noticed that people present did not talk to each other, but every one talked for himself. One could not understand what they said either, and whenever one tried to draw just a step closer, one already came to stand near an exit again. One could hear only this consistent, muffled din of words. Stirner talked and noticed that he himself failed to understand what he was saying. [...] The din of words went on undisturbed" (our trans.).

[22] "The leftists cannot write, these are simply failed writers,...social commitment..., fiddlesticks, where does aesthetics come in?... this is nothing but proletkult, propaganda" (our trans.).

[23] "the cautious type" (our trans.).

[24] "subversive thoughts" (our trans.).

[25] "belonged to the tolerated authors, not forbidden, tolerated" (our trans.).

[26] "This meant that one could have something printed from time to time. Maybe also only to show this to those abroad. You see, we print their stuff. They are not persecuted. We print this, too. We are not happy with it, but it can come out" (our trans.).

[27] The Securitate was the Secret Police.

[28] "Stirner is a very eloquent name: one associates it with the 'thinker', who has to cope with life's vicissitudes ('die Stirn bietet')" (our trans.).

[29] "There had been long no use living there.[...] the next shortage comes, the next weeks come without milk, the days without bread, the evening without electric power, the next media garbage comes, the next humiliation and the another one. It was enough. Stirner gazed over the stadium. Behind it lay the bleak steaming industry. The silent country. He stood up, went up to the cupboard, heaved the typewriter onto the table, laid the lid aside, inserted two sheets of paper into it with carbon paper in between, started typing: To the Passport Office. We herewith submit the emigration application. Our motives are" (our trans.).

[30] "When he lived in Berlin, he always had the impression he was abroad when he was in West Germany. On each and every trip there were pass checks. Each journey was a trip abroad" (our trans.).
[31] "Somebody shows me the city and I show him my life", "Places had something to do with my life, says Stirner" (our trans.).
[32] "on the run" (our trans.).
[33] "He glanced at this watch. It was seven. In Romania it is eight o'clock, he mused" (our trans.).
[34] "In Romania they always said: 'You, the German,' said Stirner. 'Here I am the Romanian'" (our trans.).
[35] "I am dallying with my observations as I am toying with my lighter. I cannot write about this yet" (our trans.).
[36] "He spoke German with a foreign accent" (our trans.).
[37] "civil servants' German", "the Romanian of the authorities" (our trans.).
[38] "German simply meant a kind of safety from far away. Holding on tight to German, he lived inside the Romanian foreignness. 'And now, in Germany? Nobody is the other's language'" (our trans.).
[39] "He spoke German with a foreign accent. You are Swiss, he was often asked. No, he said, and he had thus already betrayed himself. [...] He struggled with his pronunciation" (our trans.).
[40] "[he] saw his face in the mirror. It was the face of a foreigner" (our trans.).
[41] "Suddenly everywhere there was still only German. It was unusual to him, for whom German had been something private. The language in which they spoke with each other, in which they read. He would slip out of the public, while they spoke German. His German did not possess the obscenity of slogans, of headlines. The powerful ones used to speak Romanian. But this became entirely different overnight" (our trans.).
[42] "Sentences from earlier times were ridiculous. More and more often" (our trans.).
[43] "His German turned different. He noticed it. He said nothing" (our trans.).
[44] "Now there was nobody in No man's land. Nothing belonged to him. He spoke the same language as the people here, but he spoke it like one who comes from abroad. His sentences sounded as if they had been translated. He wrote, but this referred to nothing. He was alone with his language" (our trans.).
[45] "At the kiosk they stood and ate sausages with fries (pommes frites). Or pommes, like they said. He often thought it over whether he should say it so or not. But when it was his turn in the queue, he still always simply said: "Pomfrits". This was correct, but this characterised him as a foreigner. Sometimes he would notice if the female assistant was surprised. No, she was not. Surely they saw him as a foreigner, this is it, said to himself, why shouldn't they see him as a foreigner? Why should he mispronounce a word, only to count as a local, as a German?" (our trans.).
[46] "It was a faraway language in him, against which he tried to shut himself off, although he secretly craved it" (our trans.).

[47] "He could write again, he was capable of observing again, what he saw he was able to classify. The grid was still very fragile, but the fact that he could write again made him calmer" (our trans.).

[48] "In the underground he was observing people [...] He wanted to know everything about them. He wanted this precisely because he knew nothing at all about them. He stood next to people who talked to each other, caught stretches of sentences, he looked at what the people were reading. He sought to draw conclusions from what he found out. He could not rid himself of the impression that everything remained hidden to him" (our trans.).

[49] "he lived in a present that had no roots for him" (our trans.).

References

Bennett, Andrew and Nicholas Royle. 2009 [1995]. *An Introduction to literature, criticism and theory*. London, etc.: Pearson & Longman.
Jacobs, Jürgen. 1989. "Mit seiner Sprache allein. Richard Wagner erzählt von der Einwanderung in die Bundesrepublik." In *Frankfurter Allgemeine Zeitung*, 17. 4.1989, 30.
Jass, Walter. 1996. "Ein ostmitteleuropäischer Zusammenhang bleibt ... Gespräch mit dem Dichter und Schriftsteller Richard Wagner". In *Allgemeine Deutsche Zeitung für Rumänien*, 1.11.1996, 5.
Kory, Beate Petra. 2012. "Der Schriftsteller als Aussiedler am Beispiel der Erzählungen Richard Wagners Ausreiseantrag und Begrüßungsgeld". In *Temeswarer Beiträge zur Germanistik*, 9/2012: 131–146.
Neidhart, Christoph. 1988. "Fremde Alptraumreportage aus einem Arbeitsparadies ohne Wirklichkeit." In *Die Weltwoche*, 14.4.1988, 89.
Nubert, Roxana. 2006. "Die sogenannte Stunde Null in der rumäniendeutschen Literatur: Die Aktionsgruppe Banat." In Mitteleuropäische Paradigmen in Südosteuropa. Ein Beitrag zur Kultur der Deutschen im Banat, edited by Roxana Nubert, and Ileana Pintilie-Teleagă. 254–268. Wien: Praesens.
Perschy, Jakob Michael. 1989. "Westberlin ist der falsche Platz, um neue Wurzeln zu schlagen." In *Die Presse*, 6./7.5.1989, IX.
Pulver, Elsbeth. 1989. "Schreiben lernen im Niemandsland. Eine Erzählung von Richard Wagner." In *Neue Zürcher Zeitung*, 7.7.1989, 39.
Wagner, Richard. 1989a. *Ausreiseantrag. Eine Erzählung*. Frankfurt am Main: Luchterhand Literaturverlag.
—. 1989b. *Begrüßungsgeld: Eine Erzählung*. Frankfurt am Main: Luchterhand Literaturverlag.

CHAPTER NINE

GROUP IDENTITY IN TEENAGE TALK FROM MADRID

ANNETTE M. MYRE JØRGENSEN

1. Vagueness

Teenagers often use vague expressions when speaking with their peers. Bertrand Russell relates to *vague language* (hereafter VL) in a theoretical way, claiming: "whatever vagueness is to be found in my words must be attributed to our ancestors for not having been predominantly interested in logic" (1923, 1). Russell's attitude towards VL is quite negative, as he relates it to laziness (Keefe 2000, 11). Teenagers are often scorned for their "lazy" speaking habits and accused of being incoherent. I want to show that teenagers do not use VL due to sheer laziness, but quite the contrary; they use vague language because they *have no desire to be clear*. This type of language serves a special purpose: it marks their *in-group identity*, since VL is a productive strategy in their interaction and helps them to express this identity.

1.1 Teenagers, Peers and In-group Identity

As Garrett and Williams remind us: "In tandem with developing more autonomy from parents, teenagers have to forge rewarding and supporting relationships with peers" (2005, 40). This means that teenage language fulfills an overall interactional function, creating rapport and expressing *social relations* (Herrero 2002, Zimmermann 2002, Jørgensen and Martínez 2010, Deppermann 2007). In this chapter, I argue for the significance of such dimensions in the analysis of VL in teenage narrative events from Madrid; I use a pragmatic linguistic approach to the examples from the COLA-corpus (www.colam.org).[1] I assume their language is an expression of a social identity, "a same age group affiliation" with their peers, rather than *a social, national or ethnic identity*.[2]

The teenagers in this study (13-19 years old) interact, using codes such as VL, which seem incomprehensible for the people around them. In this way, they construct a special *in-group identity* (Brown and Levinson 1987). Carter and McCarthy (2006) assert that VL expressions are an indication of assumed shared knowledge and that they mark in-group membership, insofar as the references of VL can be assumed to be known to the listener. Cutting also argues that speech communities use VL as a sign of in-group membership: "It could be concluded that using VL is a high involvement strategy for claiming in-group membership" (Cutting 2007, 226).

The Madrid teenagers' overuse of VL as general extenders in narrative events through expressions such as *y eso (and so), y todo eso (and all that), no sé qué (I don't know what), no sé qué no sé cuántas (and this and that)* as in-group membership signs is obvious in the following conversation extract:

1. MAR: vale dijo el tío vale vale vale vale
right the guy said right right right
   LUZ: no fue
he didn't go
   MAR: pues voy a ir hoy pues el domingo que viene a Caná no *sé qué* yo voy porque yo la
well I'm going today because next Sunday to Caná God knows what because I have
tengo que volver <u>a ver **no sé qué**</u> y tengo que conseguir su teléfono **y tal** porque
to I have to see her and God knows what I have to get her telephone number and so on because
claro le dijo no pides%
of course he told her don't ask%
pídeselo a ella que no te lo doy sabes estoy dispuesto a conseguir su teléfono **_no_**
ask her for it because I'm not giving it to you, you know? I'm willing to get her telephone and
sé qué yo voy a hablar con ella porque me encanta **_no sé qué y tal_**   maore2-01
I know that I'm going to talk with her because I like her a lot and all that

These same teenagers also have their own uses of VL such as *movida/s*. *Movida/s* is a noun which originally had a quite specific meaning,[3] but which has acquired an utterly unspecific meaning in their language, and as such is used for a variety of purposes when telling a story.

2. MARIO: y el que lo lee es el que hace el papel del más tonto de todos
and he who reads it is the one who plays the role of the most stupid of all
y está leyendo un texto de ***movidas de la música*** a
he is reading some stuff on music
historia de la música y eh eh confunde mazo de cosas y y y
the history of music and he is mixing up lots of stuff and and and
por ejemplo dice ***no se qué*** de batir un huevo
for example, he says something about whipping an egg
y y y no no ***no se qué no se qué*** que es muy parecido sabes\ malcb2-01a
and and and no no it's very alike you know

In the following, I focus on the VL conveyed through the use of the noun *movida(s) or move(s)* as a productive in-group identity marker in informal conversations among teenagers from Madrid, as recorded in the COLAm-corpus (www.colam.org).

This chapter has five sections, including this introduction. In Section two I present relevant theories on identity and identity construction in teenage language; I present the COLAm-corpus, and discuss VL in narrative events. The third section comprises a presentation of the methodology used in my study. The analysis of the Madrid teenagers' vague language is the subject of Section four. In the final section, I discuss identity creation, before summing up with some concluding remarks.

2. Theories

2.1 Identity

Postmodernists conceive of identity as fragmented and in flux, as an accomplishment, not something that is stable. Identity can be changed to suit the necessities of the moment (Tracy 2002), so it can be seen as *dynamically enacted through talk, which changes from one occasion to the next*. Tracy (2002) proposes four types of identity, some of which are stable. Firstly, she argues for a master identity; something each person possesses–it is stable and fixed, prior to any particular situation, and encompasses the individual's nationality, gender, etc., (e.g., a woman from Trinidad and Tobago, a teenager from Madrid). On top of this, one can build the second type of identity–one's personal identity–which is also stable and unique (e.g., pro-EU, against the EU, pro-Manchester United, pro-Real Madrid). The third kind is interactional identity, which refers to the specific role that people take on in a communicative context with regard to particular people (e.g., friend or Pizza Hut employee, teenager from a Madrid school). The fourth, and final type of identity, according to Tracy, would be one's relational identity; the kind of relationship that a person enacts with a particular conversation partner in a specific situation (e.g., hostile, distant, close).

The differences between these types of identity lead to an important insight, because as in Keupp, Ahbe and Gmür (1999), identity can be conceptualized as something stable and permanent. This is similar to Tracy's (2002) master and personal identities, just presented. Recent approaches, in contrast, emphasize the dynamic and interactive, more constructive nature of identity: "social identities tend to be indeterminate, situational rather than permanent, dynamic and interactively constructed" (Deppermann 2007, 2). Social identity theory states that the individual's self-concept comprises two parts: personal and social identity. The personal identity would be Tracy's master and personal identities, expanded on by the social, the interactional and relational identities. These three types of identity are combined in the creation of an in-group identity.

2.1.1 Teenagers' Group-identity

There are certain features that make us "who we are", different from others, and make us one person and not another (Tracy 2002). Identity is built up over the years, through our own experiences and perceptions, interaction with others and the world surrounding us, according to Erikson (1992). The negotiation of identity is *the* crucial question of adolescence (Deppermann 2007). Adolescence is a process, not an end-product. It is a period where teenagers move away from establishing their individual identity, among other concerns, to embrace a group identity, as the experts argue (Contreras Romero et al. 2009; Erikson 1992; Garrett and Williams 2005). According to Erikson (1992), it is during adolescence (13-19 years old) that teenagers start socializing in an independent way, constructing their own identity. In this task, friends and interactions with friends are obviously crucial; they are the persons they spend most time with, according to Gómez Lavín (1996) and Dávila León (2004). Teenagers distance themselves from the childhood they are leaving behind as well as from the world of the grown up generation, turning to peers who are in the same situation (Garrett and Williams 2005; Thurlow 2005). Thus, "Peer-group interactions are a most important arena for the conversational construction and assessment of social identities of self and others" (Deppermann 2007, 273).

Researchers who study identities need to study these interactive processes, since the individual's idea of self and others, especially the relational and interactional self, are also built through interaction. Antaki and Widdicombe (1998) emphasize the importance of discourse and interaction in the study of identities with their concept of "identity-in-interaction". According to Widdicombe, "the important analytic question is not [...] whether someone can be described in a particular way, but to show how this identity is made relevant or ascribed to self or others" (1998, 191). Talk-in-interaction is where social facts are established.

In order to understand why people talk as they do, and how they negotiate their identities, it is important to look at the groups in which they have spent long periods of time: speech communities (Hymes and Gumperz 1972), discourse communities (Swales 1998), or communities of practice (Eckert and McConnell-Ginet 1992; Eckert 2005). In these groups, individuals acquire beliefs about appropriate ways of speaking and interpreting their surroundings. The system of belief is shared by other members of that same community, as are their speech codes–and ways of making sense of the world the teenagers share. VL is one such shared speech code.

According to Eckert & McConnell-Ginet (1992, 464), teenage groups can be conceptualized as a "Community of Practice" (CoP), that is to say: an "aggregate of people who come together around mutual engagement in an endeavor" in an informal setting. Tracy (2002) claims that the negotiation of identity is omnipresent in everyday interactions. In the analysis of teenage talk, knowledge of the CoP is necessary in order to understand the interaction: "what from a distance may look 'all the same' may display a filigrane [sic!] pattern of distinctive differences when seen under the looking-glass of the social group directly involved" (Auer 2007, 13).

The concept of the CoP is a useful tool for investigating subtle aspects of social interactions. Through their regular gatherings, teenagers in a CoP develop shared values, norms and communicative practices. These common resources are the result of an extended period of mutual interaction and are, thus, frequently indexical resources, i.e. "short-cut devices that can evoke a whole range of meanings and connotations for the participants" (Georgapoulou 2005, 171). Androutsopoulos points out that "high intimacy in the group, an unstructured situation, and a lively and emotional atmosphere" can be considered "as the main contextual parameters for the development of adolescent speech styles" (2005, 1496) and identity, all of which are important factors in the relational and interpersonal identities. Eckert and Mc Connell-Ginet have shown that social practices construct aspects of identity (1999). The analysis of a sample episode of the teenagers' interactions in peer-groups shows that the construction of their group-identity is intertwined with the negotiation of other identity aspects in their narrative events.

Narratives are a means of constructing norms and group identity, and for building cohesion as well. In an adolescent group, having something to say and the right to speak, gives social status (Schuman 1986). Narrative events also emphasize the group as a CoP, where *group cohesion,* created by verbal interaction, gives status as well as leading to identity differentiation. Collaborative narration is a well-used strategy in turning speech codes into group property as well as settling on the different linguistic group identity markers, and establishing events as part of group memory (Eder 1988).

2.1.3 Linguistic Markers of Group Identity

People communicate their identities through the ways they use language. Part of the meaning of the everyday interaction has to do with the views of self and other that are built up and reflected in talk, and by telling stories. When we talk, we impart information, but other activities take place as well, for instance identity work, which has two aspects: 1) Identity is established through common agreement on how to talk. 2) Nationality, age, profession and social class influence how one talks. The relationship between discursive practices and identities is a reciprocal one in the interaction where there is a *self-presentational aspect* and a *partner directed one*.

Research on identity should be considered when constructing explanations for language use. Different factors contribute to the shaping of adolescent group-identity; VL in narrative events is one such factor (Gómez Lavín 1996; Castillo 2009; Stenström and Jørgensen 2008). Teenagers break the rules and make new ones for themselves in creating their own identity, and this affects their language. As an example of this, I explore teenagers' *group identity-construction* based on their use of VL in narrative events. I am particularly interested in "movidas", *(moves)*–a vague language expression which requires the group's common experience to be understood.

2.2 Vague Language

Language can be vague in different ways (Zhang 2011). One is through hedging,[4] which is rare in teenage talk, where exaggeration, instead, tends to be dominant (Jørgensen 2009). Approximators such as *about, around* and *approximately*, as well as *sort of, kind of* and *basically*, like shields, have the effect of withholding commitment to a proposition (Overstreet 1999; Andersen 2010; Zhang 2011), which, can, for instance, be explained by the general insecurity of teenagers (Contreras Romero et al. 2009).

VL may be defined as "that which modifies a linguistic item, phrase or utterance to make its meaning less precise" (Channell 1994, 20). It is commonly assumed that language should ideally be precise and that vagueness is a defect to be avoided whenever possible. The definition of vague language has been discussed in depth by philosophers (Pierce 1902; Russell 1923; Wright 1975), linguists (Ullmann 1962; Crystal and Davy 1975; Channell 1994; Williamson 1994) and psychologists (Deese 1974). When it comes to conversation, Crystal and Davy (1975) disagree with Russell (1923), because they claim that lack of precision "is one of the most important features of the vocabulary of informal conversation" (1975, 111-112). Due to temporary memory loss, they say, or not knowing the exact word, the subject of the conversation does not need an exact word, and the choice of vagueness is deliberate in order to preserve an atmosphere. Philosophers like Wright (1975) also suggest that we could not operate with a language free of vagueness. Williamson (1994) proposes that precise language is not necessarily more efficient than VL. He describes vagueness as a positive feature of human language, "Vague words often suffice for the purpose in hand, and too much precision can lead to timewasting inflexibility" (Williamson 1994, 4869). For instance, the following utterances are a bit pedantic and *time-wastingly inflexible*: "Please, open the window 47 degrees", or if I say to my sister, "I'll be at your place at 15:37 this afternoon."

Channell's view is that "what matters is that VL is used appropriately" (1994, 3), and this opinion is supported by Deemter (2010) and Ruzaité (2007). Jucker (2003) suggests that vague or precise language should be based on context, and considers that the ability to vary the precision of utterances and to use them in appropriate contexts is part of the speakers' communicative competence. He also insists that the interpretation of VL is an inherent part of natural language use when the *cooperation principle* is activated, because VL is an interactional strategy:

> Speakers are faced with a number of communicative tasks, and they are vague for strategic reasons. Varying the level of vagueness may help guide the addressee to make the intended representation of entities and events and to draw intended implications from them. (Jucker, Smith, and Lüdge 2003, 1739)

Speakers, or as we shall see in this case, teenage speakers, use VL when they are unable or unwilling to give accurate information, or when they think it is either unnecessary or socially inappropriate to do so, for instance, by rounding off numbers when telling the time.

In teenage talk from Madrid we will see that VL is frequently used in order to create a certain atmosphere. The noun analysed here–*una(s)/la(s) movida(s)*–belongs to what Crystal and Davy classify as "nouns that express total vagueness" (Crystal and Davy 1975, 111). This kind of VL is frequent, along with other ways of being vague, in teenage talk. In this section, I focus on the vagueness of this noun used with a non-specific referential meaning, but where its meaning is inferred by the speakers who belong to the same group, thus creating a special group identity. Example 2 provides just one example of the vague use of nouns like *movida(s)*. The references are supposed to be to the world that the teenagers know and share. The accommodation of vague utterances thereby enables the teenagers to get by with a relatively small, general-purpose lexicon. The teenager can adjust the extension of a vague predicate to suit his/her referential needs. One example, among many others, would be the noun *movida/movidas* in the COLAm-corpus: which can only be understood by being familiar with and sharing the all-important context (Kyburg and Morreau 1996, 2000; Cheng 2007) and setting of the peer-group.

In teenage talk, the listener does not expect that the meaning the speaker wants to convey is a literal one. A literal interpretation is neither always necessary nor always appropriate for successful communication (Sperber and Wilson 1991), let alone among teenagers where part of their group identity is to *share knowledge in a way only they can understand*. Regarding vague uses of language, the speaker presents only some of the analytical and contextual implications of the proposition. The listener is expected to construct a subset of contextual implications as intended by the speaker to achieve discourse goals, by *means of shared knowledge*. Teenage talk as such, is indeed a process in which the understanding of utterances is always involved. It implies the speaker's assumption that the listener is able to discover the implications the teenager wants to convey, so the choice of the propositional form of an utterance also depends on the speaker's evaluation of the listener's cognitive abilities as well as on her assumptions about the common ground that he/she shares with him/her.

VL is interpersonal and is used in informal style and relaxed settings (Andersen 2010). The use of vague nouns like *movida(s)* with varying degrees of strictness and cooperation from the interactants contributes not only to the expressiveness of teenage language (Zhang 2011; Overstreet 2005; Overstreet and Yule 2002), but to the construction of a group-identity marker. This chapter departs from Grice's (1975) Cooperative Principle (CP) for the understanding of the vague expressions in a CoP when telling stories.

I argue for an interactional approach to the concept of vagueness in language, since it is not only an inherent feature of natural language but–crucially–an interactional strategy. Teenagers are faced with a number of communicative tasks, and they are vague for strategic reasons. Varying the level of vagueness may help guide the addressee to make the intended representation of entities and events and to draw the intended implications from them. As we see, when using the noun *una movida*, the teenagers collaborate within the group to find the specific meaning of the generic word. The major function of VL in teenage talk, tailoring conversational contributions to the informational needs of the other participants, is accomplished, since VL maintains and enhances the ongoing relationship by collaboration in the narrative events.

The focus of this section has been on the nature and role of vague expressions in the narrative events, stressing the role of common ground in the use of them. The teenagers constantly negotiate their common ground, seeking and providing clues as to the partner's beliefs and the current accessibility of beliefs that are relevant to the group's interpretation of the utterance. I want to explore the interplay between contexts and meanings of vague expressions in a discourse type in which vagueness plays an important role, i.e., in the story telling in teenagers' everyday conversations. I concentrate on how the vague noun *movida(s)* is used. It is not just a poor, although adequate substitute for precise expressions; vague expressions of this kind are to be preferred over precise expressions because of their greater interactive efficiency (Sperber and Wilson, 1995).

3. Theoretical Frame

Pragmatic meaning, direct and indirect as such, is an important tool for the analysis of the interactional function of teenage language. One insight especially into indirectness in teenage talk is provided by the theory of "vagueness" developed in the late 1970s, 80's and 90's, which Channell (1994, 20) claims is paradigmatic. Her claim is supported and expanded on by Jucker (2003), who applies Sperber & Wilson's relevance theory (Sperber and Wilson 1986). Eder (1988) and Schuman (1986) contribute with the theoretical frame for the narrative events.

3.1 Methodology: Corpus Oral de Lenguaje Adolescente, COLA

Corpus Linguistics, a line of work that has become more and more popular among linguists, is characterized by an empirical methodology, and carries out investigations on large collections of natural data called *corpora*. Biber says that "empirical investigation of corpora can shed light on previously intractable research questions in linguistics" (2006, ix). This fully justifies the empirical corpus based inductive methodology. The COLA-corpus offers many advantages for the study of language in use: we analyse the mentioned aspects of oral language among teenagers by looking at real examples gathered in order to see what really happens among them.

Briz (2003), agrees with Zimmermann (2002, 141) who insists that the study of teenage language should be based on real interactions: "The point of departure for its study should be the communicative act, the conversation among the teenagers: the elements of their speech should not be taken separatedly or in an isolated way".[5] This is what the Corpus Oral de Lenguaje Adolescente Madrid, the COLAm-corpus, has made possible: the observation of teenage language in real interactions (www.colam.org). The COLA-corpus has a strategic point of departure, we record the teenagers talking with their friends, since this is when we get the most natural and analyzable data. Conversations about issues such as parents, teachers, love relations, or drinking, are treated as if they were questions of paramount importance, and are frequent among our Madrid youngsters (Jørgensen 2008; Hofland et al. 2005; Jørgensen and Eguía Padilla 2014).

The entire COLA-corpus consists of teenage talk from three different metropoles: the COLAm (Madrid), COLAba (Buenos Aires) and COLAs (Chile) (Jørgensen and Eguía Padilla 2014; Jørgensen and Drange 2012). The Madrid, or COLAm-corpus was recorded in Madrid in 2003-2007 by school recruits, who volunteered to record their conversations with their friends of the same age and a similar social background for three or four days. The speakers, including the recruits, were boys and girls, aged from 13 to 19 from working-, middle-, and upper-class schools in the Madrid metropolitan area.[6] The COLAm-corpus, which currently consists of roughly 500.000 words, is large enough to reflect the Madrid teenagers' speech habits. The corpus has samples of conversations held among teenagers made accessible to investigation through computational programs. The way the data are collected and the dimensions, organisation and design of the COLA-corpus, allow us to study the functions of the different elements of Spanish teenage talk, which we can access through special search engines. One of the advantages of this corpus is that it presents the speakers' voices along with the transcribed speech, offering the researcher the opportunity to capture the speakers' different moods and expressions of emotions and thus enabling the interpretation of the utterances. Having access to their intonation helps us account for other aspects as well (Hofland et al. 2005; Jørgensen and Eguía Padilla 2014). I have chosen examples where *movida(s)* is used from the 130 cases found, where there was a short storytelling or narrative event. The term *utterance* is used to refer to the linguistic units analysed in teenage language. An utterance can consist of any element, from a pause filler to a long utterance (Bañon 1993; Tracy 2002).

4. VL in Teenage Talk

There are different types of VL found in the COLAm-corpus such as hedges, so-called *general extenders* (Channell 1994; Overstreet 1999; Terraschke 2007)[7] and generic terms, or *verba omnibus*, such as the noun *movida(s)* analysed here in the teenagers' narrative events. *Movida(s)* is an emblematic example of Spanish vague teenage talk, frequent in the COLAm-corpus (130 tokens of five types), which, to my knowledge, has not been studied by any other linguist. It is the context that determines the meaning of the noun *Movida(s)*. In the following narrative events, the noun *movida(s)* is used as a generic term, instead of a precise word. It has no referential content, but invites the listener to infer a referent or a meaning.

Movida(s) means everything from a *linguistic investigation* for instance, in the story (3), beneath, to a *special drink* in example (7) and *the things a cat can do in story number* (8):

3. MARISOL: y y y entonces estoy grabando ahora
   and and and then I'm recording it now
   MANOLO: ya pero para qué/
   yes but what for?
   MARISOL: sí para porque hacen una **_una movida de e_** lenguaje coloquial
   yes, it is for an oral language thing
   MANOLO: y eso \
   and so?
   mi madre
   my mother
   big brother
   big brother
   MARISOL: qué hacen una cosa del lenguaje colloquial \ maesb2-04
   they are doing something on everyday language

In the next little story, constructed through the common efforts of both speakers, one boy tells the others what happened at school, and *unas movidas* means *eczema* or skin rash.

4. MANUEL: al allí y nos ha mandao a Gómez nos ha dicho a (xxx)
    otro que está enfermo
    to there he has sent us to Gómez he told him that the
    other is sick
    JOSELUIS: si se ha ido esta mañana (xxx) dicho que le habían salido
    unas movidas raras
    yes he went off this morning because he got some
    strange things on his hand
    y y había llamado
    and and he had called
    MANUEL: a su madre
    malcc2-03
    his mother

In the dramatic story told in (5) *movida* means a bone in the forearm. The listeners are collaborating in initiating as well as telling the story:

5. LUZMARI: jo con tu padre chaval le querías pegar
    wow with your father man you wanted to hit him
    MANUEL: hace un pedazo de años sí
    it's a piece of (many) years ago yes (it has been
    going on for many years)
    y me metió una somanta de hostias
    and he gave me lots of blows (he hit me a lot)
    JUAN: a mí también se me fue una vez
    I also lost it with him once
    MANUEL: **_y le rompí una movida de la muñeca_**
    and I broke some things in his hands
    JUAN: pues a mí no me dió tiempo me llevó a de bofetones
    well I didn't have time for that he brought me
    kicking from
    desde la cocina hasta el cuarto de mi hermana
    malcc2-13e
    the kitchen to my sister's room

In the following narrative event (8) *movidas* means *lifeguard*, and it is also a beautiful example of collaboration in the telling of the story:

6. MANUEL: parece mentira que tú que has sido socorrista
it's kind of unreal that you have been a lifeguard
LUZMARI: ya. que tú tenías que **_llevar lo deee todas las movidas esas no_**/
yeah. you had to be in charge of all those strange things no?
PEDRO: si eso lo he llevado durante. tres meses
yes I have been doing that for three months
luego ya no vuelves a tratarlo y se te olvida y
then you get back you don't do it and you forget
JUAN: se te olvida/
you forget?
PEDRO: y que luego que cada piscina lo tiene diferente
and then every pool has it in different ways
todos los tubos y toda malcc2-13c
all the tubes and all the

In story (9) Marta starts telling her friends about a strange drink, *una movida rarísima*, she and her friends were invited to try, but Juan takes over telling the story and finishes it:

7. MARTA: y nos invitaron a un chupito también
they invited us for a little sip as well
JUAN: no no y el pibe ese nos vió ahí
no no and that guy saw us there
un rato ya incluso bebiendo y comiendo y nos dijo
for a while even drinking and eating and then he said
queréis unos chupos de **_una movida rarísima_**
do you want a sip of this very strange thing
CARMEN: sí tío qué asco
yes man how gross
JUAN: **_una movida_** que la botella era suya
the thing is the bottle was his
CARMEN: soda con algo
soda with something
JUAN: era de esas botellas que no pone de qué es
it was one of those small bottles that don't tell you what is inside
y es con un tapón es porque tiene un barril él

malcc2-13
and it was with a cork because he has a barrel

In the following story (8) Marta tells her friends about a very smart cat her sister's boyfriend has:

8. MARTA: el talentito del gato del novio de mi hermana que tiene quince años trae ratones
the little talent of my sister's boyfriend's cat who is fifteen years old brings mice
 CARMEN: quince años\ tiene/
is it fifteen years old?
 LUZMA: pues como debe de estar el gato de mal con quince años no/
then how must that cat look like when it is fifteen years old no?
 MARTA: que va tronca es increible
not at all it is unbelievable
es un gato que hace _unas movidas_
it is a cat who does all kind if things
que es mazo de inteligente agarra y roba
it is very intelligent it takes and steals
 PEDRO: Mimi Mimi sí que roba eh/
Mimi Mimi really steals right?
 MARTA: le roba le roba a la vecina los filetes de carne
malcc2-11
it steals the steaks from the neighbour

The noun, in both definite and indefinite forms–*la(s)/una(s)movida/s*–is very productive, since it is also used as an interjection expressing admiration, an intensifier and as a general extender; it is the general expression, or *verba omibus*, most frequently used in the narratives of the Madrid teenagers.[8]

These expressions do not interrupt the fluency of the story because of the lack of a precise word. The social functions of vagueness are undoubtedly *all in action* in the COLAm teenage talk. In the examples of narrative events presented, the teenagers do not lack communicative competence, since they are able to vary the precision in their utterances according to the listeners. They use *movida(s)* as an interactional device as well as an in-group identity marker. In addition to this competence, they have a common ground, and share beliefs, so they do not have to negotiate the common ground relevant for the interpretation of the linguistic relevance (Sperber and Wilson 1986) of the utterances in the narrations. These substitutions for the precise expression (Jucker et al. 2003), are possible, thanks to their group-identity, where one of the aspects is collaboration, as we have seen in the examples.

The fact that the generic word *movida(s)* has different functions as a generic term, interjection and general extender, is a reflection of the teenagers' relaxed attitude towards normativity in general and linguistic normativity in particular. In the COLAm conversations there is no questioning about what *movidas* means and it causes no interruptions in the conversation for explanations. There are no reactions of surprise or indications that listeners do not understand the word in the conversations analysed. On the contrary, these words are used in an utterly confident and friendly interaction. What is interesting about *movida(s)* is that it is totally context-dependent, and nobody but the speakers in the conversations knows its true meaning, or uses it in its original meaning, thereby potentially causing a misunderstanding (http://lema.rae.es/drae/).

The noun *movida(s)*, used in Madrid teenage language, is an example of how an in-group identity can be shaped by the collaborative use of a noun in their stories. It serves a special function and conveys meanings that only the in-group members understand, thanks to their shared world and context.

5. Final Remarks

Members of a *community of practice*, a CP of adolescents like the ones observed, understand the subtle processes of social interaction in which they express themselves and interpret the utterances of others, and negotiate in-group identity. Having looked at the examples of the stories in which *movida(s)* occurs, I think we are in a position to claim that it is a phenomenon of teenage talk and that VL works as a context-dependent mark of group identity, because of its versatility and frequency of use in the narratives analysed here and in other conversations. A special contextual feature to be considered is the adolescent *culture of leisure* and playfulness; teenagers have time to play with the words and think about the contexts.

The configuration of an identity through language is complex, and its construction through interaction is gradual, and as such, *hard to define*. Depperman, for example, views identity as a conduit for the scientific constitution of the individual as an agent:

> By relating them to a common identity, the different, ephemeral actions of an individual are bundled and projected onto timeless, more or less stable dimensions of attributes, and these are understood as being related to one another by a uniform, overarching structure of subjectivity. 'Identity' thus builds a bridge between individuals and society. (2007, 274)

The configuration of *adolescent identity* is not exactly simple either, because adolescence is, above all, an economic and institutional construction, established through formal education, law and employment in the marketplace, more than by biology and age, according to Garrett and Williams (2005, 37), who also ask: "where does adolescence begin and end?" Coleman (1974, ix) would answer that "Adolescence can be defined in various ways depending on one's perspective, and social, economic or political notions do not always accord with a psychological viewpoint."

Ambadiang, García Parejo and Palacios Alcaine (2009) claim that identity studies in linguistics are based on a specific concept of identity, which is related more to *groups* than to personal identity. Identity is, as mentioned, a difficult concept with a double dimension: the individual and the social. According to Coupland: "There are certainly occasions when people purposively and rationally target identities for themselves in talk [...] But identity is often less coherent, less rationalized, more elusive, more negotiated, and more emergent than this" (2008, 269). Furthermore, Andersen and Mørch (2005) point out that there is a general tendency to consider personal identity as a psychological phenomenon constructed from social logic. As a consequence, identity has to do with the components it is analysed *under* and the way *it is interpreted*. A question not answered in the discussion of identity creation through language is how much of it is based on *free will* and how much is *unintentional*? Are the speakers always aware of the consequences of their choices during the creation of identity through shared speech?

No doubt Duszak has a point when he says that it is not clear whether social identities can be ascertained by words alone, or if the particular words can mark people as carriers of definite social values (2002). In the case of our Madrid teenagers, it is safe to say that vagueness is one of the markers of their group identity. However, Auer (2007, 6) points out that people sometimes engage in an identity act: "A (linguistic) act of identity can then be defined as the selection of a linguistic element which indexes some social group A and which is chosen on a particular occasion [...] in order to affiliate oneself with or disaffiliate oneself from a social group B".

5.1 Conclusions

VL specified as the *use of movida(s)* is one of the markers of these teenagers' group-identity, corresponding with Tracy's (2002) definitions of relational and in-group identity. Although I have presented one aspect of VL, a general expression, there are many more examples of VL in teenage interaction: frequent use of discourse markers, general extenders, generic terms (*cosa, cacharro, movida*). Furthermore, because vague expressions in teenage language are understood within the group, they do not demand explanation, which might interrupt the fluency of their conversations. If we were to compare these findings with those from an adult interaction corpus we would probably find fewer or possibly different, types of incidences of VL. There certainly is a propositional attitude in some of the utterances, especially in example 4. *movidas raras*, which would be interesting to dig deeper into in future analyses.

In spite of the fact that teenagers are generally considered to use imprecise, vague language and seem unwilling to improve (Eckert 2005), I hope to have shown that this vagueness is a powerful interactive tool, as well as a device that creates an in-group identity. Their special use of the language is not simply a result of laziness.

Notes

[1] The COLA-corpus has three parts: the COLAm (Madrid), COLAba (Buenos Aires) and COLAs (Chile). In this chapter I will talk in general terms about the COLA corpus, but the analysis is realised on the Madrid part: COLAm.
[2] The characteristics of this age group's language are considered to contrast to the standard language.
[3] http://lema.rae.es/drae/ *Movida* in Spanish means move/*s, movement/s*.
[4] Lakoff coined the term "hedge" for a word or phrase that makes a proposition "fuzzy" or vague in some way (1972). A hedge can be categorized either as a "shield" or as an "approximator".
[5] "La base de partida para su estudio ha de ser el acto comunicativo, la conversación de o entre jóvenes: no pueden tomarse los elementos por separado o de manera aislada [...]"

[6] The teenage conversations were recorded with SONY (MZN10) recorders, and the files have been transferred to CDs for transcriptions using the program Transcriber. The variables that have been registered are age, sex and the teenager's social class. The teenagers are treated anonymously, avoiding the personal identification of the recruits. The recordings are an efficient way of recording informal conversations, because the 'observer's paradox' is avoided: "Find out how the people speak when they are not being observed; when it is only through the observation one could get to know it" (Labov 1994).

[7] "Set marking tags" (Dines 1980), "general list completers" (Jefferson 1990), "extension particles" (Dubois 1992) or Vague Category Markers VCM (Evison, McCarthy, and O'Keeffe 2007).

[8] *Las/una(s)movida(s)* has been transformed into an interjective form, expressing admiration: *qué movida*, which I have found only as a reaction to an intervention in the COLAm-corpus.

References

Ambadiang, Théophile, Isabel García Parejo and Azucena Palacios Alcaine. 2009. "Discurso, rutinas comunicativas y construcción de la identidad en situación de contacto dialectal: el caso de los adolescentes ecuatorianos en Madrid." In *Palabras fuera del nido. Vertiente sincrónica y diacrónica del español de contacto dialectal* edited by Julio Calvo Pérez (coord.) and Luis Miranda (coord.), 66−88. Lima: Universidad de San Martín de Porres.

Andersen, Gisle. 2010. "A Contrastive approach to vague nouns." *New Approaches to Hedging* Vol. 9:35−48. DOI: 9789004253247.

Androutsopoulos, Jannis K. 2005. "Research on Youth Language/ Jugendsprachforschung." In S*ociolinguistics/Sozioliguistik: An International Handbook of the Science of Language and Society/ Ein internationales Handbuch zur Wissenschaft von Sprache und Gesellschaft*, edited by Norbert Dittmar Ulrich Ammon, Klaus Mattheier & Peter Trudgill, 1496−1505. Berlin/New York: Mouton de Gruyter.

Antaki, Charles and Sue Widdicombe. 1998. *Identities in talk*. London: Sage.

Auer, Peter. 2007. *Style and Social Identity: Alternative approaches to linguistic heterogeneity*. Berlin: Walter de Gruyter.

Bañon, Antonio Miguel 1993. *El vocativo en español: propuestas para su análisis lingüístico*. Barcelona: Octaedro.

Briz, Antonio. 2003. "La interacción entre jóvenes: Español coloquial, argot y lenguaje juvenil." In *Lexicografía y Lexicología en Europa y América: Homenaje a Günther Hensch*, edited by María Teresa Echenique Elizondo and Juan Pedro Sánchez Méndez, 141−154. Madrid: Gredos.

Brown, Penelope and Stephen Levinson. 1987. *Politeness: Some Universals in Language Usage Studies in Interactional Sociolinguistics*. Cambridge: Cambridge University Press.

Carter, Ronald and Michael Mc Carthy. 2006. *Cambridge grammar of English: a comprehensive guide: spoken and written English grammar and usage*. Cambridge: Cambridge University Press.

Castillo, Gerardo. 2009. *El adolescente y sus retos: La aventura de hacerse mayor, Ojos solares. Desarrollo*. Madrid: Pirámide.

Channell, Janet. 1994. *Vague Language*. Oxford: Oxford University Press.

Cheng, Winnie. 2007. "The use of Vague Language across spoken genres in an intercultural Hong Kong Corpus." In *Vague Language Explored*, 161−181. Oxford: Oxford University Press.

Contreras Romero, Graciela Josefina, Patricia Balcázar Nava, Gloria Margarita Gurrola Peña, and Geovany Miguel González Arce. 2009. "Factores que influyen en la construcción de la identidad en adolescentes." *Revista científica electrónica de psicología* Vol. No 8:107–128.
Coupland, Nikolas. 2008. "The delicate constitution of identity in face-to-face communication: A response to Trudgill." *Language in Society* 37 (2):267–270. DOI: 10.1017/0S0047404508080329.
Crystal, David and Derek Davy. 1975. *Advanced Conversational English (Applied Linguistics and Language Study)* London: Longman.
Cutting, Joan. 2007. *Vague Language Explored*. New York: Palgrave.
Dávila León, Oscar. 2004. "Adolescencia y juventud: de las nociones a los abordajes." *Ultima Década* 21:83–104.
Deese, James. 1974. "Towards a psychological theory of the meaning of sentences." In *Human Communication: Theoretical Explorations*, 67–80. Hillsdale: Lawrence Erlbaum Ass.
Deppermann, Arnulf 2007. "Conversational practices of representing out-group-members among adolescents." *Selves and Identities in Narrative and Discourse*, edited by Michael Bamberg, Anna De Fina and Deborah Schiffrin, 273–301. Amsterdam: Benjamins.
Dines, Elizabeth R. 1980. "And Stuff like That." *Language in Society* 9 (1): 13–31.
Dubois, Sylvie. 1992. "Extension Particles." *Language and Variation Change* 4 (2):179–203.
Duszak, Ana. 2002. *Us and the others*. Amsterdam/New York: Benjamin's Publishing Company.
Eckert, Penelope. 2005. "Stylistic practice and the adolescent social order." In *Talking Adolescence* edited by Peter Thurlow and Angie Williams. New York: Peter Lang.
Eckert, Penelope and Sally McConnell-Ginet. 1992. "Communities of practice: Where language, gender, and power all live." In *Locating Power, Proceedings of the 1992 Berkeley Women and Language Conference*, edited by Kira Hall, Mary Bucholtz and Birch Moonwomon, 11.
—. 1999. "New generalizations and explanations in language and gender research." *Language in Society* Vol. No:185–201.
Eder, Donna. 1988. "Building cohesion through collaborative narration." *Social Psychology Quarterly* Vol. 51:225–235.
Erikson, Erik H. 1992. *Identitet: ungdom og kriser*. København: Reitzel.
Evison, Jane, Michael McCarthy and Anne O'Keeffe. 2007. "Looking out for love and all the rest of it: Vague category markers as shared

social space." In *Vague Language Explored*, edited by Joan Cutting, 138−157. Hampshire: Palgrave.
Garrett, Peter and Angie Williams. 2005. "Adults' perceptions of communication with young people." In *Talking adolescence*, edited by Angie Williams and Crispin Thurlow. New York: Peter Lang.
Georgapoulou, Alexandra. 2005. "Styling men and masculinities: Interactional and identity aspects at work." *Language in Society*, 34 (2):163−184. Vol. 34, No 2 DOI: 10.1017/S0047404505050074.
Gómez Lavín, Carmen. 1996. *Psicología evolutiva. Características psicológicas de las distintas etapas de la vida*: Gómez Lavín, Carmen.
Herrero, Gemma. 2002. "Aspectos sintácticos del lenguaje juvenil." In *El lenguaje de los jóvenes*, edited by Felix Rodríguez, 67−96. Madrid: Ariel Social.
Hofland, Knut, Annette Myre Jørgensen, Eli-Marie Drange and Anna-Brita Stenström. 2005. "COLA: A Spanish spoken corpus of youth language." In *Proceedings from the Corpus Linguistics Conference Series*, edited by University of Birmingham Centre for Corpus Research. Birmingham: Centre for Corpus Research, University of Birmingham.
Hymes, Dell and John J. Gumperz. 1972. *Directions in sociolinguistics: the ethnography of communication*. New York: Holt Rinehart and Winston.
Jefferson, Gail. 1990. "List construction as a task and resource." In *Interaction Competence*, edited by George Psathas, 63-92. Washington, D.C: International Institute for Ethnomethodology and Conversation Analysis: University Press of America.
Jucker, Andreas H., Sara W. Smith and Tanja Lüdge. 2003. "Interactive aspects of vagueness in conversation." *Journal of Pragmatics* 35:1737−1769.
Jørgensen, Annette Myre. 2008. "COLA: Un corpus oral de lenguaje adolescente." In *Discurso y Oralidad. Homenaje al Profesor José Jesús de Bustos Tovar*, edited by A.M. Bañón Hernández L. Cortés Rodríguez, Ma del Mar Espejo Muriel, J. L. Muñío Valverde, 10. Almería: Arco Libros.
—. 2009. "En plan used as a hedge in Spanish teenage language." In *Youngspeak in a Multilingual Perspective*, edited by Anna Brita Stenström and Annette Myre Jørgensen, 95-118. Amsterdam: John Benjamins Publishing Company.
Jørgensen, Annette Myre and Eli-Marie Drange. 2012. "La lengua juvenil de las metrópolis Madrid y Santiago de Chile." *Arena Romanistica* Vol. 9:74−96.

Jørgensen, Annette Myre and Esperanza Eguía Padilla. 2014. "Presentación de COLA, un corpus oral de lenguaje adolescente en línea." XIX Congreso de romanistas escandinavos, Reykjavik.
Jørgensen, Annette Myre and Juan Antonio Martínez. 2010. "Vocatives and phatic communion in Spanish teenage talk." In *Love ya hate ya- The sociolinguistic study of youth language and youth identities*, edited by J. Normann Jørgensen, 193–209. Cambridge: Cambridge Scholars Publishing.
Keefe, Rosanna. 2000. *The phenomenon of vagueness*. Edited by Rosanna Keefe, *Theories of Vagueness*. Cambridge: Cambridge University Press.
Kyburg, Alice and Michael Morreau. 1996. "Vague Utterances and Context Change." *AAAI Technical Report FS-96-04*:92−100.
—. 2000. "Vague Language in Context." *Linguistics and Philosophy* 23 (6):577−597.
Labov, William. 1994. *Principios de cambio lingüístico*. Vol. 77, *Biblioteca Románica Hispánica*. Madrid: Gredos.
Overstreet, Maryann. 2005. "And stuff und so: Investigating pragmatic expressions in English and German." *Journal of Pragmatics* 37:1845−1864.
Overstreet, Maryann E. 1999. *Whales, candlelight, and stuff like that: general extenders in English discourse, Oxford studies in sociolinguistics*. New York: Oxford University Press.
Overstreet, Maryann and George Yule. 2002. "The metapragmatics of and everything." *Journal of Pragmatics* 34 (6):785−794.
Pierce, Charles Sanders. 1902. "Vagueness." In *Dictionary of Philosophy and Psychology II*, edited by M. Baldwin. London: Macmillan.
Russell, Bertrand. 1923. "Vagueness." *Australasian Journal of Philosophy and Psychology* Vol. 1:84−92.
Ruzaité, Jurate. 2007. "Vague Language in Educational Settings. Quantifiers and Approximators in British and American English." *Lodz Papers in Pragmatics* Vol. 3:157−178.
Schuman, Amy. 1986. *Storytelling rights*. Cambridge: Cambridge University Press.
Sperber, Dan and Deirdre Wilson. 1986. *Relevance: Communication and Cognition*. Oxford: Blackwell Publisher.
Stenström, Anna-Brita and Annette Myre Jørgensen. 2008. "La función fática de los apelativos en el habla juvenil de Madrid y Londres. Estudio contrastivo." In *Actas del III Coloquio EDICE*, edited by Antonio Briz, Antonio Hidalgo, Marta Albelda, Josefa Contreras and

Nieves Hernández Flores, 355– 365. Valencia: Universidad de Valencia.
Swales, John. 1998. *Other floors, other voices: a textography of a small university building*: Lawrence Erlbaum Associates.
Terraschke, Agnes. 2007. "Und tralala: Vagueness and general extenders in German and New Zealand English." In *Vague Language Explored*, edited by Joan Cutting. Hampshire: Palgrave.
Thurlow, Crispin. 2005. "Deconstructing adolescent communication." In *Talking Adolescence*, edited by Angie Williams and Peter Thurlow, 1–20. New York: Peter Lang.
Tracy, Karen. 2002. *Everyday talk building and reflecting identities, The Guilford communication series*. New York: Guilford Press.
Ullmann, Stephen. 1962. *The Principles of Semantics—a linguistic approach to meaning*. Oxford: Blackwell.
van Deemter, Kees. 2010. *Not Exactly: In Praise of Vagueness*. Oxford: Oxford University Press.
Williamson, Timothy. 1994. "Vagueness." In *The Encyclopedia of Language and Linguistics*, edited by D. Bolinger and A. McIntosh et al., 4869–4871. Oxford: Pergamon.
Wright, Crispin. 1975. "On the coherence of vague predicates." *Synthese* 30:325–365.
Zhang, Grace. 2011. "Elasticity of vague language." *Intercultural Pragmatics* 8 (4):571–599.
Zimmermann, Klaus. 2002. "La variedad juvenil y la interacción verbal entre jóvenes." In *El lenguaje de los jóvenes*, edited by Félix Rodríguez, 137–161. Barcelona: Ariel.

IDENTITY, PROFESSION AND GENDER

CHAPTER TEN

"IT'S DOABLE": WOMEN'S JOURNEYS TO ACADEMIA IN SOUTH AFRICA AND THEIR SENSE OF SELF

EVA LAMBERTSSON BJÖRK, JUTTA ESCHENBACH, MATHABO KHAU AND LYNETTE WEBB

1. Introduction

Many African communities have a patriarchal gender order which privileges male superiority and female subordination, both in the private and public spheres. Women remain in the background while enabling men to prosper and succeed (Bakare-Yusuf 2003). This creates challenges for them in the public sphere of education and work, and they do not get as far as their male counterparts (Arndt 2002). Many African women may however have access to education and work, but they do not necessarily have the support to see them through because of gender inequalities and stereotyping.

Women all over the world face many challenges when entering academia, and negotiating their places there. They are discriminated against and marginalized because of gender and ethnicity (e.g., Walker 1998; Marbley et al. 2011; Idahosa and Vincent 2014). Women are often seen as the "other" in academia (Acker 1994 in Walker 1998). Due to traditional gender role positions, they also have to juggle family responsibilities with building an academic career (e.g. Acker and Armenti 2004).

Being first generation academics poses a number of additional challenges for women, but little has been written about their particular situation. In the US, Sandra Jones (2004) found that higher education for this group of women meant "a way out" of being oppressed because of class, gender and race. Further higher education meant "a place where [they] belong", a place where they could fulfill their deeply felt wish to work intellectually (74). In South Africa, Grace Idahosa and Louse Vincent (2014) have also explored first generation academic women and their experiences of being marginalized and their negotiation of this marginality, with similar results.

In this chapter, we continue to look at first generation academic women in South Africa. However, we focus on the *journey* they took to academia. Being the first in their families to obtain an academic degree means being the first to accomplish something that may imply a break with traditions–it may entail gains, but simultaneously it may also entail losses. Obviously, it involves changing identities. We interview three women, exploring how they construct their sense of self. We look at how they position themselves and, in turn, are themselves positioned, and we examine how they view themselves in relation to their journey.

In order to understand these women's positioning we turn to Pierre Bourdieu and Judith Butler. Bourdieu's concept of field is useful in explaining social contexts. He compares it to the site of a game with specific rules that specify what is allowed and what is not. In a field, players have different positions, depending on the specific capital at their disposal. Some people have more valued capital, others less (Bourdieu 1993, 72–76). In this chapter, we discuss three types of such capital– economic, social and cultural. Economic capital consists of financial assets. Social capital can be understood as "connections" (ibid., 32), the social networks that people have access to as members of a certain group, and that give them valuable resources for success as players in a particular field (Bourdieu and Wacquant 1992, 119). Cultural capital concerns the consumption and expressions of culture (ibid., 160), and may be explained as "the knowledge and tastes that are transmitted within families and schools, and that mark those who possess them as socially superior to those who do not" (Cheal 2005, 159). Needless to say, access to all three forms of capital will influence any attempt at becoming a successful player in academia.

Butler (2006 [1990]) observes that the construction of identity is performative in that gender is constructed as a "repeated stylization […], a set of repeated acts" (45). This theory comes with a caveat, which is that women have little intentional control over their performances in their lives; this means that the lived experiences of women academics are subjected to the dominant discourses of performing both womanhood and academia. In spite of this, performativity sometimes allows women to err inadvertently, causing gaps in the repetition of gender stylization. With this in mind, we use the notion of performance–one component at play in Butler's idea–to highlight how women's lives are metaphorical stages upon which they perform their gendered scripts. In any stage performance actors in general are subjected to the director's power, but they may also actively influence how they perform and bring to life their given scripts. In performance, actors may actively challenge and resist–even within narrow confines–these scripted performances. For us this means that the women in this study, like stage performers, can make use of gaps in their scripts and thus influence the performance of their gendered and academic identities.[1]

2. The Stories

In May 2015 eight women at a university in the Eastern Cape, South Africa were interviewed to elicit their life stories about their journey to academia. The women were members of the same faculty, but differed in ethnic background and age. For this study, we selected three of the participants who were first generation academics. Clearly, this is not a representative selection for a population. However, we are not looking for representativeness, but for in-depth information.

To this end, we chose life stories. We tell stories to make sense of our lives, Jerome Bruner claims (1990). In stories we try to organize our experiences (ibid., 35); we interpret the events in our lives from a certain perspective and thereby give meaning to them. In narratives we describe what we have done and why; and this description may, or may not, as the case may be, tally with facts (ibid., 119). A life story expresses "our sense of self: who we are and how we got that way" according to Charlotte Linde (1993, 3). Therefore, studying narratives as part of someone's life story yields insights into how this person's sense of self is constructed. Narratives offer "insight into how meaning is made from experience and how identities are constructed –as well as [...] insight into the social and cultural setting within which those experiences arise" (Idahosa and Vincent 2014, 62), since "culture is constitutive for mind"–as Bruner argues (1990, 33).

The participants, whose names are fictitious here, originally came from Lesotho, South Africa and Uganda. They were all black. "Black" is used to indicate a position that has impacted on their lives and their opportunities for education and work. The interviewees' ages ranged from 32 to 57.

The individual, semi-structured interviews were conducted, recorded and transcribed by two of the present authors, and lasted between 25 to 46 minutes. The questions related to the life stories were first about the start of the journey and the interviewees' dreams and hopes for the future as young girls. Second, they were asked about challenges and highlights during the journey, and, finally, about how they viewed their journey from their present vantage point as academics.

3. The Journey

3.1 Point of Departure

The three women, Buhle, Jane and Mpho, come from different ethnic backgrounds. However, their early years were governed by similar structures and rules. They were positioned, and also originally positioned themselves, within the broader framework of *African woman*, as most clearly expressed by Jane:

> living up-country I was bound by the culture (.) of an African woman I knew my life was predestined by my parents I had to do and live the way my parents expected me to

Living up-country as a woman entails performing on a set stage with a predetermined script, she must live the life she is given. The expectations of how one can be a woman in the context of *up-country* determine how a woman performs her womanhood in relation to the script. A woman's identity is *predestined*, be it in a village in Lesotho or Uganda, or in a township in South Africa. As made clear by the overarching category of *African woman*, the predetermination goes beyond ethnic groups. An *African woman* is inevitably steered towards the life of her mother, a life characterized by hard physical work and poverty (see also Arndt 2002).

Poverty also runs through the descriptions of their parents' lives; they lack education, do not have *decent jobs*, and struggle to make ends meet. Buhle says:

> I grew up in a family where both my parents never got matric my mother grade eleven my dad grade ten I think so (.) I had to they didn't have decent jobs they weren't able to provide for us

Getting an education does not seem to be an option for Mpho either as she is left behind with her siblings when her mother runs away from her abusive husband. Her father then directs his abuse towards his children and there is neither will nor means to send her to school. Mpho concludes: "well ehm (.) I don't think if things were left to my father anything would ever have happened in terms of us going to school or even going beyond primary school education."

The three women bear witness to life as repetition. Buhle explains that life is not *progressive*, there is no movement. The chances of breaking the mould are close to non-existent, as they are effectively barred from making their own choices. According to Bourdieu these women are predetermined to remain players in their original fields as described in their narratives. They have little of Bourdieu's traditional capital. They are short on cultural capital as their identity formation is subject to strong cultural norms and fixed gender roles. They all but lack the social networks that would show them how to change the scripts they are performing. Finally, they also have precious little economic capital.

3.2 A Valid Ticket

These women beat the odds–they change and they move, escape routes open up and create gaps in their life scripts (see Butler 2006 [1990]). The gaps give them the opportunity to break the traditional mould of *African woman* and bring new content to the role. Inside themselves they find the agency needed to pursue a different future. This agency is reinforced by the support they receive from others, and as their agency grows, it simultaneously causes the support to increase in a self-reinforcing spiral. Let us have a closer look.

Already as children they dream of a different life. All three imagine "a way out" and the only valid ticket for a journey such as they plan, is education. Their dreams are similar, but also different. Buhle's dreams are initially linked to a collective dream:

> Most of us you know we always like to (.) to help because of our background where we come from you see all the struggles all the difficulties that you experience in terms of finances education so you always want to (.) to make your life better you see you always want to (.) like our role models were mostly doctors because we saw doctors people who were highly educated and you know they have easy access to education they are progressive their lives are moving forward so my aspiration MY dream actually was to become a medical doctor ((…)) as I said earlier it's because of circumstances because I saw people around me who were educated their lives were much better they got better jobs they got everything they wanted so I thought to myself I I don't want to struggle

> I don't want to (.) if I ever have kids I don't want them to go through what I went through with my parents

Buhle establishes a "we-identity", *most of us you know we*, she speaks for her community and she is one with her culture. As the narrative develops, Buhle goes on to link the characteristics of her people–helping others and improving life–to the medical profession. Being a doctor means having a *progressive* life, a life that is not forever moving in circles. *Doctors* have *easy access to education*, and later: *they got better jobs they got everything*. From this Buhle moves on to an individual level, talking about *my aspiration MY dream*–she wants a different life for herself and for her future children. She underlines the strength of her dreams by dissociating herself from her background, repeatedly stating *I don't want*. Her dreams spring from a comparison between life as it is set for her and another life that seems feasible, although only just. Her escape route, she recognizes, is by way of education.

As a young girl, Mpho also dreams of becoming a doctor. However, her dream is of a more individual nature, linked to creating a sorely lacked identity for herself; *back home I was nothing*, she says. Becoming a doctor would mean being seen by others:

> I was brought up to believe that doctors were more important than anyone and I wanted to BE important because I was never made to feel important in any way so I wanted something that would FORce people to see me as (.) someone worth recognizing

Mpho contrasts her background, in which she is unimportant, with the dream of becoming someone important. As a child, she does not know her full worth, but she wants to be recognized as unique; she thus stresses her individual identity more than that of a group.

Jane also dreams of escaping the script of *African woman*, she does not want her mother's life:

> my dreams was NOT to live my mother's life because my mother had made sure that she educates us so that we don't live on the land tilling ( ) the land doing that was hard labour so that was my dream was to work on my education and find a paying job (.) I wasn't ambitious anything of paying job teaching nursing anything would do I could be very comfortable with that as long as I don't go to work on the land (.) so that was my dreams

Her way out is non-specific, *anything of paying job*, she says, *would do*. However, like the others, her escape depends on education.

As instigators of change, dreams may prove ineffectual. These women dream, but more than that, they are agents in their own lives. In their narratives, they constantly return to their own agency. They present themselves as acting, seizing every opportunity to make something new out of their lives. Jane says:

> I knew the power of working hard academically can change and can add to my life and I GRABBED the bull by its horn and I said I'm going to STUDY come what may (.) that's my early my young time

Buhle, Mpho and Jane aim to enter a new stage and become players in a more rewarding field. They are intelligent and very hard-working. They dedicate themselves to their studies, often late at night when the rest of the family is asleep and there is blessed silence. Jane tells the following story:

> my grand-father used to come and I remember when he asked me Jane is your father buying paraffin for you for your for you to burn midnight oil and I said <<in a voice of fond remembrance> yes he does and he asked me again are you burning midnight oil and I said (.) grand-pa I am and I passed>

Buhle further explains that in addition to hard work, the desired change also entails being different and being seen as different. Her ambitions and her love of reading prevent her from socializing, an important value in her culture:

> I thought to myself let me just push myself in in the side of education and see where that takes me (.) because at home I'm the only one who actually has matric to even come to university (.) is highest level see (.) so that's why I thought () continue with schooling and I always I grew up loving to read and I wasn't much of a socializing person so I was always at home I was sort of like a bookworm ((...)) you know in in our culture when you are seen as this child who who is like NOT very sociable who's always at home you go to school you go to church or stay at home in our African culture we are used to visiting neighbours sitting all day talking and doing whatever I was not very much into that so because of that I got a lot of (.) comments because <<mimicking the neighbours> you know she thinks she is better>

She presents herself as different and *NOT very sociable*, as a *bookworm*. Her cultural background would entail *visiting neighbours sitting all day talking and doing whatever*, but this clashes with her personal values.

Buhle underlines her deviance by repeating others' positioning of her as different; *she thinks she is better*. This evaluative comment highlights her dilemma. Buhle has found her escape route in education, but because she escapes, she is considered a traitor of her own culture.

All interviewees position themselves as deviant. Jane and Mpho are different from other children in terms of school performance. Jane says: *my mother liked the way I was performing because I was doing well compared to other children*, and Mpho: *I was the teacher's pet ((...)) and I liked the way she made me feel special in front of all the others*. So, while all three position themselves as different, it is only Buhle who presents herself as socially inept in the eyes of others. However, she is also the only one who refers to a social group other than parents/teachers.

Intelligence and agency make it possible for them to make use of the gaps that become available. However, they also receive a lot of support from others who recognize their qualities. Such support includes, for example, general motivation and positive attitudes, concrete help providing time and space in which to study, and financial contributions. Their developing identities are positively reinforced by family members as well as by official agencies, in the form of bursaries.

Their parents do their best to contribute, but their financial resources are very limited. Mpho's mother is a housemaid and earns little, but *she was very supportive with her little means*. Jane's parents have to sell *seven goats to dress* her. The financial limitations are also made clear by Buhle:

> they [parents] would give me they would support me whenever they can but they couldn't pay for my tuition but my transportation they made sure that I had clothes to wear at school they couldn't buy my books or pay for my tuition

School fees present an enormous challenge, and Mpho, for one, has to trust in her teachers for support:

> So the teachers in my school you know they would have they would have in the morning during assembly they would have this list to call out those who have not paid fees ((...)) and then everyone knows that you haven't paid and then we would be told that we should pack our bags and go then I would go to my class-room pick up my bag <<whispers> am I ( ) to go out and I remember (once) there was a teacher came and said no you are not going anywhere> and I said but I haven't paid my fees she said my classroom would be barren without you let's go to the staff room, I'll pay for you and she paid so that is what happened almost all the time

Her teacher recognizes her young student's potential and comes to her rescue. This is a reaction that Mpho seems to elicit throughout her schooling, it *happened almost all the time*. Although financing schooling remains a constant struggle, support also comes in other forms, such as the provision of time and space for daughters to study. Jane explains that her mother *would say you don't do anything all you do is to study so the cooking cleaning the house going to the fields to dig that was other people she said I want you to study*. There is also positive support in form of recognition from neighbours as Mpho says: *they'd encourage me and sometimes they'd even call me teacher even though I was not a teacher then*.

Through supportive families, teachers and, in some instances, neighbours, the women collect capital. Their social networks, although a far cry from the powerful networks necessary for movement according to Bourdieu, make it possible for them to secure a valid ticket for their journey towards academia.

Additional support comes in the form of their early experience of how they may profit from going to school and working hard. For Jane it means to gain a new identity:

> I cried I said I want to study so they [parents] accepted to take me to boarding school they had sold SEVEN goats to dress me it was my first time to buy shoes when (during my time up there in) going to school barefeeted was normal absolutely normal for a child so it was after primary seven going to S one it was my first time to buy a towel for myself new clothes new shoes because I was going to a boarding school I was a new girl and <<in a voice of wonder and pride> THAT changed MY CHANGED my outlook and I said working hard is very very nice>

Jane is sent off to boarding school with new clothes, ready to explore a new world. The singularity of this situation is underlined by Jane's choice of words. She repeats *my first time*; the reflexive pronoun *myself* in *a towel for myself* emphasizes how she is singled out from the collective group, and she repeats the word *new-new clothes new shoes*. The repetition culminates in her overall conclusion *I was a new girl*. Jane experiences how education may result in high, tangible profits, not only in terms of a new identity, but also in terms of future expectations, it *CHANGED my outlook*. Immediate, concrete rewards, such as new clothes, change her position. She realizes that it is possible for her to shape her own life.

For Mpho the profit is even higher, for the very first time she has an identity:

> the neighbours were very supportive because I remember times when they would tell their children to go to my house for me to help them with their homework ( ) and for that they would give us whatever they had food clothes anything that they could give yea so it was like actually earning ((laughing)) so on that I think they they could see that this it sparked something I don't know and they were very supportive and they'd encourage me and sometimes they'd even call me teacher even though I was not a teacher then ((...)) it was the one place where I felt really alive because apart from THAT going back home I was nothing but out there I was someone yes so I loved that I enjoyed it all the time

The neighbours give Mpho payment in kind, and limited as it is, it is still *like actually earning*. Further they boost her confidence through their positive attitudes. They call her teacher, and she is recognized. The contrasts between her two worlds are made clear, at home she does not exist, is *nothing*, but *out there* she is *someone* and *alive*.

3.3 The Journey

Buhle, Jane and Mpho now have their tickets for their journey towards academia. They meet many hindrances. They all three testify that lack of funding is a major issue in their lives. Buhle and Mpho never know when and if they will receive their next grant, and for Buhle there are occasions when she has to abandon her studies as there simply is no money. There are also financial obligations that must be met when it comes to supporting family members. Further, there is the challenge of being the first women in their families to embark on such a journey, and they have no one to show them the way. Mpho says*: I had to find out everything for myself and apply I did everything for myself in terms of finding a scholarship applying getting a placement at university.*

In addition, Mpho stresses her struggle against "traditional" expectations of the predetermined identity of *African woman* and her traditional role as a spouse:

> after I got my first degree I got married and the man I was married to at that time when I got my first degree he had a diploma in electrical engineering and well while we were dating it was fine then we got married and his mother started telling him that his married woman was more educated than him and therefore she will not respect him because she will bring more money into the house so I think the only thing that my husband

was left with was to be violent and to be a womanizer ((...)) so within a year and a half of marriage we were divorced and I had a daughter out of that marriage and after that I had a series of problems in my career

Her mother-in-law argues that Mpho, as the major breadwinner, will be unable to show her husband proper respect. Higher education and an income to match cannot be combined with the role of being a good wife. Mpho's husband struggles with his identity as his position is threatened, and resorts to violence and extra-marital affairs. The break-up of the marriage leads to *a series of problems in her career*. As a divorcée and single mother she falls short of fulfilling the expectations of a Catholic wife and mother. However, when refused a position in a school on account of her private life, she objects to the limiting script that others have dictated. She contests the school's decision and, as she says, *I won it and they gave me the position anyway*. Again her agency and tenacity serve her well on the journey.

However, in spite of all the obstacles, the women also talk about a joyful journey. Having changed the script of *African woman* fills them with pride. Buhle sums up her academic journey at this point in her life, referring to her graduation:

> Yea it was very nice yea it's a nice feeling (.) especially as much as it was difficult it was a nice feeling for my parents as well (.) because I was their first child to even come to university let alone to graduate so they were very proud and also to show others that it's doable you can do it with hard work you can (.) get to where you want to be

She sums up what kind of person she is now, and how she became that person. The extraordinariness of the journey that she has managed is underlined by her parents' recognition. Buhle is the very first in the family to achieve an academic degree. Her life narrative serves as an example illustrating that in spite her lack of traditional capital it is still possible to construct a new reality. Through using the gaps that occur it is possible to change status, and, in fact, the entire script.

Mpho also tells the story of her graduation, a story that accentuates her as a unique human being and gives her the recognition she dreamed of as a young girl:

> I had gotten a summa cum laude and I was the only one and I was a black student and no one thought a black woman student would pass not cum laude but summa yea so when I walked across the stage everyone stood up in the audience and it was very significant because when I graduated for

> my Honours no one from my family was there so everyone else in the audience and in the academic procession became my family because all of them like WOOOH all of them at the same time

Her achievements are listed in increasingly superlative terms as her story develops and escalates: *summa cum laude–the only one–a black student– no one thought a black woman student would pass* summa cum laude. Her uniqueness is underlined by including the categories of race and gender. It all ends up in the jubilant conclusion: *so this is how you do things for yourself YES*. Like Buhle, Mpho presents her story as an example for others and she stresses the aspect of agency. She enters a new stage, with a new script, quite different from the original script of *African woman*. The same goes for Jane. Her hard work gives her the opportunity to work in the USA, she manages to rewrite the script and enter a stage that is far from *up-country rural*.

3.4 Looking Back on the Journey

The three women's identities have continued developing with their changing lives, and they are no longer the girls who once set out for academia, escaping the preset script for *African woman*. From their present vantage point they are able to reflect on their journey's losses and gains.

Regrets and losses come in different shapes and hues. Buhle returns to her failed dream of becoming a medical doctor, she imagines an alternative life story where she would have been practicing by now:

> I wish that year when I finished my degree my my BSc degree I could've gone straight to the medical school I would've been finished by now (.) I would be practicing now as a doctor but because I saw what was happening THERE (.) in front of me I thought no I didn't think of the future I just thought no let me just now thinking about it and thinking maybe I should have

She reflects on why things turned out as they did, *I saw what was THERE (.) happening in front of me*. She had to contribute to supporting her family and was forced to abandon her studies temporarily. In retrospect, she also criticizes her young self for not planning ahead. She explains how her dream was lost because of external financial factors, and because of her own character traits.

Jane also imagines a different life story. She wishes that she had set herself higher goals from the beginning. She was, for a long time, content with being a school-teacher because:

> I was no longer going to work as an upcountry girl ((…)) I did not add on anything I was not a life-long learner I was relaxed I was comfortable in myself and I could have added I could have made additional choices of being a life-long learner so those are some of the differences I would have made at that time and I would have done my master's at a much younger age ((…)) but after getting the master's then I realized oh this is what I should've done a long time ago and those are some of the stupid mistakes that I made ((…)) I would have done even a PhD and what have you but time look simply I woke up late

Jane berates herself for being sedate and for lacking ambition, regretting the late start that she got. While Buhle and Jane lament academic routes not taken, Mpho comments on having to fight to maintain her hard-earned identity. She explains that she was forced to develop *not only a tough shell but also a very tough interior* to

> face the rest of the world that was looking at me raising a daughter on my own and being a divorced Catholic CHILD which Catholic divorces they don't divorce so I was the bad child and studying in South Africa as a black person is HELL it is HELL and being a black person of non-South African origin is twice that and being a black person of non-South African origin and a woman is three times that so I had to be able to bear all that

Mpho positions herself as alone against *the rest of the world*. The Catholic Church judges her as lapsed and worse. Academia offers rampant racism, xenophobia and prejudice. As she is black, a foreigner and a woman to boot, her identity is predetermined by others. Her white lecturer makes her feel as if she were *a nasty piece of something that he doesn't want to see in his lecture hall* […] *you don't belong*, she says. Not being a natural player in the academic field, Mpho is certainly not made welcome:

> I managed to do my PhD in two years (.) it was examined in two years and passed but they refused for me to graduate (.) they said who can do a PhD in two years only Indian people only Indian people can do a PhD in two years who is she? ah that one from Lesotho should wait for graduation next year

There have certainly been both regrets and losses during the journey. However, these women have found a different way of performing being *African woman*. Buhle has succeeded in building a supportive academic network where she is involved in community research projects. In

Bourdieu's wording, she has acquired the necessary social capital and become a player in a field originally closed to her. She positions herself as different from her siblings, her life has changed:

> now I've got a family am married I own my own house at least things are getting better every day I've two kids now I have a three year old and a eight month old (.) a girl and a boy and (.) we manage with my husband to get at least a decent house in one of the suburbs around of [city] so at least life is slowly is is progressive is progressive much better we've achieved a LOT in comparison to our siblings because I'm the first one ((…)) to own a house they are still staying with my parents all my other siblings are still staying at home and I'm the only one to own a house to own a car the first one you see so at least things are are progressive

She is the first in her family who has managed to change the script and enter a new stage. Buhle represents the first generation to be able to offer her children, both daughter and son, a life different from her own. It will be *progressive*, just as she once considered doctors' lives to be.

Jane is also happy to have been able to rewrite her childhood script:

> I feel the biggest thing I've gained is THAT freedom to make my personal choices I'm no longer that little girl who thought my parents (.) determined my destiny now I'm an adult independently who makes my personal choices and who lives by their choices and I feel I'm an independent individual and I feel absolutely happy in myself because (.) that is now my focus remaining with two years to retirement I'm beginning to think of writing a book about my life story that could benefit those young children who are growing up who may feel that there's something they can learn from reading my own life story I feel convinced that I have a story to share

She underlines how she has dodged a life that was culturally predetermined. She has managed to make her own *personal choices*. She has managed to break with the values and norms that she, as *African woman*, is supposed to abide by, and replaced them with values such as freedom and independence. Jane has created her own identity and now performs being *African woman* outside the set script. She is happy with the woman she has become, and concludes *I feel absolutely happy in myself*. Her happiness even manifests itself in her wish to share her story for the benefit of others.

Finally then, Mpho regrets the struggles she had to go through in shaping her identity during the journey. However, after all the hardships, she has gradually gained a new identity. This is an identity that she loves:

I'm strong I think I've gained a stronger fighting spirit I can fight anything anyone anyhow and (.) I think I've become a better person and a better academic because of all these KNOCKS and BUMPS and things along the way yeah so I think it was necessary because I love the person that I am today

4. Having Reached the Destination

The three women, Buhle, Jane and Mpho, break free from the fixed gendered script of *African woman*, and its repetitive patterns. In spite of initially lacking any capital in the traditional sense, they seize the opportunities, the gaps, that open up for them and they use them. This is made possible by their eliciting both social and financial support through their extraordinary character traits.

In their life stories about the journey towards academia, they position themselves, and are positioned, as different from others. In this vying for positions, they are able to construct a new sense of self. Their journeys have given them the possibility to perform the role of *African woman* in a new way.

Notes

[1] We thank Dr. Johanna Wagner, Østfold University College, for many fruitful discussions about Judith Butler.

References

Acker, Sandra and Carmen Armenti. 2004. "Sleepless in academia." *Gender and Education*, Vol: 16, No. 1: 3–24.

Arndt, Susan. 2002. *The dynamics of African feminism: Defining and classifying African feminist literatures*. Trenton, NJ: Africa World Press, Inc.

Bakare-Yusuf, Bibi. 2003. "Determinism: The phenomenology of African female existence." *Feminist Africa*, Vol: 2, http://www.agi.ac.za/sites/default/files/image_tool/images/429/feminist_africa_journals/archive/02/fa_2_feature_article_1.pdf [Accessed 27.02.2019].

Bourdieu, Pierre. 1993 [1984]. *Sociology in Question*. Translated from the French by Richard Nice. London: Sage.

Bourdieu, Pierre and Loïc J. D. Wacquant. 1992. *An Invitation to Reflexive Sociology*. Cambridge: Polity Press.

Bruner, Jerome. 1990. *Acts of Meaning*. Cambridge, Massachusetts: Harvard University Press.

Butler, Judith. 2006 [1990]. *Gender Trouble. Feminism and the Subversion of Identity*. New York, London: Routledge.

Cheal, David. 2005. *Dimensions of social theory*. Basingstoke: Palgrave Macmillan.

Idahosa, Grace and Louise Vincent. 2014. "Losing, using, refusing, cruising: First-generation South African women academics narrate the complexity of marginality". *Agenda*, Vol: 28, No. 1: 59–71.

Jones, Sandra J. 2004. "A Place Where I Belong: Working-Class Women's Pursuit of Higher Education." *Race, Gender & Class*, Vol: 11, No. 3: 74–93.

Linde, Charlotte. 1993. *Life Stories. The Creation of Coherence*. New York: Oxford University Press.

Marbley, Aretha Faye, Aliza Wong, Sheryl L. Santos-Hatchett, Comfort Pratt and Lahib Jaddo. 2011. "Women faculty of color: voices, gender, and the expression of our multiple identities within academia." *Advancing Women in Leadership*, Vol: 31: 166–174.

Walker, Melanie. 1998. "Academic identities: women on a South African landscape." *British Journal of Sociology of Education*, Vol: 19, No. 3: 335–354.

Appendix

Transcription Conventions

(.)	pause
ACcent	main accent
?	pitch rising
((nodding))	non-verbal actions
<<surprised> >	interpreting comments indicating length
( )	unintelligible passage
(such)	presumed wording
((…))	omissions in transcript

CHAPTER ELEVEN

FICTION AS THE "FIRST LABORATORY OF MORAL JUDGMENT": PRE-SERVICE TEACHERS AND THE DEVELOPMENT OF A PROFESSIONAL IDENTITY

KAREN PATRICK KNUTSEN

Narratives and Professional Identity

The majority of pre-service teachers in Norway start their studies directly after completing upper-secondary school when they are approximately 19 or 20 years old, and can thus be categorized as young adults. Most of them, however, will still be in the process of negotiating their own adult identities, even though they are no longer adolescents. This becomes more complicated when they begin developing their professional identities as teachers,[1] responsible for guiding children and adolescents in increasingly multicultural classrooms. Multicultural literature can be a gateway to raising these pre-service teachers' awareness of their own personal identities and values while helping them build their professional identities.[2] This in turn can help them to implement the goals of the Norwegian National curriculum (LK 06) in their future classrooms.

The core curriculum lays the ethical foundation of education in Norway, as established by the Ministry of Education and Training, and mandated in educational law. The curriculum acknowledges that the school system comprises many pupils from minority cultures and languages in Norway and states that education should thus convey knowledge about other cultures and show how we can take advantage of the potential they represent. The curriculum states that "Knowledge of other peoples gives us the chance to test our own values and the values of others" (Norway

2011). This is important because the goals of the core curriculum are very ambitious in this respect:

> Education should counteract prejudice and discrimination, and foster mutual respect and tolerance between groups with differing modes of life. Education should provide training in cooperation between persons of different capacities and groups with diverse cultures. But it must also expose the conflicts that can arise in encounters between different cultures. Intellectual freedom implies not only allowance for other points of view, but also courage to take a stand, confidence to stand alone, and the strength of character to think and act according to one's own convictions. Tolerance is not the same as detachment and indifference. Education should develop resolve to assert one's rights and those of others, and to stand up against their violation. (ibid.)

Obviously, knowledge of other peoples and cultures is important. But students must also be aware of their own values if they are to test them in intercultural encounters. The goals of the curriculum apply to all the subjects taught. As an educator responsible for preparing students as ESL (English as a Second Language) teachers in Norway, I am concerned with how we can straddle the division between raising the students' consciousness of their own values and personal identities while simultaneously equipping them with methods or tools that can help them to meet these core curricular goals in their future English classrooms. Both are constitutive of their professional identities as teachers.

English literature has a natural place in teacher education, providing authentic input for language learning and information about English-speaking cultures. Literature often thematizes ethical decisions and moral dilemmas. In this connection, the philosopher Paul Ricoeur argues that narrative in itself contributes to the constitution of the self (1994, 114). For Ricoeur, "Literature is a vast laboratory in which we experiment with estimations, evaluations, and judgments of approval and condemnation through which narrativity serves as a propaedeutic to ethics" (ibid., 115). He maintains that we come to grips with our own identities by creating our own life stories, inspired by literature and drawing on literary elements:

> Following the intuitive preunderstanding we have of these things, do we not consider human lives to be more readable when they have been interpreted in terms of the stories that people tell about them? And are not these life stories in turn made more intelligible when the narrative models of plots–borrowed from history or from fiction (drama or novel)–are applied to them? It therefore seems plausible to take the following chain of assertions as valid: self-understanding is an interpretation; interpretation of

the self, in turn, finds in the narrative, among other signs and symbols, a privileged form of mediation; the latter borrows from history as well as from fiction, making a life story a fictional history or, if one prefers, a historical fiction, interweaving the historiographic style of biographies with the novelistic style of imaginary biographies. (ibid., 114, footnote 1)

Reading fiction allows us to reflect on our own values as we follow the characters and plots. For Ricoeur narrative is never ethically neutral and it functions as the first *laboratory of moral judgment* (ibid., 140, my emphasis).

The pleasure we take in following the fate of the characters implies, to be sure, that we suspend all real moral judgment at the same time that we suspend action itself. But in the unreal sphere of fiction we never tire of exploring new ways of evaluating actions and characters. The thought experiments we conduct in the great laboratory of the imaginary are also explorations in the realm of good and evil. Transvaluing, even devaluing, is still evaluating. Moral judgment has not been abolished; it is rather itself subjected to the imaginative variations proper to fiction. (ibid., 164)[3]

In this chapter, I explore the potential of and problems involved in using multicultural literature as a laboratory of moral judgment in ESL classes. Can reading multicultural young adult literature in English help pre-service teachers develop a deeper understanding of themselves and different others, augmenting their professional identities? Can the appreciation of diversity gained in such reading in turn be implemented by these teachers in the classroom?

In an attempt to answer these questions, I have collected and analyzed reading logs based on Anglo-Indian writer Bali Rai's young adult novel *(Un)arranged Marriage* (2001),[4] written by students from four cohorts of pre-service teacher trainees studying during the period between 2012 and 2015 at a small university college in Norway. The reading logs are based on an assignment focusing on different ways of using literature in the classroom. We were exploring the theme of multiculturalism and how teachers could use multicultural literature to work with this topic. The students had first carried out a traditional literary analysis of a different novel. I now wanted them to focus on reader-response methodology by writing a reading log, where they could voice their own opinions and associations more freely than in a conventional literary analysis.[5] In the following, I give a brief synopsis of the novel before describing the writing assignment and the student groups. Finally, I discuss my analysis of the students' writing logs, relating them to Ricoeur's theories on narrative and identity.

Synopsis of *(Un)arranged Marriage*

Bali Rai's debut novel *(Un)arranged Marriage* was published in 2001 to great acclaim. It tells the story of Manjit, whose parents have immigrated to England from the Punjab province in India. Manjit, or Manny, as he prefers to be called, was born in England and has never visited India. He has four older siblings, all of whom have accepted arranged marriages with partners with an Indian background, in accordance with their parents' wishes. When the novel opens, Manjit is thirteen, and his brother Harry is soon to be married. In this connection, Manny learns that his father is also planning to marry him off, according to the Punjabi tradition, at age seventeen. This comes as a shock, as he has his own goals for the future: getting a university education and choosing his own mate. None of his plans include following Punjabi family traditions, which he rejects in favor of the culture and values of the British society he has grown up in. With only four years to go, Manny concocts a plan, his "cheat", aiming to sabotage his parents' plan by making himself unattractive as a marriage partner.

The novel takes up a number of issues that have to do with growing up between two cultures. This is relevant for teachers in Norway who will have the responsibility of teaching many pupils with non-Norwegian backgrounds, whether the latter are first generation immigrants or the children or grandchildren of immigrants from other cultures. Manny is growing up as part of an ethnic minority in England, but as a second-generation Anglo-Indian he has also been better integrated into the local community and culture than his parents and perhaps his older siblings as well. The individualistic culture and values of the Western world are contrasted with the collective, family-centered cultures of Asia, illustrating the gap that Manny and children like him have to straddle. Religious differences, discrimination and cultural clashes both within and between ethnic groups shape his life. Manny's father, for example, despises many of the cultural aspects of his adopted country Britain, seeing whites, or "Gorah" and all other races than the Indian as immoral or inferior. He disapproves of both Manny's white and black friends.

In addition to growing up between two cultures, Manny shares most of the problems and temptations that other teenagers face in their daily lives:

drug abuse, school truancy, shoplifting, peer pressure, and negotiating his adult identity. Teen rebellion and family conflicts are staple subjects in young adult novels, as are alienation, first love and sexual relationships.[6] Manny also has to cope with his father's alcoholism, which often leads to violence and psychological abuse.

The book is divided into four parts and an epilogue. In the first, we are filled in on the family situation and follow Manny at school and with his friends and classmates. In part two, as part of his cheat, Manny's behavior deteriorates. He is skipping school with the result that his grades are falling. He and his friend Ady shoplift, drink, use drugs and get in trouble with the police. His behavior gets him expelled from school. He is truly making himself undesirable as a future husband, but also spoiling his own prospects of getting a higher education and securing his future.

In part three, the family decide to travel to Punjab to visit relatives, and they trick their rebellious son, leaving him behind with the extended family hoping that he will finally agree to the marriage they have planned for him. With the help of an unconventional uncle, Manny returns to Britain, only to be beaten by his father.

In the penultimate section of the book, Manny appears to have given in. He works at a supermarket, goes to pubs with his father and brothers, and even meets his bride-to-be and her family. However, he plans to punish his family by escaping from the three-day wedding celebrations at the last minute, and carries out this plan with Ady's help.

In the epilogue, the protagonist, now 19, looks back on his actions. He was forced to make a complete break with his family. He has destroyed their honor–and he is "dead" to them. Manny now lives with the parents of his ex-girlfriend, Lisa, while he works and completes his school certificate. He does not regret his decision to break with his family, but he does feel badly about how he treated his bride-to-be and her family. He also feels that he has been immature in terms of considering his own heritage as a Punjabi and a Sikh. He is learning about Sikh traditions and admits:

> I confused all the hate that I felt for my family and their stupid traditions with being a Sikh or being a Punjabi. It was all one big whole to me, maybe because I was too young to see the difference. (Rai 2001, 269–270)

Participants in the Study

Year	F	M	Nor.	Non-Nor.	1 - 7	5-10
2012 (22)	14	9	15	4	3	19
2013 (20)	11	9	14	2	4	16
2014 (24)	14	10	14	3	7	17
2015 (20)	19	8	19	1	6	14
Total 86	58	36	62	10	20	66

Figure 1: A total of 86 students wrote reading logs and consented in having them used for research purposes. Of these, 58 were female, 36 were male. The majority (62) were ethnically Norwegian, whereas 10 had assorted other heritages (marked as "Non-Nor."). 20 of the students were specializing as teachers for grades 1-7; the remaining 66 were specializing for grades 5-10.

The students specializing for grades 1-7 were third year students, whereas the 5-10 students were in their second year of the four-year teacher education program. The participants' median age was 20, with a smaller number (5) of mature students (35 years and older). The sample used can be described as a sample of convenience, as I had access to them through a 15 credit (ECTS) course in British Civilization and Literature that I taught each fall. The students have all attended the same course and university college and completed an identical assignment. The sample size, however, suggests that the reading logs give a representative picture of how reading literature can affect pre-service teachers in terms of understanding their own values and their professional development.

The Reading-log Assignment

The assignment asks students to try out a literary didactic method in their work with *(Un)arranged Marriage*. The main aim of writing a reading log was to document their thoughts and feelings in the encounter with the text. The log was to be handed in as an obligatory assignment, and it was also used in class; students read and discussed their draft logs in groups. I asked those who were willing to let me use their anonymized logs in my research to sign a consent form. All of the students agreed.

Students were given the box of suggestions below, containing elements they might include in their logs. They were asked to structure the logs with four entries, one for each major part of the book. In addition I asked them to write a brief reflection on the reading log method. I noted that I was not primarily concerned with their language or the structure of their entries. It was the responses that were important rather than correct grammar or cohesion; and here, all quotations from the reading logs are unedited. They did not have to use all the suggestions in each entry, but could choose freely. Many of the students commented that this way of working with literature was new to them; they felt rather uncertain about whether they were doing the assignment "correctly". As one student writes: "I used some time to find out how to organize my reading log and I am still not sure if the way I did it is the best" (9 12 F N).

Reading Log

While you are reading the book write down all the things that go on in your head in a "stream of consciousness" style. As you read, you will be making a record of images, associations, feelings, thoughts, judgments, etc. You will probably find that this record will contain:

Questions that you ask yourself about characters and events as you read. (Answer these yourself when you can).
Memories from your own experience provoked by the reading.
Guesses about how you think the story will develop, and why.
Reflections on striking moments and ideas in the book.
Comparisons between how you behave and how the characters in the novel are behaving.
Thoughts and feelings about characters and events.
Comments on how the story is being told. For example, any words or phrases or even whole passages that make an impression on you, or motifs which you notice the author keeps using.
Connections to other texts, ideas and courses.
An outline of the chapter [or section], no longer than a paragraph.

Please date each entry, and note down the time and place, as well as the mood you are in while reading. Please note down the page number you are reading when you make an entry. Please take pleasure and pride in your log. *Please do not try to rewrite the book.*

Figure 2: From: Anthony Carlisle. "Reading Logs: An Application of Reader Response Theory in ELT." *ELT Journal,* Vol. 54, No.1, 2000: 14.

Results and Discussion

During my first reading of the logs, I saw that students, as expected, tended to combine simple plot summary with their personal reactions to the story.[7] The assignment itself opens for this type of response, encouraging students to make text-to-world and text-to-self connections. To systematize the logs, I created a matrix divided into four columns, categorizing comments connected to 1) their future profession, 2) moral judgements, 3) their own experiences and identity, and 4) considerations of the reading log as a teaching method.

A closer reading of the logs revealed that all but three of the 86 students (two from 2012 and one from 2013) make comments which may be construed as moral judgements about the characters or events in the story; these comments comprise the longest column in the matrix, revealing a lot about the values and beliefs of the log-writers themselves. Comments which contain moral judgments, tend to cluster around particular themes or topics which I sub-categorize as follows: dysfunctional families, arranged marriages, the importance of education, Manjit's "cheat", and racism/the tolerance of difference. Below I present findings which demonstrate that the readers have indeed used the text as a laboratory of moral judgement.[8]

Dysfunctional Families

Of the 86 students, 29 comment on the physical and psychological abuse that Manjit is subjected to in his family. One student writes:

> I have read about children being [physically] abused like this many times, but to actually read it in a novel where you get to 'witness' everything that is going through someone's mind makes me feel very privileged to come from a society where that is not acceptable. (13 15 F N)

Another writes:

> This violent way of raising a child is so far away from my perspective, and how I have been raised myself, and that is probably why I am just filled with anger and sadness, feeling that Manny deserves so much more. (17 15 F N)

Many of these respondents say that reading about the abuse made them feel sick: "Dear God, isn't his father a human being? Can't he see the pain in his son's eyes?" (19 12 F NN). Another student writes that

> Manny's father is a poor excuse for a human being. He is an abusive, racist man who clearly has a problem with alcohol. [...] I want to jump into the book and give that man a proper beating and, pardon my French, get his sorry ass thrown in jail. [...] Not what you would call great parenting. (22 12 F N)

Other comments discuss family dynamics and parenting in the novel. Twenty-five students feel provoked by the family relationships described in the novel where bullying and hatred predominate in relations between siblings and between parents and children. As one student puts it,

> Home is where your support should be. His parents should guide him in some direction. They don't do that [...] They don't understand that he is torn between two cultures and trying to find himself in the middle. (19 15 F N)

Ten students add that they are especially disappointed by the behavior of Manny's mother.

> I really do not like Manny's mother. She seems cold. The only thing she does is to make him feel bad about himself. In my opinion, that is not what a mother should do. (11 12 F N)

Another is more adamant in condemning the mother's behavior:

> I feel so much rage and disgust for those who stand by and watch their children being hit by their fathers or anybody else. I can understand that Manny's mother is chained by both the fear of her husband and by the idea that the man is the head of the house. But her mother's instinct, the mother lion inside her, should be outraged and put a final stop to his abuse. [...] I am a mother to a 3-year-old boy and I will stop at nothing to protect my child. I would never let something like tradition stand in my way, which is exactly what she is doing. (22 12 F N)

These comments reveal the students' beliefs about the nurturing and protective role of parents, and mothers in particular, in their own society.

Twenty-two students find the parents' behavior deplorable in leaving Manjit behind in India to teach him to be more obedient and to accept the marriage his father has planned for him. "It is totally absurd to me that someone would just leave their child, but so is the concept that beating up your child is acceptable" one student writes (14 12 M N). Another notes:

> When Manny's family leaves him in India, I actually felt sick to my stomach. This is in my head considered child abuse and was a sad part to read through. […] I think it's a little funny how Manny's father always talks about keeping the family together and holding the 'pure' traditions strong, when he drinks heavily, beats his son and leaves him in India. He acts as the complete opposite of his own words and is a morally appalling figure in my opinion. (20 12 M N)

Ten students remark on the fact that Manjit's family seems to care more about family honor than about the welfare of their own children: "Personally, I find it difficult to understand how pride, status and reputation can be valued more than a son or a daughter", one student remarks (17 15 F N). This student goes on to reflect "But again, I have completely different perspectives in life, growing up in a different culture, religion, traditions and values" (ibid.), demonstrating an awareness of her own ethnocentricity.

Arranged Marriages

Obviously, the tradition of arranged marriages is the center of conflict in the novel and the catalyst for the events. Twenty-five students condemn the tradition outright:

> I can't imagine being told by my own father who I was supposed to marry! And at the age of 17!! I'm disgusted. This is for me an ancient tradition that does not belong in the 21st century. (22 12 F N)

Another student is also very negative, but seems to develop her thinking about the matter as she continues reading.

> I think I would have considered murder if my parents had tried to force me into marrying someone. Whether it would have been my murder or theirs, I am honestly not sure. I do know that arranged marriages always have been a part of some cultures, even my own a few centuries back, but I just cannot imagine being forced to do something against my will. 'Married off' is too nice a description. Sold is more like it. (11 14 F N)

Later this student remarks: "If both parties are willing, who am I to condemn arranged marriage? There is a difference between arranged and forced marriage" (ibid.). Three students react to the fact that planned marriages could be return favors to family acquaintances or that marriages are contracted to acquire citizenship in Britain for relatives or friends living in India.

Three readers comment on the novelty of getting the male perspective on arranged marriage and write that they previously had thought of this cultural tradition as mainly affecting girls. A male student notes:

> We hear all the time stories about young girls forced into marriage, but we rarely hear about the boys. I honestly must say that this bothers me, and I think Bali Rai made me realize that. (22 14 M N)

In connection with the tradition of arranged marriages, five students comment on the custom of the women moving in with their in-laws, as Manjit's older sisters and sisters-in-law have done. "I think it's strange how they just lose contact with his sisters because they have to live with their husbands' families" (6 15 F N). Others find the idea of living in an extended family claustrophobic and stress the importance of having your own space and privacy, even if you do get along with your in-laws. Ten students comment on the importance of individual choice in terms of marriage partners, but also in relation to other life-determining situations.

Another aspect of arranged marriages that is condemned is the young age of the couple. Eight students believe that teenagers are children themselves and are not ready to take on the responsibilities of marriage and parenthood. In this connection, six students also condemn teenage pregnancy. Manjit's Jamaican friend Ady and his girlfriend become parents while in their teens, even though they are not subjected to an arranged marriage.

The topic of teenage sexuality is also touched on, and unsurprisingly, draws diametrically opposed responses. Lisa's parents have a conversation with Manjit and Lisa on sexuality and the importance of using birth control measures. Whereas five students find this very positive, believing the parents are acting responsibly, three others condemn this behavior, saying that they are encouraging the teenagers to have sex when they are not emotionally mature enough to handle such a relationship. Two students comment on how embarrassed they would have been about experiencing such a talk with their own parents.

Education

Manjit's father insists that education is not important; a real Punjabi man should begin working early, marry and establish a family. Rai balances this view in the novel, as Manny's uncle is a doctor and his son, Ekbal, is going to attend university, and a number of students point this out. Several students draw on their own experiences with friends in Norway with an Asian background and say that Asian parents on the contrary really want their children to excel at school in order to go into high-status professions like medicine and law. Likewise, in the novel Uncle Jag has a university education and broke with his family to avoid an arranged marriage. Obviously, not all Punjabis in the novel stick blindly to the old traditions. Nine students note that parents should encourage education, and eight say that not getting an education is certainly not an option. Two students point out that if Manjit really wants to oppose his parents he should continue doing well in school rather than dropping out:

> And if his family has little understanding of the value of education, why isn't Manny's rebellion more concentrated around opposing his family, studying hard and then staying at Lisa's or receiving help from Mr. Sandhu? (15 13 F N)

Manjit's "Cheat"

Another aspect of the novel which elicits many comments is Manjit's delinquent behavior in trying to get out of the arranged marriage. Twenty-seven students condemn his rebellious behavior, and eighteen condemn his "cheat". They sometimes seem to forget that Manny is a constructed character and only thirteen when he starts acting out, in order to make himself undesirable as a son-in-law:

> Manny can complain and blame his family all he wants, but at the end of the day it is his own fault for getting kicked out of school and losing his only break from home (13 15 F N),

as one student puts it. Several students ask why Manjit doesn't simply move out and live on his own. Others note that they understand why Manjit is acting the way he does, remembering the powerlessness of adolescence. At the age of thirteen, one is both emotionally and financially dependent on adults, and surviving on one's own is not an option. In this connection, many students comment on Manjit's conference with his teacher Mr. Sandhu, expressing sadness that Manjit is unwilling to explain his behavior and problems at home to a man who most likely would understand and perhaps be able to help. They also comment on the fact that they must remember this in the future when they are teachers and have students who behave rebelliously: there can be underlying problems that need to be tackled.

Here the students express a wide spectrum of moral judgements, from condemning Manjit's behavior outright to understanding the powerlessness and immaturity of adolescence. When getting himself arrested for shoplifting and expelled from school fails to stop his father's plans for him, his cheat changes direction. After his return from India Manjit decides to play along, acting as if he has accepted the contracted marriage. However, his real plan is to flee from the ceremony on his wedding day, getting his revenge. Two students consider this to be a positive turn:

> I also hoped that Manjit would get an even more brutal revenge [...] for all the harassment and violence he endured from his family. [...] I wanted to see physical or psychological torture imposed on the mob of his family (12 14 M N),

as one male student writes. However, eighteen students feel that Manjit should have found a different solution, and they feel especially sorry for the bride who is left at the altar and her family:

> The only thing Manjit admits that he regrets is the fact that he disrespected the girl he was supposed to marry, her family, the Sikh temple and religion. He was too busy planning his cheating and revenge on his folks to notice and think about this earlier. He was probably too young and not mature enough to see it. (10 12 F NN)

Those who dislike Manjit's "cheat" also feel that it is wrong of him to accept money from his father and to allow the family to use so much money on the wedding when he does not plan to carry through with it.

Although most of the students view Uncle Jag as a fellow spirit and Manjit's savior, eight comment on the way Jag puts marijuana in the family's breakfast so that they fall asleep, giving him and Manjit the chance to escape to the airport.

> [...] sneaking narcotics into other people's food is an awful thing to do. So is lying and holding people 'captive'. [...] putting stuff into people's food and drinks is a cruel thing to do and completely unacceptable. (15 13 F N)

Others simply seem amused by this trick.

Racism and the Tolerance of Difference

As pointed out in the synopsis of the novel, Manjit's father despises both the British and people of other ethnicities than Indian. This reversal of racism elicits comments from twenty-one students. One student writes:

> It is nice to read about racism which is not mainly about white people discriminating black people, although this is mentioned when Manny tells us how Leicester is divided into parts and that one part is unjustly seen as a ghetto. (15 13 F N)

Another comments:

> I feel annoyed by the display of racism in the book so far. The ignorance and cheap attitudes of Manjit's father and brother. It feels like they are puppets following their traditions without question, being convinced that that is the way to live life. But in today's modern society with multiculturalism and diversity, I think it is more important than ever to accept difference, as long as it does not interfere with the laws or values of the country you live in. (7 15 M N)

Whereas the first student comments on the novelty of the reversal of racism, the second focuses more on the overt racism of Manjit's father and brother and highlights his own belief that we must tolerate difference to a certain degree. Eleven students are particularly upset by the way Manjit's father condemns British society and western values:

> Why did they choose to move to England and stay there if the Punjabi culture is so much better than the English? His family talk condescendingly not only about English culture, but also about everything and everyone who is not Indian and who does not share the Punjabi culture. (26 15 F N)

Six students note that the caste system in India is also an expression of racism. They are pleased that both Manjit and Uncle Jag choose to befriend the servant Mohan from the lower caste, and that they react against the system. Students remark that Manjit's stay in India also makes him aware of his own privileged status as a citizen in the western world. His camera, clothing and other possessions which he has not seen as especially opulent are signs of his privilege in India where so many are obviously suffering from poverty.

> Manny wanted to give all the poor beggars around him some money, but realized he couldn't due to the number of people. Harry, on the other hand, is again depicted as a real 'full-blooded' jerk, as he would prefer to just shoot all these people and get rid of them. (10 13 M N)

As this student points out,

> Manny's experience with this journey gives him a small revelation as well. As he now, for the first time in his life, gets to put his life and existence in a wider perspective. In my opinion, that's always a useful experience. (ibid.)

Summary and Implications

As the students' log entries show, these pre-service teachers have engaged in passing moral judgments during the course of their reading. Their observations are often individualistic and idiosyncratic, but the majority of judgments tend to cluster around the topics of dysfunctional families, arranged marriages, the importance of education, Manjit's "cheat", and racism/the tolerance of difference. In a number of cases, they contrast their own experiences with those of Manjit, thus becoming more aware of their own values and preferences. This leads to reflections on their own identities and development. Some of them openly condemn almost every aspect of the foreign culture/traditions portrayed in the novel, whereas others realize that their beliefs are very much a result of their own upbringing in an individualistic, western society. Only two students, for example, comment on how Rai juxtaposes the individualistic values of British society in the scenes set in Leicester with the collective, family values described in part three, set in India.

In the reflection note on using the reading-log as a teaching method, most students are ambivalent. They see the potential of the method, saying that they thought more deeply and remembered more from the book after writing the reading log and discussing it in class.[9] But the majority also feels that having to take notes and write often inhibits the pleasure of reading and makes it feel like a duty. A number of students suggest using the method in school with shorter texts, perhaps with a chapter or a poem, and then using the logs as a basis for a broader discussion, as we did.

The story itself caused students to think about their future profession as teachers. It is clear that understanding how children from a non-Norwegian background may struggle to accommodate two cultures and differing sets of expectations in their lives is important for teachers. However, a number of students basically read the story mimetically, identifying with the protagonist rather than seeing him as a figure constructed by the author for specific purposes. Reader-response methodology of course encourages a mimetic reading, focusing on emotional interaction with the text, rather than on analysis. They often judge him from their more mature perspective and are disappointed that he does not behave more rationally or make better choices. Others feel they learned a lot about adolescent behavior and its causes, and this is knowledge they want to take with them into the classroom.

Focusing on multicultural literature is particularly useful if students are to teach in a way that helps their pupils meet the goals of the National Curriculum. Working with these books can "expose the conflicts that can arise in encounters between different cultures" (Norway 2011). Furthermore, thinking freely about and responding to multicultural texts involves

> not only allowance for other points of view, but also courage to take a stand, confidence to stand alone, and the strength of character to think and act according to one's own convictions. (ibid.)

As a teacher, this project has taught me that studying literature should not be restricted to teaching the rudiments of literary analysis or using literature solely as language input. Allowing students to respond associatively and reflectively to the ideas and conflicts in a text can be just as important for their development as future teachers and citizens. Studying literature and using reader-response methodology corroborates Ricoeur's hypothesis that literature can function as the first laboratory of moral judgment. Reading multicultural literature can help them reflect on the ethical values and cultural differences focused on in the Norwegian National Curriculum. Further research could be done to contrast the responses of the ten non-Norwegian students with those of their Norwegian classmates.

To sum up, using reader-response methods such as reading-logs allows students to make text-to-world and text-to-self connections that lead to moral judgments. If they understand that they actually make moral judgments on events, dilemmas and choices in fictional worlds while reading, they can become more aware of their own values, supporting their personal identity formation as well as their development as practitioners.

Additionally, discussing their observations and moral judgments with their classmates and teacher further augments this development.

Notes

[1] Sachs (2001) discusses competing discourses and outcomes within teacher professional identity. Beauchamp and Thomas (2009) focus on issues involved in understanding teacher identity, particularly the identity of pre-service teachers and new practitioners.

[2] For information on multicultural literature suitable for children and adolescents see Landt (2006); Mitchell (2003); and Stephens (2010). Cai (2002) covers a number of the on-going debates on this kind of literature.

[3] Ricoeur (1994) also discusses how the complexity of a human life becomes easier to understand when put in a narrative format. He explains that we can make sense of our own and of others' biographies the same way we understand stories: by following a plot and the protagonist featured in it. For more on Ricoeur's theory, see Venema (2000), "Paul Ricoeur on Refigurative Reading and Narrative Identity." For a brief discussion of the connections established by different philosophers between narrative and identity, see Ritivoi (2010).

[4] *(Un)arranged Marriage* received many positive reviews and was shortlisted for nine regional book prizes. It won the Angus, Stockport, North Lanarkshire and Leicester Book awards. By 2014 the novel was available in eleven different languages and it has been popular on school reading lists in Scandinavia and Germany, among others. In Britain the novel is now on the General Certificate of Secondary Education reading list. Rai has continued to write young adult novels, some of which target reluctant readers. He is a popular speaker at schools and festivals and has launched books across Europe, in Singapore and Nepal. https://en.wikipedia.org/wiki/Bali_Rai [Accessed 27.02.2019].

[5] See e.g., Maria Nikolajeva (2003; 2010) for more on the difference between reading mimetically, as one does for a reading log, and semiotically, as is usual for conventional literary analysis. She explains that reader-response methodology often encourages the former, especially in young readers.

[6] As Robyn McCallum (2006) explains, young adult literature also tends to be characterized by common thematic or ideological concerns, such as the formation of an adult identity, solidarity with a group's ideals and the experience of sexual maturity. McCallum (1999) has also focused on literature and adolescent identity in *Ideologies of Identity in Adolescent Fiction: The Dialogic Construction of Subjectivity*. See also Stephens (2010b) on adolescence and literature.

[7] For more insight into the reader-response method see e.g., Robert E. Probst's "Dialogue with a Text" (1988); Sandra L. McKay's "Literature in the ESL Classroom" (1982); Aly Anwar Amer's "Teaching EFL/ESL Literature" (2003); or Perry Nodelman and Mavis Reimer's *The Pleasures of Children's Literature* (2003, 218–222).

[8] Quotes from the logs are coded with a student number, year, gender and ethnicity (e.g., 12 14 F N, indicating student number 12, cohort year 2014, Female, Norwegian).

[9] See Johnson (2011) for an investigation into multiple selves and multiple identities in pre-service teachers. Her study shows how students linked the experience of reading young adult literature to their possible teacher selves when they were allowed to read aesthetically, attending to their own responses, rather than efferently, or reading for information.

References

Amer, Aly Anwar. 2003. "Teaching EFL/ESL Literature." *The Reading Matrix.* Vol. 3, No. 2, Sept.: 69–70.

Beauchamp, Catherine and Lynn Thomas. 2009. "Understanding teacher identity: an overview of issues in the literature and implications for teacher education." *Cambridge Journal of Education*, Vol. 39, No. 2: 175–189.

Cai, Mingshui. 2002. *Multicultural Literature for Children and Young Adults.* Westport, CT and London: Greenwood.

Carlisle, Anthony. 2000. "Reading Logs: An Application of Reader-Response Theory in ELT." *ELT Journal.* Vol. 54, No. 1: 12–18.

Johnson, Angela B. 2011. "Multiple Selves and Multiple Sites of Influence: Perceptions of Young Adult Literature in the Classroom." *Theory into Practice*, Vol. 50: 215–222.

Landt, Susan M. 2006. "Multicultural literature and young adolescents: A kaleidoscope of opportunity." *Journal of Adolescent & Adult Literacy.* Vol. 49, No. 8: 690–697.

McCallum, Robyn. 2006. "Young Adult Literature." In *The Oxford Encyclopedia of Children's Literature.* Oxford University Press. (e-reference edition), edited by Jack Zipes. Oxford: Oxford UP.

—. 1999. *Ideologies of Identity in Adolescent Fiction: The Dialogic Construction of Subjectivity.* New York and London: Garland.

McKay, Sandra. 1982. "Literature in the ESL Classroom." *TESOL Quarterly*, Vol. 16, No. 4: 529–536.

Mitchell, Diana. 2003. "Multicultural and International Literature." In *Children's Literature: An Invitation to the World.* Boston, etc.: Pearson Education, 198–225.

Nikolajeva, Maria. 2003. "Beyond the Grammar of Story, or How Can Children's Literature Criticism Benefit from Narrative Theory?" *Children's Literature Association Quarterly*, Vol. 28, No. 1: 5–16.

—. 2010. "The Identification Fallacy." In *Telling Children's Stories: Narrative Theory and Children's Literature*, edited by Mike Cadden, 187–208. Lincoln and London: Nebraska UP.

Nodelman, Perry and Mavis Reimer. 2003. *The Pleasures of Children's Literature.* 3rd ed. Boston, New York, etc.: Allyn and Bacon.

Norway. 2011. The Norwegian Ministry of Education and Research. "Knowledge Promotion–Kunnskapsløftet." Available through: http://www.udir.no/Stottemeny/English/Curriculum-in-English/_english/Knowledge-promotion---Kunnskapsloftet/ [Accessed 19.02.2017].

Probst, Robert E. 1988. "Dialogue with a Text." *The English Journal*, Vol. 77, No. 1: 32–38.
Rai, Bali. 2001. *(Un)arranged Marriage*. Reading, UK: Corgi Books.
—. 2014. "Interview with Barbara Matthews at De Monfort University, Leicester". Available through: http://www.dmu.ac.uk/about-dmu/events/events-calendar/2014/october/in-conversation-with-bali-rai.aspx#sthash.1bHyqfZH.dpuf [Accessed 22.06.2017].
Ricoeur, Paul. 1994 [1992]. *Oneself as Another*. Trans. Kathleen Blamey. Chicago and London: Chicago UP.
Ritivoi, Andreea Deciu. 2010 [2005]. "Identity and Narrative." In *Routledge Encyclopedia of Narrative Theory*, edited by David Herman, Manfred Jahn, and Marie-Laure Ryan, 231–235. London and New York: Routledge.
Sachs, Judyth. 2001. "Teacher professional identity: competing discourses, competing outcomes." *Journal of Educational Policy*, Vol. 16, No. 2,
Stephens, John. 2010. "Multiculturalism." In *The Routledge Companion to Children's Literature*, edited by David Rudd, 212–213. London and New York: Routledge.
—. "Adolescence." 2010b. In *The Routledge Companion to Children's Literature*, edited by David Rudd, 140–141. London and New York: Routledge.
Venema, Henry. 2000. "Paul Ricoeur on Refigurative Reading and Narrative Identity." *Symposium*, Vol 4, No. 2: 237–248.

CHAPTER TWELVE

NEGOTIATING AND INTRODUCING IDENTITIES: THE "ÉCRITURE COLLECTIVE" OF ARIANE MNOUCHKINE, HÉLÈNE CIXOUS AND THE THÉÂTRE DU SOLEIL

GABRIELE C. PFEIFFER

On August 28, 2017, the Goethe Prize of the City of Frankfurt am Main was awarded to the French theater manager and directrice Ariane Mnouchkine, a co-founder of the Théâtre du Soleil in Paris. For more than 50 years, Mnouchkine and her theater have been consistently staging successful productions in Paris and abroad. The theater, a free living collective, is evidence of how productive a political approach to the theater can be. Through her life's work, Mnouchkine has rendered enormous services to the theater, yet her political commitment always supercedes her artistic work–she shows political responsibility in both her art and her work.

This chapter presents Ariane Mnouchkine's work, focusing on the process of creating professional identity in the theater. Mnouchkine and her ensemble have established and developed a collective ensemble identity, based on the idea of collaborative work in all aspects of their productions, spanning the whole range from initial concept to actual performance. The chapter follows the development of the commitment to collective identity at every level–personally, artistically, and from the perspective of the character on-stage. The tension created from the interactions between these identities is then elaborated on via the theater's collaboration with the feminist writer, Hélène Cixous. Her involvement with the Théâtre du Soleil triggered a transformative process in her writing.

Identification with a Theater Collective

Mnouchkine, born in 1939,[1] was educated at Oxford (one of her contemporaries was the British filmmaker Ken Loach) and the Sorbonne. During her Parisian period she co-founded the student theater group ATEP (Association Théâtrale des Étudiants de Paris). She produced the outstanding production *Genghis Khan* (1961) and it is said that she knew already from the start that she would never become a good actress, but rather a good director, or directrice. Her numerous trips to the Far East, where she grew familiar with Asian theater, had a profound influence on her theater work (especially in the 1980s). Upon returning from her first trip to Asia she reassembled the student theater group and in 1964 the Théâtre du Soleil (Theater of the Sun) was born, alluding to the sun in the sense of its warmth, light and sensuality. It is notable that the theater was not named after Mnouchkine herself, which was the usual practice at this time. She therefore signals that she is only *one* of the co-founders of the Théâtre du Soleil, which from the beginning defined itself as a collective. The theater celebrated its 50th anniversary a couple of years ago, staging Shakespeare's *Macbeth* (2014).

Early productions were considered brilliant because they were set up in unique locations such as an abandoned circus in Montmartre (*La Cuisine* 1967 (*The Kitchen*)), or due to collective improvisations, such as as those found in *Les Clowns* (1969 (*The Clowns*)), or because of their adaptations of such classical works as Shakespeare's *Le Songe d'une nuit d'été* (1968 (*A Midsummer Night's Dream*)). The latter production was due to go on tour, but was prevented from doing so by the events of May 1968, while the earlier mentioned production, *The Kitchen*, went on tour, playing in occupied factories in France. Three characteristics define the essence of the Théâtre du Soleil's work: the nature of their particular choices of locations, such as the factories just mentioned, or the old disused ammunition warehouse–the so-called Cartoucherie–which later became their permanent site on the periphery of Paris; their chosen method and style of acting (namely creating their performances through improvisation, as collective works in process); and their reaction to current socio-political developments, incorporated in their performances.

Although the political intentions and positionings contained in the plays are paramount, the theater troupe goes a step further. They have been politically consistent with regard to their work-aesthetics and employee morale: in fact, their artistic work is based on the idea of collaborative work in all senses, including parity of salaries among all troupe members up to the present day. In contrast to regular theater companies, which aim to stage and finalize theater productions as quickly as possible, the Théâtre du Soleil allows time for a lengthy creative process. This is apparent in their so-called rehearsal periods, which are characterized by collaborative work methods. They have "established a reputation for detailed textual work, moving away from the constrained acting style of the naturalistic theater towards a more overtly theatrical performance style which celebrated the visual, sensory and musical power" (Delgado and Heritage 1996, 176). The results are magical–opening a vision of another, utopian world. Mnouchkine expressed part of her rigid credo in an interview: "It's all immediately transformed. Probably, little by little, we tried to find forms for each play. But I do hate naturalism and realism–that's not theatre" (ibid., 190). The result is a theater that has broken with many of the conventional European forms of theater on various levels, such as the "early non-single authored texts, breaking with the two-hour slot, [and] a commitment to collective working methods" (ibid., 184).

Finding One's Identity: Authorship within the Theater Collective

The Théâtre du Soleil works with collaboratively authored texts. But how can this work? One of the first methods they explored provides an answer: only a couple of years after the theater was established in 1970, the ensemble and Ariane Mnouchkine created a piece called *1789*, which is about the French Revolution. Their well-tried method of working with improvisations and as a collective rather than working within the relationship between an actor and a director led them to the so-called *création collective* (collective creation). This approach enabled everyone to try every part (free disposition of roles)[2] and Mnouchkine as directrice served solely as a kind of first spectator, helping the actors and actresses to find their respective roles as if she were a midwife helping to deliver a child. Because there was no authoritative text, competences, tasks and duties rotated among all parties. *1789* was not the very first production without a written text as a foundation, but it was the first production with a complete, elaborated plot. They were therefore forced to develop and *write a text* and not simply to *create the mise en scène*. The members of the Théâtre du Soleil met this challenge by using a method they already were familiar with, namely by working together. Thus the method of *écriture collective* (collective writing) was born. In a conventional context the basis for a production is the text of the play. In the situation at hand, however, the creator of the text is already part of the theater collective–the playwright is the collective. Simone Seym (1992, 73) elaborates as follows:

> *Création collective* bedeutet aber nicht nur, daß die Schauspieler und Ariane Mnouchkine im Sinne einer *écriture collective* gleichzeitig ihre eigenen Autoren sind, sondern auch, daß die Entstehung der Kostüme, des Bühnenbilds, der Lichtregie und der Musik in diesen gemeinsamen Schaffensprozeß eingebunden sind und einander durchdringen.[3]

Each member relies on his or her special competence. It is their craft they identify with. But they cannot claim to be (just) an actress, a musician, a writer, a costume designer, in finding their professional identities. Everyone is involved at every single step, including the cleaning of the floors; Ariane Mnouchkine herself is famous for tearing off the ticket stubs. "In this situation", as Adrian Kiernander (2008, 15) emphasizes, "it is clearly an advantage that the actors should feel that they are not simply small cogs in a larger machine, but fully contributing members of a social organization who support one another, teach one another, and amongst whom they can afford to step out into the unknown". When the theater was focusing on the French Revolution they created two spectacles: in 1970 the performance *1789* and two years later the second one entitled *1793*. Both productions gained the ensemble and its directrice fame within the international theater landscape. And it was these "inventive ensemble pieces which provided imaginative multiple-perspective commentaries on the events of *1789* and its aftermath. These productions were also the first to evolve in what has become the permanent home of the Théâtre du Soleil, the Cartoucherie" (cf. Delgado and Heritage 1996, 177). The Cartoucherie proved to be a secure home for the theater people. "It's an island", says Mnouchkine, "so we protect each other in a way, although we are very fragile sometimes" (ibid., 186). Troupe members cannot escape the demanding daily work of the theater to focus on their own professional identities or to compete with everyone else. They cannot simply focus on being an actor or actress; they are expected to take part in the work of the writer or musician or vice versa. Instead, the effort and the struggle with *oneself* is enormous. The theater itself provides an island, a secure "home". Rather than identifying with their profession, the troupe of the Théâtre du Soleil relate to and identify with the place and their theatrical community. This seems to be an unwritten law, validated by all, irrespective of professional background. Nevertheless it is important to understand that the individual person is not ignored or negated, as Ariane Mnouchkine also clarifies:

A collective is not the negation of the individuals of which it's composed. It would be dangerous to think that a collective can exist without eyes, without mouths, without hands. A collective is the grouping of several creators. (Mnouchkine 2005, 60)

Among these is the creator of an indispensable part of the theater production, the text of the play itself. Traditionally, playwrights, like the French feminist writer Hélène Cixous, work as individual contributors. When Cixous came in contact with the Théâtre du Soleil she had already developed her sense and perspective of writing, known as *écriture féminine* (a feminine mode of writing), and also had experience of writing for the theater. She wrote her first play in 1971: *La Pupulle* (*The Pupil*). More than a decade later, Cixous' debut with Ariane Mnouchkine and the Théâtre du Soleil changed her understanding of what being an author means substantially; instead of writing *for* a theater she started to write *with* a theater, as illustrated in the piece called *L'Histoire terrible mais inachevée de Norodom Sihanouk, roi du Cambodge* (*The Terrible but Unfinished Story of Norodom Sihanouk, King of Cambodia*) (1985).[4] This was followed by other collaborations between Cixous and the Théâtre du Soleil: in 1987 *L'Indiade, ou l'Inde de leurs rêves* (*The Indiada or the India of their Dreams*);[5] in 1992 *Les Euménides d'Eschyle* (translation by Cixous); in 1994 *La Ville parjure ou le Réveil des Érinyes* (*The Perjured City, or The Awakening of the Furies*);[6] in 1997 *Et soudain des nuits d'éveil* (*Suddenly Nights without Sleep in century*);[7] in 1999 *Tambours sur la digue* (*Drums on the Dam*);[8] in 2003 *Le Dernier Caravansérail* (*The Last Caravanserai* (*Odysees*));[9] in 2010 *Les Naufragés du Fol Espoir* (*The Castaways of the Fol Espoir*);[10] and recently in 2016 *Une chambre en Inde* (*A Room in India*).[11]

What does it mean writing for a theater ensemble that commits itself to a collective method of working, of creating a *pièce théâtral*? What are the consequences for the author, the *authority*, and in what way does this change one's perception of being a writer? Hélène Cixous–as Susan Sellers (2007, 75) describes in her book about the French author–"outlines her motivations and experience of writing for the theatre in a series of postscripts."[12] One of these postscripts enlightens us on Cixous' understanding of the relationship between the writer (herself) and the theater, based on her understanding of theater, which "is by definition 'the land of others'" (ibid., 76). One consequence of course is that Cixous was forced to change her habit of writing of *The Self* to writing of *The Others*. The writer can no longer focus on him–or herself as the center of a text. She argues that writing for the theater means being inhabited by the others, and "her task is to give birth to these others by listening to what they say" (ibid., 77).[13]

> Writing for the theatre, I am haunted by a universe of fictitious but real people. It's the strangest, most magical experience. I live, inhabited by my characters, who give me the same feelings real people give me, except that they live inside me, I am their home. (Cixous, qtd. in ibid., 77)[14]

In this remarkable process, both writer and actor/actress have to abandon their own respective egos and make room for the *Other*. Cixous calls this phenomenon "the gift the theater gives to the author: incarnation" (qtd. in ibid., 80). "Cixous suggests", writes Susan Sellers, "that unlike the writing of fiction, […] the theatre requires [that] the author does not write alone but at the behest of and in conjunction with others" (ibid., 85).

Being on Stage: Creating Identities

The most recent production created by the Théâtre du Soleil in 2016 was another collaboration with Cixous, "en harmonie avec Hélène Cixous"[15] (in harmony with Hélène Cixous): *Une chambre en Inde,* and is outlined in the program. The setting of the story presents meta-theater par excellence: A Parisian theater company is on tour in India. The director, feeling overwhelmed and weak after a terror attack, leaves the group; now the group has to create a play within a couple of days on its own. The former assistant and new directrice has a series of dreams triggered by her current situation. She thinks about the role of theater in general but in the context of the current world and the widespread fear of terrorism. In those dreams she is visited by Shakespeare, Chekhov, and an Indian theater group, as well as Ghandi, and members of the Taliban. The whole history and cosmos of the Théâtre du Soleil as well as of Ariane Mnouchkine appear on stage, including the elements of Western and Eastern theater. Mnouchkine's alter ego–obviously–is played by the writer Hélène Cixous. Here she has indeed flipped her professional role.

In its past, the Théâtre du Soleil produced numerous extraordinary *mises en scène* without having either an author or a written text at all. One of these productions, from 2006/2007 was *Les Éphémeres* (*Ephemera*),[16] which probably showed the most intimate relation between the theater, Ariane Mnouchkine and the other members of the ensemble. She always kept her private life very private, avoided speaking about her family–her Russian emigré father, who was a filmmaker, and her English mother, an actress. In this spectacle though "there is a trace of remoteness about her"

(Dickson 2012), as a critic writes. Bonnie Marranca points out that "*Les Éphémères*, the disappearance of the human race, [...is] to celebrate the everyday life of human beings in varieties of the emotional register, passing through joy, grief, anger, generosity, and everything in between." (2010, 60)

The play encompasses and reflects the life experiences of the members of the Théâtre du Soleil, which by this time was composed of more than 20 nationalities and four generations. Each of these members plays multiple roles and stories, each of which are narrated in separate episodes. "It truly has the feel", writes Charles Isherwood (2017), "of a production that draws not so much on a single director's vision, let alone a single writer's voice, but on a field of experience to which the whole company–numbering 70, including technicians, musicians and backstage workers–has contributed." Some of the characters are related, some appear several times, some only once, some are seen in different stages of their lives. The story itself is simple: after her mother's death, a daughter sells their house, a couple sits together and has dinner, one person is tracing her family story during the Nazi occupation, another one is celebrating a birthday,–all 29 scenes are set in domestic situations, living–or dining rooms, garden or kitchen, just ordinary stories in ordinary places. The focus is on their interior lives and relationships. Each story takes place on a kind of miniplatform which is constantly moving:

> The concept of the staging is to have all the scenes acted on rolling platforms (chariots) that are slowly pushed out of the shimmering broad curtains at either end of the long horizontal performance space between the two sets of audience rows. (Marranca 2010, 63)

These moving platforms seem to be floating islands and do give "the idea of life as constant flux, a journey marked by a series of sometimes obvious, sometimes obscure inflection points" (Isherwood 2017). The characters are stimulated by grief, trauma, and the horror of death. They act out different actions and reactions, and sometimes find themselves in representative life situations. The whole world seems to be captured on the little platforms which rotate and rotate, just like "the Earth's constant rotation" (Marranca 2010, 63).

The performance is an approach to contemporary human existence, with all our qualities and dysfunctionalities, embedded in the history of the 20th century with the background of both world wars. It attempts to answer all kinds of unresolved questions, but it primarily addresses the issue of who we are–who can we identify with. The Théâtre du Soleil simply and at the same time complexly suggests: "Who you are is the way you interact with others" (Marranca 2010, 63). This seems to be a *sine qua non* in the context of theater, regardless of form and content. As actor, directrice or author you always give birth to a character on stage interacting with the *Other*. Cixous was reflecting on precisely this metaphor. This is how a character finds his or her own identity on stage–as well as off-stage. During rehearsals for *Les Èphémères* there were lots of improvisations and the theater troupe brought their own stories and identities with them, to a greater extent than ever before. While telling their own private stories they were expecting a character to appear. Even Ariane Mnouchkine herself had begun to tell stories about her childhood and her family members during the rehearsal period. Much to her surprise, she could find *her* own story on stage despite her constant desire for well-guarded privacy. Mnouchkine certainly did not intend to become production material herself. But some of the actors used details of her stories and integrated them. She thus unintentionally provided material for the actors and actresses in the end.

Ariane Mnouchkine was only half-aware of her family situation as she admits during a film interview (2009).[17] She had remembered an episode during summertime which she had spent with her grandparents. Foggy memories emerged: A garden, a beach, she was walking along that beach, collecting shells. This little story reveals a time before their deportation in connection with the Second World War. Although Mnouchkine had learned about the deportation early on in her life, she was 17 years old before she found out why they had been deported. As an adult, she had to ask herself why she had not asked about this earlier; why and when and what she had believed in. Once she understood the complete story, the circumstances and her family's history, she could confront herself directly without closing her eyes, as a spectator of her *mise en scène* later on. In addition to the little girl on stage, there was also a group of grown up women looking for her Jewish grandparents. The members of the Théâtre du Soleil troupe staged Ariane Mnouchkine's story, honoring her and her family's history. She was very surprised when she realized that the actresses and actors had chosen her life story instead of their own stories for the performance. At the same time, she was also very grateful and touched.

Ariane Mnouchkine–as a human being, a woman, a directrice, a member of the Théâtre du Soleil and as the first spectator of its productions–now saw herself on stage. And many others did so too. The audience can recognize and learn about its own behavior, shape and identity even though they do not function as models for the actors and actresses. As Bonnie Marranca summarizes in her study about *Les Èphémères,* "it is one of the many lessons in the cultivation of the heart found in this wise work. Sometimes theatre can feel like a gift to disconsolate souls" (2010, 66).

The Collective as One's Identity

In summing up my discussion of professional identity, personal identity, the character's identity in the artistic work of the Théâtre du Soleil in Paris, I would like to cite Dario Fo, who was the first and only actor to win the Nobel Prize in Literature. On that occasion Fo (1997) pointed out that he accepted the Prize as a representative for all "giullari", or jesters, in the whole, wide world and especially including his wife, the actress Franca Rame.[18] He could never have succeeded both on- and off-stage without acting as a team player. Fo's speech points out the importance of working together, being part of a team, and creating theater as a member of an ensemble. This is exactly what Ariane Mnouchkine has been doing throughout her career in the theater–emphasizing the importance of and practicing collaborative theater work as a *collective*.

(I would like to acknowledge the support of Ingrid Fuchs, Reinhard Kraxner and Dan Cordeiro in developing this chapter in English.)

Notes

[1] "Ariane Mnouchkine was born on March 3, 1939 in Boulogne-sur-Seine, into an environment in which film was omnipresent since her Russian father, Alexandre Mnouchkine (1903–1993), who immigrated to France after the Russian Revolution, was a well known film producer" (Féral 2009.)
[2] Cfr. exemplification in Pfeiffer 2018, 38; cfr. the appandant website of the project "(Re)Presenting Theatrical Concepts of Being: Histrionic Explorations by Ariane Mnouchkien, Carmelo Bene, and Jerzy Grotowski" http://theatricalbeing.univie.ac.at/en/home/ [Accessed 12.7.2017].
[3] "*Création collective* does not only mean that in the sense of an *écriture collective* the actors and Ariane Mnouchkine are their own authors, but also that in this collective creative process the development of costumes, stage, light design, and music are integrated as well, and that all of these elements are intertwined with each other." (my trans.).
[4] The translation of the title follows the official version by Donald Watson published in *The Hélène Cixous Reader*, edited by Susan Sellers, 1994. There you can also find an extract of the play in English, 142–146.

[5] The translation of the title follows the official version by Donald Watson published in *The Hélène Cixous Reader*, ibid. There you can also find an extract of the play in English, 159–162.
[6] The translation of the title *The Perjured City* by Bernadette Fort follows the official version published in: *Selected Plays of Hélène Cioxus* (2004). Other titles also exist, e.g., *The Treacherous City or the Awakening of the Furies* or *And suddenly nights of awakening.*
[7] Translation follows the dictionary entry "Hélène Cixous (1937-)", in *The Columbia history of twentieth-century French thought* (2006).
[8] The translation of the title *Drums on the Dam* by Judith Miller and Brian J. Mallet follows the official version published in: *Selected Plays of Hélène Cioxus* (2004). Other translations of the title exist, e.g. *The Flood Drummers.*
[9] This is the official translation used at the Avignon festival, where the Théâtre du Soleil showed up as a guest performance, available online http://www.festival-avignon.com/en/shows/2003/le-dernier-caravanserail-odyssees-the-last-caravanserai-odysees [Accessed 6.8. 2017].
[10] This translation is the official version of the Théâtre du Soleil cfr. http://www.theatre-du-soleil.fr/thsol/IMG/pdf/100916_scenario_nfe-2.pdf [Accessed 7.8.2017]. It has also been translated as *The castaways of the mad hope* by Eric Singleton, published in his article "Performing Orientalist, Intercultural, and Globalized Modernities", in: *The politics of interweaving performance cultures: beyond postcolonialism,* edited by Erika Fischer-Lichte, Torsten Jost, and Saskya Iris ain. New York, London: Routledge 2014, 77–94.
[11] The more common translation in the media is *A Room in India*, but there is also one another translation: *A Bedroom in India.* An official translation does not yet exist.
[12] She refers to *Le Lieu du Crime, le lieu du Pardon* (*The Place of Cirme, The Place of Forgiveness*), *L'Ourse, la Tombe, les Etoiles* (*The Bear, the Tomb, the Stars*), *Qui es-tu* (*Who Are You*), *L'Incarnation* (*The Incarnation*), 136. The English translation, a revised translation by Chatherine MacGillivray of *Le Lieu du Crime, le lieu du Pardon* (*The Place of Crime, The Place of Forgiveness*) is published in: *The Hélène Cixous Reader* (1994), 149–156.
[13] Similar to Cixous, who sees her role as a writer who gives birth to the *Other*, Mnouchkine stated that she considers herself a midwife, who assists the actors and actresses in giving birth to their figures.
[14] Susan Sellers is quoting from Hélène Cixous' article "The Place of Crime, The Place of Forgiveness".
[15] Cfr. several productions in collaboration with Hélène Cixous and the Théâtre du Soleil are available at the theater's website, for example the mentioned one: http://www.theatre-du-soleil.fr/thsol/nos-spectacles-et-nos-films/nos-spectacles/2016-une-chambre-en-inde-2016/ [Accessed 6.6.2017].
[16] This rough translation was used by media, cfr. https://www.theguardian.com/culture/2012/aug/10/ariane-mnouchkine-life-in-theatre and
http://www.nytimes.com/2009/07/10/theater/reviews/10ephemeres.html?n=Top%2

52FReference%252FTimes%2520Topics%252FSubjects%252FT%252FTheater [Accessed 6.8.2017].

[17] Documentary film *Ariane Mnouchkine–l'aventure du Théâtre du Soleil* von Catherine Vilpoux, Arte France Produktion, Koproduktion Agat Films & Cie, 2009.

[18] Franca Rame (1929–2013) made her debut when she was eight years old. She belonged to an old theater family consisting of actors and actresses for generations, who passed on their knowledge just as actors did in the Middle Ages.

References

Anonym. 2006: "Hélène Cixous (1937-)." *The Columbia history of twentieth-century French thought*, edited by Lawrence D. Kritzman, 484–486. New York: Columbia Univ. Press 2006.

Cioxus, Hélène 2004. *Selected Plays of Hélène Cioxus,* edited by Eric Prenowitz, London: Routledge.

Delgado, Maria M. and Paul Heritage. 1996. "Ariane Mnouchkine." *In contact with the Gods? Directors talk theatre,* edited by Maria M. Delgado & Paul Heritage, 175–190. Manchester and New York: Manchester University Press.

Dickson, Andrew. 2012. "Ariane Mnouchkine and the Théâtre du Soleil: a life in theatre." *the guardian*, 10 August 2012. https://www.theguardian.com/culture/2012/aug/10/ariane-mnouchkine-life-in-theatre [Accessed 6.8.2017].

Féral, Josette. 2009. "Ariane Mnouchkine." *Jewish Women: A Comprehensive Historical Encyclopedia.* 1 March 2009. Jewish Women's Archive. https://jwa.org/encyclopedia/article/mnouchkine-ariane [Accessed 12.7.2017].

Fischer-Lichte, Erika, Torsten Jost and Saskya Iris Jain., eds. 2014 *The politics of interweaving performance cultures: beyond postcolonialism,* New York, London: Routledge.

Fo, Dario. 1997. "Nobel Lecture: Contra Jogulatores Obloquentes | Against Jesters Who Defame and Insult." Nobel Lecture, December 7, 1997. Nobelprize.org. Nobel Media AB 2014. Web. 28 Jul 2017. http://www.nobelprize.org/nobel_prizes/literature/laureates/1997/fo-lecture.html [Accessed 25.7.2017].

Isherwood, Charles. 2017. "Everyday Intimacies and the Intensity of a Ringing Phone." *The New York Times*, 26 April 2017. http://www.nytimes.com/2009/07/10/theater/reviews/10ephemeres.html?n=Top%252FReference%252FTimes%2520Topics%252FSubjects%252FT%252FTheater [Accessed 6.8.2017]

Kiernander, Adrian. 2008. *Ariane Mnouchkine and the Théâtre du Soleil,* first published 1993, digitally printed version 2008. Cambridge: University Press.

Marranca, Bonnie. 2010. "Ordinary Life. Les Éphémères by Ariane Mnouchkine." *PAJ, Performing Arts Journal,* Vol. 32, No. 1 (Jan., 2010): 60–66, published by The MIT Press on behalf of the performing Arts Journal, Inc. 5. http://www.jstor.org/stable/20627958 [Accessed 5.8.2017].

Mnouchkine, Ariane. 2005. "The individual and the collective", from an interview with Ariane Mnouhckine by the editors of Théâtre/Public. In *Collaborative Theatre: The Théâtre du Soleil sourcebook*, compiled and edited by David Williams, new translations by Eric Prenowitz and David Williams, first published 1999: 59–64. London / New York: Routledge.

Pfeiffer, Gabriele C. 2018. *Ephemer und leibhaftig, Schauspielerische Erkundungen von Ariane Mnouchkine, Carmelo Bene, and Jerzy Grotowski*, Wien: habilitation treatise.

Sellers, Susan. 2007. *Hélène Cixous, Authorship, Autobiography and Love*, first published 1996. Malden: Polity Press.

—. ed 1994. *The Hélène Cixous Reader, with a preface by Hélène Cixous and foreword by Jacques Derrida*. London: Routledge.

Seym, Simone. 1992. *Das Théâtre du Soleil. Ariane Mnouchkines Ästhetik des Theaters*. Stuttgart: Metzler.

The Official Web Site of the Nobel Prize | Nobelprize.org. 2017. "The Nobel Prize in Literature 1997." https://www.nobelprize.org/nobel_prizes/literature/laureates/1997/ [Accessed 25.7.2017].

CHAPTER THIRTEEN

ALIENATED AND EVANESCENT IDENTITIES IN THE CONTEMPORARY WORLD OF AUSTRIAN AUTHOR KATHRIN RÖGGLA

ALESSANDRA SCHININÀ

Work is an essential part of individual identity. Austrian writer Kathrin Röggla shows how alienation can lead to loss of self in a globalized environment. In her work, she deals with current affairs, such as the world economic crisis, environmental catastrophes, terrorism and the omnipresent media. The author concentrates particularly on the world of work in the service sector in the context of a global society that is both neoliberalist and interconnected, as well as being precarious and transmutable. The characters that inhabit her works are employed in international associations or in the media. They are scientists, interpreters, politicians, managers, journalists, technicians and programmers, who live in a permanent and conscious state of self-representation, which is characterized by the omnipresence of the media and a sense of precariousness. They are intermediate level, specialized workers who are successful, with no apparent income problems, yet they find themselves in situations where they lose control of themselves. This often happens through the intervention of a third figure, for example an interviewer, who allows the characters to talk until they come to realize the absurdity of their own existence, or through an unexpected, disturbing event that sweeps away all certainty. Their occupational-existential identities, which are sustained by a particular lifestyle and language, collapse and nothing remains. Röggla's characters increasingly dissolve and, in the end, they move like ghosts or zombies in disturbing urban landscapes and non-places.

Instead of individual, original identities, the author presents us with patterns of identity or "Identitätsmuster", which are externally imposed and based on certain linguistic and conceptual characteristics, internalized and passed on from their work lives to the private sphere, with dramatic consequences. In order to highlight this process of loss of an autonomous identity, Röggla uses a particular narrative style, which can even involve the figure of the narrator in a process of self-representation and dissolution (Kormann 2015). Röggla aspires to represent an "absence" (Röggla 2015, 30) and creates characters who are there and not there, voices in a world where every certainty has disappeared. In particular, the elements that characterize the model of neoliberalist society are seen in their effects on the individual personality, including its extreme consequences. This involves all aspects of our being and appearance in public and Röggla mercilessly unmasks every illusion. The loss of identity occurs through the loss of one's own language, of one's own feelings, of one's own physical needs and even of one's own body in the name of the absolute imperative of efficiency and productivity. Finally, one becomes a ghost, unable to go backward or forward, in an eternal present of the living dead. Röggla's works always lead to a disconcerting hyperrealism.

Identity, as social positioning, comes about primarily through language. In one of her most famous works, *wir schlafen nicht (we never sleep)*, from 2004, Röggla tackles the consequences of the New Economy for the job market. The author presents its effects on everyday life, simultaneously reproducing and unmasking its language and the ideals it expresses. Her characters are manifestations of the dominant system and are not described, instead they reveal themselves through interviews and dialogue. We do not have access to their thoughts but only their speech; we "hear" them speak during a giant, alienating congress of management consultants. They are, in reality, people who embody certain behaviours and linguistic habits (Vilar 2010). Their professions are as fashionable as they are hard to define concretely, and the use of anglicisms and abbreviations only makes them more elusive. This can be noted already in the foreword where the various types considered are listed: "diesem text liegen gespräche mit consultants, coaches, key account managerinnen, programmierern, praktikanten usw. zugrunde" (Röggla 2004).[1] The six characters who are interviewed identify themselves from the start based on their specialist jargon, incomprehensible to those who do not work in such a context:

> *der senior associate*: man solle ihn ruhig warnen, wenn er mit zu vielen anglizismen um sich schmeiße, das gehe ihm nämlich schon automatisch. manchmal merke er gar nicht mehr, in welchem fachjargon er wieder einmal rede und was für vokabular er wieder rauslasse. das passiere

schnell, daß man für außenstehende einfach nicht mehr verständlich sei. [...] aber die unverständlichkeit sei ja genau einer der gründe, warum es überhaupt beratungen gebe– (Röggla 2004, 9–10)[2]

They have adopted jargon and they have automatized it to such an extent that they have lost control, at some point, not only of their words but also of their own voices, of their own organs. We therefore find statements such as: "irgendwann merkst du nicht mehr, daß du am reden bist" (ibid., 8–9)[3] or the characters meet to "sich reden hören, während man spricht" (ibid, 23).[4] It is paradoxical that in her poetics lectures, Röggla protests against this continuous public chatter while there is silence concerning how things really are (Röggla 2015, 19).

Röggla insists on the nature of performance in modern society, the so-called society of spectacle. The "actors" in her works, drawn from the contemporary world of work, do not produce anything concrete, they hide behind fairly vague definitions, adhering to the mentality of "selling yourself in the best way possible" ("Sich-am-besten-Verkaufen"). They define themselves, not based on what they are, but on what they are not, and above all, they talk about themselves using indirect affirmations. In the case of the interviews, the words are reported by another person and so they talk about themselves in the third person and in the formal subjunctive verbal form (Kremer 2008, 114–137; Krauthausen 2015). This schizophrenic situation corresponds to their state of alienation. The more they move away from the preformed linguistic schema, from the "business management German" ("bwler-deutsch") that determines their lifestyle during the interviews and events, the more the system collapses around them.

In the face of unpleasant situations, such as being forced to plan and communicate redundancies, one of the interviewees states:

> anfangs sei er da ja mehr rangegangen mit der haltung–"sozusagen". das sei ja nicht er, der den job mache. er spiele vielmehr eine rolle, er spiele vielmehr mit uns schaue sich das sozusagen an, oder eine art experiment, das er mit sich durchführe, unter dem motto: mal sehen, wie sich diese welt so anfühlt. das sei eine haltung, die man so nicht durchziehen könne [...] weil das eben ein job sei, der einen 100% fordere. [...] möglicherweise könnten das andere, aber er sei nicht der typ, der 24 stunden eine rolle spiele, nein, das sei er nicht. (Röggla 2004, 14)[5]

From the contradictory words of the interviewee it seems that an internal schism is the only way to survive the psychological pressure from their type of work, even though another self, dedicated 100% to work performance, takes over fairly quickly. Indeed, their performance of a social role extends from work to private life, from the type of car they drive, to the clothes they wear. Above all, one learns "man müsse [...] den mund halten, sich zumindest etwas zurückhalten mit der eigenen Meinung. wisse man doch: was dürfe man sagen und was nicht" (ibid., 32).[6]

This situation of continuous self-representation and displacement ends up provoking a conflict between individual personality and work experience. The characters presented by Röggla constantly sideline their own ideas and attitudes in order to "fulfil themselves" within a dominant logic imposed from outside. The words of the efficient champions of the New Economy create a sense of nausea emerging from a life made up of quick and irregular meals, hotel rooms, airplane flights resembling bus journeys and a lack of sleep. All of this is endured in the name of the logic of growth that turns against them, destroying their psychological and physical individuality. Like the travelling salesperson, the protagonist of Kafka's *Metamorphosis*, who complains about the same type of alienating work and then is transformed into a foul insect, there is a mutation here as well. The author's new "monsters" have a disturbed relationship with their own homes, families, emotions and desires. Their identification with the company, the loss of loving relationships and their drug-like dependence on work, results in a series of physical ailments, of reactions of denial that are turned in on themselves: allergies, panic attacks and aphasia.

In particular, the loss of one's voice, the tool of one's trade, is considered to be disastrous in the communication branch:

> ja, er habe seine stimme verloren, also komplett verloren. "da ging nichts mehr", und in seinem job müsse man eben eine stimme haben, ohne stimme laufe da gar nichts. ihm scheine, so im nachhinein, daß die stimme mitunter sein wichtiges werkzeug sei, das sei ja etwas fürchterlich interaktives, so eine arbeitssituation, andauernd kommunizieren, rücksprache halten, kommunizieren, meetings abhalten und nochmals kommunizieren. (ibid., 107)[7]

If you do not communicate you do not exist, and communicating means selling, and also selling oneself. In consumer society, each interlocutor becomes a client. The more we insist on talking about people, the more we mask the reality of the transformation of people into consumers. Moreover, following the logic of business efficiency, people are catalogued into types a, b or c, according to their work performance, reduced to numbers and cogs in a dehumanizing machine.

Other watchwords of contemporary society are flexibility, speed, efficiency, and multi-tasking. We are subjected to continuous demands ("könnte man nicht doch ein wenig schneller sein? könnte es nicht doch etwas effizienter ablaufen? wo könnte man den arbeitsprozeß noch optimieren?" (ibid., 130[8])). Röggla shows us the other face of the so-called "Leistungsgesellschaft", the society based on productivity and efficiency, on the entrepreneur of the self, who ends up being a frustrated self whose intellectual capacity and physical strength are exhausted. The imperative of success, and of having to better ourselves, mutates into a continuous state of stress and fear: fear of losing your job, of being made redundant, of not keeping up with the competition, as is the case with one of the managers interviewed:

> *der partner:* ja, so ein bißchen was von gehirnwäsche habe es schon, wenn man sich hier länger aufhalte, aber ein bißchen was von gehirnwäsche müsse es auch haben, das sei ja der sinn der sache, das sei ja das programm jeder messe, sonst mache man ja auch keine geschäfte (lacht). aber mit der zeit komme man dann doch auf seltsame gedanken. da müsse man nur aufpassen, daß es sich auf einen übertrage, diese ganze irrsinnsstimmung hier [...] mit der zeit träten einige störungen auf, so wahrnehmungsstörungen. ja, da komme es zu kognitiven dissonanzen, wenn man nicht achtgebe, auch mit dem gedächtnis. aber um ihn müsse man sich wirklich keine sorgen machen, er sei nur ein wenig überspannt, und da könnten schon die nerven mit einem etwas durchgehen. (ibid., 129)[9]

The fact is that this brainwashing occurs voluntarily. The characters, stressed by the rhythms of the trade convention, talk about being "addicted to work" and argue:

> –und außerdem: man ist ja nicht direkt hierher entführt worden, nein, das kann man nicht sagen, man ist ja aus freien stücken hierhergelangt. –nein, von einer entführung kann man nicht reden [...]–wenn, dann müßte es sich um eine länger angelegte entführung handeln, also eine, die schon länger am laufen ist. (ibid., 128)[10]

Captured "a long time ago", the new middle class of the information society represented in Röggla's stories finds itself in a tunnel from which it cannot escape without the risk of self-destruction (cf. Röggla 2009, 181). We are no longer masters of our own lives; our own identities dissolve and become empty containers, we become living dead or ghosts in a collective hallucination:

> *die key account managerin*: [...] ob sie immer mehr zum gespenst werde, wisse sie nicht [...] sie könne nur sagen: "wie das gespenst immer mehr stimmt, zu dem man verdonnert wurde, ja wie das gespenst in einem immer mehr zunimmt". (Röggla 2004, 197)[11]

Röggla's works characteristically involve combining a sociological approach to societal analysis with the analysis of language. The language of her characters corresponds to a lifestyle based on rationality, flexibility, individual initiative, the continuous performance of the self, and conformism. In order to enact this, fundamental elements of the individual are removed, such as autonomous thinking, or aspects of a social nature, like solidarity. In the fractures, pauses, repeated responses, in the interaction with an interlocutor, all of the weaknesses of the protagonists, and those of the system they embody, are revealed (Allkemper 2012). Röggla's works follow the Austrian tradition of unmasking the self through language to deal with the ills of contemporary society. However, unlike Elfriede Jelinek, she does not try to use words to bring out the depths of the human soul, or an unelaborated, personal, historical past, but rather to unmask the clichés of global society. The voices that we hear speaking appear without a past and without a future, prisoners of an anxiety-provoking present, they are alienated, passive, trained for continuous competition and performance. Insomnia and anxiety are the consequences of a distorted work ideology. Using estrangement and a form of ironic hyperrealism, the author forces the reader to go beneath the surface.

Another element that erodes the individual personality is the context in which people move and undertake work activity. Röggla places her characters in typical, contemporary non-places: exhibition halls, meeting rooms, car parks, airports, seminar rooms, and supermarkets. Even their domestic indoor surroundings are depersonalized. There are no descriptions of particular furnishings, nor are there family scenes, only isolated individuals locked in claustrophobic rooms, sitting in front of the television, on the telephone or near windows in buildings in cold cities in which you are either a tourist or a stranger, like aliens or illegal immigrants. Rather than acting, they observe others and themselves as foreign bodies. The sense of threat is constant, fuelled by the media. In *die alarmbereiten* (Röggla 2010), the author gathers seven "stories", unusual in their form and content, where the protagonists have to face environmental and financial catastrophes, climate change, pandemics, terrorism, the nefarious dealings of humanitarian organizations, and the invasiveness of the media in search of sensational stories. The characters, reduced to mere voices, live immersed in these real or virtual catastrophic scenarios, which mirror their own workplaces, and in the end, succumb to their own fixations. Moreover, their anxieties and paranoia are fuelled by the media bombardment, which prevents the individual from thinking freely, leading to final dissolution. In the place of individual identity, we have, yet again, social typologies that correspond to people's own work activity. There are the "observers", the experts who, when faced with the unmanageable situation, literally disappear from the hotel seminar room where they are meeting to organize yet another emergency plan. Then there are the "talkers", those who try in vain to overcome their own fear through a continuous flow of words that they dump on others during public meetings, private appointments or on the telephone. Even the translators, the word professionals, are no longer able to translate the absurdity of the ideology and terminology of business speak that is dehumanizing and self-destructive.

Similarly, in the sequence of scenes dedicated to the reactions to 9/11 entitled *fake reports*, included in the collection of works *besser wäre: keine* (it would be better: nothing–Röggla 2013), people are replaced with typologies of human beings that are labelled and act like machines ("präsenzmaschinen", "medienmaschinen", "mythenmaschinen"). Included are workers from various sectors, such as the media, photographers, technicians, public relations, journalists, politicians; all are of an intermediate level and use prefabricated language. The author writes in the initial stage directions:

> rhetoriken, formate, gesten, narrative strukturen sind für sie genauso bestimmend wie mentalitäten, politische haltungen oder auch kulturalismen [...] sie versuchen sich zurechtzufinden, betreiben mimikry an dem, was sie nicht verstehen. (Röggla 2013, 39)[12]

Reduced to mere numbers in a giant media theatre, they participate in a "Katastrophennetzwerk" made up of a network of people who are constantly on the move (NGO and international organization workers, economists, engineers, scientists), who in the end lose control of events and of themselves. In Röggla's literary world, identities are not determined by geographical provenance or by family ties. Instead, ordinary people become bearers of the dominant discourse, imposed upon them by the global capitalist economy. There are no dissenting voices; the feeling of estrangement leads to social death and self-dissolution in a ghostly universe, all animated, however, by a certain irony, by a bizarre "coupling of the disconcerting and the comic" (Röggla 2010, 178).

In *Nachtsendung* (night mission) from 2016, a collection of short stories, the author presents us with a sample of men and women overwhelmed by the absurdity of their everyday normality. Compared to her previous works these stories apparently use a more traditional type of narration. This time, all of the characters have a Christian name and a surname; we have access to their thoughts and the events are narrated from their perspectives. But this apparent normality turns into a nightmare, in the empty feeling that manifests itself above all in the perception of the individual. This is what inadvertently happens during an invasive work activity that determines a way of thinking, based on the imperatives of efficiency, flexibility and mobility, revealing its inhumanity. It is no coincidence that the characters are often seen during a journey, for work or for a supposed holiday: in a car, on a bus, on an airplane. They rarely drive themselves, more often they are "transported" through wastelands or eerie urban scenery that is never described in detail, but only conveyed through the disturbed vision of the characters. Significantly, the collection begins with a description of a group of passengers who are waiting inside an airplane stuck on the runway. It is as if the next 40 stories are born out of this anxiety-provoking wait. At the end of the volume, we revisit the airplane and its occupants, who are finally taking off as if nothing has happened, thereby perpetuating the collective madness in which they are all immersed.

Almost all of the stories narrated have the hallmarks of a tragicomic sensation of estrangement that is suddenly felt in the surrounding environment, usually a work context or that of a "holiday", which turns out to be even more devastating. The unexpected disorientation experienced defamiliarizes that which has seemed normal, culminating in the dissolution of the personality. The dominant economic discourse, which until now has determined the language and lifestyle of the characters, gets stuck, and the subject is no longer able to go backward or forward: an insurer, after a system fault, is no longer able to rediscover any threads of normality; an office clerk misses a Thursday and soon she cannot remember anything about all of the days in which she has done something unscrupulous, yet profitable for her company and career; a journalist at an international discussion forum is the only one who notices a speaker who is invisible to the others; a professor wanders absent-mindedly through a hotel that is hosting a conference of 1400 Germanists and historians until he is the only survivor; a talk show host finds himself facing guests who are no longer able to speak. These are apocalyptic scenarios, in which particular catastrophes are not described, nor are the ruins displayed. But the feeling that something ominous is looming or that perhaps it has already happened, provokes feelings of annihilation, of losing track of time and space. The self loses temporal and spatial coordinates in an alienation that extends itself from the world of work to every sphere of life.

The false identity that Röggla wants to unmask is that of a middle class that has lost contact with reality, it lives as if it were in a media bubble with a sense of precariousness and anxiety. It is a sort of sleep that is both hyperactive and dull at the same time. Just as the average person is in crisis, so is the concept of collectivity, it shatters into momentary, ephemeral and illusory associations, such as collecting petition signatures online or a flash mob (Röggla 2015, 49). In her lectures on poetics, *Die falsche Frage* (The wrong question 2015), Röggla treats the concept of teamwork as a problem. There is always talk of cooperation at every level, but what is really behind it, what remains after the moment of social connection once the individual is off the Internet? In contrast, democratic participation in the life of the state is continually diminishing and there are increasing numbers of individuals with narcissistic personality disorders (Röggla 2015, 52–54). Taking inspiration from sociology, Röggla aspires to translate a crisis that involves both individuals and the democratic system into new literary forms:

> In liquiden spätkapitalistischen Demokratien sind es flexible Subjekte, dynamisierte und fragmentierte, die unsere *role models* darstellen. Inszenierung und "Vernetzung", "Mobilität", "Multitasking" und "Virtualisierung" sind Idealbegriffe unserer Zeit, die keinen Rahmen mehr für die alten Vorstellungen von identitären Subjekt abgeben. [...] Meine Figuren sind paradoxe Kollektive, Teams, die eher Nichtteams sind, die eigentlich immer gegeneinander arbeiten, die kein Produkt herstellen, sondern da sind, um sich zu rechtfertigen, die den anderen immer eher ausstechen wollen. (ibid., 61)[13]

Just as the non-stop talk hides uncomfortable truths, this movement similarly hides a real static state, an underlying inertia. For Röggla it is as if individuals live by continuously moving from one interruption to another, and this also modifies how things are perceived (ibid., 67). We are constantly looking for confirmation of ourselves, through the images of ourselves that the media send out. The self no longer exists as such, but only to the extent to which it is represented. We sell our own images to the highest bidder, to a public that in turn, is completely absorbed by the drive to represent themselves, because otherwise they no longer exist (ibid., 70). Here, the unease, the evanescence of the self or the dissolving identity of Röggla's characters is obvious. She plays ironically with the disappearance of the self, which means disappearance of the capacity to imagine a different future.

Victims of a general flattening, of a surface two-dimensionality ("Die Welt ist flach", The World is Flat, is the title of one of her *Nachtsendung* stories in which the characters feel squashed inside a postcard), Röggla's characters are determined and trapped by a system that impedes free, individual development. Literature and literary discourse thus become the author's tool for denouncing the dominant economic discourses and for reflecting on social identities and on the loss of liberty and essential democracy for the autonomous, conscious development of identity.

Notes

[1] The English quotations from *wir schlafen nicht* are from the translation by Rebecca S. Thomas 2009, *we never sleep*. "this text is based on conversations with *consultants, coaches, key account managers, programmers, interns*, etc." (Röggla 2009).

[2] "*the senior associate:* one should feel free to warn him if he started throwing around too many english expressions. this had actually become automatic with him by now, sometimes he didn't even notice what trade jargon he was actually using and what kinds of vocabulary he was letting slip all this time. very quickly you simply became incomprehensible to outsiders. [...] but this mutual incomprehensibility was one of the exact reasons why consulting existed anyway" (ibid., 7).

[3] "at some point you don't even notice that you're talking anymore" (ibid., 6).

[4] "you hear yourself talking while you're speaking" (ibid., 21).

[5] "at the beginning he had approached it with the attitude - "so to speak": it wasn't really him doing the job. it was more that he was playing a role, he was just playing along and checking it out, so to speak. or it was some kind of experiment that he was performing on himself along the lines of: let's see how this world feels. that is an attitude that you just can't maintain [...] because of the fact that this job demanded 100%. [...] maybe others could, but he was not the type who could fake it 24 hours a day, no that he wasn't." (ibid., 11–12).

[6] "to keep your mouth shut [...] at least hold back somewhat with your opinions. everyone knew: what you could say and what you couldn't" (ibid., 29).

[7] "yes, he had lost his voice, really completely lost it. "it didn't work at all anymore", and in his job you really had to have a voice, without a voice nothing worked at all. after the fact, it seemed to him that his voice was his most important tool, his work situation was just incredibly interactive, continually communicating,

conferring with people, communicate, hold meetings and communicate some more." (Röggla 2009, 92)

[8] "couldn't you be just a little bit faster? couldn't things run just a little bit more efficiently? where could you optimize the work process?" (ibid., 114).

[9] "*the partner:* yes, there was a little bit of brainwashing that went on if you stayed around here for a while, but a little bit of brainwashing would have to be involved. that was the point of the whole thing. that was the agenda of every trade fair. otherwise, you'd never do any business (laughs). but over time you really did start having some odd thoughts. you just had to watch out that it didn't get transmitted to you, this whole insane atmosphere here. [...] with time a few disturbances did appear, various disturbances in perception, for example. there could even be cognitive dissonances if you weren't careful, with the memory too. but you really didn't have to worry about him, no, he was just a little tense, and under the circumstances you could lose your temper at times..." (ibid., 113).

[10] "and besides that: no one has been kidnapped and brought here against their will. no, you couldn't say that, they had all come here of their own free will. - no, you couldn't call it a kidnapping. [...] - if it were, then it would have to be about a kidnapping with a longer term of investment, one that had been going on for a longer period of time" (ibid., 112).

[11] "*the key account manager:* [...] but whether or not she was continually turning into more of a ghost, that she didn't know. [...] but she could only say: »how the ghost in her grew and grew, and how the ghostly existence one had been sentenced to became increasingly real" (ibid., 175).

[12] "[...] rhetoric, formats, gestures, narrative structures mark them as much as mentality, political attitudes or culturalisms [...] they try to make sense of it all, they use mimicry for what they do not understand" (my trans.).

[13] "In liquid, late capitalist societies it is flexible, dynamized and fragmented subjects who represent our *role models*. To perform and "to be online", "mobility", "multitasking" and "virtualization" are ideal concepts of our time, which provide no more the frame for the old images of subjective identities [...] My figures are paradoxical collectives, teams, which are, rather, non–teams , which, in reality, work always one against the other, not realizing a product, but they exist in order to justify themselves, they always want to overtake each other." (my trans.).

References

Allkemper, Alo. 2012. "Kathrin Röggla: 'stottern'." In *Gegenwartsliteratur Schreiben*, edited by Alo Allkemper, Norbert Otto Elke, and Helmut Steinecke, 417–430. München: Fink.

Kormann, Eva. 2015. "Risiko Schreiben in der flüchtigen Moderne: Kathrin Rögglas Variante einer littérature engagée." In *Gegenwartsliteratur: Ein Germanistisches Jahrbuch*, Bd. 14, edited by Paul Michael Lützeler, Erin McGlothlin, and Jennifer Kapczynski, 171–195. Tübingen: Stauffenburg.

Krauthausen, Karin. 2010. "Gespräche mit Untoten, Das konjunktivische Interview in Kathrin Rögglas Roman *wir schlafen nicht*." In *Schreibweisen Poetologien 2 Zeigenössische österreichische Literatur von Frauen*, edited by Hilde Kernmayer, 191–215. Wien: Milena.

Kremer, Christian. 2008. *Milieu und Performativität. Deutsche Gegenwartsprosa von John von Duffel, Georg M. Oswald und Kathrin Röggla,* Marburg: Tectum.

Loreto Vilar, Maria, 2010. "Decoding Images: Top-Dog-Jobs für Frauen in Kathrin Rögglas *wir schlafen nicht*." In *Die gläserne Decke: Fakt oder Fiktion,* edited by Dolors Sabaté Planes, and Marion Schulz, 129–142. Frankfurt am Main: Peter Lang.

—. 2013. "Gegen die mediale Krisendramaturgie: Zur Performativität des Katastrophischen im Theater von Hilling, Röggla und Jelinek." In *Literatur als Performance,* edited by Ana R. Calero Valera, and Birgitte E. Jirka, 109–123. Würzburg: Königshausen & Neumann.

Pümpel, Daniela. 2014. "Burnout als Thema der Literatur–Kathrin Rögglas Roman *wir schlafen nicht* als literarisches Abbild einer Leistungsgesellschaft." In *Arbeit und Kultur: Positionen in Kunst und Theorie,* edited by Martin Mader, 25–63, Innsbruck: Studia.

Röggla, Kathrin. 2013 [2004] *wir schlafen nicht.* Frankfurt am Main: Fischer Taschenbuch.

—. 2009. *We never sleep*, transl. by Rebecca S. Thomas. Riverside, Cal.: Ariadne Press.

—. 2010. "Ironie, Kritik und Performance." In *Schreibweisen Poetologien 2 Zeigenössische österreichische Literatur von Frauen*, edited by Hilde Kernmayer, 178–190. Wien: Milena.

—. 2012. *die alarmbereiten.* Frankfurt am Main: Fischer.

—. 2013. *besser wäre: keine: essays und theater.* Frankfurt am Main: Fischer.

—. 2015. *Die falsche Frage: Theater, Politik und die Kunst, das Fürchten nicht zu verlernen.* Berlin: Theater der Zeit.

—. 2016. *Nachtsendung*. Frankfurt am Main: Fischer.

CHAPTER FOURTEEN

HOW THE "OTHER" BECOMES "AGENT" THROUGH THE RUPTURE OF WAR: A NEW LOOK AT JACQUELINE WINSPEAR'S MAISIE DOBBS NOVELS

JANE M. EKSTAM

The fourteen Maisie Dobbs novels by Jacqueline Winspear[1] follow the gradual development of private investigator Maisie Dobbs' identity from "the other" to "agent". War changes Maisie's life forever, develops one of her greatest strengths, natural empathy, and leads her into a professional path that allows her to take control over her life despite her humble beginnings and gender. Maisie is "the other" in three main respects: social class, gender, and profession (there were few female private investigators in the inter-war years). In this chapter, I explore these three kinds of "otherness" and how they contribute to and/or inhibit Maisie's identity development.

Winspear's novels explore crimes whose origins can be traced back to World War One, a war in which Maisie herself has participated. She is a young woman in her thirties at the beginning of the series. As her career progresses, she solves an impressively wide variety of crimes, primarily murders. Her success as a private investigator, however, changes her status forever: she becomes a successful, educated, well-trained and self-assured professional whose qualities, albeit grudgingly, are recognised by male colleagues, and whose services are requested by both Scotland Yard and the British Secret Service.

Like many working-class girls at the time, the fictional Maisie becomes a servant at the age of thirteen. Noting her passion for books and learning, her employer allows Maisie to be tutored by the well-known scholar and detective, Maurice Blanche. Maisie passes the entrance examinations to

Girton College (Cambridge University) but defers her studies until after the war, where she serves as a Voluntary Aid Detached nurse (VAD). Her years at the front prove to be invaluable experience when she starts her private investigation agency. By the eleventh novel, *A Dangerous Place*, Maisie becomes Lady Compton through marriage. Characteristically, however, she prefers to be addressed by her maiden name, Dobbs, and particularly after the early death of her husband in an aeroplane crash.

As a detective, Maisie is middle class. She can move easily between the lower, middle and upper classes but is never quite at home in any class. She is always "the other" socially. Professionally, she is also "the other", at least in the eyes of some of the male colleagues with whom she must work on occasions at Scotland Yard. However, as a self-employed private investigator, she becomes her own as "agent", one who, in the Ricoeurian sense, is capable of action not only on her own behalf but also that of others (Ricoeur 1995). She is her own boss, and establishes a reputation as a highly successful investigator. She knows who she is and what she can do. And equally importantly, she remains true to herself throughout the series. She holds to her ideals and to the values and expectations of her profession and not only accepts but capitalises on the lessons she learns at different stages of her life and career; she demonstrates a broad understanding of human nature and the influence of the environment on it; and she remains proud of her origins and the social and professional journey that she makes throughout the thirteen novels. Whatever her situation, we can trust Maisie to remain true to herself.

Death, and individual death in particular, is at the centre of detective fiction. As Susan Rowland has demonstrated, the genre attempts "to compensate for, or rebalance, the cultural psyche in a time when war seems to efface the meaning of an individual death" (2015a, 39).[2] Death becomes meaningful and thus "solvable at the level of self-conscious fiction" (Rowland, 2015, 39). Maisie must identify with the murdered victim so "that she undergoes, symbolically, the same method of death as the victim, but she survives" (Jackson 2002, 15). Because it is impossible to "know" death completely, Maisie can only be "other", looking on from the outside. It is one of her greatest strengths that she feels empathy for not only the victim but also the perpetrator.[3] This is an important part of the appeal of the novels and of their authenticity as detective stories because, as I have argued elsewhere, "the authenticity of detective stories lies in the way they use imaginative resources to foster empathy" (Ekstam 2015, 804). Empathy leads to sympathy, which, by its very nature, is "other-directed" (Keen 2006, 208). Maisie is thus "the other" in terms of social class, gender and profession; she is also "the other" because death is unknowable for the living. And her empathy for victim and perpetrator alike is "other-directed".

Writing in 1938, Virginia Woolf observed that "[t]o fight has always been the man's habit, not the woman's" (92). Maisie is a fighter but her primary task, in war as well as peace, is to save lives. She accepts the truth that fighting is "the habit of our culture" (Hanley 1991, 148), but the chief "habit" of Maisie's life is to alleviate the suffering arising directly from war. As the series encompasses both world wars (the most recent novel, *In This Grave Hour*, 2017, is set at the beginning of World War Two), Maisie has accumulated two decades' of war experience.

As a middle-class woman by profession, Maisie represents the change in middle-class femininity brought about by World War One as she adopts and develops "what had formerly been regarded as distinctly masculine qualities: in particular the ethics of a code of self-control and a language of reticence [...]" (Light 1991, 210). With the guidance of her mentor, Maurice Blanche, and, to a lesser extent, a mystic called Basil Khan, Maisie learns that she must always be in control of herself, and must say as little as possible until she is sure of the facts. Even then, she does not impart the latter until she can be sure that she can protect all concerned: victim(s), survivor(s), and perpetrator(s) alike. It is all about finding as satisfactory and as harmonious a conclusion as possible.

Stories, like life, need an ending. As Frank Kermode claims,

> in much the same way as the end of the Bible transforms all its contents, our sense of, or need for, an ending transforms our lives 'between the *tick* of birth and the *tock* of death', and stories simulate this transformation but must not do so too simply. (Kermode 2000, 197)

The detective story promises a resolution; the path that this follows is twisting and unpredictable, and if it is to be effective, it is certainly anything but simple. At the same time, the Maisie Dobbs novels maintain realism and credibility, two essential features of detective fiction today (James 2009, 5). And, as Maureen T. Reddy has demonstrated, detective fiction engages "the reader's interest in the extremes of human passion. There are very few other crimes that hold attention in quite the same way" (1988, 5). We can be sure that Maisie will find the perpetrator, show empathy for all involved, and that life will go on.

Three Kinds of "Otherness"

The three kinds of otherness, social, gender and professional, which are discussed below and contribute to and/or inhibit the development of Maisie's identity are viewed here from both a feminist perspective (Simone de Beauvoir), and from the perspective of empathy (Suzanne Keen).

The feminist theorist and philosopher Simone de Beauvoir claims that the concept of "the other" is "as primordial as consciousness itself" (1997, 16). It presupposes a duality of the "self" and "the other". The concept of "the other", she argues, loses its absolute sense in time of war as individuals and groups are forced "to realize the reciprocity of their relations" (ibid., 17). The same duality, de Beauvoir argues, can be applied to the nature of truth, which is neither absolute nor fixed, but is subject to interpretation. This is a fact of the masculine world that women can and must learn:

> Woman does not entertain the positive belief that the truth is something *other* than men claim; she recognizes, rather, that there *is* not any fixed truth. It is not only the changing nature of life that makes her suspicious of the principle of constant identity, nor is it the magic phenomena with which she is surrounded that destroy the notion of causality. It is at the heart of the masculine world itself, it is in herself belonging to this world that she comes upon the ambiguity of all principle, of all value, of everything that exists. (ibid., 624, original emphases)

It is above all how a woman "carries on her profession and her devotion to it" that determines the "total pattern of her life" (ibid., 1949, 691). As de Beauvoir goes on to explain, even in 1949 (two decades after Maisie becomes a private investigator; *The Second Sex* was first published in 1949), the independent woman was viewed with some scepticism: "It must be said that the independent woman is justifiably disturbed by the idea that people do not have confidence in her. As a general rule, the superior caste is hostile to newcomers from the inferior caste" (ibid. 1949, 710).

Maisie earns respect, as she is always successful, primarily due to her innovative and peculiarly feminine methods, of which more below. Her success is also due in no small part to the fact that she upholds a high level of moral conduct. As Joseph Campbell explains, the battle between good and evil is an essential feature of the field of ethics (2013, 247). M. E. Evans takes this further as she argues that detective fiction by tradition has tended to focus on the tension between a moral code that appears to be "omnipresent and relevant to all" and "the very considerable differences in social power (and influence), which are the consequences of societies divided by class, race and gender" (2009, 2–3). Because detective fiction is restorative, i.e. the social world is returned to its pre-crime state, it is also healing and redemptive. In the following, I hope to demonstrate that while Maisie Dobbs is "the other" in terms of social class, gender and choice of profession–it is only through her that we can make sense of the story. We can trust her because, whatever and whomever she faces, her role as private investigator provides her with the "reassuring stable identity" (Rowland 2001, 23) that is an important pre-requisite of detective fiction.

As already established, one of the most prominent features of Maisie's stable identity is her natural empathy. Keen defines empathy as "a vicarious, spontaneous sharing of affect, [which] can be provoked by witnessing another's emotional state, by hearing about another's condition, or even by reading" (2006a, 208). Empathy is a precursor to sympathy because it is focused on what a person might be expected to feel in a given situation or context.[4] Empathy, which leads to sympathy, is by definition, other-directed as it leads to feelings *for* another. As will be revealed shortly, in the description of Maisie's methods as a private investigator, empathy and sympathy are important features of Maisie's success as well as her appeal. They are also important reasons why the Maisie Dobbs series is so successful, with approximately one novel a year being produced since 2003.

In the following discussion of Maisie as "the other" who becomes "an agent", it is important to bear in mind the social and historical context of the novels, which encompasses pre-World War One Britain, Britain between the two world wars, and the beginning of World War Two. Individuals define themselves "in terms of what is relevant in their time and place" (Oyserman et al. 2014, 76). Maisie's journey from being "the other" to becoming an "agent" encompasses the effect of the past on her present and encompasses the most formative events in her identity development. This includes her studies at Girton College, her period of service as a VAD at the front during World War One, her apprenticeship under Maurice Blanche, including his continued influence on her life and career after his death, and the lessons she learns as she becomes an increasingly experienced and well-respected private investigator. The focus here is on her professional identity. Like all identities, this must be endorsed by others, and not least, by her male colleagues at Scotland Yard.

The Past and Maisie's Search for Truth: The Hindrances of Class

Maisie is happiest when she is asking questions. Answering questions, on the other hand, and particularly those pertaining to her past, is a particular problem for her. This is established in the first novel, *Maisie Dobbs*, where the narrator records that the questions "likely to be most difficult [for Maisie] were those that pertained to her past" (Winspear 2003, 220). In the third novel in the series, *Pardonable Lies*, the narrator notes that, "Maisie knew only too well [that] her job demanded that she reside in the past for most of her working life. And the past was a dark abyss into which she was quickly descending" (Winspear 2005, 132). The past is dark for Maisie because she lost her mother when she was only twelve years old, her period as a servant was arduous, and her time at the front as a VAD was painful emotionally and spiritually. It also resulted in the serious wounding of her lover, Dr Simon Lynch (who never recovers from shell shock and does not recognise Maisie when she visits him in the home for shell-shocked soldiers). Maisie recognises that the "wounds of the past" can be "camouflaged" (Winspear 2010, 217); it is a greater challenge to extinguish them entirely. At the same time, Maisie acknowledges that "looking back at the past" is the best way "to understand the present" (Winspear 2005, 62), and in the ninth novel of the series, *Elegy for Eddie*, the narrator emphasises that one of Maisie's greatest fears is that "she might lose touch with the past, and in so doing lose herself" (2012, 51). It is also the only way that her future will "spread out in front of her" (Winspear 2003, 287).

It is above all Maisie's work that is the means of recovering from the past. In the fourth novel of the series, *Messenger of Truth*, she admits both to herself and to Dr Dene that her work is her security, it gives her "some sort of mastery over circumstance […] *order* makes me feel safe, gives me battlements and a moat" (2006, 186. Original emphases). And, seven novels later, in *A Dangerous Place*, her job has become her salvation as she investigates the mysterious death of Babayoff. She remembers not just the war but also the loss of her child as a result of her miscarriage. This took place after having witnessed the plane her husband was piloting crash to the ground:

> Perhaps she would find the person she used to be, before tragedy struck her a second time, cutting deeper into her soul, a still-open wound more livid than anything left by the war. Now she was in business–and that

responsibility to another would give her a reason to live. (Winspear 2016, 62)

Maisie's profession is a means of survival, but it is more than that: it offers the promise of establishing the truth, which "has a certain buoyancy–it makes its way to the surface, in time" (Winspear 2017, 328). While the narrator is referring to the truth about the murder of a man who escaped occupied Belgium as a boy during World War One, the comment applies equally well to Maisie's personal position: the truth of her background and of her losses during World War One is never far from her thoughts. Indeed, it is one of the paramount reasons why she is so successful as a private investigator. She knows what suffering is, what it can do to you, and how it can be alleviated. She also knows how one's gender, social position and profession can either open or close doors. The point made by de Beauvoir about the special challenges facing an independent woman are particularly relevant to Maisie:

> The way [a woman] carries on her profession, and her devotion to it depend on the context supplied by the total pattern of her life. For when she begins her adult life she does not have behind her the same past as does a boy; she is not viewed by society in the same way; the universe presents itself to her in a different perspective. The fact of being a woman today poses peculiar problems for an independent human individual. (1949, 691)

Maisie strives to overcome the limitations of her gender, social position and choice of profession not only for herself but for those whom she serves. An important starting point is her studies with the earlier mentioned Maurice Blanche, which lead to her passing the entrance examinations for Girton College, Cambridge University (she studies psychology, ethics and philosophy). Few details are provided of her period at Girton College: it is her passing of the entrance examinations and the award of her degree along with her deferment of her studies in order to serve her country during World War One that are of primary importance. To understand just what a huge academic achievement it was for a woman in Maisie's position to be admitted to and graduate from Girton College it is necessary to understand something about higher education at Girton College.

Maisie and the Academic Life: Gaining Agency through Education

Girton College was founded by Emily Davies,[5] Barbara Bodichon and Lady Stanley of Alderley in 1869 to provide women with the same higher education and employment opportunities as men. The majority (approximately 95%) of Girtonians were from the middle class (Thane 2004, 349). They were the daughters of clerks, clergymen and schoolmasters, businessmen and colonial officials. The fictional Maisie, with her servant background and with a father whose profession was that of a costermonger, automatically belongs to a much lower class. The female students saw Girton as a means of acquiring professional skills, achieving social mobility, or, at the very least, gaining personal security (Thane 2004, 350). The standard middle-class Girton graduate was expected to become a schoolteacher, a tradition that continued until the 1960s (Thane 2004, 354). Here again, the fictional Maisie is an exception: she does not become a schoolteacher, although she does a short spell of teaching at St Francis College, Cambridge, where, fittingly, her chief task is not to teach (although she succeeds brilliantly at this) but to discover the truth behind the murder of a senior member of the academic staff.

It is notable that where Girtonians entered mixed-sex occupations, they were subjected to discrimination. This state of affairs, according to Thane, continued until the 1960s and included tensions and/or hostility (2004, 357). The fictional Maisie encounters similar problems. Already by the second novel, however, she begins to earn the respect of Inspector Stratton of Scotland Yard. She is called in as a pupil of Maurice Blanche, who has a reputation for solving difficult crimes efficiently, but Maisie quickly demonstrates that she is worthy of consultation in her own right. And, by the fourth novel in the series, *The Messenger of Truth*, Stratton is forced to admit, albeit somewhat grudgingly, that "Miss Dobbs has certain skills, certain [...] methods, that seem to bear fruit" (Winspear 2006, 3).

Maisie as a VAD: The School of Life

There are two important foundations for Maisie's "certain skills" and methods: her studies at Girton College, and more particularly those relating to moral philosophy, and her period of service as a VAD on the Western Front. The work of a VAD was varied, and included nursing, transport duties, and organisation of rest stations, working parties and auxiliary hospitals. VADs were required to pass examinations in order to gain first aid and nursing certificates. Many VADs were drawn from the middle- and upper classes. The fictional Maisie finds herself between classes. She learns quickly, however, that there is yet another class: the regular nurse, who must be deferred to at all times:

> The nurse who spoke to her was one of the regulars, not a volunteer, and Maisie immediately reverted to the bobbed curtsy of her days in service. The seniority of the regular nurses demanded respect, immediate attention, and complete deference. (Winspear 2003, 161)

At the front, Maisie drives ambulances and also serves at casualty clearing stations, which were behind the front lines. The lessons she learns prove invaluable in solving the crimes she will investigate after the War. It is not only practical skills that she learns as a VAD but also the importance of empathy and sympathy in her relations with the men she tends. It is at the front that Maisie learns about the extraordinary ability of human beings to suffer, to hide their suffering and to store it until it becomes unbearable– and what happens when human beings break, physically or emotionally.

In the very first novel, Maisie declares that her experience at the front and her period of service at a secure mental hospital after the War have helped her to "understand the wounds […] Those of the body–and of the soul" (Winspear 2002, 38). But when these wounds are inflicted on herself, she struggles: the loss of a husband and their unborn baby is almost too much to bear, even for Maisie. It is significant that it is to nursing that she turns first–only after her work as a nurse at an isolated hospital in Spain during the Spanish Civil War is she able to return to England to her private investigation agency. Nursing

> was all she needed. She would do work she knew she was good at in the service of those who needed her. She knew she would grow strong here, putting others before herself. And because she had always worked, and accepted that working was part of who she was, she thought that in time, after she'd returned to England, she might even feel compelled to go back to her old business. (Winspear 2015, 316)

Working as a nurse, and working as a private investigator are indeed integral parts of who Maisie is. And at the end of the most recent novel in the series, *In This Grave Hour*, we find Maisie joining the London Auxiliary Ambulance Service. When the recruiting officer asks her, "ready to do your bit?" (Winspear 2017, 332), Maisie not only replies in the affirmative but has a smile on her face. She is clearly determined to keep both her professions running at the same time. Her mentor, Maurice Blanche, would have been proud of her.

Maisie and Maurice Blanche: The Importance of Mentors in Developing Agency

Maurice Blanche and the lessons he teaches Maisie occupy a prominent position in all thirteen novels. Not surprisingly, it is in the first novel that we receive most detail but the same lessons re-appear, sometimes in slightly different forms, in the following novels. It is Maurice who understands Maisie best, and who has greatest influence over her intellectual, social and professional development. The values and skills that he teaches her serve her well at Girton College, at the Western front, and in her career as a private investigator. Before discussing these skills, I wish to turn briefly to the situation of women and police/detective work in the 1920s and 1930s.

As a result of the 1919 Sex Disqualification (Removal) Act, women started to train as barristers. The Act also paved the way for the appointment of female magistrates, though very few women took the opportunity (the 1921 census recorded twenty female barristers and seventeen solicitors. Horn 2013, 30). For women in the police force the situation was particularly challenging due to intense anti-female prejudice. The Police Federation of England and Wales claimed that police work "'was a man's job alone' and that women were useless" (Horn 2013, 135). The situation improved by 1931, when "there were almost two hundred female barristers and solicitors, compared with thirty-seven recorded in 1921, and none at all before 1919" (Horn 2013, 137). While Maisie does not train to be either a barrister or a solicitor, it is clear that the position of women in legal service was tenuous to say the least.

Starting up one's own business, albeit as a private investigator, was a brave decision at the time. This made it all the more important that the fictional Maisie should be trained by one who not only understands the law but also has the important contacts, social and professional, that Maisie lacks. Blanche is also a male, and at this time, it was common for men to teach and validate women.

What are the primary lessons that Maisie learns from Blanche? Maisie learns the importance of asking questions and leaving the door open to truth. "Truth walks toward us on the paths of our questions" (Winspear

2002, 32), Blanche tells Maisie at a very early stage of her career. In *Pardonable Lies*, Maisie is both able and feels satisfaction that she can teach her assistant, Billy Beale that "questions […] are at the heart of our success" (Winspear 2005, 39). A frequently recalled lesson is that coincidence is the messenger of truth, and it is one that is recalled in the most recent novel, *In This Grave Hour*, where the narrator reminds the reader that "Maisie would never discount a coincidence" (Winspear 2017, 87).

Blanche constantly reminds Maisie that she must always show respect. "Respect is crucial, on both sides, as is tolerance, and a depth of understanding of those influences that sculpt a character" (Winspear 2006, 151).

Maisie is also constantly reminded that she must allow the dead body to speak immediately after death:

> She heard Maurice's voice in her mind. 'If we are afforded the time, Maisie, those moments of quiet in the company of the dead give the one who has passed an opportunity to tell of their passing–in their position, their belongings, and the obvious causes of death. Allow yourself that moment, if you can'. (Winspear 2011, 96)

By the fifth novel in the series, *An Incomplete Revenge*, Maurice is able to tell Maisie that "You are no longer my pupil or assistant, Maisie. You are accomplished in your own right. You have little need of me now" (Winspear 2008, 227). Even at this early stage, Maurice recognises Maisie's potential and recognises that she will go on to be an unusually brave and competent private investigator. It is in the last two novels in the series, where Maisie finds herself in Munich shortly before the outbreak of war (Winspear 2016) and in the 2017 novel, *In This Grave Hour* (where she is in occupied Belgium) that she has cause to remember all the lessons she has learned from Maurice. She realises that she can stand on her own two feet. Maurice's lessons have become her own. She is no longer "the other" but is an agent in her own right. She has taken risks that few men would take, even in war, she has succeeded where others have failed, and has remained true to her own ideals as well as those of her most important teacher, Maurice Blanche. She retains what she is trained for, i.e. to run a private investigation agency, she returns to what she has discovered about herself in World War One as she volunteers for the London Auxiliary Ambulance Service, but she never forgets where she comes from.

The fourteen Maisie Dobbs novels by Jacqueline Winspear follow the gradual development of Maisie Dobbs' identity from being classified as "the other" in terms of gender, class and profession to becoming an agent in her own life. The fourteen novels published thus far in the series excite empathy and are thus other-directed, they focus on individual death, whose importance is recognised but will always, as the unknown, be "the other". Maisie, however, clearly emerges as an agent in her own life. She is in control of herself, her past and present, and is recognised by male and female colleagues as the one to call on where others have failed. She is indomitable.

Notes

[1] The fourteenth novel in the series, *To Die But Once*, was released on March 27, 2018.

[2] Rowland makes several references to Maisie Dobbs in her study, claiming, for example, that, while Maisie is willing to work with male colleagues, and even agrees to become a British intelligence agent in order to combat a Nazi spy ring in 1930s England (*A Lesson in Secrets*, 2011), she nonetheless "prefers to work alone, with a well-founded distrust of pervasively masculine institutions like the police" (55). Maisie is her own institution and agent; men must come to her if they require help.

[3] Susan Rowland describes "Maisie's ability to increase skills of empathy, to the point where she can trace deeply buried threads of twisted relationships leading to murder" (104).

[4] Keen distinguishes between empathy and sympathy as follows: **Empathy**–I feel what you feel. **Sympathy**–I feel a supportive emotion. **Empathy**–I feel your pain. **Sympathy**–I feel pity for your pain (Keen 2006, 209).

[5] For further information regarding the establishment of Girton College and Emily Davies's philosophy of education, see Emily Davies. 1866. *The Higher Education of Women*. Reprinted 1988. London: The Hambledon Press.

References

Campbell, Joseph. 1999. *Transformations of Myth Through Time*. New York: Harper Perennial.
Davies. Emily. 1988 [1866]. *The Higher Education of Women*. London: The Hambledon Press.
de Beauvoir, Simone. 1997. *The Second Sex*. London: Vintage Classics.
Ekstam, Jane M. 2015. "Modern Detective Fiction and World War One: A Symbiotic Relationship." *English Studies*, Vol. 96, No. 7. DOI: 10.1080/0013838X.2015.1051872.
Evans, Mary E. 2009. *The Imagination of Evil. Detective Fiction and the Modern World*. New York: Continuum.
Hanley, Lynne. 1991. *Writing War, Gender & Memory*. Amherst: University of Massachusetts.
Horn, Pamela. 2013. *Flappers*. Gloucestershire: Amberley Publishing.
Jackson, Christine A. 2002. *Myth and Ritual. Women's Detective Fiction*. North Carolina and London: McFarland.
James. P(hyllis) D(orothy). 2009. *Talking about Detective Fiction*. Oxford: Faber and Faber.
Keen, Suzanne. 2006. "A Theory of Narrative Empathy." *Narrative*, Vol. 14, No. 3, 207–236. DOI: 10.1353/nar.2006.0015.
—. 2010. *Empathy and the Novel*. Oxford: Oxford University Press.
Kermode, Frank. 2000 [1966]. *The Sense of an Ending. Studies in the Theory of Fiction with a New Epilogue*. Oxford: Oxford University Press.
Light, Alison. 1991. *Forever England. Femininity, Literature and Conservatism between the wars*. London: Routledge.
Oyserman, Daphna, Kristin Elmore and George Smith. 2014. "Self, Self-Concept, and Identity." In *Handbook of Self and Identity,* edited by Mark R. Leary and Jane P. Tangney, 69–104. New York and London: The Guilford Press.
Reddy, Maureen T. 1988. *Sisters in Crime. Feminism and the Crime Novel*. New York: Continuum.
Ricoeur, Paul. 1995. *Oneself as Another*. Chicago: Chicago University Press.
Rowland, Susan. 2015. *The Sleuth and the Goddess. Hestia, Artemis, Athena and Aphrodite in Women's Detective Fiction*. Louisiana, USA: Spring Journal.
—. 2001. *From Agatha Christie to Ruth Rendell*. Houndmills: Palgrave.

Thane, Pat. 2004. "Girton Graduates: earning and learning, 1920s-1980s." *Women's History Review*, 13.4. DOI: 10.1080/09612020400200398.
Winspear, Jacqueline. 2003. *Maisie Dobbs*. London: John Murray.
—. 2005. *Pardonable Lies*. New York: Picador.
—. 2006. *Messenger of Truth*. London: John Murray.
—. 2008. *An Incomplete Revenge*. New York: Picador.
—. 2010. *The Mapping of Love and Death*. London: Allison and Busby.
—. 2011. *A Lesson in Secrets*. London: Allison and Busby.
—. 2012. *Elegy for Eddie*. London: Allison and Busby.
—. 2016. *A Dangerous Place*. London: Allison and Busby.
—. 2017. *In This Grave Hour*. New York: HarperCollins.
—. 2018. *To Die But Once*. New York: HarperCollins.
Woolf, Virginia. 1938. *Three Guineas*. Oxford: Oxford University Press.

CHAPTER FIFTEEN

IN SEARCH OF "THE MESSAGE HIDDEN IN THE BEAUTY OF THE WORDS": VIRGINIA WOOLF'S NOVEL *MRS DALLOWAY*

BRITT ANDERSEN

Introduction

When Virginia Woolf published her famous modernist novel *Mrs Dalloway* in 1925, same-sex-love had for several decades been "the Love that dare not speak its name".[1] This chapter will focus on how negotiations of identity were expressed in literary texts in an early phase of modernism. The tabooed issues of lesbianism and homosexuality at this time were of course handled very differently from the way they are handled in post-modern take-offs on *Mrs Dalloway*. Michael Cunningham's novel *The Hours* (1998) and later the Oscar-winning movie of the same name (Daldry 2002)[2] have taken Woolf's "message hidden in the beauty of the words" (1925, 86) about sexualities and reworked her hidden cues explicitly. Although Cunningham draws heavily on the original novel, he illustrates a new openness to homosexuality and lesbianism. During the nearly eighty years separating these two novels, a sexual revolution has taken place.

Judith Butler, Eve Kosofsky Sedgwick, Michel Foucault, Teresa de Lauretis and many others have developed what has been called queer theory, which is central to my understanding of Woolf's novel. Foucault's *Sexual History* (1990) described how our ideas about sexuality and identity are historical constructs, approximately one hundred and fifty years old.[3] The construction of the homosexual as a person with special characteristics, made the homosexual different from the "normal" heterosexual person. The philosopher Jacques Derrida criticised people in the West for thinking in binary oppositions (1998). Academics within feminism and gender studies have focused a lot of attention on deconstructing the binary system of homo and hetero. Literary scholars have further been inspired by the American philosopher, Professor Judith Butler, who published *Gender Trouble* in 1990. This book examined how *both* the categories of homosexual and heterosexual are cultural constructs. According to Butler, continual repetition of heterosexuality defines gender and produces images of heterosexuality as something natural, free from social and cultural conditions. Since our repetition is not perfect, however, we can act subversively and contribute to change.

In this chapter, I critique a pervasive heteronormative misreading of Virginia Woolf's modernist masterpiece *Mrs Dalloway*. Already in her debut novel *The Voyage Out* (1915), Woolf wrote about an author who wanted to write about silence. What is silenced in the text is a taboo, that is, what is not spoken of.[4] Same-sex-love is described and at the same time silenced and kept secret: the heroine dies after the male artist asks her to marry him, but critics have not been able to explain why she dies.

I begin by examining a previously overlooked character, Miss Kilman, in *Mrs Dalloway*. By reading the subtext carefully, we will see how the author simultaneously expresses and disguises tabooed issues of sexuality. Woolf was one of the first authors to defy the contempt for same-sex love, so the reader should take the meta-comment on the "message hidden" in *Mrs Dalloway* very seriously. The aim of my analysis is to show that Miss Kilman is an important character, as she is the uncanny return of Clarissa Dalloway's own repressed desire. Owing to Woolf's literary construction of lesbianism, she is overloaded with stereotypical lesbian traits. Those who have not seen the grotesque humour in this portrait have missed out on some really interesting and entertaining descriptions.

New Aesthetics, New Issues

With modernism came a totally new aesthetics, with novelists copying Freud's method of free association. Yet, issues of sexual identity are often blurred–they can be found in the characters' pasts as well as in doubles or parallel characters. In *Mrs Dalloway*, the reader feels as if she is inside the characters' minds. Woolf thus adopted a more fluent, poetic style, with long, almost all-inclusive sentences, asking the reader to abandon a structured concept of the self for the semiotic, and give ourselves over to rhythms. The omniscient narrator, previously used to guide the reader, was now removed, requiring greater effort from the reader, who must assemble disparate bits of information. The result is a more fluent, poetic style, where tabooed issues could be expressed, but also hidden in the subtext.

Modernism also ushered in a new interest in perception, owing to a new awareness that we do not all share the same unified gaze. The omniscient narrator is more or less invisible, giving the illusion of direct access to the characters' minds. Perception is now inextricably intertwined with a given character's particular constellation of ethnicity, class, gender and sexuality. Woolf's novels are famous for delegating point of view to characters with different statuses, enabling the reader to observe a more multifaceted reality. With modernism, new and more daring topics were introduced into art. In her feminist essay "Mr Bennett and Mrs Brown" from 1924, Woolf herself argued that authors could write about themes that had been suppressed and "write about women as women have never been written about before" (Woolf 1968, 49). Woolf criticised male contemporaries for an "I" that relinquished all others to the shadow. One wants to know what is behind this male "I", she wrote.[5] However, Woolf also criticised female writers for their tendency to write with an anger that Woolf considered misplaced in a novel for the ways in which it destroyed a work's literary qualities. Woolf herself abandoned an overly dominant "I" and opted to write in the less oppressive third-person mode. However, in an essay from 1940, Virginia Woolf claimed somewhat surprisingly that she and her generation had revealed the "unpleasant truth" about themselves:

> Consider how difficult it is to tell the truth about oneself–the unpleasant truth... The nineteenth-century writers never told that kind of truth [...] The leaning-tower writer has had the courage at any rate...to tell the truth, the unpleasant truth about himself... By analysing themselves honestly, with help from Dr Freud, these writers have done a great deal to free us from the nineteenth century suppressions. (Woolf 1966, 149)

The preceding text was communicated on Sigmund Freud's 80th birthday, enabling Woolf to honour Freud's work by offering up her generation's gratitude. Virginia and her husband Leonard Woolf had had a lasting relationship to Freud through the Hogarth Press, which they founded, and which became the first official organ for psychoanalysis in England: "Between 1924 and 1939 we published an English translation of every book [Freud] wrote, and after his death, we published his complete works, 24 volumes, in the Standard Edition", Leonard wrote (L. Woolf 1967, 166). Virginia Woolf did not agree with Freud's theories on sexuality, but her generation did nonetheless use psychoanalytical insights in their writing. Woolf undoubtedly, for example, made use of Freud's theories on grief and melancholia,[6] as she had access to Freud's theories in her innermost circle. Her younger brother, Adrian, was in fact a practicing psychoanalyst, and he debated Sigmund Freud's theories on melancholia with Virginia Woolf in 1923, the year she started writing *Mrs Dalloway*. In the novel, she is surprisingly open about the psychic illness affecting both her own and Freud's lives,[7] as both suffered from periods of melancholia[8] and inhibition. The first attack of illness Woolf had appeared following her mother's death, while the second arose in 1915 upon the publication of her first novel *The Voyage Out*. Woolf had used nine years and burned somewhere between seven and eleven drafts before the manuscript was finally published. In her debut, heterosexual expectations and forbidden feelings result in the young female artist's hallucinations and subsequent death. However, the heteronormative critiques blame her death on tropical fever and poorly washed vegetables, while failing to note the tabooed issue of same-sex-love.

A Plotter in the Plot

Woolf, who was soon to be recognized as modernism's first lady, had now departed from the linear story to represent inner psychology in the so-called stream-of-consciousness-technique. Like James Joyce's novel *Ulysses* (1922), *Mrs Dalloway* describes the stream of consciousness and unconsciousness during one single day from morning to evening, but whereas *Ulysses* draws on Homer's epic poem the *Odyssey*, Woolf's novel appears to adopt Shakespeare's tragedy *Hamlet* as an important intertextual reference. Furthermore, the character Hamlet served as Freud's exemplary literary reference to a melancholic.

Mrs Dalloway tells the story of a group of friends who are to assemble at Mrs Dalloway's party that same evening. As they meet again, the various events from their past connect the different characters, thereby bringing their common past into the present. Woolf's particular method insists that what happened thirty years ago is crucial to who the characters are today. The main character Clarissa Dalloway is married to an MP (Member of Parliament), which confers on the couple a certain social standing. In the morning, as the servants prepare for the party, Clarissa calls out to the staff that she plans to buy the flowers for the party herself. During the day, Clarissa and her friends Peter, Sally, and Hugh, along with her husband Richard reminisce about their summers by the sea at Bourton. Clarissa herself, recalls parts of a quarrel she had with Peter, who was madly in love with Clarissa at the time. She remembers he is coming back from India one of these days.

While traditional scholarship has tended to focus on Clarissa's introspection and relationships with the members of her immediate entourage, I will begin my reading by analysing Clarissa's relationship to an overlooked figure of the periphery, namely the intriguing Miss Kilman. Kilman is responsible for teaching Clarissa's daughter Elizabeth Modern History. She is fanatically religious and self-righteous, and perspires heavily in her green raincoat, which serves as a symbol of her belonging to a lower social class and distinguishes her as different. Despite her robustness, however, Kilman is seldom mentioned by critics, except as a pretext to level accusations of class prejudice against Woolf. However, the character Kilman should not be read as a realistic portrait of a lower-class woman, since she actually resembles a gothic figure from the 1800s more closely, adding great portions of humour to parts of the novel. As mentioned, she remains important to our understanding of the main character's identity, since she demonstrates how marginalisation inextricably is linked to sexuality, norms and social power.

The Revenge of Repressed Desire

Mrs Dalloway takes place in the city of London in the aftermath of the First World War. In the imperial capital, an overwhelming sense of grief reigns. This is paralleled in the private sorrows of the main character Clarissa, who, in spite of her beauty and prestigious social standing, is drawn between sad and more blissful feelings. As she goes out into the busy streets of London, we encounter a character precipitously subjected to one affect after another, with no stable sense of identity. Abruptly the point of view shifts to a woman living next door, providing the reader with an external point-of-view describing the protagonist as Clarissa crosses the street: "a touch of the bird about her, of jay, blue-green, light, vivacious, though she was over fifty, and grown very white since her illness [...] (but that might be her heart, affected, they said, by influenza) before Big Ben strikes" (Woolf 1990, 1–2). As this excerpt suggests, Clarissa is middle-aged and has an ailing heart, suggesting a possible connection to love. As she crosses the street, she thinks she is past everything, feeling "far out to sea and alone." A quote from Shakespeare's play *Cymbeline* runs like a refrain through her thoughts: "Fear no more the heat o' the sun / Nor the furious winter's rages". In *Cymbeline* this quotation is connected to a funeral dirge, but in the play reality is not what it seems, as the "dead" person wakes up. From the beginning Clarissa is not described as authentic, she is rather a spectator to her own life:

> She felt very young; at the same time unspeakably aged. She sliced like a knife through everything; at the same time was outside, looking on. She had a perpetual sense, as she watched the taxi cabs, of being out, out, far out to sea and alone; she always had the feeling that it was very, very dangerous to live even one day. (Woolf 1990, 5–6)

Further on, the main character mourns her loss of identity in connection with her marriage: "this being Mrs Richard Dalloway, not even Clarissa any more" (Woolf 1990, 8). But passing through lively London she suddenly shifts into another mood and the text becomes more fluent and gay. The many stimuli of the city–all the sounds and sights of modernity are described fluently and simultaneously:

> Such fools we are, she thought, crossing Victoria Street. For heaven only knows why one loves it so, how one sees it so, making it up, building it round one, tumbling it, creating it every moment afresh; but [...] the most dejected of miseries sitting on doorsteps (drink their downfall) do the same [...] they love life [...]. In people's eyes, in the swing, tramp and trudge; in the bellow and the uproar; the carriages, motor cars, omnibuses, vans, sandwich men shuffling and swinging; brass bands; barrel organs; in the triumph and the jingle and the strange high singing of some aeroplane overhead was what she loved; life; London; this moment of June. (Woolf 1990, 2)

Into each life, a little rain must fall, and in Clarissa's mind this translates into thoughts of Miss Kilman, thoughts that intrude and invade her mind many times during the day, filling Clarissa with fear and hate: "It rasped her, though, to have stirring about in her this brutal monster! to hear twigs cracking and feel hooves planted down in the depths of that leaf-encumbered forest, the soul, never be content, or quite secure, for at any moment the brute would be stirring, this hatred..." (Woolf 1990, 9). Kilman evokes strong feelings in Clarissa due to her exceptionally dominating personality and for the ways in which she attacks Clarissa's self-esteem: "especially since her illness, (the brute) had power to make her feel scraped, hurt in her spine; gave her physical pain, and made all pleasure in beauty, in friendship, in being well, in being loved and making her home delightful rock, quiver and bend..." (ibid.). Kilman attacks Clarissa's feeling of well-being, her feeling of being loved and even erodes the delight she takes in her interior home space. Could it be that she threatens her heterosexual image? This is the question we will explore.

Clarissa tries to distance herself from thoughts of Miss Kilman, but this distancing suddenly seems to make Kilman even more powerful:

> For it was not her one hated but the idea of her, which undoubtedly had gathered in to itself a great deal that was not Miss Kilman; had become one of those spectres with which one battles at night; one of those spectres who stand aside us and suck up half our life-blood, dominators and tyrants; for no doubt with another throw of the dice, had the black been uppermost and not the white, she would have loved Miss Kilman! But not in this world. No. (ibid.)

Clarissa suspects that her daughter and Miss Kilman are having an affair, but in talking to her husband about her distress, he minimizes the problem, attributing such behaviours to a period all girls go through.

In Sigmund Freud's article entitled "The Uncanny" (2003), he shows how something that has once been known to us, is supressed and turned into something threatening through the mechanism of repression. This unfamiliar, yet well-known reality is called the "Unheimliche". What is uncanny and supressed can also be quite frightening. To fully understand the importance of Miss Kilman, we must examine the effect that Clarissa has on her:

> It was the flesh that she must control. Clarissa Dalloway had insulted her. That she expected. But she had not triumphed; she had not mastered the flesh. Ugly, clumsy, Clarissa Dalloway had laughed at her for being that; and had revived the fleshly desires [...] It is the flesh, it is the flesh, she muttered [...] trying to subdue this turbulent and painful feeling as she walked down Victoria Street. (Woolf 1990, 113)

Miss Kilman gets the message loud and clear; Clarissa is doing her best to remind her that she needs to take control of "the flesh" or desire. Through the text's use of hyperbole–Kilman is tall, sweaty and unwomanly–we get a glimpse of a marginalised femaleness totally out of control. But Kilman will not cede to Clarissa's imperatives; she is self-righteous and strong. Even in church she demonstrates her power:

> But Mr. Fletcher had to go. He had to pass her, and being himself neat as a new pin, could not help being a little distressed by the poor lady's disorder; her hair down; her parcel on the floor. She did not at once let him pass [...] her largeness, robustness and power as she sat there [...] (it was so rough the approach to God–so tough her desires) impressed him... (Woolf 1990, 118)

In this way, Miss Kilman seeks revenge for being rejected. She demands that others bow and obey–not to the Holy Father's–but to *her* will. It is as if she can see through Clarissa, who is to obey: "Fool! Simpleton! You who have known neither sorrow nor pleasure; who have trifled your life away! And there rose in her an overmastering desire to overcome her; to unmask her" (Woolf 1990, 110). The wish to "unmask her" comes right after Clarissa has been reflecting upon her sexless marriage.

In a hilarious scene, we meet Kilman and Clarissa's daughter Elizabeth in the Army and Navy stores where Miss Kilman buys her underwear. It is there that she burns with lust as she comfort eats, wanting to hug Elizabeth while cramming big bites of cream-cake into her mouth: "She was about to split asunder […] if she only could grasp her, if she could clasp her, if she could make her hers absolutely and for ever and then die; that was all she wanted" (Woolf 1990, 116). The wish to make her hers and then die, is actually a thwarted repetition of Clarissa's own wish after being kissed by her girlfriend Sally Seton at Bourton.

Kilman plays an important role in the novel as a whole, and she is crucially important to an in-depth understanding of the main character. She even cries out a message to the reader: "Don't quite forget me!" (Woolf 1990, 117). Her cry is an echo from one of British literature's greatest plays, *Hamlet,* where the ghost of Hamlet's father cries out: "Remember me!" However–when it comes to the reception of *Mrs Dalloway–that* is exactly what the critics have done. The portrait of Kilman has been rebuffed as indicative of her creator's snobbishness. Critics have not been prepared to meet a gothic figure in modern literature. Kilman is a monster, a figure well known from the 17th-century gothic novel in which male authors create a female monster to express their rage against women. During the eighteenth century, however, female novelists re-appropriated this image and gave it a more positive connotation, allowing for the expression of forbidden female anger and desire.[9]

Kilman is nothing other than a lesbian monster, turning parts of the novel into humour. Still she has a rather important mission, as she comments upon the main character's repression of her "fleshly desires". What Clarissa mourns above all is her heterosexual marriage ("this being Mrs Richard Dalloway, not even Clarissa any more"). However, the monster introduces doubt and suggests that the main character may be hiding her true self behind a mask. Scholars have surprisingly defined Kilman as a psychologically truthful portrait. English researcher David Dowling claims to sum up fifty articles on *Mrs Dalloway*, defending the monster in a rather peculiar way:

> Try as she will to be an extremist and despite her name, Miss Kilman is a civilized woman, and it is her failure as social being that Clarissa criticizes [...] Because we get to know Clarissa so intimately, we see that Miss Kilman is mistaken in her judgement that Clarissa is one of those who have 'known neither sorrow nor pleasure; who have trifled her [their] life away!' On the contrary, Clarissa has felt, and still feels, the gamut of human emotions. Indeed she feels both love and hatred toward Miss Kilman [...] No, Clarissa is alive and feeling; it is Miss Kilman who is denying her total being. (Dowling 1991, 107)

Not only does Dowling mistake the representation of Miss Kilman for the psychologically faithful portrait of *a civilized woman*, he overlooks the function of the monster and argues *against* the doubling of the main character and is mistaken about which character "is denying her total being" (ibid.). As we have seen, the character who is denying her being is Clarissa, and it is Kilman who reveals her masquerade. Still, critics have continued to defend Kilman, instead attacking her creator, the author. Here, one of the most respected researchers, Makiko Minow-Pinkney writes: "Kilman falls out of favour because she has poor enough taste to be adhering to socialist principles in her forties. But she is not only an abstract revolutionary, but also represents the middle-class fear of the lower orders as 'mob', as a pre-rational body clamouring for gratification, violently overturning social constraints" (Minow-Pinkney 1987, 75–76). Minow-Pinkney here comes close to the blind orthodoxy surrounding Miss Kilman, who has engaged in martyrdom and despises normality and normativity, as she has no place there. Kilman has a mission; she reveals the extent to which Clarissa is fighting to maintain her normality, as she has chosen to represent morality and reason–both despised by Kilman. In recent years, a few scholars have seen that the novel thematises same-sex-love,[10] however, Miss Kilman was–and still is–the undiscovered secret in *Mrs Dalloway*.

Lighting up a Dark Room

In society, Miss Kilman is met with contempt and pity. What transforms this situation into humour is that she knows how to get revenge. What the figure Kilman reveals to us, in an extremely funny way, is the disgust and marginalisation same-sex-love is met with in society, since she embodies a sexuality that others want to deny and control. In "concrete" meetings,

Kilman stubbornly insists on the main character's false, heterosexual existence, toward which she feels disgust and superiority. In contrast to the main character, the monster is able to express her feelings without shame, in return for which she expects respect. Through textual hyperbole, Kilman makes the reader conscious of the price Clarissa is paying for her bourgeois lifestyle.

During the day, layer after layer of consciousness is uncovered in Clarissa's mind. Clarissa remembers herself dressed in white, and finally she remembers it clearly; the day Sally gave her a kiss, an event she still thinks of as her happiest moment. The quarrel she remembered very little of in the opening scene, involved a jealous Peter, who wanted to destroy this moment, as he intruded on the kiss:

> 'Star-gazing?' said Peter.
> It was like running one's face against a granite wall in the darkness! It was shocking; it was horrible.
> Not for herself. She felt only how Sally was being mauled already, maltreated, she felt his hostility; his jealousy; his determination to break into their companionship. (Woolf 1990, 29)

Scholars have insisted that Clarissa shared Peter's infatuation: "Yet, after thirty years, it is still Peter who dominates her imagination–which lives not in the London of the present, but in the Bourton of her late adolescence. It was there that she had refused Peter and accepted Richard" (Harper 1992, 113). What the novel *does* tell the reader, however, is that Peter loved Clarissa, but that he failed to understand her. He kept asking her to tell him the truth, but she remained silent, causing him to leave Bourton in anger.

Peter returns from India the day during which the novel takes place and already at lunchtime he pops up in Clarissa's home, disturbing her as she is repairing a seam in her dress. As they sit down to talk, she has a needle in hand and he is described as tampering with a knife. These "weapons" illustrate an interpersonal psychology–that the meeting between the two old friends is a "fight" to gain the upper hand. When he tells her he is in London to help a much younger woman, married to a major in the Indian Army, to get a divorce so they can marry, she looks at him scornfully–how could he, at his age? Suddenly she is conscious of him having "this", while she has nothing. He thinks she has become what he predicted, a "brilliant and cold" woman, the "perfect hostess", married to the conservative "fool"

Richard Dalloway. Suddenly he starts crying and she is happy to comfort him.

The Melancholic Double

Clarissa's sadness is said to be caused by not daring to choose Peter as her husband. But Peter, critics explain, is too demanding, the knife showing that he would have claimed too much of her. In contrast, Richard is seen as kind and caring, and it is only through her marriage to Richard that she has survived. This particular explanation has always seemed rather unsatisfactory to me as it has little hold in the text itself. Instead, I have taken account of a self-referential comment in the novel, which reads as follows: "the message hidden in the beauty of the words. The secret signal which one generation passes, under disguise, to the next is loathing, hatred, despair" (Woolf 1990, 78). Loathing, hate and despair are the price homosexuals must pay for marginalisation. The only acceptable love for women was in marriage. The novel describes love between women at a time when same-sex-desire was connected to monstrosity, sin, prostitution and criminality.

There are references to Shakespeare throughout the novel. Another character, the traumatized ex-soldier Septimus Warren Smith reflects, on reading Shakespeare's *Antony and Cleopatra*: "Love between man and woman was repulsive to Shakespeare. The business of copulation was filth to him before the end" (Woolf 1990, 78). In an earlier scene that takes place in Clarissa's private bedroom, we get a glimpse of Clarissa's true self: "Like a nun withdrawing, or a child exploring a tower, she went upstairs, paused at the window, came to the bathroom. There was the green linoleum and a tap dripping. There was an emptiness about the heart of life; an attic room" (Woolf 1990, 26). Thanks to Charlotte Brontë's novel *Jane Eyre* (1847) the attic room is forever associated with a female monster. The image of the attic also has connotations to the melancholic author, withdrawing to an isolated room. The bedroom is in the attic where Clarissa undresses so that we as readers are allowed to see behind the mask. She "feared time itself [...] how year by year her share was sliced; how little the margin that remained was capable of stretching, of absorbing, as in the youthful years, the colours, salts, tones of existence..." (Woolf 1990, 25). Without the possibility to project herself into beautiful surroundings, she feels empty and desolate: "feeling herself suddenly shrivelled, aged, breastless..." (Woolf 1990, 26). Critics have insisted that Clarissa is frigid, but in the attic we are able to glimpse something else: "She could see what she lacked. It was not beauty, it was not mind. It was something central which broke up surfaces and rippled the contact between man and woman, or of women together. For *that* she could dimly perceive" (ibid.). In contact with other women, we learn, Clarissa is prone to lose control and give way to pleasure:

> Yet she could not resist sometimes yielding to the charm of a woman, not a girl, of a woman confessing, as to her they often did, some scrape, some folly. And whether it was pity, or their beauty, or that she was older, or some accident – like a faint scent, [...] she did undoubtedly then feel what men felt. Only for a moment; but it was enough. It was like a sudden revelation, a tinge like a blush which one tried to check and then, as it spread, one yielded to its expansion, and rushed to the farthest verge and there quivered... (Woolf 1990, 26)

Prominent feminist researcher Elaine Showalter has overlooked the lesbian issue due to her interpretation of the novel as a story about menopause:

> But menopause involves reintegration as well as loss, and can lead to growth of a woman who confronts both consciously and unconsciously issues regarding femininity, sexuality and identity. Indeed, Clarissa works through some of these feelings during her day [...]. In part, Clarissa's concern about her lack of sexual responsiveness–after thirty years of happy marriage–reflects the changes in attitude after the war... (Showalter 1994, 147).

The text tells us nothing about thirty years of happy marriage, but rather about the need for safety within marriage and the price Clarissa has paid for it.

The depiction of a woman expressing same-sex-love in 1925 was unheard of and brave. It is not the novel that is to blame when scholars have had such difficulty defining Clarissa's desire. Woolf herself in fact said she was the only woman free to write just what she wanted.[11] With the possibility of publishing at the Hogarth Press, Woolf felt free to write experimentally, and in doing so, reshaped modern literature at the same time as she expressed tabooed sexual feelings.

I will end my analysis with a cross-reading of Clarissa's other double, the one she herself found it necessary to explain to her American readers, namely the ex-soldier Septimus Warren Smith, who served in the army during the First World War and is mentally ill. Psychiatrists diagnose him with shell-shock. Showalter explains that the understanding of shell-shock and war trauma during World War One had more to do with the patient's sexuality than with war trauma: "some Freudians argued that unconscious homosexual impulses contributed to the development of shell-shock, a view that both scandalized conservative doctors and confirmed their view that only the unmanly and effeminate could succumb to war neurosis" (ibid.). Septimus, who is described as having a close relationship to his senior officer in the army–a man called Evans who was killed during the war–was unable to feel grief when he died. The fact that the two of them were described as two puppies playing together, suggests a love-affair. Septimus later married an Italian girl, but by then, we learn, his feelings were frozen in grief.

In the portrait of the melancholic and psychotic Septimus, Woolf portrays many of her own experiences with mental illness.[12] Like him, she detested food and was unable to sleep. Septimus also hears birds singing in Greek outside the window, just as his creator did. In the introduction to an American publication of *Mrs Dalloway*, Woolf herself explains that Septimus was Clarissa's double and that Clarissa was originally intended to commit suicide at the end of the party. Instead, it is Septimus who throws himself out of the window. This happens just as a psychiatrist comes to fetch him. The cure the psychiatrist had recommended was "proportion"–career and family life (ibid.).

In her book *Fictions of Psychoanalysis* (1989), Elisabeth Abel reads *Mrs Dalloway* in conjunction with Freud's three essays on female sexuality and argues that the shift from an intimate bond with her mother to a heterosexual attraction to her father represents a troublesome shift in the direction of the desire for girls: "By recalling to Clarissa the power of the past *and* the only method eternalizing it, Septimus enables Clarissa to acknowledge and renounce its hold to embrace the imperfect pleasures of adulthood more completely" (Abel 1989, 40). However, the novel does not acknowledge the necessity of a heterosexual shift, where the little girl goes from loving her mother to feeling attracted to her father. As in Shakespeare's play *Hamlet,* Freud's literary example of melancholy, it is a question of losing oneself when losing a beloved object. The author's knowledge of Freud's use of *Hamlet* makes *Mrs Dalloway* a daring statement, since this is not a Freudian novel but a critique of the sad effects heteronormative psychological theories have had on homosexuals. Here are Clarissa's thoughts about Septimus and the psychiatrist: "Suppose he had had that passion, and had gone to Sir William Bradsaw, a great doctor, yet to her obscurely evil, without sex or lust" (Woolf 1990, 163). Woolf, who loathed anger in women's novels, now wrote in anger about "the great doctor". The psychiatrist is described without focalisation, it is the author's own anger.[13] Septimus commits suicide as the doctor arrives, and when Clarissa later in the evening hears about his suicide, she identifies with his death and gains insight into the life and death of her homosexual sisters and brothers: "It was her punishment to see sink and disappear here a man, there a woman, in this profound darkness, and she forced to stand here in her evening dress" (Woolf 1990, 164). Experiencing difference meant marginalisation, melancholia, pain and death. Clarissa has survived, but psychological incomprehension killed many homosexuals, as the solution was sadly often suicide.

The literary psychologist Jean Starobinski took an interest in melancholy in literary texts when he saw melancholy in conjunction with what we do with our time. In an interview, he mentions *Mrs Dalloway* in connection with the ways in which the characters structure the hours of their day. *Mrs Dalloway*, he claims, is of central interest, as the novel's rigid structure–Big Ben striking every hour throughout the day–seems to keep melancholy at bay (Birnbaum and Olsson 1992, 456). Mechanical time breaks into the fictional characters' mental time, making them aware of time passing. But more important is the structuring of the novel, and I like the idea that the rigid temporality in *Mrs Dalloway* wards off melancholy; for example no flat language can be found. The main character has no stable feeling of inner self but rather intense moments of alternating happiness and unhappiness. Like Septimus, she goes precipitously from a feeling of abandonment to intense moments of bliss. And like Septimus, she has a melancholy longing for a lost, forbidden love object. Still the novel is filled to the brim with impressions, colours, life, rather than grey slowness.[14] As we have seen, Clarissa started out trying to find that which has become alien to her: "What was she trying to recover? [...] what image of white dawn in the country..." (Woolf 1990, 6). The image of white–the colour of innocence–turns out to be her own lost self together with her friend Sally Seton. During the day, she remembers and understands more of herself as she acknowledges her true feelings.

At the end of the novel, we attend Clarissa Dalloway's party, where the friends from Bourton are gathered: Peter, Richard, Clarissa, and the beloved Sally Seton meet, but Clarissa is busy, whirling around between her many prominent guests. The party is described somewhat like a carnival, turning things upside down. "'I have five sons!'" says Sally

Seton (Woolf 1990, 165). Clarissa must admit it is lovely to see her, but she is less attractive. Peter, however, is just like before, as he criticises Clarissa. She is at her worst, he thinks, superficial and false.

The novel's timespan goes from morning until night like the Greek tragedy. There the audience could feel catharsis, being freed from fear after they had watched the tragic fall of the hero. At the end of the party, after having heard about Septimus' suicide, Clarissa feels this sort of purification: "No pleasure could equal, she thought [...] this having done with the triumphs of youth, lost herself in the process of living, to find it, with a shock of delight, as the sun rose, as the day sank" (Woolf 1990, 164). Living through melancholy, we know, can give us a strengthened feeling of life afterwards. Clarissa sees an old woman going to bed in the window of the house next door and feels comforted. She hears the clocks striking the hour and then returns to her party. "It is a gift, she thinks, to assemble, to create. 'That's what I do it for' she said, speaking aloud, 'to life'" (Woolf 1990, 107). During the party, Clarissa's melancholy suddenly is turned into well-being. Suddenly the mood shifts to anger against Miss Kilman: "Kilman her enemy. That was satisfying: that was real. Ah, how she hated her–hot, hypocritical, corrupt; with all that power; Elizabeth's seducer; the woman who had crept in to steal and defile [...] She hated her; she loved her. It was enemies one wanted, not friends..." (Woolf 1990, 154). Kilman is connected to strong feelings like love and hate. As we see Kilman is connected to stealing, Clarissa thinks she is a thief. This might be a subversive critique of psychoanalysis, which interpreted homosexuality as a neurosis and compared it to kleptomania.

While Clarissa has been away in a small room, her old friends are talking about their youth at Bourton. Suddenly Peter is aware that something is missing:

> What is this terror? What is this ecstasy? he thought to himself. What is it that fills me with extraordinary excitement?
> It is Clarissa, he said.
> For there she was. (Woolf 1990, 172)

Peter's observation of Clarissa ends the novel. I interpret his statement as follows: the reader has gotten to know Clarissa behind masks, lies and illusions. Thanks to her parallel characters, Clarissa has now become someone who can be seen, so the novel ends in a triumphant way: "For there she was" (ibid.).

While readings of Clarissa's double, Septimus, have recently demonstrated an understanding of the "hidden message" on sexuality in *Mrs Dalloway*, the character Miss Kilman has remained in the shadow. Woolf thematises sexual orientation through her associative, stream-of-consciousness technique. Through the use of doubling, she expresses tabooed issues at the same time as she hides them well. With Miss Kilman, she created not only a hilarious portrait of a lesbian monster, she created a character who manifests many of the understandings and prejudices against lesbianism of her day. Kilman is hot, huge, and unwomanly. She is described as a thief, in accordance with early psychological theories. The lesbian turns out to be ugly, dominant and unkind. This chapter has uncovered the humour evident in the portrayal of Kilman, but also explains how hetero-normativity has resulted in misreadings of Clarissa's desire and identity.

Normativity has to do with the power to define and maintain certain norms; it thereby condemns those who cannot or do not want to be part of a compulsory norm-system to powerlessness. However, Woolf managed, in both her life and her writing, to break with this norm-system. Through subversive strategies, she articulated counter-discourses to the dominant discourses in the fields of psychology and psychoanalysis at the beginning of the 20th century. Both fields were intensely involved in the strict definitions of gender and sexual identities.

Notes

[1] From Lord Douglas' poem "Two Loves": "I am the Love that dare not speak its name". Lord Douglas was a close friend of Oscar Wilde. The poem was used as evidence in the trial against Oscar Wilde in 1895 and is quoted in *The Voyage Out*.
[2] The novel won the Pulitzer Prize for Fiction in 1999. A film version was released in 2002, starring Nicole Kidman as Virginia Woolf. Kidman won both a Golden Globe Award and an Oscar.
[3] Foucault, Michel. 1990 [1976].
[4] *The Voyage Out* (1915).
[5] In a letter to Hugh Walpole, dated 28 December 1932, Woolf writes: "I hate any writer who talks about himself; anonymity I adore. And this may be an obsession."
[6] Freud's article "Trauer und Melancholie" ("Mourning and Melancholia") from 1917 was translated and published at the Hogarth Press in 1925.
[7] Virginia and Leonard Woolf met Sigmund Freud in 1939. When Leonard writes about this meeting, he recounts that Freud had an aura, not of fame, but of greatness (L. Woolf 1988, 233–231). Freud had an expression of gentleness, Leonard explains, but behind the gentleness lay a great strength. Leonard did not relate the most important part of the meeting, how Freud bowed to Virginia and

gave her a flower, a narcissus. Freud might have read some of Virginia Woolf's novels and observed that they had the issue of melancholy in common.

[8] Jones's biography on Freud describes: "intense alternations of mood, between periods of elation, excitement and self-confidence on the one hand, and periods of extreme depression, doubt and inhibition on the other. In the depressed moods he could neither write nor concentrate his thoughts [...] he had attacks of extreme depression, which left him feeling apathetic, useless, and somewhat incapable of writing. The depression that followed each publication was temporarily somewhat alleviated by reassurance and praise from his students" (Haynal 1985, 165). Freud began his self-analysis to cure his depression.

[9] In their literary history *The Mad Woman in the Attic* (1979) Sandra Gilbert and Susan Gubar argue that the female monster expresses the female author's own "forbidden" feelings. These were feelings the female character was too inhibited to express, such as desire and anger.

[10] See for example Ronchetti (2004).

[11] To me, it seems as if Vita Sackville-West changed her writing style, as she suddenly wrote in a much more fluent way. Woolf wrote what are considered to be her two greatest novels, *Mrs Dalloway* (1925) and *To the Lighthouse* (1927) at the height of their love affair. She also wrote *Orlando* (1928) and *The Waves* (1931) during her relationship with Sackville-West.

[12] Woolf even wrote an essay entitled "On being ill" (1930).

[13] Woolf normally delegated the point of view to her characters.

[14] Woolf and Vita Sackville-West went to Paris together, with Sackville-West dressed as a man, so that they could live like husband and wife.

References

Abel, Elizabeth. 1989. *Virginia Woolf and the Fictions of Psychoanalysis.* Chicago, London: University of Chicago Press.
Bell, Anne Olivier, ed. 1981 [1980]. *The Diary of Virginia Woolf*, Vol. 3: 1925–30, San Diego, New York: Harcourt Brace & Company.
Birnbaum, Daniel and Anders Olsson. 1992. *Den andra födan, en essä om melankoli och kannibalism.* Stockholm: Bonniers.
Butler, Judith. 1990. *Gender Trouble. Feminism and the Subversion of Identity.* New York, London: Routledge.
Cunningham, Michael. 2006 [1999]. *The Hours.* London: Harper.
Daldry, Stephen. (Dir.). 2002. *The Hours* [Film]. With Meryl Streep, Nicole Kidman, and Juliane Moore. Miramax.
Dowling, David. 1991. *Mrs Dalloway: Mapping Streams of Consciousness.* Boston: Twayne Publishers.
Foucault, Michel. 1990 [1976]. *The History of Sexuality: Volumes 1-2*, Harmondsworth: Penguin.
Freud, Sigmund. 1978 [1917]. "Mourning and Melancholia." In *The Standard Edition of the complete Psychological Works of Sigmund Freud*, Vol. XIV. London: Hogarth Press.
—. 2003 [1919]. "The Uncanny." London: *Penguin Books*.
Gilbert, Sandra and Gubar, Susan. 1979. *The Madwoman in the Attic. The woman writer and the nineteenth-century literary Imagination.* New Haven and London: Yale University Press.
Harper, Howard. 1982. *Between Language and Silence. The Novels of Virginia Woolf.* Baton Rouge and London: Louisiana State University Press.
Haynal, André. 1985. *Depression and Creativity.* New York: International University Press.
Minow-Pinkney, Makiko. 2011 [1987]. *Virginia Woolf & the Problem of the Subject.* Edinburgh: Edinburg University Press.
Ronchetti, Ann. 2004. *The Artist, Society, and Sexuality in Virginia Woolf's Novels.* New York: Routledge.
Showalter, Elaine. 1994. "*Mrs Dalloway*, Introduction." In *Virginia Woolf. Introductions to the major works*, edited by Julia Briggs. London: Virago.
Woolf, Leonard, ed. 1987 [1960]. *Autobiography.* London: Hogarth Press.
—. ed. 1988 [1967]. *Downhill all the Way: An Autobiography of the years 1919-1939.* New York: Harcourt, Brace and World.
Woolf, Virginia. 1968 [1925]. *Mrs Dalloway.* London: Hogarth Press.

—. 1968 [1924]. "Mr. Bennett and Mrs. Brown." In *Collected Essays*, Vol.1, London: Hogarth Press.
—. 1966 [1940]. "The Leaning Tower." In *Collected Essays*, Vol. 2. London: Hogarth Press.

Identity and Illness

Chapter Sixteen

Writing with One's Eyes: Identity and Communicative Strategies in Masahiro Fujita's *99% Thank You* and Leo Montero's *Muñeca de Trapo*

Wladimir Chávez Vaca

Introduction

Narratives about illness, which John Wiltshire considers a "wild, disordered field" (2006, 22), are also called pathographies, a term that is not only little known within autobiographical or testimonial literature, but whose relationship to both trauma studies and catastrophe narratives remains unclear. In addition, there are only a few academic papers that highlight the literary strategies used in this sort of narrative, which is also related to identity issues, since a person's sense of self is highly likely to change with the advent of a serious disease.

My research focuses on two books that tell stories of illness: *99 % Thank you*, by Masahiro "Hiro" Fujita, and *Muñeca de Trapo* [*Rag Doll*],[1] by Leo Montero. Both texts were published in 2013 by patients with Amyotrophic Lateral Sclerosis (ALS), an incurable disease that progressively weakens the muscles, causing paralysis and, in its final stage, death by respiratory failure. Due to the complexity of the subject, I have chosen to analyze these books within a theoretical framework which includes the reflections of several scholars, among them John Wiltshire (2006), Lars Christen Hydén (1997), Jeffrey Aronson (2000), Valentina Adami (2008) and Miriam Fuchs (2004).[2]

Autopathography, Trauma Studies and Catastrophe Narratives

Anne Hunsaker Hawkins is the first contemporary scholar to use the term pathography in her research *Reconstructing Illness: Studies in Pathography* (1993). She defines it as "a form of autobiography or biography that describes personal experiences of illness, treatment, and sometimes death" (1). In an effort to contextualize this definition, John Wiltshire points out that "Narratives or poems about illness experience [...] have also been produced since the inauguration of modern medical conditions in the late eighteenth century" (2006, 25). And according to Jeffrey Aronson (2000, 1599), "pathography" was already included in Dunglinson's *Medical Lexicon* (1853) and later mentioned by Sigmund Freud in *Leonardo da Vinci and A Memory of His Childhood* (1910). In any case, the word has not been used widely in the field; for instance, researchers Lars Christen Hydén and Jan Frich prefer more generic terminology like narrative of illness or narrative-based medicine, which can be related to tales by patients, doctors or relatives of the sick person, but also to more scholarly papers. The same applies to autopathography, a term coined by Jeffrey Aronson and not necessarily used as conventional terminology by his peers. Aronson (2000) describes it strictly as patients' stories.

Lars Christen Hydén (1997, 52) reminds us that a central element in stories about illness can be an experience or an unhealthy habit, and not necessarily a disease. As already stated, the term pathography also comprises the testimony of physicians or family, and not just that of patients. However, first-person narratives of patients or autopathographies have attracted the most attention, and they seem to be quite similar to the testimonies found in trauma studies because "Patients' narratives give voice to suffering in a way that lies outside the domain of the biomedical voice. This is probably one of the main reasons for the emerging interest in narratives among social scientists engaged in research on biomedicine, illness and suffering" (Hydén 1997, 49).

From a non-literary perspective, the therapeutic effect that the patient can obtain by writing about his or her experiences seems clear. In this sense, part of the corpus of illness narratives could be included in trauma studies, especially in the case of serious illnesses that appear suddenly, disrupting normal life. Both illness narratives and trauma studies are cross-disciplinary and include areas of interest such as psychology, anthropology and sociology. Valentina Adami (2008, 5), a specialist on trauma narratives, also mentions neurobiology, history and psychoanalysis, and theorists in the same field such as Martin Modlinger and Philipp Sonntag (2011) have focused specifically on ethical issues.

The difference between the texts in focus in trauma studies and illness narratives lies perhaps in the existence of a *surviving* subject in the former. Although the traumatic event in some way or another affects the victim in the present–the experience tends to be re-lived over and over again–the danger or the terrible incident occurred at a specific point in the past and ended there. It is the perspective of a survivor, despite the fact that we are speaking about an event that comes back to haunt and disturb. From the point of view of illness narratives, this would be the case in the stories of women with breast cancer who have been healed and now re-count their previous experiences. However, there are other stories of a different nature, such as those about chronically ill or terminally ill patients. They are alive at the time of their testimony, but are not technically *survivors*, they have neither reached a stage of physical improvement nor do they have the possibility to change their condition. In such cases, it is valid to question whether this affects the focus and attitude of the narrators.

The problems of categorization connected to these narratives have not made them less palatable to readers. On the contrary, testimonial accounts in general have continued to grow in popularity. Leigh Gilmore (2001, 1), states that between 1940 and 1990, the number of books in English categorized as memoirs or autobiographies has tripled, while Elie Wiesel found them to be a feature of identity of our time: "If the Greeks invented tragedy, the Romans the epistle, and the Renaissance the sonnet, our generation invented a new literature, that of testimony" (Wiesel 1990, 9). However, some types of testimony, despite their proliferation, do not seem to attract too much attention from scholars in autobiographical studies. Autopathography or the autobiography of a sick person, is among the subgenera partially forgotten by those skilled in hybrid texts (combining historical and literary events), probably because they are sometimes considered "depressing", or "too narrow in focus, too confined in theme" (Couser 1997, 1). A good example is the anthology edited by Jan Campwell and Janet Harbord, *Temporalities, Autobiography and Everyday Life* (2002). Of the 16 papers presented, only one–"Heroes", by Jackie Stacey–develops the theme of illness. Stacey focuses on the testimonies of people suffering from cancer and tangentially also addresses the issue of AIDS. Moreover, the typology of testimonial modality developed by

Nubya Celina Casas (1981, 49–64) does not discuss illness narratives within the genre of memoir. Nor is the subject of disease mentioned as belonging to the genre of testimony in Catherine N. Parke's expansive general overview, which even includes some proposals for categorization in subgenres (2002, 29).

This study definitely considers autobiography as a literary genre, and autopathography as a separate sub-category, acknowledging its particularities, one of them mentioned by Aronson: "Indeed there is probably more fiction in autobiography than there is autobiography in fiction" (2000, 1601). In the same line of thought, John Wiltshire points out: "Things left out, puzzles unresolved, partners and carers drawn through rose-coloured spectacles: illness narratives can be troubled by these and other inadequacies" (2006, 27). Autobiography (and autopathography as a subgroup) needs to take into consideration the author and his or her intentions, due to its mixed nature; it is a genre that is neither completely literary nor completely historical. For a literary approach, we rely on Miriam Fuchs and her theory on catastrophe narratives, which share some of the same characteristics as trauma narratives.[3] In her research, Fuchs argues that autobiography "may be a pretext for trying to reconstruct what the catastrophe has damaged" (2004, 4). She defines her terminology: "I used the term 'catastrophe' for situations that occur rapidly, with immediate and shocking effects and, additionally, that bar direct intervention" (Fuchs 2004, 6). She analyzes the book *Paula* as an example. The book is a memoir about Paula Frías Allende's struggle with disease. She was Isabel Allende's daughter, and her mother wrote the book in the first person. Paula was in a coma for several months as a result of the disease porphyria, and died in 1992. Regarding this type of experience, it is stated that:

> [Fuchs' theoretical approach] also examines ways in which life writing about terminal illness–whether written by the dying person or collaboratively–can also be a form of catastrophe narration. When death is not the consequence of a long life disease but rather an anomalous event of horrendous proportions, it has dimensions of catastrophe that inevitably affect the writing of the narrative. (Fuchs 2004, 9)

Heba M. Sharobeem applies Fuchs' theories for a literary approach in "The Poetics of Pain and Cancer and the Question of Genre in Two Catastrophe Narratives" (2008). Sharobeem analyzes biographical texts on cancer written by both a woman, the Egyptian writer Abla al-Reweiny, and a man, the poet Donald Hall.[4] Both Al-Reweiny and Hall are professional writers like Isabel Allende, and this feature distinguishes them from other authors of testimonies of illness. However, these are not autopathographies: Al-Reweiny and Hall do not relate their personal experiences of illness, but focus on the lives of their partners, the poets Amal Dunqol and Jane Kenyon respectively, who both lost the battle against cancer. As in Allende's narrative, the testimonies are not narrated by the protagonist but related by someone close to him or her.

There are just a few studies regarding illness narratives which focus on textual aspects like expressions of form, style and discourse strategies, despite the fact that these literary characteristics could also have practical value and help relatives and practitioners better understand the way a patient fights the disease or accepts a disability. It has been claimed that "Words and trauma have a reciprocal influence. Therefore, the main concern of trauma studies in literature is analyzing the effects of trauma on words, and the way words deal with trauma" (Adami 2008, 4). At the same time, trauma challenges the ability of language to describe painful experiences in all their magnitude:

> Something of a consensus has already developed that takes trauma as the unrepresentable to assert that trauma is beyond language in some crucial way that language fails in the face of trauma, and that trauma mocks language and confronts it with its insufficiency. (Gilmore 2001, 6)

Identity Issues as "Shipwrecks" and the Voices of Resistance in *99% Thank You* and *Muñeca de Trapo*

Both *99% Thank you,* by "Hiro" Fujita, and *Muñeca de Trapo*, by Leo Montero, are testimonies written in 2013 by patients with Amyotrophic Lateral Sclerosis (ALS),[5] also known as Lou Gehrig's disease. Although it is a rare disease, a number of other testimonies have been published by patients affected by this condition. The famous scientist Stephen Hawking, who died in 2018, suffered from ALS, and references to the illness are found in his autobiography *My Brief History* (2013) from the chapter that depicts his experiences in Cambridge in the 1960s. However, Hawking assigns a secondary role to his disease here, less important than his family relationships and academic work. The famous Norwegian author Axel Jensen (1932-2003) was also diagnosed with ALS. His first testimonial work, *Pasienten i sentrum* (From the Patient's View, 1998), is a collection of articles focused on his health and his struggle against the inevitable, but he also uses the book to present some social criticism. A second work,

Livet sett fra Nimbus [Life Seen from Nimbus, my trans.] (2002), was written in collaboration with journalist Petter Mejlænder and refers to his disease and gives his reflections on death, without an excessive emphasis on either of these issues. It should be noted that both Hawking and Jensen are among the small percentage of sick people who have managed to live longer than the average ALS patient.[6]

99% Thank you is a Japanese-English bilingual book. It consists of 208 pages divided into six chapters, plus an introduction and acknowledgments. It also includes many color photographs from the personal archive of the author, "Hiro" Fujita (1979), an employee of a major advertising agency network in Tokyo. The work tells us about the important events in Fujita's life in chronological order. However, chapter five speaks specifically of the disease and is the longest chapter. Fujita was diagnosed with ALS at the age of 30. Some time ago he underwent a tracheotomy and now communicates through an eye tracking computer, and the book was recorded by monitoring the movement of his eyes. He blogs (some of these texts have been slightly edited for inclusion in the book) and has been interviewed by major media. Additionally, he has founded an organization, END ALS, encouraging Japanese government funding for iPS stem cell based clinical trials on ALS patients.

Muñeca de Trapo was written by Leo Montero (1967), a Spanish woman who worked as an auxiliary nurse. Married and with two daughters, she was diagnosed with ALS in 2006. Her testimony, like that of Fujita, includes a large number of photos. Montero travelled to Peru after hearing about a doctor who, purportedly, could improve her physical condition. Her experience was far from successful and she underwent a tracheotomy. She cannot move her hands, so she wrote the book aided by a head mouse. Montero has been interviewed by national and international media and published with some frequency in the local newspaper *Canfali Marina Alta*. *Muñeca de Trapo* is composed of five parts: a description of the disease (the information comes from a scientific source), an autobiography, a transcript of her publications in *Canfali Marina Alta*, personal stories from other patients with ALS and finally, the opinions of medical personnel on ALS. Strictly speaking, only the autobiography and the transcripts are Montero's testimonial material, i.e. autopathography. Montero follows a tradition already mentioned by John Wiltshire: "Many first-person illness narratives include heteroglossaic material, such as doctors' reports which give an outside perspective on the illness" (2006, 24).

Although I suggest a close reading as the main approach in an analysis, one cannot ignore the cultural and social aspects of both works and neither can one ignore the intentions of the authors. Hydén supports the idea that illness narratives can be a strategic device: they help "to achieve certain effects in the social interaction" (1997, 59), in addition to describing an individual experience (the illness) as a phenomenon that affects a community. In this sense, from a literary point of view, both books utilize comparisons and metaphors, small fragments in the form of poems, irony, paratextual elements (colors and photos), intertextuality, polyphonic narrative and the motif of paradise lost. All these strategies, which will be covered in detail below, focus on goals that the authors of illness narratives usually try to achieve, in this case as a result of a new identity created because of ALS: "to construct an illness experience, to reconstruct life history, to make disease and illness understandable, and to collectivise the illness experience" (Hydén 1997, 64).

Both *99% Thank you* and *Muñeca de Trapo* are written by non-professional authors, therefore their style is simple and direct. The sentences are usually short and resort to ellipsis. Certainly, autobiography as a genre is not usually associated with complex rhetoric. In these examples, a sincere voice is heard through "plate glass", as described by Isaac Asimov: "It is the kind of writing in which the direct sentence is preferred to the involved subordinated clause; the familiar word to the unfamiliar word; and the short word to the long word" (1981, 61). It is precisely this simple, straightforward language, along with the honesty and credibility of the few anecdotes, which help Fujita and Montero accomplish one of their primary purposes: to contribute to drawing the attention of society to the situation of patients with ALS. Fujita (2013, 18) explains: "I want as many people as possible to know about this disease and help to find a cure. This is why I am exposing my life. I think this is my mission [...] Why I was chosen". These testimonials make the efforts of the authors to raise funds in the fight against the disease visible, along with promotion of stem cell experimentation.

In both works, literary tropes such as the metaphor are not very common. In the same line of thought, Susan Sontag conducted a study on metaphors and illness used in distinct contexts. Indirectly, she supports a simple and clear narrative about the disease told in the first person: "My point is that illness is *not* a metaphor, and that the most truthful way of regarding illness–and that the healthiest way of being ill–is one most purified of, most resistant to, metaphoric thinking" (1991, 3. Emphasis in the original).

However, there are some incidences of comparison and use of literary tropes in the testimonies of Fujita and Montero:

> In that moment [after the diagnosis], a crazy cocktail of every emotion pierced through my body. It was chaos, dizziness, and an unexplainable scale of frustration and anger [...] (Fujita 2013, 10)

> Ya tenía dos flores que adornaban mi vida. (Montero 2013, 43)[7]

Montero titled her work *Muñeca de Trapo* which is, in itself, a comparison to the way ALS destroys the body. In fact, the paradox that the muscles lose the ability to move but the mind remains intact, has caught the attention of both Fujita and Montero. For Fujita (2013, 14), it is about "a glass coffin, the body as your jail cell". Montero uses expressions like "caparazón" (2013, 89),[8] or compares herself to an inanimate object: "He perdido mi movimiento. Me convertí en una figura de porcelana hecha mil añicos al caerse al suelo, salvándose únicamente la cabeza" (ibid., 105).[9] Throughout her work, Montero includes poems and versified narratives with a certain frequency, all published in *Canfali Marina Alta*. They are colloquial texts whose central theme is her status as an ALS patient. For example, one of them refers to her husband Juan, and it is about intimacy and physical contact:

> E.L.A: Me acostumbré
> Me acostumbré a tenerte sin ser como antes.
> Me acostumbré a que simplemente tus labios rocen los míos,
> con tanto cariño que llego a estremecerme, como cuando
> éramos novios.
> Me acostumbré a no abrazarte en la cama cuando siento
> frío, porque mis brazos están muertos [...] (82)[10]

In another text, Montero uses a poetic voice that speaks out against disease, personifying it:

> Eres cruel, aprovechada, cara, falsa, ruin [...] Te apoderaste de mí cuando estaba en lo mejor de mi vida, un día cualquiera de agosto, invadiendo mi pierna derecha, luego la izquierda. No contenta a los tres meses me quitaste los brazos, y ya en el colmo de tu maldad, y que más me dolió, me robaste la voz [...]Eres una gran ladrona, pero lo que no me has robado, ni podrás, es la gran ilusión por vivir (80–81)[11]

On one occasion, Fujita also speaks to the disease, personifying it: "ALS, thank you for reminding me of the essence, the true value of life. But I am going to have to kill you" (2013, 21). While not a very common strategy in his account of the facts, some of Fujita's texts can be considered versified prose:

> I notice…
> "You talk too much… because you can"
> Too many unnecessary words
> "You move too much… because you can"
> Because your bodies are too quick to find discomfort
> "You eat too much, drink too much, and pleasure yourself too much and then complain too much"
> **I can't wait to do the same because that's living.** (169, emphasis in the original)

As expected, the lives of Montero (2013, 78) and Fujita (2013, 10) were never the same again after the diagnosis. The issue of identity is common in illness narratives (Hydén 1997, 51), in catastrophe narratives (Fuchs 2004, 4) and trauma studies (Whitehead 2004, 3–11). Jan C. Frich (2010, 42) confers with other theorists in describing the situation as a "shipwreck". Due to the illness, the patient is disoriented, no longer the person he or she was, and, in order to find his or her new place in the world, tries to comprehend this new "I" he or she has become. Certain values can change, other principles take priority. One example is Montero's turn to religion after being diagnosed, and how she thus finds strength and support. Moreover, her social life has changed. Thanks to the Internet, many friends with similar health problems have invited her to travel and visit, often outside Spain. In the same line, she and Fujita give advice about the value of details in everyday life, and often reflect on happiness, love, life, and death. They describe some of their values and beliefs which have changed after the ALS diagnosis. Fujita (2013, 182; 203) emphasizes the beauty of life in small, everyday events. Montero concludes at the bottom of her short texts, with a sentence that commands the reader: "Sed felices."[12]

On many occasions, Fujita and Montero use their books as a platform for social criticism. Montero, especially, but also Fujita, reports that there is a lack of political will to improve the lives of patients with ALS. They criticize society in the hopes of changing their health condition. In fact, the struggle for life, depicted through stories, dreams and anecdotes that alternate between hope and despair, characterize both *Muñeca de Trapo* and *99% Thank You*. Montero and Fujita believe that in the near future, healing through stem cell treatments will be possible, and this explains their cautious optimism. While there are passages full of despair and fear, hope is still present: "No hay que abandonarse, dejarse morir, pensar 'total ya lo que me queda' y hundirse" (Montero 2013, 87–88),[13] or as Fujita points out: "So many things to do, and so many fights to win. I have to make a comeback [...]" (2013, 199). However, the testimonies do not hide painful stories based on that hope. For instance, Montero visits a doctor in Peru who promises to improve her health with an operation. After the surgery, she returns to Spain in even worse condition, with a tracheostomy, pneumonia and salmonella. A photo of Fujita's withered legs has the caption, "I had sexy legs, I swear!" (Fujita 2013, 162–163). Here we see how Fujita mixes mockery with seriousness, in an attempt to demystify death and disease. This position is undoubtedly the result of a point of view that now enables him to distance himself from specific and painful events related to his disease. For instance, the day he was diagnosed, what he heard the doctors saying sounded like a game-show program:

> "The name of the disease is amyotrophic something something.
> You will gradually lose your ability to move and die.
> It's unclear how long you will live but it's not long…
> It depends on the patient.
> There is no cure. We don't know the cause.
> There is no hope.
> Thank you for playing
> **Shhiiiieeeett…**" (Fujita 2013, 11, emphasis in the original)

As pointed out, *Muñeca de Trapo* and *99% Thank You* alternate between hope and despair. Moreover, the paratextual elements emphasize these thoughts: the drawings on pages 14 and 15 in Fujita's book are on a black background; the terrifying possibility of sinking into a totally locked-in state where no part of the body can move, not even the eyes, is envisioned. He reflects: "I only hope I have the courage to overcome this challenge" (Fujita 2013, 14). In contrast, the following two pages have photos of blue sky over Tokyo as a background. Here he reflects on his personal struggle and how important it is to be visible for the ALS community. For further emphasis, both authors also use other typographic elements, e.g., bold type (Fujita) or capitalization (Montero).

Muñeca de Trapo and *99% Thank You* contain some of the characteristics of catastrophe narratives such as "story segments and intertextuality" (Fuchs 2004, 18), which are also typical in trauma fiction: "There are, however, a number of key stylistic features which tend to recur in these narratives. These include intertextuality, repetition and a dispersed or fragmented narrative voice" (Whitehead 2004, 84). As mentioned, Montero's sentences, as well as those of Fujita, are usually short, and their works are divided into a number of sub-chapters, resulting in a fragmented view of their lives. Likewise, Montero's narrative style is definitely polyphonic. Her voice in *Muñeca de Trapo* is complemented with more than 40 first-person testimonies, among them, those of patients, relatives and doctors. Although Fujita does not use this strategy extensively, he too includes other voices in certain dialogues. Examples of intertextuality also exist in Montero when she incorporates the scientific explanation of ALS, although this resource stands within its own discourse and does not include her interspersed thoughts, with a notable exception when she quotes *The Book of Proverbs* (Montero 2013, 147).

Fujita and Montero repeat a specific event in their narrations: the actual moment they receive the ALS diagnosis. Both mention the event in their introductions and later return to it in specific subsections. In this regard, it has been said: "Repetition is inherently ambivalent, suspended between trauma and catharsis" (Whitehead 2004, 84). Fujita describes a violently strong emotion of invasion. Montero, on the other hand, fainted. For both, the event is experienced as a turning point or fall from grace, akin to the literary motif of paradise lost. Literary motifs are not an invention of fiction, but a reflection of human behavior that is transferred to the written text. As their origin is in human nature, they are perfectly applicable to the autobiography. Paul Socken (1993, 92) pointed out that in such texts: "There is a personal search and hope for unity and harmony, more like recovering something lost than creating something new". Both Fujita and Montero refer frequently to a lost past. Two examples will suffice:

> Then when I stepped out of the office, I went back to being a teenager again. It was a good life. My days were blessed with joy and happiness. I had big plans and dreams for the future... Who knows, I might have been walking down the street with my wife and baby by now. (Fujita 2013, 9)
> Añoro mi voz. Me gustaba cantar. Hasta nos compramos un karaoke [...]
>
> Añoro acabar agotada por ir a acompañarlas [a sus hijas] a un centro comercial a comprarse ropa.
> Añoro cuando sufría haciendo régimen para perder peso.
> Ahora me voy consumiendo, no tengo hambre.
> Añoro hablar por teléfono con todos. (Montero 2013, 79)[14]

Fujita and Montero struggle constantly. At first, there is acceptance, but this is subsequently replaced by the desire to resist. Although they recognize the lethal nature of the disease, they nevertheless deny the possibility of its final victory. Neither of them adopt an attitude of resignation. Both are on the warpath:

It's been three and a half years since my fight with ALS began.
I've picked a fight that can't be won.
But I have too many reasons why I can't lose.
So I guess I am just going to have to win [...] (Fujita 2013, 19, emphasis in the original)

Te desafío en que mis ojos vean la cura, ya sé que te las das de fuerte, pero no. ¿Sabes? No hay más fuerza que el amor de madre. ¿Privarlas de mí? Ah no, eso no. Lucharé hasta que mi último latido deje de oírse. Me has dejado como una muñeca de trapo físicamente, pero moralmente, buf, no puedes conmigo y se lo voy a demostrar a todos. Me río en tu cara. (Montero 2013, 81)[15]

Conclusion

Both *99% Thank you* and *Muñeca de Trapo* contain literary features that serve social purposes. Their accounts reveal a transformed identity after the eruption of an unexpected, violent event (the disease), a feature that is of interest both in trauma studies as well as in catastrophe narratives. The testimony as a genre has personal value, but is also socially important (Adami 2008, 32), and Montero and Fujita give a voice to patients with ALS. Their stories represent the fears, aspirations and hopes of a collective, and find legitimacy in strategies such as direct speech or the use of personal photographs that give force to their message.

Writing a testimony about suffering from a disease has clear therapeutic effects. Patients face a situation that is not desirable, but when they are given the chance to express themselves, their efforts to tackle the disease are foregrounded. The disease is capable of stealing the patient's voice; it darkens and overwhelms their powers of speech. Formulating their testimonies helps the patients in their quest to regain control of the situation and, in some cases, to overcome the illness. Moreover, in memoirs written by terminally ill patients, it is remarkable to note that the fighting spirit is still there.

Granted that the printed word–literature–functions as a portrait of different aspects of our nature, both *99% Thank you* and *Muñeca de Trapo* show us not only the human soul facing forces which cannot be controlled; from their subjective point of view, Fujita and Montero also reflect upon the essential questions of mankind: happiness, life, death and love. At the same time, these testimonies are salient for all readers, since disease can affect us or one of our loved ones at any given moment. As Fujita and

Montero prove, however, human nature mobilizes us to fight, even against overwhelming odds.

Notes

[1] At the time of writing, *Muñeca de trapo* had not yet been published in English. In this chapter, all translations are mine.

[2] This research was supported by Convocatoria Pública Nacional para Proyectos Artísticos y Culturales 2018-2019 [the Institute for the Development of Arts, Innovation and Creativity (Ecuador)].

[3] There are clear similarities between trauma studies and catastrophe narratives, despite Heba M. Sharobeem's statement that "Fuchs distinguishes catastrophe from trauma" (2008, 295). Actually, the difference is too narrow: Fuchs (2004, 7) refers specifically to traumas that occurred during childhood. She is not interested in a psychoanalytic approach or in events in the distant past: "Rather than look for past conflicts lingering on into the present, I concentrate on life writing characterized by a volatile occurrence *in* the present time of the writing or close enough to be a significant element in the mnemonic, creative process" (8, emphasis in the original).

[4] Fuchs (2004, 4) has made it clear that despite the restrictive title of her work, *The Text is Myself: Women's Life Writing and Catastrophe*, her theory does not apply exclusively to studies with a feminist approach.

[5] In the summer of 2014, the Ice Bucket Challenge marketing campaign raised money for ALS research and promoted awareness of the disease. The event was successful.

[6] Another autobiographical work associated with this disease, *Una caricia de Dios* (A Caress of God, 2012), was published in Mexico by Raúl Castro Bonilla and his wife María Grisela Mondragón. For more information, see Chávez Vaca 2016.

[7] "I already had two flowers [Montero's daughters] decorating my life" (my trans.).

[8] "Shell".

[9] "I lost my movement. I became a porcelain figurine, shattered in pieces after dropping to the floor; only the head was saved" (my trans.).

[10] "ALS. I got used to it.
I got used to having you [Juan] without being the way I used to be.
I got used to just rubbing your lips against mine,
with so much love that I started to tremble, just like when
we were dating.
I got used to not cuddling up to you in bed when I feel
cold, because my arms are dead. [...]" (my trans.).

[11] "You are cruel, exploitative, shameless, false, mean [...] You stole my power when I was in the prime of my life, one day in August, invading my right leg, then the left. Not content after three months, you took my arms, and to top your wickedness, and what hurt me the most, you stole my voice [...] You're a thief, but what you have not stolen, nor can you, is the great desire to live" (my trans.).

[12] "Be happy" (my trans.).

[13] "One cannot give up, let go of life, thinking 'and that's all that's left for me' and collapse" (my trans.).

[14] "I miss my voice, I loved to sing. We even bought a karaoke recorder [...]
I long to end up exhausted accompanying [her daughters] to a mall to buy clothes.
I miss the suffering of a weight loss diet.
This illness is wasting me away, I feel no hunger.
I long to talk on the phone with everyone" (my trans.).

[15] "[Montero talks to a personified ALS] I challenge you. My eyes will see the cure. You think you're the stronger, but you're not, you know? You're not stronger than a mother's love. Leave them? [Montero's daughters] without me? Oh no, never. I will fight until my last heartbeat no longer can be heard. You have turned me into a rag doll physically, but morally, pfff, you can't defeat me and I'm going to show everyone. I laugh in your face" (my trans.).

References

Adami, Valentina. 2008. *Trauma Studies and Literature*. Frankfurt am Main, Berlin: Peter Lang.
Allende, Isabel. 1994. *Paula*. Barcelona: Sudamericana/Plaza & Janés.
Aronson, Jeffery. 2000. "Autopathography: The Patient's Tale." *British Medical Journal*, Vol. 321, No. 7276: 1599–1602.
Asimov, Isaac. 1981. *Asimov on Science Fiction*. Garden City: Doubleday.
Campwell, Jan and Janet Harbord, eds. 2002. *Temporalities, Autobiography and Everyday Life*. Manchester: Manchester University.
Casas, Nubya Celina. 1981. *Novela-testimonio: historia y literatura*. Ann Arbor, Michigan: UMI.
Castro Bonilla, Raúl and María Grisela Mondragón. 2012. *Una caricia de Dios*. Tlaquepaque: Ediciones Alba.
Chávez Vaca, Wladimir. 2016. "Cuando el paciente se vuelve biógrafo. Las narrativas de la enfermedad en *Una caricia de Dios*." *Dialogía*, Vol.10.
Couser, Thomas. 1997. *Recovering bodies: illness, disability, and life-writing*. Madison: University of Wisconsin.
Freud, Sigmund. 1989 [1910]. *Leonardo da Vinci and A Memory of His Childhood*. Norton: New York.
Frich, Jan C. 2010. "Dialogue and Creativity: Narrative in the Clinical Encounter." In *Illness in Context*, edited by Knut Stene-Johansen and Frederik Tygstrup, 37–50. Amsterdam: Rodopi.
Fuchs, Miriam. 2004. *Women's Life Writing and Catastrophe*. Madison: University of Wisconsin.
Fujita, Masahiro. 2013. *99% Thank You*. Tokyo: Poplar.
Gilmore, Leigh. 2001. *The Limits of Autobiography. Trauma and Testimony*. Ithaca and London: Cornell University.
Hawking, Stephen. 2013. *My Brief History*. New York: Bantam Books.
Hunsaker Hawkins, Anne. 1999 [1993]. *Reconstructing Illness: Studies in Pathography*. West Lafayette: Purdue University Press.
Hydén, Lars Christer. 1997. "Illness and Narrative." *Sociology of Health & Illness*, Vol. 19, No. 1: 48–69.
Jensen, Axel. 1998. *Pasienten i Sentrum*. Oslo: Cappelen.
Jensen, Axel and Petter Mejlænder. 2002. *Livet sett fra Nimbus*. Oslo: Spartacus.
Modlinger, Martin and Philipp Sonntag, eds. 2011. *Other People's Pain: Narratives of Trauma and the Questions of Ethics*. New York: Peter Lang.
Montero, Leo. 2013. *Muñeca de trapo*. Málaga: Editorial Seleer.

Parke, Catherine N. 2002. *Biography: Writing Lives*. New York: Routledge.

Sharobeem, Heba M. 2008. "The Poetics of Pain and Cancer and the Question of Genre in Two Catastrophe Narratives." *Canadian Review of Comparative Literature*, Vol. 35, No. 4: 294–327.

Socken, Paul. 1993. *The Myth of the Lost Paradise in the Novels of Jacques Poulin*. Rutherford: Fairleigh Dickinson University.

Sontag, Susan. 1991. *Illness as metaphor; and AIDS and its metaphors*. London: Penguin Books.

Stacey, Jackie. 2002. *'Heroes' in Temporalities, Autobiography and Everyday Life*, edited by Jan Campbell and Janet Harbord. Manchester: Manchester University.

Whitehead, Anne. 2004. *Trauma fiction*. Edinburgh: Edinburgh University.

Wiesel, Elie. 1990. *Dimensions of the Holocaust*. Evanston: Northwestern University.

Wiltshire, John. 2006. "Pathography? Medical Progress and Medical Experience from the Viewpoint of the Patient." *Southerly*, Vol. 66, No. 1: 22–36.

IDENTITY AND CHILDHOOD

CHAPTER SEVENTEEN

"EACH HOMELESS PERSON HAS A DIFFERENT STORY TO TELL": HOMELESS IDENTITY IN DAVID WALLIAMS' METAFICTIVE CHILDREN'S BOOK *MR STINK* (2009)

GRO-ANITA MYKLEVOLD

This chapter discusses the construction of a homeless identity in the contemporary children's book *Mr Stink* (2009) by David Walliams. Childhood plays an important role in identity development and Mia Österlund claims that "How children in different time periods and societies deal with marginalization, exclusion and exile says a great deal about the nature of the social order of that time and place" (Österlund 2013, 1). I will thus examine how Walliams' child protagonist, Chloe, interprets a homeless person's individual self-biography, and investigate how the portrayal of the eponymous hero Mr Stink prevents or confirms stereotypical images of a large and heterogeneous group. I will also discuss how metafiction, or "books about books and the writing of books" (Nikolajeva 2016 [1996], 190), may aid children in becoming more critical readers and more tolerant of diversity and ambiguity (Pantaleo and Sipe 2012).

Home and Homelessness in Children's Literature

Home is an essential component of childhood and for many children the idea of home is a safe haven where they are allowed to grow up in a stable environment. The plot development of home–away–home is a prominent one in many children's books (Österlund 2013). The canonical works *Alice's Adventures in Wonderland* (1865) by Lewis Carroll and *The Wizard of Oz* (1900) by F. L. Baum follow this pattern; both Alice and

Dorothy are initially home, then they become temporarily homeless and finally return home in the denouement of the books. The character of the homeless child is also portrayed in several other classical works in children's literature, for example in *Oliver Twist* (1836) by Charles Dickens and *Rasmus and the Vagabond* (1956) by Astrid Lindgren. However, homeless *identity* in children's books has not been the subject of much research, and deserves more attention.

Theories of Identity

The social scientist Lindsey McCarthy argues that the construction and implications of a "homeless identity" are both oversimplified and under-researched. She points out that:

> Within the news media and literature, alike, people experiencing homelessness are often categorised into various stereotypes revolving around their lack of abode. In such a practice a 'homeless identity' becomes the defining feature of a person's character. Very few theoretical studies have critically addressed this discursive construction and its implications. (McCarthy 2013, 46)

In both literature and the media, the homeless person is typically portrayed as a white, "bearded, dirty male" and a "male panhandler" (ibid., 46–47). Such stereotypes are obviously counter-productive as regards tolerance and respect for other people and different ways of living in a postmodern society.

Postmodern human beings are divided into two groups by the famous sociologist and philosopher Zygmunt Bauman (1996): the tourists and the vagabonds. Although these are only metaphors of postmodern life, the first group is portrayed as a group with many resources, which enable them to travel voluntarily, whereas the latter group is constantly on the move and lacks important privileges. As Bauman puts it, "The tourists travel because they want to; the vagabonds–because they have *no other choice*" (Bauman 1996, 14, italics in original).

"Identity" may be seen as both an individual and a social concept; and the famous British sociologist Anthony Giddens claims that in late-modern cultures "the self becomes a *reflexive project*" (Giddens 1991, 32, italics in original). He views identity as something which "has to be routinely created and sustained in the reflexive activities of the individual" (ibid.). Identity is thus seen not as something that is received or fixed, but something that has to be individually created and continually adjusted through each individual's storytelling:

> A person's identity is not to be found in behavior, nor–important though it is–in the reactions of others, but in the capacity to keep a narrative going. The individual's biography, if she is to maintain regular interaction with others in the day-to-day world, cannot be wholly fictive. It must continually integrate events which occur in the external world, and sort them into the ongoing 'story' about the self. (ibid., 54)

Giddens thus argues that each person has a narrative and a life biography that constitutes the foundation of his or her identity; it is an ongoing activity and something that is negotiated through social interaction with others.

Identity in Fiction

Unlike Giddens, Monika Fludernik claims that identity is explicitly linked to "otherness" and how we mirror ourselves in other people (Fludernik 2007, 260). She puts forward the idea of a narrative identity which is dominant in all conversational and natural narrative settings and, like the feminist Judith Butler, Fludernik argues that identity is "performative"; something "which we create inside our social roles" (ibid., 261). She expands on this through asserting that "identities are constructed in the interplay of individuals with other people in social contexts of family, work, study, leisure activities, etc." (ibid.).

Maria Nikolajeva emphasizes how reading fiction moulds the readers' identities and advocates a cognitive approach to literature. She claims that reading fiction enhances our cognitive and empathic skills (Nikolajeva, 2014) and underlines the importance of memory in shaping the readers' identities:

> Memory is doubtless the greatest narrative engine in fiction. Not only does it mould the fictional character's identity, making it fluid and more resemblant of a real human being; it also evokes readers' memories and thus affects their identities in interaction with fiction. Again, this is why we read fiction: it has the power to shape our identities. (ibid., 88–89)

My chapter will utilize all these aspects of identity construction to focus on how homeless identity is narrated and interpreted in this contemporary children's book. I will place particular emphasis on how Mr Stink narrates his own self-biography through storytelling, and examine how this is interpreted by the child protagonist, Chloe.

Children's Literature by David Walliams

As previously mentioned, in this chapter I use the book *Mr Stink* (2009) by David Walliams to examine the identity construction of a homeless person in children's literature. Walliams recently started writing children's books and is at large a *tabula rasa* in the field of children's literature criticism. He has, within a short period of time, established himself as one of the world's most popular children's writers, together with Roald Dahl, J. K. Rowling, Julia Donaldson and Jeff Kinney.[1] During the period between 2008 and 2018, Walliams has published nine children's books and five picture books, and in 2014, his books even surpassed *Harry Potter* in popularity in UK schools.[2] Despite the fact that several book reviewers and readers have argued that David Walliams is "the new Roald Dahl,"[3] little academic research has been devoted to examining Walliams' fiction for children and even less on the alleged similarity between the two authors. One exception is Myklevold (2017), who examines how David Walliams and Roald Dahl make use of metanarration and metafiction in two of their books.

Walliams' first two books were *The Boy in the Dress* (2008) and *Mr Stink* (2009), both illustrated by Roald Dahl's famous illustrator Quentin Blake. The first book thematized cross-dressing and this, in addition to Walliams already being a famous comedian who himself frequently cross-dresses, earned the book lots of publicity and acclaim. The second book, however, did not receive that much attention despite the fact that it also contains controversial themes, namely homelessness, politics and adult hypocrisy.

Mr Stink is a warm, well-written book about Chloe, her dysfunctional family and her new vagabond friend, Mr Stink. Already in the title, *Mr Stink*, we get an indication of where the main thematic emphasis is: not only on the child protagonist Chloe, but on helping the eponymous hero, her new, homeless friend Mr Stink. This is a distinct attempt to change the reader's focus and perspective; from the well-off to the marginalized homeless, from the family arena to those who live out on the streets, from "the haves" to "the have nots", from those who have a choice to those who cannot choose, or in Bauman's terms from the "tourist" Chloe to the "vagabond" Mr Stink (Bauman 1996).

Chloe's Identity in a Dysfunctional Family

Nikolajeva argues that if a children's story focuses on a family, it is best if it is a dysfunctional one in order to stimulate children's cognitive activities:

> [...] if family is the focus of a narrative it should preferably be dysfunctional in some way. A happy, harmonious family does not provide a good plot. Moreover, I would argue, harmony does not stimulate cognitive activity. In plain words, readers need a deviation from 'the happy family' script to get engaged with the story. Thus a dysfunctional family may be dictated by the plot rather than reflect a representative state of society. Absent parents are a frequent trope in children's fiction. The narrative function of an absent parent is to allow the child protagonist to explore the world without restriction and protection. The symbolic function of an absent parent is to allow the child protagonist to develop their own identity. (Nikolajeva 2014, 37–38)

It is indeed a dysfunctional family and (mentally) absent parents we are presented with in *Mr Stink*. Chloe's hypocritical mother, Mrs Crombe, favorizes her other daughter Annabelle, and Mr Crombe is so ashamed that he has lost his job that he hides in the closet every day instead of admitting that he is unemployed. Chloe's mother is so superficial that she "even sprayed air-freshener in the garden" (Walliams 2009, 29) and makes Chloe wear clothes that in her opinion make her look "like a Quality Street" (ibid., 121) even though Chloe "desperately wanted to be a Goth" (ibid.). Chloe's desire to develop her own identity and achieve her own personal style, particularly important for a 12-year old, is crushed by her mother's political ambitions and urgent desire to identify herself with Members of Parliament (MP). Chloe's mum lacks empathy and compassion, and desperately wants to become an MP for the Conservative Party. She makes a long list of harsh and absurd policies. Point 20 on her list reads "Finally, all homeless people, or 'soap-dodgers', are to be banned from our streets. They are a menace to society" (ibid., 88).

The fake and inhospitable qualities of her mother are juxtaposed with Chloe's empathy and courage. One incident illustrating these aspects of her character is when she befriends and, after a while, takes in, the town tramp Mr Stink and lodges him in the garden shed. By getting to know him and a homeless person's individual biography (Giddens 1991), she, unlike the grown-ups, looks behind his appearance to try to find the essence of his identity and his individual traits. Perhaps because she comes from a dysfunctional family and is "emotionally homeless", Chloe, "who loved being alone with her thoughts" (Walliams 2009, 15), asks herself many questions about the homeless man and thus further develops her cognitive skills and her own identity as a reflective, curious and intelligent girl. Instead of ignoring the homeless man, she starts thinking about "Why did he live on the streets? Had he ever had a home? What did his dog eat? Did he have any friends or family? If so, did they know he was homeless?" (ibid.). Through interaction with fiction, children and adolescent readers of *Mr Stink* may become more reflective and nuanced as well, since fictional characters resemble real human beings (Nikolajeva 2014, 88–89), so that the readers might start asking the same questions in real life, thus viewing the homeless as heterogeneous individuals, each with their own unique story or self-biography. Chloe early realizes this and is, from the very beginning of the narrative, presented as the most courageous and tolerant character in the book:

> One morning, Mr Stink simply appeared in the town and took up residence on an old wooden bench. No one knew where he had come from, or where he might be going. The town folk were mostly nice to him. They sometimes dropped a few coins at his feet, before rushing off with their eyes watering. But no one was really *friendly* towards him. No one stopped for a chat. At least, not till the day that a little girl finally plucked up the courage to speak to him–and that's where our story begins. (Walliams 2009, 14)

When Chloe and Mr Stink later appear on a TV programme about politics and homelessness, Chloe's humane and individual approach to the homeless is contrasted with the treatment the UK's more than 100,000 people living on the streets receive from the general public:

> Part of the problem stems from the fact that we are seen as statistics rather than people. [...] 'We all have different reasons for being homeless', continued Mr Stink. 'Each homeless person has a different story to tell. Perhaps if people in the audience tonight, or out there watching at home, stopped to *talk* to the homeless people in their town, they would realise that.' (ibid., 186–187, italics in original)

This is exactly what Chloe does in the beginning of the narrative; she stops to talk to the vagabond and thus challenges her own fears and develops her own mature identity in getting to know him, as well as defying her mother:

> 'Hello', said the girl, her voice trembling a little with nerves. The girl was called Chloe. She was only twelve and she had never spoken to a tramp before. Her mother had forbidden her to speak to 'such creatures'. Mother even disapproved of her daughter talking to kids from the local council

estate. But Chloe didn't think Mr Stink *was* a creature. She thought he was a man who looked like he had a very interesting story to tell–and if there was one thing Chloe loved, it was stories. (ibid., 13–14)

Contrary to the advice from her cold mother, Chloe befriends Mr Stink and wants to find out more about his story. She asks him about his background, but at first he is unwilling to share his life narrative. Both Chloe's empathy for the individual and her fascination for stories, make her stop and talk to Mr Stink. These aspects are both linked to metafiction in children's literature.

Metafiction in Children's Literature

Metafiction may simply be defined as "books about books and the writing of books" (Nikolajeva 1996, 190) and the whole idea is to "erase the illusion of a boundary between fantasy and reality, and in so doing it also questions the reality of 'reality'" (ibid., 202). This may assist young readers of children's literature in becoming more active, philosophical, inquisitive and critical. Chloe herself is a philosophical and curious girl who asks herself and Mr Stink many questions about their existence. Chloe dreams of becoming a writer, but Chloe's hypocritical mother, who is shallow and fixated on appearances, humiliates her writing aspirations, tears apart her storybooks and orders her to use more time on maths. Nevertheless, Chloe tells Mr Stink vampire stories she has made up and gets positive feedback from him, which is important for her identity, something I will return to below.

Nikolajeva claims that "[o]ne way to call into question the narrative and its truthfulness is to let the protagonist at the end of the book start (or contemplate) writing precisely the book we have just read" (ibid., 193). When Chloe starts writing the exact same book that we have just read at the end of the story, she exemplifies this point: "She opened her maths exercise book and began to write the first words of her new story. *Mr Stink stank*..." (Walliams 2009, 267). At the same time as it is a way of questioning the "reality" of the narrative and distancing the readers, it also shows us that Chloe's identity as an aspiring writer has begun to take shape. At the end of the book, she is in charge of her own destiny and is no longer dependent on her mother or bullied at school. She is now narrating her own biography, and this development is largely due to befriending and being encouraged by her vagabond friend Mr Stink.

This respect for people that are somewhat "different" that Chloe displays is an important theme to communicate to children, and Pantaleo and Sipe (2012) argue that different kinds of narratives and metafiction may make young readers simultaneously more critical and more tolerant:

> by reading and discussing books with narrative diversity and metafictive devices, students may become aware of their own and (and others') thinking and reasoning strategies, making them better problem-solvers in general, which may lead to greater metacognition. [...] They learn that stories may be told from various points of view, and that these points of view do not necessarily overlap easily with one another. Therefore, children learn about and experience the importance of accepting ambiguity and multiple interpretations, not a single answer or a single viewpoint. These abilities have many implications for how they approach stories, but also how they approach real life. (Pantaleo and Sipe 2012, 13)

Reading metafictive children's fiction can thus assist in heightening awareness of both one's own and others' viewpoints and perceptions, which can also be transferred to how youngsters behave and think in their daily lives. Nikolajeva contends that reading metafictional narratives aids readers in developing empathy (Nikolajeva 2014). The ability to think critically, to develop self-distance and the ability to reflect on your own and others' identities are all important aspects to learn when growing up, since this may lead to more empathy and tolerance for different cultures and different life styles. As parents, teachers or teacher educators, this is yet another incentive for utilizing more metafictive children's and young adult literature in schools and at home.

Since Chloe is an aspiring author, the metafictional references in this book are abundant, and in the end of the novel she is depicted narrating the book *Mr Stink* in the same way that it starts, both implying that she is the author and that she has a writer's career ahead of her. Walliams is a children's writer who frequently employs metafiction (Myklevold 2017). Nikolajeva views metafiction as a dominant and constructive literary device in contemporary children's literature. She claims that "Both metafiction and polyphony overturn our conventional ideas of realism and allow us to approach the essence of a children's book as a work of art" (Nikolajeva 2016 [1996], 10). The self-referentiality and polyphony, or multi-voicedness, of children's literature thus seems to aid us in understanding the significance and topicality of contemporary children's books (ibid.).

Homeless *within* a Home

Since Chloe's Mum openly favors her sister and rebukes Chloe for being more interested in story writing than maths, the notion of "homelessness" can be utilized in a new context: "She thought of Mr Stink, sitting on his bench [...]. She wasn't homeless like him, but she *felt* homeless in her heart" (Walliams 2009, 61). As previously touched upon, this is an important part of Chloe's development: realizing that a feeling of loneliness and homelessness can also appear *within* a house and a family. Since the family is so dysfunctional, Chloe feels left out and alienated from her family, so she communicates much better with her postmodern, extended family: Raj and Mr Stink. Raj is the local, Indian newsagent, who contradicts the fake images of several other grown-ups in the book. He is a genuinely warm, tolerant and jovial character. He is described as Chloe's close friend and confidante: "Chloe loved talking to Raj. He wasn't a parent or a teacher, and whatever you said to him, he would never judge you" (ibid., 53). Raj is a tolerant and reflective character who says "[a]ny of us could become homeless one day. I can see nothing wrong with talking to a tramp, just like you would anyone else" (ibid., 54).

Interestingly, whereas Chloe feels more and more "homeless" and alienated from her own family, Mr Stink, feels more and more at home:

> Mr Stink had made the shed quite homely. He had fashioned a bed out of some piles of old newspapers. An old piece of tarpaulin was his duvet, with a grow bag for a pillow. It looked almost comfy. An old hosepipe had been arranged in the shape of a dog-basket for the Duchess. A plant-pot full of water sat beside for a bowl. In chalk he'd expertly drawn some old-fashioned portraits on the dark wooden creosoted walls, like the ones you see in museums or old country houses, depicting people from history. On one side he'd even drawn a window, complete with curtains and a sea view. –You seem to be settling in then, said Chloe. –Oh, yes, I can't thank you enough, child. I love it. I feel like I finally have a home again. (ibid., 106–107)

However, as Bauman points out, "The tourists travel because they want to; the vagabonds–because they have *no other choice*" (Bauman 1996, 14). Chloe, as the resourceful "tourist" that she is, has a choice, she can contemplate whether to leave or not, whereas Mr Stink does not have this privilege and will soon be pushed out of his temporary home. As Chloe finds out towards the end of the narrative, Mr Stink used to have a permanent home, before he became a vagabond. Through observing her new friend, Chloe sees that he has good manners, eats with silver cutlery, draws historical motifs on the garden shed walls, and has a photograph of a woman and a stately home. Chloe speculates a lot about who he really is, and she eventually finds out that Mr Stink's former identity was noble; his name was Lord Darlington:

> Mr Stink took a breath. 'Well, I had it all, child. More money than I could ever spend, a beautiful house with its own lake. My life was like an endless summer. Croquet, tea on the lawn, long lion days spent playing cricket. And to make things even more perfect I married this beautiful, clever, funny, adorable woman, my childhood sweetheart. Violet.' (Walliams 2009, 230–231)

After losing his wife in a fire, Mr Stink could no longer bear to be in the house: "Being there gave me terrible nightmares. I kept seeing her face in flames. [...] So one day I started walking and I never came back" (ibid., 234). From being a nobleman, or in Bauman's term a tourist (1996), he adopts the identity of a vagabond, in both a metaphorical and a literal sense. The only grown-up character who realizes that such a sudden metamorphosis is possible is the friendly, multicultural and flexible Raj, who logically states that "[a]ny of us could become homeless one day" (Walliams 2009, 54). His genuinely compassionate and reflective nature is juxtaposed with that of the Prime Minister, who only pretends to be a caring leader, but who actually is an obnoxious man. He "performs" his identity (Fludernik 2006) as a statesman, but he cares more about power than about his constituents. He reveals this in the way he treats–and talks– to Mr Stink. The PM's hypocrisy is clearly revealed when he wants Mr Stink to become a member of the Conservative Party, and later Minister for the Homeless, only to gain more votes in the upcoming election:

> 'If you joined the party it would fool the public into thinking we *cared* about the homeless! Maybe one day I could even make you a Minister for Soap-Dodgers'. –'Soap-Dodgers?' said Mr Stink. –'Yeah, you know, the homeless.' (Walliams 2009, 223)

Language Awareness as Metafiction and as a Means of Defining Identity

Calling the homeless and Mr Stink "Soap-Dodgers" means, despite the obvious element of comedy, using a derogatory term to describe a large, heterogeneous group. In many ways, Mr Stink, through his name and avoidance of baths, confirms some of the stereotypes of the homeless, but in other areas, like his speech, his vocabulary and his posh manners, he contradicts stereotypes.

Normally, Walliams uses a lot of comedy and humorous remarks in his children's writing, but this literary device is usually utilized between groups that are more, or less equal, in social status and power. Here, it is the opposite: the Prime Minister talks in a degrading way about a marginalized group to a homeless person. The PM blatantly admits it himself when he says to Mr Stink: "You're just so *funny*. I mean to laugh *at*, not really with" (ibid., 223). When Mr Stink is hesitant about taking on a Minister-post for the homeless, the PM goes so far in his demeaning speech to Mr Stink that Chloe reacts strongly:

-'Right', said Mr Stink. 'And as Minister for the Homeless, I would be able to help other homeless people?'

-'Well, no', said the Prime Minister. 'It wouldn't *mean* anything, just make me look like a fantastic tramp-loving guy. Well, wadda you say, Mr Stinky-poo?'

Mr Stink looked very ill at ease. −'I don't...I mean...I'm not sure...'

-'Are you *kidding* me?' laughed the Prime Minister. 'You're a tramp! You can't have anything better to do!'

The suited herd laughed too. Suddenly Chloe had a flashback to her school. The Prime Minister and his aides were behaving exactly like the gang of mean girls in her year. Still stumbling for words, Mr Stink looked over to her for help.

-'Prime Minister...?' Said Chloe.

-'Yes?' He answered with an expectant smile.

-'Why don't you stick it up your fat bum!' (ibid., 223–224)

The comparison of the PM's administration and a gang of bullies in school is a fitting one, and explains why the normally quite shy Chloe can respond with such anger. Here, she identifies with Mr Stink as a victim of bullying, and takes his side against the oppressive, powerful PM.

The fact that Mr Stink, who is usually so verbal, is lost for words signifies helplessness and displays the effects of how it feels to be marginalized and ridiculed by someone much more powerful. The fact that Chloe stands up for her homeless friend against bullying grown-ups, shows how contemporary society, although fictionally illustrated, displays both tolerance in the younger generation and intolerance in the older generation.

Even though Mr Stink needs Chloe's help against the PM, he is normally very specific and conscious of which word he prefers when describing himself and his own identity. When referring to himself, he states that:

> –'I don't like the word 'tramp'. It makes you think of someone who smells' [...] Chloe tried to conceal her surprise. Even the Duchess looked puzzled and she didn't even speak English, only Dog.
>
> –'I prefer vagabond or wanderer', continued Mr Stink. The way he put it, thought Chloe, it sounded almost poetic. Especially 'wanderer.' She would love to be a wanderer. (ibid., 39–40)

Chloe's artistic identity of course gives her a conscious and creative relationship to words, stories and literature, and Mr Stink is equally conscious of defining himself and his identity with the right words and flare: "I am but a humble wanderer. A vagrant maybe, certainly a vagabond, a street dreamer if you will..." (ibid., 209).

This metafictive and linguistic consciousness of both Chloe and Mr Stink, through Chloe's interest in writing and Mr Stink's ardent play with words, can also signal the importance and powerfulness of language to young readers. Language can be both a powerful and a painful tool, since terms and names may contain beautiful connotations, but the wrong names can also cause pain. Walliams utilizes metafiction in many of his books and one of the reasons may be to illustrate the importance of reading, language, and the potential imaginative power and playfulness of utilizing the right vocabulary.

When Chloe is going to tell the vampire story to Mr Stink, she is reluctant to read her own text because it is personal–a feeling that most authors (and academics) can relate to. Chloe doubts herself and her writing abilities, since she links writing to her identity, it becomes personal: "These were her words. It was much more private, more personal, and she suddenly felt like she wasn't ready to share it with anyone" (ibid., 115).

However, she finally reads it, and Mr Stink acts as an encouraging audience and editor. He tells her among other things: "Wonderful opening!" (ibid.); he states that it is a success, that she must make a sequel, and suggests that her next story could be about flesh-eating zombies. Chloe then realizes that just as she has changed through her friendship with the vagabond, stories may be altered and revised by her.

Throughout the book, we see that to Chloe, the defining feature of Mr Stink is not his lack of abode or lack of a bath, but his story and the individual behind his somewhat shabby appearance. In sharp contrast to several of the grown-ups in the story, the child protagonist develops into a reflective, mature and tolerant character. Through their unique friendship, Chloe and Mr Stink communicate to young readers that tolerance and respect for people and customs that are different, is an essential skill in today's heterogeneous society. By assisting marginalized individuals, one can simultaneously develop a broader understanding of the world and of oneself.

Reciprocally, when Chloe provides a homeless individual with shelter, Mr Stink provides Chloe with nuanced views on homelessness, her family and herself. Chloe gets Mr Stink to reveal his "true" identity, but he also assists Chloe in finding hers. Mr Stink, who himself is out of work is the one who encourages Chloe's future profession as a writer. Since he is the eponymous hero, the stereotypes are reversed and give us a more nuanced view of a marginalized group: the homeless person is the most responsible and balanced grown-up, and the "establishment" with the politicians are the irresponsible ones. The book also reminds us that people's circumstances may change at any time, and a vagabond may become a tourist and a tourist may become a vagabond (Bauman 1996). After interpreting Mr Stink's individual story, Chloe realizes this. She also comprehends that, like "reality" and "identity", "a story" is not an entirely fixed entity. Stories, like persons' identities, are continually changed and recreated. Consequently, Chloe closes the narrative of the book by creating a new one.

Notes

[1] According to Imogen Russel Williams in the *Guardian*, Sept. 4, 2013.
[2] Cf. the article "David Walliams overtakes J. K. Rowling among readers in UK schools", *The Guardian*, March 5, 2014.
[3] Cf. "Why David Walliams really is the new Roald Dahl", Beverly Turner in *The Telegraph*, Sept. 5, 2013.

References

Bauman, Zygmunt. 1996. "Tourists and Vagabonds: Heroes and Victims of Postmodernity." Institut für Höhere Studien (HIS): Wien. https://www.ssoar.info/ssoar/bitstream/handle/document/26687/ssoar-1996-baumann-tourists_and_vagabonds.pdf [Accessed 10.1.2018].

Butler, Judith. 1990. *Gender Trouble: Feminism and the Subversion of Identity.* New York: Routledge.

Fludernik, Monika. 2007. "Identity/alterity." In *The Cambridge Companion to Narrative*, edited by David Herman, 260–273. Cambridge: Cambridge University Press.

Giddens, Anthony. 1991. *Modernity and Self-Identity. Self and Society in the Late Modern Age.* Stanford: Stanford University Press.

McCarthy, Lindsey. 2013. "Homelessness and identity: a critical review of the literature and theory". In *People, Place and Policy Online*, 7/1, 46–58. Sheffield: Sheffield Hallam University. http://extra.shu.ac.uk/ppp-online/wp-content/uploads/2013/09/homelessness_identity_review_literature_theory.pdf [Accessed 23.5.2016].

Myklevold, Gro-Anita (2017). "'I dare not write it, even hint it. Nobody will ever print it': Metanarration and Metafiction in Contemporary Children's Books." In *Narratology Plus: Recent International Narratives for Children and Young Adults,* edited by Peter Langemeyer & Karen Patrick Knutsen, 145–164. Frankfurt am Main: Peter Lang Edition.

Nikolajeva, Maria. 2016 [1996]. *Children's Literature Comes of Age: Toward a New Aesthetic.* New York and London: Garland.

—. 2014. "Memory of the Present: Empathy and Identity in Young Adult Fiction." In Special issue: narrative emotions and the shaping (s) of identity. *Narrative Works: Issues, Investigations and Interventions.* https://journals.lib.unb.ca/index.php/NW/article/viewFile/22784/26462 [Accessed 11.1.2018].

—. 2014. *Reading for Learning: Cognitive approaches to children's literature.* Amsterdam/Philadelphia: John Benjamins Publishing Company.

Pantaleo, Sylvia. 2010. "Mutinous Fiction: Narrative and Illustrative Metalepsis in Three Postmodern Picturebooks." In *Children's Literature in Education*, 41, 12–27. Springer.

Pantaleo, Sylvia and Lawrence P. Sipe. 2012. "Diverse Narrative Structures in Contemporary Picturebooks: Opportunities for Children's

Meaning-Making." *Journal of Children's Literature*, vol. 38, No.1, Spring 2012.
Turner, Beverly. 2013. "Why David Walliams really is the new Roald Dahl". In *The Telegraph*, Sept. 5, 2013. https://www.telegraph.co.uk/women/mother-tongue/10291436/Why-David-Walliams-really-is-the-new-Roald-Dahl.html [Accessed 13.3.2018].
Walliams, David. 2008. *The Boy in the Dress*. London: HarperCollins Publishers.
—. 2009. *Mr Stink*. London: HarperCollins Publishers.
Williams, Imogen Russel. 2014. "David Walliams overtakes J K Rowling among readers in UK schools". In *The Guardian*, March 5, 2014. https://www.theguardian.com/books/2014/mar/05/david-walliams-jk-rowling-uk-schools [Accessed 13.3.2018].
—. 2013. "Is David Walliams the new Roald Dahl?» In *The Guardian*, Sept. 4, 2013. https://www.theguardian.com/books/booksblog/2013/sep/04/david-walliams-booksforchildrenandteenagers [Accessed 1.4.2017].
Österlund, Mia. 2013. *Barnboken: Journal of Children's Literature Research,* 42. Http://www.barnboken.net/index.php/clr/article/view/163/311 [Accessed 12.1.2018].

CHAPTER EIGHTEEN

"THE RIGHT ALICE": A CYBERTEXT PERSPECTIVE ON NARRATED IDENTITY IN FILM ADAPTATIONS OF LEWIS CARROLL'S NOVELS

BRITT W. SVENHARD

Introduction

At the time of writing, science fiction enthusiasts around the world are eagerly awaiting the second season of the American television series *Westworld*, first released by HBO in 2016 (Nolan and Joy 2016). Westworld is a future Wild West-themed amusement park where android hosts, who look exactly like humans, are programmed to play out the same pre-scripted narratives for high-paying guests to take part in every day, as in a videogame. The visitors have unlimited freedom to do what they want with the hosts without retribution and each day, the staff repairs and wipes out the memories of the hosts. When the android Dolores–dressed in a blue Victorian frock and with yellow hair–starts having visions that resemble memories, she slowly comes to terms with her true reality and starts questioning her existence. As more hosts learn the truth about themselves, a desire for narrative control is stirred, and a robot uprising looms.

The *Westworld* series is only one example of the many references in popular culture to Lewis Carroll's *Alice* stories, and the series follows two very successful *Alice* inspired films of the last decade: Tim Burton's *Alice in Wonderland* (2010) and James Bobin's *Alice Through the Looking Glass* (2016). The discussion of these films in this chapter should be read against the backdrop of the iconic status of the originals: their omnipresence in postmodern culture and the impressive body of scholarly work available. The scope of this chapter, however, allows us only to explore a fragment of this work, and Carroll's original stories[1] will receive less (and perhaps somewhat irreverent) treatment. This is also the case with regard to the narrative possibilities of film, which, ironically, is the medium of the narratives under scrutiny. Film theory will have to take a backseat to literature and cybertexts in my discussion of how certain motifs in the films link up with theories on narrativization and identity construction as described in philosophy and narrative theory.

Newer forms of multi-level narrative, such as cybertext, challenge traditional ideas about identity construction via a linear plot. Here, I argue, however, that the medium of film can function as a tool that can convey the multi-level structure of such texts. The classical fantasy stories about *Alice* in both films emphasize how cybertext structures can shape viable models for life narratives and identity construction.

Theory: Narrative and Identity

When Carroll's Alice falls down the rabbit hole, her perspectives on time, space and distance start to change. These perspectives are also defining elements in video and computer games, and the fact that Burton's *Alice in Wonderland* was influenced by earlier video games[2] as well as inspiring new game versions,[3] illustrates how the different media of literature, film and video games mutually influence each other and diverge.

In *Narrative and Identity* (2008), Bo Petterson, on behalf of narratology studies, makes "[a] Plea for a Truly Interdisciplinary Study of Narrative" (32). He argues that in order to explain the relation between narration and identity, it is necessary to compare definitions found within different disciplines, because, "like any other science, literary studies should not be conducted in a vacuum but be aware of and learn from other disciplines as it pursues its own goals" (33). For narratologists, the question is whether other literary-aesthetic modes and cultural patterns may be involved in self-making processes as much as narration is (Hallet 2008, 50).

Birgit Neumann and Ansgar Nünning write that in narrative psychology, narratives function as a cognitive tool used as an organizational and problem-solving strategy (2008, 4). Narrativization is the structuring of the sequence of events into a coherent story, "a process by which the effect of contingency, as unpredictability and randomness, is converted into the effect of necessity or probability exerted by the configuring act of the storyline"–hence, identity also "emerges from the relative unity of character and action imposed by the unity of narrative" (Ritivoi cited in

Neumann and Nünning 2008, 5–6). However, Birgit Neumann points out that contemporary novels

> raise questions about the constructive aspects of identity and challenge humanist notions of an autonomous self [and that] this understanding influences the structure and aesthetics of contemporary novels. The current preoccupation of literature with questions of identity expresses itself clearly in the form of self-reflexive, doubtful exploration rather than straightforward assertion. (Neumann 2008, 53)

The structure of such novels is usually one that "alternates between the simple chronological succession of the frame narrative and the multi-temporal levels of the embedded memory streams, […] [depicting] the retrospective narrative as intertwined with the contexts in which it is created" (Neumann and Nünning 2008, 14). Furthermore,

> [t]he narrativization of experience and the construction of a narrative identity are guided and constrained by culture, which offers its members a set or stock of canonical, culturally accepted plots, symbols and characters through which they can interpret their experience and negotiate–or even make–their identity. (ibid., 9)

Neumann and Nünning also cite Bruner, who claims that individuals make sense of their personal experience by ordering it along the lines of literary genres, and that "one important way of characterizing a culture is by the narrative models it makes available for describing the course of a life" (Bruner, cited in Neumann and Nünning 2008, 9). The scope of this chapter does not allow for a discussion of a hierarchy of different modern narratives accepted as identity formation narratives. I would, however, like to point out that the adventure genre to which the two films under discussion belong has traditionally not been counted among the conventional models for life-narratives and identity construction, irrespective of medium (Constandinides 2010). This, however, is also, to follow Pettersson's plea, what makes it worthy of study.

Cybertext and Identity Construction: "But is it narrative?"

For more than two decades, video game theorists have been preoccupied with the relationship between videogames, film and literature and many have drawn parallels between their narrative modes and their affiliations (Laurel 1991; Murray 1997; Jenkins 2006). Espen J. Aarseth, on the other hand, has looked at the textual organization of the different media and, in his early writings, has questioned whether such parallels are (even) possible (1997).

In his early work *Cybertext: Perspectives on Ergodic Literature* (1997), Aarseth discusses adventure games and the intrinsic qualities of the genre and questions the common approach of addressing it from the perspectives of literary theory and criticism. Aarseth defines cybertexts (such as nonlinear hypertexts, adventure games and multi-user dungeons) as involving a process where the user (reader) engages with the text's mechanical organization and effectuates semiotic sequences as part of the literary exchange (1997, 2). Aarseth calls this process *ergodic* and sets it apart from reader-response theories:

> [...] when you read from a cybertext, you are constantly reminded of inaccessible strategies and paths not taken, voices not heard. [...] This is very different from the ambiguities of a linear text. And inaccessibility, it must be noted, does not imply ambiguity but, rather, an absence of possibility–an aporia. (1997, 3)

Burton and Bobin's films are usually categorized as fantasy adventure films and they both abound with overt references to adventure videogames. For the purpose of my discussion on narrative identity processes, I will take a closer look at what Aarseth calls "the ideal reader" of adventure games. Aarseth explains that in the early adventure games, the ideal reader

> would solve all the riddles of the text and thereby extricate the one definite, intended plotline. Eventually, this strategy changed, and now the reader's role is becoming less ideal (both in a structural and a moral sense) and more flexible, less dependable (hence more responsible), and freer. (1997, 105)

More interestingly, Aarseth points out what he calls a systematic misrepresentation in literary theory of the relationship between the narrative text and the reader; the idea that a narrative text is like "a labyrinth, a game, or an imaginary world, in which the reader can explore at will [...] [is] a spatiodynamic fallacy where the narrative is not perceived as a presentation of the world but rather as that world itself" (ibid., 3–4). According to Aarseth, historically, two labyrinth metaphors coexisted as one: One where the labyrinth is linear and unicursal–one path leading towards a centre. The other is more like a maze; it is multicursal– where the wanderer faces a series of critical choices (ibid., 6). With the Renaissance, the old metaphor of the text as labyrinth, "which in medieval poetics could signify both a difficult, winding, but potentially rewarding linear process *and* a spatial, artistically complex, and confusing artifact, was restricted to the latter sense" (ibid., 7). The result was that the labyrinth ceased to denote linear progress and teleology and hence could no longer serve as a model for narrative texts. The problem of narrative theory and literary criticism, maintains Aarseth, is that although they continue to unabashedly apply metaphors "like *labyrinth, game,* and *world*" (ibid., 8) in analyses of unicursal works, they leave the concept of the labyrinth and the existence of multicursal literary structures unexplored, and do not attempt any reassessment of terms and concepts applied.

Even so, Aarseth concludes that since the dynamic of searching and finding so typical of games in general seems to satisfy a desire in us for closure, it cannot be seen as a narrative structure, but rather as a fundamental layer of human experience, "from which narratives are spun" (ibid., 92). In my further discussion, I will explore the use of Aarseth's concept of the ideal reader of the adventure game in the films and develop the idea that the labyrinthine principle that informs the organization of cybertexts is also a viable tool for identity construction in the *Alice* films.

The Real Alice or The Right Alice?–The Dream Motif in Burton's *Alice in Wonderland*

Tim Burton's *Alice in Wonderland* draws its narrative structure and it characters first and foremost from the diegetic levels of *Alice in Wonderland* (Carroll, 1865 [2001]) and *Through the Looking Glass and What Alice Found There* (Carroll, 1871 [2001]). The frame story of the film takes us to Victorian England where Alice faces restrictions and gender discrimination. Here, the bored and rebellious Alice of Carroll's frame story has developed into a nineteen year old who, inspired by her deceased father–an adventurous merchant who wanted to explore trade routes to China–is looking for an alternative way of life to that of a lady of leisure which her mother and sister would like to see her settled into. The setting of the frame story is Alice's own engagement party on the estate of her intended fiancé, Hamish. Having run away from the situation, she follows a white rabbit in a waistcoat, falls down a rabbit hole and ends up in Underland. The diegetic level seems to be identical to Carroll's Wonderland, aesthetically and in terms of characters and storyline. But, we soon realize that Carroll's story is already in the past, asserting itself only in the form of Alice's recurring nightmares: The opening scenes of the film are a flashback that works as a prologue before the setting of the engagement party. It shows Alice Kingsley as a child, appearing in the doorway in her nightdress, interrupting a meeting her father is having with the partners of his trading company. When her father tucks her back into bed, she tells him about the recurring nightmare, where she falls down a hole and meets a rabbit in a waistcoat and a caterpillar. He tells her it is only a dream and that if she gets too frightened, she can always wake up.

Burton replaces the non-linear, episodic narratives of the original, with a linear adventure structure, in the form of a quest inspired by the poem "Jabberwocky", which appears in Carroll's second book. This poem tells the nonsensical story of the slaying of the monster Jabberwock on a "frabjous day", and includes characters like the Bandersnatch and the weapon the "vorpal sword". Having read it, Alice can only conclude that: "[S]omebody killed something: that's clear, at any rate..." (Carroll 1871 [2001], 156). In the film, the Mad Hatter recites the poem and then informs Alice: "It's all about you, you know". We learn that Underland is now subjected to the rule of the tyrannical Red Queen, who usurped the throne from the White Queen, her sister. They have all been waiting for Frabjous Day, when, it is foretold in the calendar the Uraculum, Alice will slay the Jabberwock, the Red Queen's monster champion, and the White Queen will return to rule Underland.

At the end of both of Carroll's *Alice* stories, the reader is led to believe that Alice's perceptions have been incorrect, that her adventures in Wonderland have been a dream, and that she is now back in the real world (Arp 2010, 134). In chapter four of *Through the Looking Glass and What Alice Found There*, Tweedledee tells Alice that it is the sleeping Red King who is dreaming her into existence. There are numerous philosophical studies discussing epistemology and metaphysics in Carroll's novels. However, I intend to sidestep the discussion of how self-identity becomes an epistemological problem in the original *Alice* stories, to look instead at how the dream motif in the film merges the diegetic levels. This creates equal dimensions similar to the multi-level structure of cybertexts, rendering the narrativization in both dimensions an integrated process of identity construction.

Following the scene where she leaves the engagement party and falls down the rabbit hole, comes a recreation of the iconic scenes of Alice testing the "Eat me" cakes and drinking potions that make her either grow or shrink, reminding herself as she is doing so that: "It's only a dream". As she struggles to become the right size in order to escape the room she is in through a tiny door, the camera suddenly frames her through a keyhole, suggesting the perspective of the camera belongs to someone else, peeping. We get a voiceover: "You'd think she would remember all this from the first time." Someone else responds: "You've brought the wrong Alice!", whereupon the first speaker pleads: "[g]ive her a chance!" Later, when she has met some of the characters who will become her companions in Underland, she confronts their accusations that she is an impostor by asking: "How can I be the wrong Alice when this is my dream?" At a loss, they take her to see an intensely petrol blue caterpillar called Absolem. When Alice introduces herself simply as "Alice", Absolem disputes that she is whom she claims to be. Alice, on the other hand, refuses to accept that she is the Alice depicted in the Uraculum, all the time insisting that it is her dream, and trying to wake herself up.

It is only when the Hatter, who is supposed to bring Alice to safety at the White Queen's palace, is arrested by the Red Queen's guards that Aarseth's ideal reader comes into play: instead of going directly to the White Queen, Alice decides to rescue the Hatter. When Bayard, a bloodhound, tells her she should instead prepare to meet the Jabberwock as foretold in the Uraculum, she says: "[T]his is *my* dream. I'll decide where it goes from here!" When Bayard then warns her about diverging from the path, Alice insists: "*I* make the path!" Upon hearing about Alice's decision, the White Queen, pleased, reassures Bayard that: "No, no, but that is exactly where she'll find the Vorpal Sword. We have our champion". Thus, from a narratological point of view, Alice can be seen to improvise in order to achieve narrative control and to command her own perspective, but in terms of the unicursal labyrinth, the options available are nevertheless strategic links that only allow for a "hyperlinear reading, the improvised selection of paths across a network structure" (Aarseth, 1997, 79).

On the morning of Frabjous Day, Alice turns to Absolem, who is half-asleep and about to transform, for advice. Absalom answers that he cannot help her if she doesn't even know who she is. Alice is provoked by this: "My name is Alice. […] My father was Charles Kingsley. He had a vision that stretched half-way round the world and nothing ever stopped him. I'm his daughter. I'm Alice Kingsley". Finally she is able to define herself, and Absolem exclaims: "Alice–at last! You were just as dimwitted the first time you were here. You called it Wonderland, as I recall". Then Alice remembers her nightmares and we are presented with a series of flashbacks of Alice when she is much younger, experiencing the same situations in Underland. Alice realizes that they were not dreams at all, but actual memories, and consequently, that Underland, although a different dimension, is real. She takes on the role of the Right Alice, slays the Jabberwock and frees Underland from the oppression of the Red Queen.

Climbing out of the rabbit hole, her dress in tatters and with visible scars from the encounter with the Bandersnatch, Alice returns to the party, where she rejects Hamish's proposal of marriage and instead goes off to discuss business with his father, who is also her father's old partner. They agree to expand the company's trade routes, as her father wanted, and she becomes an apprentice with the company. Having completed her quest and defined herself, this knowledge is transferred to the "real" mimetic world/level. But the issue was never of an epistemological kind in Burton's film. Rather than exploring who she really *is*, if there is such a thing as the Real Alice, the quest is about Alice deciding who she *wants to be*.

The Duchess in Carroll's *Alice's Adventures in Wonderland* tells Alice to: "[b]e what you would seem to be" "(Carroll, 1865 [2001], 96). According to Rick Mayock, Alice resembles one of Nietzsche's free spirits because she takes control of her perspectives, knowing that her mode of life is not the only possible mode. "Reality is not something behind appearances; rather, we arrange our appearances into a perspective that enables us to survive and make sense of an otherwise formless flux, or what Nietzsche calls arrangements of 'wills to power'" (Mayock, 2010, 157). According to Nietzsche, there is no real "self" or "ego" apart from our experiences. Because we endure dramatic changes in life, both in terms of life situations and appearances, there is a need for the concepts of "I" and "self", as "static, unchanging mental constructs" (ibid., 158). This is what allows us to make decisions about how to proceed in life. However, if identity "emerges from the relative unity of character and action imposed by the unity of narrative" (Ritivoi cited in Neumann and Nünning, 2008, 6), this means that Alice as someone who believes "as many as six impossible things before breakfast", *needs* to constantly narrate herself through action, to narrate herself into being.

"Remember who you are!"–The Memory Motif in Bobin's *Alice Through the Looking Glass*

In Carroll's *Through the Looking Glass and What Alice Found There*, the White Queen tells Alice "remember who you are!" (Carroll, 1871, [2001], 176). In Bobin's *Alice Through the Looking Glass*, the non-linear, multilevel structure inspired by Carroll's stories, is itself an important motif, as it problematizes the way we understand our experiences and arrange our memories of them. Although the chessboard, another type of game, is introduced in the very first scenes at the diegetic level, suggesting that the film will follow the same rules (albeit skewed ones!) of Carroll's novel, it quickly becomes clear that memory and our narrativization of ourselves through memories are the main motifs. Particularly interesting in the context of this discussion of the potential of the cybertext as a cultural model for self-narration, is Jürgen Schlaeger's observation that the time concept of traditional narrativity is challenged in contemporary texts and that we see a clear shift towards spatialization (cited in Neumann and Nünning, 2008, 11). Neumann and Nünning explain that "[n]umerous texts exploit representations of the physical environment to stage the present as 'an extended space' [...] in which the past and future are 'arranged around the present and not before or after it' [...] Different temporal levels fuse and resist being structured in any linear way" (11). In literature, this "failure to join together temporally differential dimensions goes along with a dissolution into disparate narrative fragments, thus indicating the instability of the meaning-making process" (ibid., 13). Having already established that the cybertext structure allows these dimensions to be integrated, it is nevertheless clear that in both films, it is in fact a state of instability and confusion–a loss of self–that brings about the adventure quest.

According to Scott F. Parker, Carroll's Alice never seems to experience true ego loss (2010, 146), but in the films, both the unintended fall down the rabbit hole and the more calculated step through the mirror, happen at a time when Alice is faced with seemingly impossible life choices. The adventures in Underland thus give her an opportunity to test her "will to power".

The "Impossible" Alice faces in the frame story of *Alice Through the Looking Glass* is giving up on her desired way of life as a captain sailing the Asian seas, and signing over her father's ship, *The Wonder*, to Hamish, in order to let her mother keep her house. Debating with herself what to do, she asks "Then who will I be?" Absolem, now transformed into a butterfly, enters the frame and asserts that "You're Alice, of course". That being settled, she follows him through a mirror to Underland. The quest Alice undertakes at this time is that of helping the Hatter re-narrate himself (and as it turns out stopping the Red Queen from gaining power again). This involves time travel, as Alice must navigate the dimensions of

Underland and the Oceans of Time that store the Hatter's memories, in the process of helping him rework his memories and reconstruct his life.

The Hatter's family were believed to have been killed on "Horunvendush Day", when the Red Queen unleashed the Jabberwock on the village of Witzend, as a revenge on the Hatter's family, the Hightops. They had embarrassed her by making her coronation crown too small, causing the crown to go to her younger sister, the White Queen. A dispute with his father estranged the Hatter from his family and left him with only sad memories when they disappeared. Having stumbled upon remnants of a small paper hat that he had once given his father, but that he had always believed his father had thrown away, the feeling of estrangement is now replaced by love and hope. The Hatter believes they may still be alive and he wants Alice to help him find them, so they can be reunited. At first, Alice, uncharacteristically, believes this to be impossible, whereupon the Hatter isolates himself, slowly deteriorating. The White Queen explains that the only way to save the Hatter and his family is if Alice, with the help of the Chromosphere, which is guarded by Time, travels back to Horunvendush Day. Time "lives in a void of infinitude, in a castle of eternity. Through here, one mile past the pendulum" and should Alice get hold of the Chromosphere, it will enable her to "travel across the Ocean of Time". The danger of undertaking time travel, however, lies in your past self seeing your future self, because then "everything will be history". In all of Underland, it is only Alice who can do this, since she is the only one of the creatures living there whose memories and experiences are limited to her recent past.

Upon arriving in Time's castle, Alice discovers Time personified as a man with blue glass eyes and a huge mustache, who keeps records of the lives and deaths of creatures living in Underland using a filing system of pocket watches representing each individual. In one room (or rather space), with a sign above the door reading "UNDERLANDIANS LIVING", pocket watches are hanging in the air, literally from the sky, in alphabetical order. When one has stopped ticking, Time finds it, closes the lid and takes it to be stored in another room called "UNDERLANDIANS DECEASED". When Alice explains her errand, asking to borrow the chromosphere, Time denies her request, saying that it would result in the disintegration of history: "You cannot change the past. Though I dare say, you might learn something from it". However, seeming about to return to her characteristic old self, able to accomplish impossible things, Alice does not seem prepared to heed Time's warning. When Alice realizes that the Red Queen also has her eyes set on the chromosphere, hoping to get even with her sister, by acquiring the power to "rule the past, present, and the future", her mission also becomes a race to make sure the Chromosphere does not fall into the wrong hands. Having managed to steal it, Alice is able to travel back through the events and discovers that there is a connection between the Hatter's memories and those of the Red Queen. She realizes that Horunvendush Day is a result of the actions of the White Queen. She lied to her parents as a child about stealing a tart, and blamed her sister instead. This caused her sister to run out of the house, fall and hit her head so that it swelled up, abnormal in shape and size. Alice, thinking she can change the course of events, tries to prevent the accident from happening, and manages to hinder one potential accident. But at the same time, she distracts the Red Queen long enough to land her straight into another–with the exact same result. Finally able to appreciate Time's warning, Alice suddenly remembers that while arranging the pocket watches of the deceased and reading their names out loud, Time had not mentioned the Hightops. Alice realizes they must be alive, and rushes back to the Hatter, who the Rabbit says is "barely ticking" at this point. She tries to wake him up, saying that he was right all the time; that she had thought it was impossible and that she should have believed him. Like Absolem before the battle of Frabjous Day, the Hatter then opens his eyes and concludes: "It's you, isn't it? I'd know you anywhere. You're Alice".

In Bobin's film, the Chromosphere is crucial as it powers Time. Mark W. Westmoreland cites Gilles Deleuze's reading of time and his concept of *chronos*, which makes the present the only time dimension, as it absorbs both the past and the future into itself. This again builds on Henri Bergson, who claims that "the past preserves itself automatically by affecting the present [and] the present [...] varies by how a person pays attention to his or her experience" (Westmoreland 2010, 176). When Time introduces himself to Alice, he explains that he is "the Infinite, the Eternal, the Immortal, the Immeasurable–unless you have a clock". We tend to think of time in terms of space and as a movement of objects from one point to another, and Westmoreland points out that "[a]s we began using clocks, temporality, as we understood it, changed from heterogeneous and qualitative to homogeneous and quantitative" (ibid., 175). Still, it is possible to see time as something we impose on the world in order to make sense of our own experiences. According to Westmoreland, in Carroll's novels, it is really the qualitative and experiential dimension of time that is important (ibid., 167). He explains that although we find a similar structuring principle in the form of the chess-board in the novel,

[w]hile space is infinitely divisible as extension, it would be a mistake to equate two simultaneous positions in space with the movement of objects across space. Although each square on a chessboard is equal in size, Alice's experiences of the Fourth Square–that of Tweedledum and Tweedledee–and the Sixth Square–that of Humpty Dumpty–are uniquely and qualitatively different. (ibid., 172–173)

As shown in the plot summary above, in *Alice Through the Looking Glass*, the past asserts itself in the form of powerful memories, influencing the characters' sense of self and their actions in the present. Tyler Shores argues that although memory can present us with a possible meaning, it is a meaning that needs to be interpreted. As with dreams, we should ask what our memories mean, and remember that they both shape and are shaped by our sense of self, and our version of the past (2010).

Having accomplished her quest to reconcile the Hatter with his family and to stop the Red Queen from returning to power, Alice has once again narrated herself across dimensions as the Right Alice who believes six impossible things before breakfast. This process is again transferred to the frame story, where she also needs to attempt the impossible to get to the next level. In London, Alice faces the choice between her career and her relationship with her mother. Much like Carroll's Alice when she realizes that the court jury are just a pack of cards (Carroll, 1865 [2001], 129), she is now able to see *The Wonder* as "just a ship". She is happy to hand over her father's pocket watch to Time and she tells Hamish upon her return from Underland that she is willing to sign over the ship in order to let her mother keep the house. I propose that it is possible to see these sacrifices as a version of the Impossible and in accordance with cybertext structures. This realization opens a new path as it has the unexpected outcome of making her mother perform a mental u-turn. She now throws convention to the wind and tears up the contract Alice has just signed: "Alice can do whatever Alice chooses. And so can I. Goodday!"

Conclusion

The idea that the "classical concepts of identity as a linear, teleological enterprise in which the individual may either succeed or fail to construct a coherent story" is no longer adequate under today's "diversifying and pluralizing cultural conditions" (Hallet 2008, 39) is disputed in this chapter. I also argue that the multi-level structure of cybertexts such as the adventure game have the potential to bring such identity narratives to the fore in film texts. In Burton and Bobin's films, the ideal reader is again a moral reader who accepts the identity narrative required by a certain genre. This allows for the idea that we can narrate ourselves into being if we just have the "will to power". According to Jens Brockmeier and Donal Carbaugh, the study of fictional narratives is "a laboratory in which we can experiment with the possibilities for culturally admissible constructions of identity" (cited in Neumann 2008, 66). In the case of the two *Alice* films, we see how they, through the adaptation of the adventure game hero and the multi-level structures of cybertexts, are able to convey a new, cultural narrative model for the construction of identity.

Notes

[1] *Alice's Adventures in Wonderland,* 1865, and *Through the Looking-Glass, and What Alice Found There,* 1872. In this chapter, references are from *The Annotated Alice: The definitive Edition,* edited by Martin Gardner, 2001. London: Penguin Books.
[2] *American McGee's Alice,* 2000, Dev. Rogue Entertainment. Dir. American McGee. Electronic Arts.
[3] *Alice in Wonderland,* 2010, Dev. Étranges Libellules. Disney Interactive Studios.

References

Aarseth, Espen J. 1997. *Cybertext. Perspectives on Ergodic Literature.* Baltimore: The Johns Hopkins University Press.
Alice in Wonderland. 2010. Dev. Étranges Libellules. Disney Interactive Studios.
American McGee's Alice. 2000. Dev. Rogue Entertainment. Dir. American McGee. Electronic Arts.
Arp, Robert. 2010. "Alice, Perception, and Reality: Jell-O Mistaken for Stones." In *Alice in Wonderland and Philosophy: Curiouser and Curiouser*, edited by Richard Brian Davis, 125–136. New Jersey: Wiley.
Bobin, James. 2016. *Alice Through the Looking Glass.* Walt Disney Studios Motion Pictures.
Burton, Tim. 2010. *Alice in Wonderland.* Walt Disney Studios Motion Pictures.
Carroll, Lewis. 2001 [1865]. *Alice's Adventures in Wonderland.* In *The Annotated Alice: The definitive Edition*, edited by Martin Gardner, 3–132. London: Penguin Books.
—. 2001 [1871]. *Through the Looking-Glass, and What Alice Found There.* In *The Annotated Alice:The definitive Edition*, edited by Martin Gardner, 133–288. London: Penguin Books.
Constandinides, Costas. 2010. *From Film Adaptation to Post-Celluloid Adaptation: Rethinking the Transition of Popular Narratives and Characters across Old and New Media.* London: Continuum.
Hallet, Wolfgang. 2008. "Plural Identities: Fictional Autobiographies as Templates of Multitextual Self-Narration." In *Narrative and Identity. Theoretical Approaches and Critical Analyses*, edited by Birgit Neuman, Ansgar Nünning, and Bo Petterson, 37–52. Trier: Wissenschaftlicher Verlag Trier.
Jenkins, Henry. 2006. *Convergence Culture. Where Old and New Media Collide.* New York: New York University Press.
Laurel, Brenda. 1991. *Computers as Theatre.* Boston, MA: Addison-Wesley Longman Publishing.
Mayock, Rick. 2010. "Perspectivism and Tragedy: A Nietzschean Interpretation of Alice's Adventure." In *Alice in Wonderland and Philosophy: Curiouser and Curiouser*, edited by Richard Brian Davis, 153–166. New Jersey: Wiley.
Murray, Janet. 1997. *Hamlet on the Holodeck.* Cambridge, MA: The MIT Press.

Neumann, Birgit. 2008. "Narrating Selves, (De-)Constructing Selves? Fictions of Identity." In *Narrative and Identity. Theoretical Approaches and Critical Analyses*, edited by Birgit Neuman, Ansgar Nünning, and Bo Petterson, 53–69. Trier: Wissenschaftlicher Verlag Trier.

Neumann, Birgit & Nünning, Ansgar. 2008. "Ways of Self-Making in (Fictional) Narrative: Interdisciplinary Perspectives on Narrative and Identity." In *Narrative and Identity. Theoretical Approaches and Critical Analyses*, edited by Birgit Neuman, Ansgar Nünning, and Bo Petterson, 3–22. Trier: Wissenschaftlicher Verlag Trier.

Nolan, Jonathan and Joy, Lisa. 2016. *Westworld.* Warner Bros. HBO.

Parker, Scott F. 2010. "How Deep Does the Rabbit-Hole Go? Drugs and Dreams, Perception and Reality." In *Alice in Wonderland and Philosophy. Curiouser and Curiouser*, edited by Richard Brian Davis, 137–151. New Jersey: Wiley.

Pettersson, Bo. 2008. "I Narrate, Therefore I Am? On Narrative, Moral Identity and Modernity." In *Narrative and Identity. Theoretical Approaches and Critical Analyses,* edited by Birgit Neuman, Ansgar Nünning and Bo Petterson, 23–36. Trier: Wissenschaftlicher Verlag Trier.

Shores, Tyler. 2010. "'Memory and Muchness': Alice and the Philosophy of Memory." In *Alice in Wonderland and Philosophy: Curiouser and Curiouser*, edited by Richard Brian Davis, 197–211. New Jersey: Wiley.

Westmoreland, Mark W. 2010. "Wishing It Were Some Other Time: The Temporal Passage of Alice." In *Alice in Wonderland and Philosophy: Curiouser and Curiouser*, edited by Richard Brian Davis, 167–180. New Jersey: Wiley.

CONTRIBUTORS

Dr. Britt **Andersen** is Professor of Comparative Literature at the Norwegian University of Science and Technology, Trondheim, Norway.
E-mail: britt.andersen@ntnu.no.

Dr. André **Avias** is Professor of French Literature and Cultural Studies at Østfold University College, Halden, Norway.
E-mail: andre.avias@hiof.no.

Dr. Guri Ellen **Barstad** is Professor of French Literature at Østfold University College, Halden, Norway.
E-mail: guri.e.barstad@hiof.no.

Dr. Eva Lambertsson **Björk** is Associate Professor of English Literature and Intercultural Communication at Østfold University College, Halden, Norway.
E-mail: eva.l.bjork@hiof.no.

Dr. Wladimir **Chávez Vaca** is Associate Professor of Spanish Literature at Østfold University College, Halden, Norway.
E-mail: wladimir.a.vaca@hiof.no.

Dr. Ana-Maria **Dascălu-Romițan** is Assistant Lecturer in German Studies at the Polytechnic University of Timisoara, Romania.
E-mail: ana.dascalu@upt.ro.

Dr. Melanie **Duckworth** is Associate Professor of English Literature and Cultural Studies at Østfold University College, Halden, Norway.
E-mail: melanie.duckworth@hiof.no.

Dr. Jane M. **Ekstam** is Professor of English Literature and Didactics at Østfold University College, Halden, Norway.
E-mail: jane.m.ekstam@hiof.no.

Dr. Jutta **Eschenbach** is Associate Professor of German and Intercultural Communication at Østfold University College, Halden, Norway.
E-mail: jutta.eschenbach@hiof.no.

Dr. Annette Myre **Jørgensen** is Professor of Spanish Linguistics at Østfold University College, Halden, Norway.
E-mail: annette.m.jorgensen@hiof.no.

Wayne **Kelly** is Assistant Professor of English at Østfold University College, Halden, Norway.
E-mail: wayne.kelly@hiof.no.

Dr. Mathabo **Khau** is Senior Lecturer in Gender Studies, Nelson Mandela University, South Africa.
E-mail: mathabo.khau@mandela.ac.za.

Dr. Karen Patrick **Knutsen** is Professor of English Literature and Didactics at Østfold University College, Halden Norway.
E-mail: karen.knutsen@hiof.no.

Gro-Anita **Myklevold** is Assistant Professor of English at Østfold University College, Halden, Norway.
E-mail: gro.a.myklevold@hiof.no.

Dr. Roxana **Nubert** is Professor of German Literature at West University of Timisoara, Romania.
E-Mail: roxana.nubert@e-uvt.ro.

Dr. Gabriele C. **Pfeiffer**, is doctor habilitatus (PD) of Theatre Studies and holds the Elise Richter Position (FWF) at the Department of Theatre, Film and Media Studies, University of Vienna, Austria.
E-mail: gabriele.c.pfeiffer@univie.ac.at.

Dr. Grazziella **Predoiu** is Professor of German Literature at West University of Timisoara, Romania.
E-mail: grazziella_predoiu@yahoo.de.

Dr. Mette **Ramstad** is Associate Professor of the Science of Religion at Østfold University College, Halden, Norway.
E-mail: mette.ramstad@hiof.no.

Dr. Alessandra **Schininà** is Professor of German Literature at the University of Ragusa, Italy.
E-mail: aschini@unict.it.

Britt W. **Svenhard** is Professor of English Studies at Østfold University College, Halden, Norway.
E-mail: britt.w.svenhard@hiof.no.

Dr. Elin Nesje **Vestli** is Professor of German Literature at Østfold University College, Halden, Norway.
E-mail: elin.n.vestli@hiof.no.

Dr. Lynette **Webb** is Senior Lecturer in Multilingualism at Nelson Mandela University, South Africa.
E-mail: lynette.webb@mandela.ac.za.